FATHERS IN CULTURAL CONTEXT

This book reviews the latest research on fathering in cultures representing over 50% of the world's population. Multidisciplinary experts on 14 countries/regions discuss cultural and historical influences, variations between and within cultures, and socioeconomic conditions and policies that impact fathering. Several hundred studies on fathering published in languages other than English are made accessible to readers around the world. Cultures were selected based on availability of research, geographical balance, and significance for a global understanding of fathering.

Empirical evidence is blended with the authors' insights and speculation about what it is like to be a father in each culture. The 14 central chapters also feature personal stories, photos, and maps, to help readers understand the many contexts of fathering. The book opens by explaining theoretical and methodological underpinnings of international research on fathers. The main chapters are organized by regions: Asia/Middle East, Africa, the Americas, Europe, and Australia. The final chapter integrates and compares all the chapters and makes suggestions for future research.

Every chapter has the same structure, making it easy for readers to compare fathers between cultures: opening case story; cultural/historical background and influences on fathers; review of research on fathering; sub-cultural variations in fathering; social/economic conditions that influence fathers; policies and laws relevant to fathering; comparisons with fathers in other societies; and a summary.

An ideal reader for graduate or advanced undergraduate courses on child development, fathering, or family processes taught in family studies, psychology, sociology, anthropology, education, gender/women's studies, and ethnic studies departments, this anthology is relevant to practitioners, educators, policymakers, and researchers interested in the study of father involvement.

DAVID W. SHWALB is a Professor in the Psychology Department at Southern Utah University. He holds a B.A. degree from Oberlin College, and a Ph.D. from the University of Michigan. He was a Fulbright Dissertation Fellow at Tokyo University and also studied at Waseda University. He is a former president of the Society for Cross-Cultural Research, and has previously held faculty positions at Koryo International College (Japan), Brigham Young University, and Southeastern Louisiana University. Along with Barbara Shwalb, he is English Abstracts editor for the *Japanese Journal of Developmental Psychology*, and the

Japanese Journal of Child Abuse & Neglect. He is the co-author or editor (along with B. Shwalb) of three volumes: *Japanese Childrearing: Two Generations of Scholarship* (1996), *Applied Developmental Psychology: Theory, Practice and Research from Japan* (2005), *Respect and Disrespect: Cultural and Developmental Origins* (2006, *New Directions for Child & Adolescence* series), and also three books published in Japanese. During his 8 years in Japan, Shwalb served as a teacher at the preschool, middle school, high school and college levels. He has conducted cross-cultural research on fathers since 1978, and his cross-cultural interests are in parenting, socialization, and personality development in family and school contexts, and in the developmental origins of respect, disrespect, and self-respect.

BARBARA J. SHWALB is retired from the Psychology Department of Southern Utah University. She holds B.S. and M.A.T. degrees from Southeast Missouri State University, and a Ph.D. from the University of Michigan (Combined Program in Education and Psychology). She was a Japan Ministry of Education Fellow (at Tokyo University), and lived in Japan for 6 years. She has previously held faculty positions at the University of Utah and Nagoya University of Business & Commerce. Along with David Shwalb, she was a research associate of the Japanese Child and Family National Research Center and the Hokkaido University Faculty of Education. She is the co-author of six volumes, and also co-edited special issues of *Evaulation in Education* ("Socialization and school achievement in Japan") and *International Journal of Educational Research* ("Cooperative learning and cultural context"). Barbara is a former public school teacher, and has taught at the elementary, junior and senior high school levels. Her research interests are cross-cultural developmental and learning issues, and affective and cognitive concept formation in the development of respect and disrespect. The Shwalbs have published papers on human development in Japan, Korea, China, Vietnam, Indonesia, South Asia, and the U.S.

MICHAEL E. LAMB is Professor of Psychology at the University of Cambridge. A native of Northern Rhodesia (now Zambia), he received his Ph.D. in psychology from Yale University (1976), honorary doctorates from the Universities of Goteborg (1995) and East Anglia (2006), and the James McKeen Cattell Award from the Association for Psychological Science for Lifetime Contributions to Applied Psychological Research (2004). He has authored or edited about 45 books, including *Development in infancy* (1981, 1987, 1992, 2004, in press), *Developmental science: An advanced textbook* (1984, 1988, 1992, 1999, 2004, 2011), *Infant-mother attachment* (1985), *The role of the father in child development* (1976, 1982, 1997, 2004, 2010), *Child care in context* (1992), *Investigative interviews of children* (1998), *Hunter-gatherer childhoods* (2005), *Child sexual abuse: Disclosure, delay and denial* (2007), *Tell me what happened: Structured investigative interviews of children* (2008), and *Children's testimony* (2011). He also has authored about 600 professional publications, and edits the APA journal, *Psychology, Public Policy, and Law*. He has written or co-authored reports of research in the U.S., U.K., Sweden, Germany (East, West, and Unified), Switzerland, Israel, Canada, the Central African Republic, the Congo, Malaysia, Taiwan, China (People's Republic), Japan, Korea, and Costa Rica.

FATHERS IN CULTURAL CONTEXT

EDITED BY

DAVID W. SHWALB

Department of Psychology, Southern Utah University,
Cedar City, UT, USA

BARBARA J. SHWALB

Department of Psychology, Southern Utah University,
Cedar City, UT, USA

MICHAEL E. LAMB

Department of Psychology, University of Cambridge,
Cambridge, UK

NEW YORK AND LONDON

First published 2013
by Routledge
711 Third Avenue, New York, NY 10017

Simultaneously published in the UK
by Routledge
27 Church Road, Hove, East Sussex BN3 2FA

Routledge is an imprint of the Taylor & Francis Group, an informa business

Library of Congress Cataloging in Publication Data
    Fathers in cultural context / edited by David W. Shwalb,
    Barbara J. Shwalb, Michael E. Lamb.\
    p. cm.
    Includes index.
    1. Fathers—Cross-cultural studies.
    2. Fatherhood—Cross-cultural studies.
    I. Shwalb, David W. II. Shwalb, Barbara J. III. Lamb, Michael E., 1953–
    HQ756.F3847 2013
    306.874'2—dc23
    2012009735

ISBN: 978–1–84872–947–6 (hbk)
ISBN: 978–1–84872–948–3 (pbk)
ISBN: 978–0–203–81600–4 (ebk)

Typeset in Palatino
by Swales & Willis Ltd, Exeter, Devon

Dedication

We dedicate this book to the memory of our fathers:

Richard Abraham Shwalb – who read us Dickens and all 14 of Baum's *Oz* books, put four children through college, instilled in us a love of books and music, and whose passion for Japan first introduced us to cultural studies.

Thomas W. Nichols – to my dad who made me feel like a princess when I was young, who danced with me at wedding receptions, and who made me feel like a grown-up when I would talk with him, and he'd pay attention.

Frank Lamb – whose nurturance, tolerance and commitment gave meaning to the concept of father involvement long before it was fashionable for fathers to be actively involved.

Richard A. Shwalb, Thomas Nichols, and Frank Lamb. Photos courtesy of David W. Shwalb, Barbara J. Shwalb, and Michael E. Lamb.

Contents

Part Six: Australia

Part Seven: Conclusions

Figures and Tables

Figures

Tables

Contributors

Ramadan A. Ahmed, Department of Psychology, Kuwait University, Kuwait City, Kuwait.

Ana Cecília de Sousa Bastos, Federal University of Bahia/Catholic University of Salvador, Salvador, Brazil.

Jennifer A. Baxter, Australian Institute of Family Studies, Melbourne, Australia.

Pedro Gomes Brasileiro, Institute of Psychology, Federal University of Bahia, Salvador, Brazil.

Nandita Chaudhary, Lady Irwin College, University of Delhi, Delhi, India.

Richard J. Fletcher, Family Action Centre, The University of Newcastle, Newcastle, Australia.

Hillary N. Fouts, Department of Child & Family Studies, University of Tennessee, Knoxville, TN, USA.

Linda L. Haas, Department of Sociology, Indiana University-Purdue University, Indianapolis, IN, USA.

Ziarat Hossain, University of New Mexico, Department of Individual, Family & Community Education, Albuquerque, NM, USA.

C. Philip Hwang, Department of Psychology, University of Gothenburg, Gothenburg, Sweden.

Jean M. Ispa, Department of Human Development & Family Studies, University of Missouri, Columbia, MO, USA.

Simone Ispa-Landa, Department of Human Development & Social Policy, Northwestern University, Evanston, IL, USA.

Michael E. Lamb, Department of Psychology, University of Cambridge, Cambridge, UK.

Charlie Lewis, Department of Psychology, Lancaster University, Lancaster, UK.

Xuan Li, Department of Psychology, University of Cambridge, Cambridge, UK.

Karen E. McFadden, Department of Applied Psychology, New York University, New York, NY, USA.

Lawrence J. Moloney, Australian Institute of Family Studies, Melbourne, Australia.

Jun Nakazawa, Faculty of Education, Chiba University, Chiba, Japan.

Joseph H. Pleck, Department of Human & Community Development, University of Illinois, Urbana-Champaign, IL, USA.

Jaipaul L. Roopnarine, Department of Child & Family Studies, Syracuse University, Syracuse, NY, USA.

Helena Martinelli Serra, Institute of Psychology, Federal University of Bahia, Salvador, Brazil.

Barbara J. Shwalb, Department of Psychology, Southern Utah University, Cedar City, UT, USA.

David W. Shwalb, Department of Psychology, Southern Utah University, Cedar City, UT, USA.

Bruce M. Smyth, Australian Demographic and Social Research Institute, Australian National University, Canberra, Australia.

Catherine S. Tamis-LeMonda, Department of Applied Psychology, New York University, New York, NY, USA.

Nicholas W. Townsend, Department of Anthropology, Brown University, Providence, RI, USA.

Jennifer Utrata, Department of Comparative Sociology, University of Puget Sound, Tacoma, WA, USA.

Vivian Volkmer-Pontes, Institute of Psychology, Federal University of Bahia, Salvador, Brazil.

Foreword

Joseph H. Pleck
University of Illinois at Urbana-Champaign, IL, USA

From the vantage point of someone who began working on fathering in the 1970s, the way that the scholarly landscape of fatherhood research has changed over the last four decades is remarkable. When I started out, "fatherhood research" meant the investigation of the consequences of father absence. Through the early 1970s, it seemed that in U.S. developmental research, fathers were absolutely towering figures in child development – but towering mainly in their absence. That perspective changed, of course, and new research emerged that focused instead on fathers who were "present" and on what they actually do (or not do) with their resident children. It is now over 35 years since the inception of this "new" study of fatherhood, marked by the publication of the first edition of Michael Lamb's *The Role of the Father in Child Development* in 1976. And over 25 years have passed since the explicit formulation of the foundational construct of "paternal involvement" (Lamb, Pleck, Charnov, & Levine, 1985; Pleck, Lamb, & Levine, 1985). From one perspective, the study of fatherhood with a contemporary slant has been going on for a long time. But taking a longer-term view, it is historically quite recent.

The new fatherhood research clearly began with a primary focus on fathers in the United States. As a result of several dynamics, in its early years only certain kinds of fathers were generally studied. First, research was usually explicitly restricted to fathers who were co-resident with their child, who were the child's biological father, who were currently married, who were not teens when they had first births, who were not physically or mentally disabled, who had typically developing children, and who were heterosexual. Second, when samples were drawn that met these restrictions, they were frequently convenience samples (e.g., recruited in university communities) that under represented non-white, non-middle class, and/or immigrant fathers. Third, when samples included fathers in one of more of these latter "exceptional" subgroups, there were too few of them to make subgroup analysis possible, and/or the researcher did not consider this possibility.

These sampling limitations were of course not unique to fatherhood research. Addressing the multiple dimensions of diversity within the U.S. has been a major challenge to the entire field of human development and family studies (HDFS) in this country. So, too, has been fully recognizing that the U.S. is not the only country in the world and that its research findings cannot be implicitly assumed to represent "universal" developmental or family processes. Scholarly publications such as the *Journal of Comparative Family Studies* and professional associations such as the International Society for Infant Studies, the International Society for the Study of Behavioural Development, and the Family Section of the International Sociological Association have made important contributions to the HDFS field in the latter area.

In my view, the new fatherhood research has actually compared favorably to many other lines of research in HDFS in terms of addressing diversity within the U.S. In U.S. studies, alongside research on resident married fathers, the proportion of investigations focusing on divorced fathers, stepfathers, adoptive fathers, teen fathers, low-income fathers, non-white fathers, and gay fathers has increased steadily since the 1980s (Goldberg, Tan, & Thorsen, 2009). More recently, there has been increasing attention to disabled fathers and fathers with atypically developing children, cohabiting fathers, immigrant fathers, and "social" fathers (men who are not the child's biological father, have neither married the child's mother, nor adopted the child, but who live with and function as a father to the child). Unfortunately, these multiple lines of research are generally conducted independently of each other, or "stove-piped." In particular, it often seems that the two single largest bodies of current fathering research – one on resident, married, middle-class fathers, and the other focusing on low-income, unmarried, often non-white fathers ("fragile families" fathers) – are, to adapt George Bernard Shaw's phrase, two research literatures separated by their common use of the term "father."

The new fatherhood research has also in my view been less prone to U.S.-centrism than has been the broader HDFS field. Fatherhood research's proactive interest beyond U.S. borders has been simultaneously reflected in, and in turn stimulated by, Michael Lamb's edited volumes. Reflecting his multinational background and professional network, Lamb included generous "helpings" of non-U.S. research in *The Role of the Father in Child Development* (beginning with the 1976 first edition, increasingly so in successive later editions); in his subsequent *Fatherhood and Family Policy* (Lamb & Sagi, 1983); and of course in *The Father's Role: Cross-Cultural Perspectives* in 1987. Other fatherhood research anthologies published in the U.S. also reflect a movement away from U.S.-centrism (Bozett & Hanson, 1991; Cabrera & Tamis-LeMonda, in press; Hewlett, 1992; Tamis-LeMonda & Cabrera, 2002). Important English-language collections have also been published in Britain (Hobson, 2002) and Canada (Ball & Daly, in press).

Fatherhood research has also drawn particularly on the time diary data collected in numerous Western and East European industrial societies for over five decades. For example, Bianchi, Robinson, and Milkie (2006) report data showing dramatic (though differential) increases in fathers' engagement time with children in three European countries, Australia, Canada, and the U.S. between 1965 and 2000. Time diary data are also increasingly available from non-Western societies (e.g., Hsin, 2007). Research on immigrant fathers in the U.S. provides a bridge between research on fatherhood diversity within the U.S. and cross-national research. At the first research conference on immigrant fathers in the U.S., I learned that fully 20% of American fathers with resident children under age 18 are foreign-born, a fact that I think is not widely known (Pleck, 2008).

Turning to this book, what does cross-cultural fatherhood research tell us, and in what new directions does it point? I defer to the editors of this volume (Chapters 1 and 16) to answer these challenging questions! Instead, I will alert the reader to two broad issues they might keep in mind as they read each chapter of this book: the "father involvement" question and the "essential father" (or "fatherhood and masculinity") question.

First, the father involvement construct has clearly been foundational in contemporary fathering research in the U.S. At the same time, from the moment of its formulation, this concept has been contested as not recognizing fathers' economic and broader social roles and as applying only to white middle-class fathers (and, the critics could have added, to native-born fathers in the U.S.). As one of the construct's co-authors, it often seemed to me during the 1990s that paternal involvement was somehow being singled out as a *piñata* by the social sciences (for an analysis of and response to these critiques, see Pleck & Stueve, 2001). However, U.S. research appears now to have moved beyond the sterile debate about what the term "father involvement" *should* mean. That is, the explicit manifestations of father involvement (behavioral engagement, warmth, and control with their children) continue to be studied, *and* fathers' economic and other social roles, fathers' affects and cognitions, and fathers' identities and self-understandings are all receiving increasing research attention as well, whether or not they are conceptualized as part of involvement.

This book's chapters on Europe, Australia, and North and South America generally employ the involvement construct, and do not seem to find it problematic. Most chapters on Africa, East and South Asia, and the Middle East also employ the involvement construct to greater or lesser degree. But it is notable that they give equal or more emphasis to fathers' economic and other social roles. In some cases, the joint focus of these chapters on paternal involvement and on the other obligations associated with fatherhood as a social status seems to be an uneasy juxtaposition.

Because of globalization, American/European cultural practices have permeated non-Western societies. It has to be said that father involvement is one of these practices. As a comparative example, Otnes and Pleck (2003) tell the fascinating story of how the Western "white wedding" has become normative around the globe. How should we view the globalization of father involvement? There is an ongoing debate about whether the diffusion of American/European cultural practices into the rest of the world is a good thing or a bad thing, an issue beyond the scope of this Foreword or book. As I argued above, in the U.S. context it now seems possible to employ the father involvement construct to non-white and non-middle-class fathers in a non-problematized way that does not implicitly devalue fathers' other roles. But in Africa, East Asia, South Asia, and the Middle East, the issues involved in using the involvement construct may be more complex.

Second, in the U.S., most popular discourse about fatherhood is organized around what I term the "essential father" hypothesis – the idea that the reason to promote greater father involvement is that fathers, by virtue of being male, make an essential and unique contribution to child development (Pleck, 2010). As evidence, a Google search on "fathers" and "essential" jointly yielded 5.35 million pages (in English) in June 2009, increasing to 30 million pages in November 2010; searching on "fathers" and "unique" yielded a similar pattern. This hypothesis can be summarized as a sequence of three linked ideas. First, fathers make a contribution to children's (and especially sons') social and personality development that is *essential*. Second, fathers make a contribution that is *unique*; what makes fathers' contribution essential is precisely that it is unique. Third, the uniqueness of fathers' contribution lies specifically in that it is *uniquely male* and *uniquely masculine*.

As I discuss elsewhere (Pleck, 2010), current research actually provides little support for the component testable propositions underlying this popular conception of paternal essentiality. And, there is an alternative perspective on the importance of fathers in child development that is fathering-affirmative, much more consistent with the evidence, and in accord with the way we think about every other protective factor in development.

This book reinforces an idea that has always been in the back of my mind about the essential father hypothesis: the notion that fathering is "essential" to children's social and personality development seems to be a uniquely American preoccupation. To be sure, European and non-Western societies embody a cultural understanding of fathers' roles as fundamental in gender relations, and as central in how gender relations are reproduced (as well as change) from one generation to the next. But the ways that European and non-Western societies valorize the roles of fathers do not seem to include the anxious undertone evident in U.S. discussions of fathers' "essential" and "unique" contributions. However, just as the American concept of father involvement has entered into fatherhood research in other countries, it is possible that the American rhetoric of paternal essentiality will also gradually infiltrate those societies' popular fathering discourse as well. Time will tell.

In conclusion, *Fathers in Cultural Context* presents cutting-edge current research about fathering in a wide range of diverse world societies, and brings the cross-cultural perspective in fathering research to a new level. In addition, its concluding chapter makes valuable recommendations for how future investigations can focus even more on culture. Altogether, this book makes a vitally important contribution in making contemporary fatherhood studies truly global and truly inclusive.

References

Ball, J., & Daly, K. (Eds.). (in press). *Father involvement in Canada: Contested terrain.* Toronto, Canada: University of Toronto Press.

Bianchi, S., Robinson, J., & Milkie, M. (2006). *Changing rhythms of American family life.* New York, NY: Russell Sage Foundation.

Bozett, F., & Hanson, S. (Eds.). (1991). *Fatherhood and families in cultural context.* New York, NY: Springer.

Cabrera, N. J., & Tamis-LeMonda, C. S. (Eds.). (in press). *Handbook of father involvement: Multidisciplinary perspectives* (2nd ed.). New York, NY: Routledge.

Goldberg, W., Tan, E., & Thorsen, K. (2009). Trends in academic attention to fathers, 1930–2006. *Fathering, 7,* 159–179.

Hewlett, B. (Ed.). (1992). *Father–child relations: Cultural and biosocial contexts.* New Brunswick, NJ: Transaction Books.

Hobson, B. (Ed.). (2002). *Making men into fathers: Men, masculinities and the social politics of fatherhood.* Cambridge, UK: Cambridge University Press.

Hsin, A. (2007). Children's time use: Labor divisions and schooling in Indonesia. *Journal of Marriage and the Family, 69,* 1297–1306.

Lamb, M. E. (Ed.). (1976). *The role of the father in child development.* New York, NY: Wiley.

Lamb, M. E. (Ed.). (1987). *The father's role: Cross-cultural perspectives.* Hillsdale, NJ: Lawrence Erlbaum Associates.

Lamb, M. E., Pleck, J. H., Charnov, E. L., & Levine, J. A. (1985). Paternal behavior in humans. *American Zoologist, 25,* 883-894.

Lamb, M. E., & Sagi, A. (Eds.). (1983). *Fatherhood and family policy.* Hillsdale, NJ: Lawrence Erlbaum Associates.

Otnes, C., & Pleck, E. H. (2003). *Cinderella dreams: The allure of the lavish wedding*. Berkeley, CA: University of California Press.

Pleck, J. H. (2008). Studying immigrant fathers: Methodological and conceptual challenges. In S. Chuang & R. Moreno (Eds.), *On new shores: Understanding immigrant fathers in North America* (pp. 255–285). Lanham, MD: Lexington Books.

Pleck, J. H. (2010). Fatherhood and masculinity. In M. E. Lamb (Ed.), *The role of the father in child development* (5th ed., pp. 32–66). Hoboken, NY: Wiley.

Pleck, J. H., Lamb, M. E., & Levine, J. A. (1985). Facilitating future change in men's family roles. *Marriage and Family Review, 9* (3–4), 11–16.

Pleck, J. H., & Stueve, J. L. (2001). Time and paternal involvement. In K. Daly (Ed.), *Minding the time in family experience: Emerging perspectives and issues* (pp. 205–226). Oxford, UK: Elsevier Science.

Tamis-LeMonda, C. S., & Cabrera, N. J. (Eds.). (2002). *Handbook of father involvement: Multidisciplinary perspectives*. Mahwah, NJ: Lawrence Erlbaum Associates.

Preface

*David W. Shwalb, Barbara J. Shwalb, and
Michael E. Lamb*

Twenty-five years ago, *The Father's Role: Cross-Cultural Perspectives* (*Father's Role*, Lamb, 1987) presented reviews of fathering research from several countries. It was a companion volume to the early editions of *The Role of the Father in Child Development* (*ROTF*, Lamb, 1976), the fifth edition of which appeared in 2010. *ROTF* has stimulated and reflected the maturation of research and theory on fathers since its initial printing, and each successive edition paid increased attention to contextual and cultural factors that affect fathers. However, there was never a second edition of the *Father's Role* volume. This book is a 25th anniversary commemoration and update of the cross-cultural volume, *and much more*.

The 1987 *Father's Role* included 13 chapters, most of which described Western fathers or applied Western research methods and theory in studies of non-Western cultures. A quarter-century later, our volume heralds a new understanding of fathers around the world. It has 14 main chapters that describe fatherhood on every continent and in societies comprising over half the world's population. International experts on fathering discuss cultural and historical influences, variations between and within cultures, and social policies that increasingly influence fathers and fatherhood.

This book confirms that internationalization and rapid changes in social conditions around the world have piqued a global interest in fathering. Although theoretical work on fathering is still dominated by North Americans and Western Europeans, with indigenous viewpoints very rare, important research on fathers has been conducted worldwide in a wide variety of cultures. Indeed, this volume breaks the language barrier by citing almost 900 studies of fathers and fatherhood previously available only in non-English languages. It thereby documents what has been accomplished but gone largely unnoticed for 25 years, recounting "a story that must be told," to use Chaudhary's words (Chapter 4).

The three of us decided to collaborate on this book when we reunited after a gap of 23 years, at the 2010 conference of the Society for Cross-Cultural Research (SCCR). We had first met in 1978 as graduate students (David and Barb) and professor (Michael) at the University of Michigan. At the SCCR meeting, we decided to solicit chapters based on four criteria: (1) availability of illustrious authors, (2) representation of all continents, (3) representation of both large and small societies, and (4) our knowledge that inclusion of a country or region added significant knowledge to a broader international understanding of fathering. Unfortunately, space limitations required us to exclude reports from several societies where considerable amounts of research have been conducted.

Each chapter is captivating to read. Anyone wanting to grasp what men in general and fathers in particular deal with in the societies under focus will be enthralled. We planned this book so that it would be of value to both scholars and practitioners interested in fathers, families, and cultures. In addition, special features (case stories, photos of fathers and children, regional maps, similar sub-sections in all chapters, summaries, speculative commentaries, and integrative conclusions in every chapter) will make this book useful for courses in many behavioral and social sciences. The chapters are not technical research reports. Instead they are thought-provoking, integrative and comprehensive reviews of data, cultural influences, and applied policy implications for fathering in societies around the world. We and the chapter contributors respect multi-disciplinary studies, and welcome readers from diverse fields including developmental and cross-cultural psychology, anthropology, comparative sociology, education, family studies, gender studies, international studies, and ethnic studies. Finally, the forward-looking conclusions of the chapters should serve as a heuristic for researchers and practitioners planning future projects, and help readers to think about the future of fathering around the world. We anticipate that this book will stimulate readers to conduct innovative research on fathering from new and more nuanced cultural perspectives.

We thank Debra Riegert and Jessica Lauffer of Routledge/Taylor & Francis for their encouragement and expert guidance, and Deborah and Andrew Gorder for the indexes, and Joan Young and Robyn Lewis for their editorial assistance. Appreciation is also due to the Psychology Department (Lynn White and Steve Barney, Chairs) and the College of Humanities & Social Sciences (James McDonald, Dean) at Southern Utah University. Paul R. Larson of the Southern Utah University Department of Physical Science expertly customized six maps to help readers see the relation between fathering and geographic location, and Rohn Solomon of

Southern Utah University Publications provided generous assistance with graphics and the cover design. We would also like to thank our reviewers: Ziarat Hossain (University of New Mexico), Linda Nielsen (Wake Forest University), and one anonymous reviewer. Most importantly, we express heartfelt gratitude to the authors of the 14 main chapters, for their patience and tolerance with our demands for multiple drafts of their contributions.

We expect that the next update of this book will not take another 25 years, and that the next edition will reflect the enthusiasm and research activity generated by reading this volume.

Part One

Introduction

Chapter One

Introduction

David W. Shwalb and Barbara J. Shwalb
Southern Utah University, Cedar City, UT, USA

Michael E. Lamb
University of Cambridge, Cambridge, UK

Each chapter of this book begins with the story of an individual father, and then places fathering in the broader contexts of community, culture and country. As a whole, this volume illustrates that contemporary young men are developing new modes of fathering that are more diverse and complicated than in the past, and that interest in and research on fathers has spread worldwide. Many readers may be surprised by the magnitude of the changes that have taken place and may be similarly unaware of the impediments to change, especially the restraining influences of "tradition" discussed by so many of the contributors.

Great progress has been made internationally in attempts to understand fathering, and the 14 central chapters of this volume portray fathering in many different nations, including some of the world's largest and smallest societies. The contributors integrate research literatures while discussing cultural and historical influences, variations in fathering between and within cultures, social and economic phenomena such as divorce, illegitimacy, immigration, and migration that increasingly influence fathers, and social policies related to fathering. Some of the chapters provide the first comprehensive English-language accounts of fathering in the cultures concerned, and the authors of every chapter are fluent in the native languages of the relevant countries. Because of the diversity represented, it is not surprising that contributors adopt various definitions of fathers (the men), fathering (the behavior), and fatherhood (conceptualizations of the role), and not surprisingly they also make different assumptions about culture. This variety of perspectives challenges readers to reconsider their own assumptions about fatherhood.

Geographical and Population Coverage

The world map (Figure 1.1) identifies the societies represented in this volume, which cumulatively comprise a majority of the world's population. Chapters 2–15 are grouped in order of the overall population of each continent: Asia, Africa, North and South America combined, Europe, and Australia. This book includes chapters about seven of the world's ten most populous nations (People's Republic of China, India, U.S., Brazil, Bangladesh, Russia, and Japan), and the size of the populations represented in the 14 chapters range from small-scale societies in Central and East Africa, to China and India (each home to about one-fifth of the world's fathers).

Table 1.1 provides comparative demographic information about the countries discussed in this book, with data on nine variables relevant to fathers and families. To represent the Caribbean, Central/Eastern Africa, Southern Africa, and Arab societies, we present demographic data for the countries most often referenced in these four respective chapters.

Chapter Themes

One purpose of this chapter is to introduce major themes pursued in the succeeding chapters. To make the volume cohesive across chapters and help readers compare the chapters, we asked all authors to include the following elements:

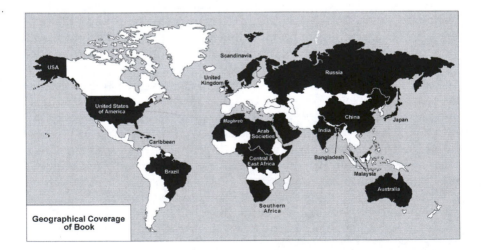

Figure 1.1 Map of the world, courtesy of Paul R. Larson.

Table 1.1 Characteristics[1] of Countries by Chapter, Reported in 2012

Chapter	Country/ Region	Population[2]	Pop. Density[3]	Mean Age[2]	Fertil. Rate[2]	% Urban Pop.[2]	Per Capita Income[4]	Infant Mort.[2]	Life Exp.[2]	Land Area (Sq km.)[2]
2.	China	1,336,718,015	139.54	35.5	1.5	47	7,600	16	75	9,569,901
3.	Japan	126,475,664	337.13	44.8	1.2	67	34,000	3	82	364,485
4.	India	1,189,172,906	360.34	26.2	2.6	30	3,500	48	67	2,973,193
5.	Bangladesh	158,570,535	1,141.84	23.3	2.6	28	1,700	51	70	130,168
	Malaysia	28,728,607	85.84	26.8	2.7	72	14,700	15	74	328,657
6.	Egypt	82,079,636	78.73	24.3	3.0	43	6,200	25	73	995,450
7.	C. African Republic	4,950,027	7.23	19.2	4.6	39	700	99	50	622,984
8.	SouthAfrica	49,004,031	40.98	25.0	2.3	62	10,700	43	49	1,214,470
9.	Jamaica	2,868,380	248.39	24.2	2.2	52	8,300	15	73	10,831
10.	Brazil	203,429,773	22.72	29.3	2.2	87	10,800	21	73	8,459,417
11.	U.S.	313,232,044	32.19	36.9	2.0	82	47,200	6	78	9,161,966
12.	Russia	138,739,892	8.31	38.7	1.4	73	15,900	10	66	16,377,742
13.	Sweden	9,088,728	20.82	42.0	1.7	85	39,100	3	81	410,335
	Norway	4,691,849	15.10	40.0	1.8	79	54,600	4	80	304,282
	Denmark	5,529,888	128.56	40.9	1.7	87	36,600	4	79	42,434
14.	UK	62,698,362	253.42	40.0	1.9	80	34,800	5	80	241,930
15.	Australia	21,766,711	2.92	37.7	1.8	89	41,000	5	82	7,682,300

Notes:

1 Population density per square mile; Mean age of entire population; Fertility rate = births per woman; Per capita income in U.S. dollars; Infant mortality = deaths per 1,000 live births; Life expectancy at birth.

2 www.cia.gov.

3 www.worldatlas.com (all information retrieved on January 27, 2012).

4 www.unicef.org.

1. **A Case Story of a specific father** – The stories not only illustrate the uniqueness of every father but also show how individual fathers in each society exemplify culturally specified characteristics. For example, authors describe Munir's extended separation from his family when he left Bangladesh to work in the Middle East (Ch. 5), Dmitri's views on the impact of alcoholism on Russian fathering (Ch. 12), and Tony's love of the outdoors and sports activities with his child in Australia (Ch. 15).

2. **Cultural and historical influences on fathering** – Fathering is both universal and cultural, and the influence of culture on fathers has evolved over generations, centuries, and millennia. For instance, contributors describe the evolution of Confucian influences on fathers in China and Japan (Chs. 2 and 3), the impact of Hinduism and patriarchy on fatherhood in India (Ch. 4), and the legacy of colonialism for Southern African, Caribbean, and Brazilian fathers (Chs. 8, 9, and 10).

3. **Comprehensive review of fathering research in the target culture(s) or region** – Most research cited in several of the chapters was published in journals and books in the authors' native languages, and this volume makes these data accessible for the first time to those who read English. The literature in some societies is broad and deep (Japan in Ch. 3, U.S. in Ch. 11, UK in Ch. 14), but it is narrow and nascent in other societies (Bangladesh/Malaysia in Ch. 5, Southern Africa in Ch. 8, Brazil in Ch. 10). Research by the contributing authors is featured in every chapter, but the authors look well beyond their own work.

4. **Social policy issues related to fathering** – Discussions of public policies and practices that affect fathering show the absence of such measures in some societies (Arab Societies in Ch. 6, Central/East Africa in Ch. 7), whereas there have been many impactful policies, laws, and interventions in other cultures (Sweden in Ch. 13, the UK in Ch. 14). In societies like Sweden, policies have had sweeping effects, while in countries like Japan extensive policies have been of less import. Policies in most countries have been formulated to increase fathers' involvement and responsibility, on the assumption that these changes are desirable, but they vary, and succeed or fail depending on the societies' level of affluence, historical values, and employment systems.

5. **Sub-cultural variations in fathering** – Fathers vary within every society and region, and the authors of several chapters (China, Ch. 2; India, Ch. 4; UK, Ch. 14; Australia, Ch. 15) assert that the appreciation of diversity is key to understanding fathers. Even in cultures once presumed to be homogeneous (Japan, Ch. 3), there are both involved

and uninvolved fathers. Further, new immigrant populations have brought with them variations in paternal behavior from many parts of the world.

6. **Contemporary social/economic conditions that affect fathering** (e.g., divorce, marital status, and economic disparities) – Demographic and societal trends provide further context for contemporary fathering. For example, current divorce rates vary among the cultures represented in this volume (e.g., particularly high in Russia and the U.S., but low in Brazil and China). Rates of non-marital births are reportedly high in the U.S., the UK, Scandinavia, and elsewhere, and the failure to acknowledge paternity is discussed in many chapters. Such social and population factors continue to change over time, as do economic disparities within cultures. For example, even in Japan where 90% of the population once identified themselves as middle class, disparities between rich and poor are predicted in Chapter 3 to intensify in the next generation.

7. **Speculation, predictions for the future, and comparisons with fathers in other societies** – We encouraged contributing authors to offer personal views, interpretations, and speculations where relevant data were not available. Their expert opinions and predictions provide thought-provoking explanations of big-picture issues, and their forward-looking approaches also distinguish this book from similar volumes.

Previous Sources of Information about Fathers in Cultural Context

Several other books and theoretical papers have focused on cultural aspects of fathering. These publications include collections of reports from multiple research groups, books about single research programs, and review articles focused on general theoretical approaches to fathering in cultural context. We recommend the following multi-disciplinary sources, each of which provided a big picture cross-cultural view of fathering.

Whiting and Whiting (1975)

Anthropologists Beatrice and John Whiting and their colleagues conducted a "Six-Culture Study" (Whiting & Whiting, 1975) in India, Okinawa, Kenya, the Philippines, the U.S., and Mexico, and showed for example the effects of societal complexity and household type on children's development. As Whiting and Edwards (1988, p. 35) wrote, culture as represented by parents is an "organizer" and "provider" of settings for children. With regard to fathers, the Whitings and their associates reported that paternal involvement varied between cultural groups as a function of division of labor (in work and family settings) and living arrangements (e.g., co-sleeping). Although these researchers focused more on mothers than fathers, the Whitings' work and that of their successors and protégées (e.g., Weisner, 1997; Harkness & Super, 2002) provided a framework that could be used to understand fathers in different cultures.

Hewlett (1992, 2010)

In his 1992 book and 2010 review chapter, Hewlett provided taxonomies to classify fathering and research on fathering in both small-scale and industrialized societies. He distinguished first between evolutionary, cross-cultural, and ethnographic research methods, as well as between adaptationist and cultural theoretical approaches. In addition, Hewlett (2010) categorized fathers' behavior patterns as "intimate" (characterized by strong attachments and frequent care giving interactions with infants), "distant" (primarily concerned with discipline and as providers), and "multiple" (whereby several men, including both biological and social fathers and others, share responsibility for children). Hewlett's categories are referenced in this volume only by Fouts (Ch. 7), but we will return to his classifications of research, theories and fathering patterns in our concluding Chapter 16.

Gray and Anderson (2010)

As in Hewlett's work, Gray and Anderson emphasized hunter-gatherer societies, but they also discussed industrial societies in observing that fathers are consistently the second most frequent sources of care for children. They concluded that "additional care" (i.e., non-maternal childcare) is necessary universally, and that fathers most often provide that needed care. Gray and Anderson claimed that changes in education, employment, media, and urbanization all contribute to changes in fatherhood and that, despite globalization, fathering is as diverse as ever worldwide. Finally, they predicted that relevant policies and laws will continue to evolve in line with changes in the nature of fathering and social conditions.

Khaleque and Rohner (2011)

Research by Rohner and his associates is as exemplary as any in the field when it comes to the use of validated measures to compare fathers across many cultures. Grounded in Parental Acceptance-Rejection Theory ("PARTheory") and their battery of measures, this group has replicated studies of fathers, mothers, and children in a wide variety of countries. Their approach is cited by several chapter contributors, especially Ahmed in Chapter 6. In a recent meta-analysis of 68 PARTheory studies, Khaleque and Rohner (2011) found that acceptance of children by their fathers was more strongly correlated with measures of children's psychological adjustment than was maternal acceptance. As we emphasize in Chapter 16, it is very difficult to integrate results from research with disparate samples and measures, and it is thus important to applaud the achievements of Rohner and his colleagues.

Bozett and Hanson (1991)

Bozett and Hanson focused on fathering in the United States, and on diversity associated with ethnicity, religion, social class, rural/urban settings, sexual orientation, and organizational culture. They proposed a theory of cultural influences on fathering that considered (1) normative paternal behavior, (2) environmental constraints on fathers, (3) mechanisms to reconcile discrepancies between normative expectations and constraints, and (4) influences of the child's and father's ages and of historical change. Several contributors to their anthology emphasized precisely these sources of influence when discussing intra-cultural diversity, which is also a consistent theme in our volume.

United Nations (2011)

Most recently, the Department of Economic and Social Affairs of the United Nations Secretariat released a 200-page report titled *Men in Families and Family Policy in a Changing World* (United Nations, 2011). This timely document focused on five topics: (1) "Men, families, gender equality and care work"; (2) "Fatherhood and families"; (3) "Fathers in challenging family contexts"; (4) "Migration, families and men in families"; and (5) "Men, families and HIV and AIDS." It also included case studies of interventions, laws, and social policies from numerous societies, as well as features about policies in several cultures highlighted in our volume (e.g., Jamaica, South Africa, Norway, Brazil, Sweden, and India). Unlike the other works summarized above, the U.N. report was primarily concerned with applications rather than theory, but it also cited international research on fathering and provided international demographic information about fathers and families.

Concluding Thoughts

In Chapter 16 ("Final Thoughts, Comparisons, and Conclusions"), we amplify the central messages provided in the substantive chapters and offer some comparisons between the countries and cultures concerned. Such comparisons can be revealing, however difficult they may be to draw. For example, immigration issues (e.g., Brazilian fathers in Japan, South Asian fathers in the UK, Caribbean fathers in the U.S.) and migrations within societies (e.g., rural-to-urban migration in China, population movements within Southern Africa) and within regions (migrations between Arab countries, Bangladeshi migration to Malaysia) all demonstrate that trans-cultural identity has become an important part of the increasingly complex picture of fatherhood in many cultures.

We also offer suggestions for the next generation of research on fathers in cultural context, and conclude with predictions for the future of fathering internationally. Because the culturally sensitive literature on fatherhood is described within this volume as "preliminary," "immature," "piecemeal," and "sparse," it is not easy to form solid conclusions, but just as we asked chapter contributors to speculate we do the same in Chapter 16. We hope that readers will conclude, as we do, that international research on fathers is essential, important, and has a bright future.

References

Bozett, F., & Hanson, S. (Eds.). (1991). *Fatherhood and families in cultural context.* New York, NY: Springer.

Gray, P.B., & Anderson, K.G. (2010). *Evolution and human paternal behavior.* Cambridge, MA: Harvard University Press.

Harkness, S., & Super, C.M. (2002). Culture and parenting. In M. Bornstein (Ed.), *Handbook of parenting: Vol. 2. Biology and ecology of parenting* (pp. 253–280). Hillsdale, NJ: Lawrence Erlbaum Associates.

Hewlett, B.S. (1992). *Father–child relations: Cultural and biosocial contexts.* Chicago, IL: Aldine.

Hewlett, B.S. (2010). Fathers' roles in hunter-gatherer and other small-scale cultures. In M.E. Lamb (Ed.), *The role of the father in child development* (5th ed., pp. 413–434). Hoboken, NJ: Wiley.

Khaleque, A., & Rohner, R. P. (2011). Pancultural associations between perceived-parental acceptance and psychological adjustment of children and adults: A meta-analytic review of worldwide research. *Journal of Cross-Cultural Psychology, 43,* 784–800.

United Nations (2011). *Men in families and family policy in a changing world.* New York, NY: United Nations Department of Economic and Social Affairs, Division for Social Policy and Development. Retrieved August 8, 2011, from http://www.un.org/esa/socdev/family/docs/men-in-families.pdf.

Weisner, T.S. (1997). The ecocultural project of human development: Why ethnography and its findings matter. *Ethos, 25,* 177–190.

Whiting, B.B., & Edwards, C.P. (1988). *Children of different worlds: The formation of social behavior.* Cambridge, MA: Harvard University Press.

Whiting, B.B., & Whiting, J.W.M. (1975). *The children of six cultures: A psychocultural analysis.* Cambridge, MA: Harvard University Press.

Part Two

Asia

Chapter Two

Fathers in Chinese Culture

From Stern Disciplinarians to Involved Parents

Xuan Li and Michael E. Lamb
University of Cambridge, Cambridge, UK

Case Story: Qiu's First Role as a New Father

Qiu and his wife, both only children, come from Guangzhou, one of the biggest cities in Mainland China. After years of gradually recognizing the instinctual desire to be a father that had begun to stir in adolescence, Qiu and his wife embraced the unexpected news of their first child's impending arrival while still pursuing postgraduate degrees in Europe, both because they wanted to have their own baby and because they were profoundly opposed to abortion. With support from both families, Qiu stayed in the UK to continue his studies after learning of his wife's pregnancy, while his wife returned to China where she could receive better care from their families while preparing for birth.

Qiu returned home a few weeks before the expected delivery and thereafter accompanied his wife to prenatal hospital checks and hospital-organized childbirth preparation classes for expectant fathers and mothers. Not without effort, he checked his wife into the best ward available at a major local hospital shortly before the delivery; an entry pass allowed him to stay with his wife day and night, soothing and encouraging her. He was supported by parents from both families, who also provided care for his wife and visited the hospital frequently with delicious meals.

Qiu, like most Chinese fathers in the hospital, was encouraged to stay with his wife during the delivery. He helped push his wife into the labour room, massaged her to ease her pain, and guided her using techniques they learned together in the prenatal classes. After the exhausting days before and during childbirth, Qiu was greatly relieved that both his wife and child were in good condition, and he was happy to have a son.

Looking back, Qiu views the inconveniences they experienced (insufficient hospital resources and poor services) as inevitable consequences of the huge Chinese population and of the increasing popularity of institutionalized childbirth by Chinese women whose forebears gave birth in their own homes with the assistance of experienced, elder female relatives and midwives. In fact, Qiu regrets that such intra-familial help is no longer available for contemporary, urban Chinese families. He also thinks that fathers, who might not always be competent assistants in matters such as childbirth, now have to participate whether or not they want to do so, because traditional resources are not available in modern Chinese society.

Participation in childbirth was an empowering experience for Qiu. Although it will be a long time before he can fully understand the meaning of fatherhood, a meaning rooted in fantasies about caring for and educating the child, Qiu is already thinking about having a second child.

Changes in paternal involvement around childbirth highlighted in this Case Story hint at the many novel features of modern Chinese fatherhood, an institution shaped by the unique historical, philosophical and cultural roots and diverse contextual influences.

Significance of research on Chinese fatherhood

Both English- and Chinese-language research on Chinese fatherhood started to emerge in the last few decades, fostered in part by recognition of the sheer number of Chinese fathers. With a male population of 686.85 million, Mainland China alone likely accounts for nearly one-fifth of the world's fathers (National Bureau of Statistics of the People's Republic of China, 2011b), and other major groups of Chinese people live in densely populated areas like Taiwan (population = 23.16 million) and Hong Kong (7.08 million) (National Bureau of Statistics of the People's Republic of China, 2011a). Chinese fathers are not only numerous; they are also culturally diverse. Jointly shaped by Confucianism, Taoism, Buddhism, the majority *Han* culture, and various ethnic minority cultures, Chinese families and fathers differ to some degree from Euro-American families with respect to parenting traditions, family structure and gender roles.

It is also necessary to consider fatherhood in the context of massive recent social changes in contemporary Chinese societies. China has transformed itself from a self-isolated society to an active participant in a globalized world after fundamental socioeconomic reforms began in the late 1970s, while Taiwan has sought to preserve and reinforce traditional Chinese values despite economic advances. Meanwhile, the end of British colonial rule and reunion with China in 1997 brought Hong Kong into increased economic and cultural exchanges with other Chinese sub-groups. At the same time, thousands of other Chinese people have moved to disparate and alien cultures and societies, boosting the number of Chinese expatriate fathers. A rough estimate suggests that there were approximately 48 million Chinese people living overseas in 2008 (Guo, Chen, Xie, Zhang, & Lin, 2009. While early Chinese immigrants were concentrated in Southeast Asian countries such as Indonesia (10.00 million Chinese, 3.1% of the total population) and Singapore (2.79 million Chinese, 74.1% of the total population), recent Chinese expatriates have extended their destinations to many continents ("Overseas Chinese", 2011), particularly North America (4.80 million Chinese), Europe (1.7 million) and Oceania (1 million). Dynamic population flows across cultures and societies, accompanied by enhanced communications between groups within and outside Chinese culture, have complicated the interaction between tradition and modernity and may also foster changes in fathering ideals, behaviour, and family relations.

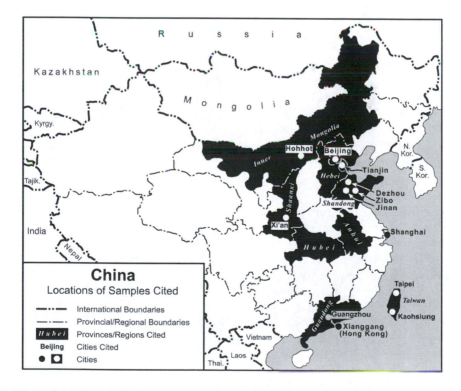

Figure 2.1 Map of China, courtesy of Paul R. Larson.

Cultural and Historical Background as It Influences Fathering

Fathers everywhere are profoundly influenced by cultural beliefs. Confucian classics as well as recent research on contemporary Chinese families reveal essential features of Chinese fatherhood, including parenting style, gender roles and family organization.

Fathering style

Chinese fathers were frequently assumed to be "authoritarian," in part because Confucius (551–479 BC) stressed parental involvement in child development and emphasized strict parental discipline using the cutting of the jade ("玉不琢，不成器") as a metaphor in both the *Book of Rites* (《禮記》), one of the most important Confucian classics, and the *Trimetric Classic* (《三字經》), a widely used textbook on Confucianism. Such discipline was primarily the responsibility of fathers, and was ideally strict, because of the popular beliefs that "strict fathers raise filial sons" ("嚴父出孝子") and that the misbehaviour of children was their fathers' fault ("養不教，父之過").

Strict social order within the family was also a recurrent theme in traditional Chinese philosophy. In Confucianism, the superiority of parents over children was determined by "natural laws," such that "The father guides the son" ("父為子綱"). In turn, the child was to be compliant, respectful, and "filial" (孝) towards his or her parents, especially the father. As noted in the *Book of Filial Piety* (《孝經》), another Confucius classic: "In filial piety there is nothing greater than reverential awe of one's father" ("孝莫大於嚴父。"). Such a hierarchy derived from the father–son relationship was not only an essential rule of family life, but also a fundamental aspect of social relationships in Chinese society (Hwang, 2001).

Interestingly, while paternal strictness (嚴) was emphasized in the upbringing of children, paternal kindness (慈) was preached as a parallel reflection of the core Confucius concept of benevolence (仁) in a family context. "As a father, he rests in kindness" ("為人父，止於慈"), said Confucius, who saw kindness as the ideal state of fatherhood. To raise an ideally filial and respectful child, "the father should be strict with the son and not improperly close; the love for one's own blood should not be spared" ("父子之嚴，不可以狎；骨肉之愛，不可以簡"), wrote Yan Zhitui (顏之推, 531–590 AD; http://ctext.org/yan-shi-jia-xun/jiao-zi), a famous scholar and advocate of Confucian education. Parental strictness and kindness were not only both emphasized, they were also viewed as compatible. In contemporary terms, Chao's (1994) comparative study of American and immigrant Taiwanese mothers, for example, showed that the concept of "guan"（管）or "training" – to govern or to restrict children with a loving, caring connotation – distinguished Chinese parenting ideology from that of Euro-Americans, who saw parental strictness and kindness as opposite and incompatible.

Gender roles

Differentiation between paternal and maternal roles was closely linked to socially defined gender roles. Guided by its agricultural origins, with labour and strength crucial to prosperity, the Chinese culture has a strong patriarchal tradition that favoured males over females. The "three cardinal guides" ("三綱") proposed by the Han Dynasty scholar Dong Zhongshu (董仲舒, 179–104 BC) and promoted officially, required that women obey their male relatives (father, brother, husband) and that men guide their wives. The imbalanced gender status was further reinforced by the influential Neo-Confucian scholar Zhu Xi (朱熹, 1130–1200 AD), who advocated strict obedience to such guidelines. The male-dominant tradition was rarely challenged until the New Culture Movement in the early 20th century, when women finally gained access to education and became involved in extra-familial business following popular criticism of traditional values. In spite of revolutionary changes in gender roles throughout the 20th century, the division of family responsibility such that men take care of "external" affairs while women takes responsibility for "interior" chores remains prominent in many Chinese families and in relevant popular proverbs ("男主外, 女主内"). Interior chores like childcare are thus the responsibility of mothers, whereas breadwinning remains the fathers' responsibility, with the extent of father–child interaction often constrained by this division of labour.

Chinese families also commonly adhered to the "strict father, affectionate mother" model, where "affectionate" also meant nurturing or kind (嚴父慈母. Ho, 1987; Shwalb, Nakazawa, Yamamoto, & Hyun, 2010). This model was first mentioned in the *Book of Jin* (《晉書》, http://zh.wikisource.org/wiki/晉書/卷055) in the 7th century AD and later became a popular idiom and well-instilled ideology for Chinese family life. According to this model, the Chinese father, by dint of his "natural" superiority and better education, was the more appropriate disciplinarian. In contrast, the mother played the role of nurturing parent, supporting the child with warmth and affection to compensate for the stern father. The mother also helped discipline the child by monitoring behaviour, especially before the child reached the "age of reason" (懂事), when the father formally became involved in the child's education. In this manner, traditional parental roles were differentiated yet intertwined.

Ideal of manhood

The Chinese father's roles as family head and role model for his wife and children were ultimately influenced by the Confucian ideal of manhood.

The suppression of emotional expression was desired in an ideal man or "an educated gentleman" (君子). Men's control over emotions ensured that the latter neither undermine personal judgement nor threaten social harmony (Tang, 1992). Taoism and Buddhism – the other two pillars of Chinese culture – agreed with Confucianism that absence of emotion was beneficial and desirable, although on different grounds. Chinese parenting practices thus tended to focus on the inculcation of socially appropriate behaviour and discouragement of individual feelings and opinions (Tang, 1992). As role models for their children, Chinese fathers were to be emotionally reserved not only towards their children, but also as individuals, as is the case in many other emotionally restrictive, collectivistic cultures.

Reminders for researchers

Researchers should be careful when attributing the behaviour of Chinese fathers to their cultural origins, because we know so little about traditional Chinese fathering. Without clear definitions of what counts as the "Chinese parenting style," or a precise understanding of whether and how Chinese fathers differ from their counterparts in other cultures, it seems inappropriate to overestimate the importance of tradition for Chinese fatherhood.

Conceptualization of Chinese fatherhood also must recognize intracultural diversity. Throughout Chinese history, regional sub-cultures and ethnic minorities have survived, thrived and even ruled. In Mainland China today, there are 55 recognized and distinct ethnic minorities comprising 113.79 million people in total, in addition to the Han majority that constitutes 91.51% of the total population (National Bureau of Statistics of the People's Republic of China, 2011b). Some minorities mingle with the Han majority, while others reside in "autonomous" provincial areas. Taiwan, too, is famous for the preservation of ethnic diversity. There are also huge regional variations in family beliefs and gender roles even within the Han. Researchers should bear in mind such variations when generalizing from Chinese research findings.

Furthermore, the Chinese culture is no more static than any other culture. On the one hand, challenges to parenting traditions from the beginning of the 20th century, such as the Cultural Revolution of the 1960s and 1970s and Western influences in recent decades have weakened the cultural link between the contemporary Chinese and their ancestors. On the other hand, traditional Chinese culture, in particular the Confucian classics, have recently regained attention and popularity, perhaps in response to increases in nationalism associated with economic advancement. Instead of assuming historical continuities, theoretical and empirical validation is needed to measure the links between contemporary Chinese families and their cultural traditions. For instance, attitudes and behaviour of new generations of Chinese parents must be described, measured and compared with those one might expect on the basis of cultural traditions. It would also be worthwhile to make intergenerational comparisons, so that we can determine whether and how changes take place across time. Tracking these changes, combined with cross-regional comparisons, would further elucidate the interplay between cultural traditions and socio-political developments, and their influence on fathers.

Contemporary Social/Economic Conditions and Policies That Impact Fathering

Cultural beliefs affect fathering styles implicitly, but current social forces affect paternal behaviour more directly. To better understand contemporary Chinese fathers, we must take into account current social, political and economic contexts.

Demographic landscape and policies

Mainland China's family planning policy is one of the most controversial yet influential social policies in the world. Often referred to as the "One Child Policy," the family planning policy was introduced in the late 1970s to control overpopulation and promote child welfare (Information Office, State Council of People's Republic of China, 1995). Restrictions on the number of children in each household were believed to enhance children's development by concentrating the available family resources. In most cases, urban Chinese families are now allowed to have only one child, although there are exceptions for members of minority ethnic groups, when children are disabled, or when both parents are themselves singletons. Rural households enjoy more flexibility and are allowed to have a second child when the firstborn is a girl. Official estimates suggested that there were over 90 million Chinese born as singleton children by the year of 2007 (90m Chinese Growing Up as Only Children, 2007), which has allegedly increased to over 100 million. This may account for a significant decrease in family size from 4.41 people per family in 1980 to 3.10 in 2010 (Ma, 2011). Nevertheless, in both urban and rural areas, parents are encouraged to offer comparable resources to their singleton children regardless of gender, which would have been unimaginable in the past.

Socioeconomic policies

One other major source of within-cultural variation is the rural/urban dichotomy, which has a variety of implications for family life and fathering. The introduction of a market economy in the late 1970s, together with the continuation of rural/urban distinctions in the household registration system (戶口制度) contributed to vast disparities in lifestyle between urban and rural families. The latest report on family finance (Survey and Research Center for China Household Finance, 2012), surveying over 8,400 families in 25 Chinese provinces, suggests that the average annual income of an urban family (21,819 Yuan – CNY) is more than three times (6,877 CNY) that of a rural family, and the medium annual family income for urban and rural families is 27,200 CNY and 10,000 CNY, respectively. Four-fifths of the rural population has been educated up to middle school or less, and the illiteracy rate is as high as 14.51%, while over half of the urban population has at least a high school diploma with the illiteracy rate of merely 4.23%. Whereas urban families enjoy modern conveniences and benefit from social policies, rural families are far more likely to suffer from economic and social hardships including more costly medical insurance and school fees, and a lack of affordable childcare, well-staffed schools, public libraries and computer access. These conditions, along with associated family problems such as parental conflicts over childcare, make family life and child rearing in the countryside and cities very different. The socio-economic gap between rural and urban families, and similarly between coastal areas and inland provinces, also affects fatherhood in Mainland China.

Gender policies and employment patterns

Gender equality and employment policies powerfully affect paternal involvement. In Mainland China, gender equality has been a constitutional right since 1954 (Article 86, *Constitution of the People's Republic of China*, 1954), and women have been encouraged to pursue education and join the labour force. At the end of 2004, for instance, 337 million Chinese women were registered as employed and made up 44.8% of the workforce, and a recent nation-wide survey of Beijing, Shanghai and Guangdong households indicated that women were no more likely than men to be unemployed (Institute of Social Science Survey, Peking University, 2010). International data also show that China has a higher female employment rate and greater gender equality than other East Asian countries, including Japan and South Korea (Hausmann, Tyson, & Zahidi, 2010). For example, while about one-third of Indian women and half of Japanese women participate in the labour market, the female labour market participation rate in China has remained at around 70% in recent decades (United Nations Secretariat, Department of Economic and Social Affairs [DESA], 2011).

It is not certain, though, whether and to what extent egalitarian policies have changed the behaviour of Chinese fathers. Is childcare fairly shared by parents in dual-earner families, which are the norm in urban China, or is it still the mothers' responsibility? Public surveys show that in 2000 the average urban Chinese woman spent 3.34 hours a day on domestic labour (household activities including but not limited to childcare), compared to 2.08 hours by the average husband, and that rural women spent as many as 4.27 hours on household chores each day, almost three times as much as their husbands (Xu, 2004). The latest governmental data also suggest that, regardless of cross-regional variations, Chinese women still take primary responsibility for household chores on both weekdays and weekends (Institute of Social Science Survey, Peking University, 2010). Such figures indicate that employment policies have not yet transformed the father's roles.

Other employment policies that affect fatherhood, such as paternal access to childbirth and paternal leave, have just started to attract attention. Chinese fathers are now entitled to ten days of paternal leave around childbirth, although this right is neither well known nor widely implemented. In large cities such as Shanghai and Guangzhou, fathers are also allowed to attend childbirth, but we do not know how many fathers know about, appreciate, or benefit from this policy (http://english.cctv.com/20090619/101165.shtml).

Family structures

Modernization of Chinese societies has brought change to family structures, too. Two aspects of family structure are particularly critical to our discussion: (1) the increase in the proportion of nuclear families and (2) father absence attributable to the "floating population" (流動人口) of men who leave their places of origin alone to find work, often moving from rural areas to cities.

In accordance with the Chinese tradition of filial piety, multiple generations often live in the same residence, usually with the paternal grandparents. According to the national census in 2000, for example, 13.3% of urban Chinese families, 14.3% of suburban families and 20.2% of rural families had three or more generations living in the same household. Among urban and suburban families, the number of multi-generational families had been decreasing, whereas the number of rural multi-generational families had increased. This is probably because urban senior citizens can usually live by themselves on their pensions, whereas rural seniors with no pension or properties must rely more on their children. Extended families are becoming problematic in a mobile society, especially as younger Chinese seek increasing independence. As a result, nuclear families have become proportionately more common, accounting for over half the households in China in 2000 (Wang, 2006). This trend is bringing about substantial changes in the ability of Chinese fathers to exert paternal authority without grandparental interference. Although fathers in nuclear families may shoulder a heavier childcare burden than those who can count on grandparental support, they may enjoy more time and freedom to inter-act with their children. Such family structures may change father–child relationships by enhancing father–child intimacy through engagement in various aspects of their children's lives, and by altering family dynamics and children's perceptions of their fathers in positive ways.

Growth of the "floating population," on the other hand, poses an impediment to fathering. The latest governmental statistics show that the floating population in Mainland China had reached 261.39 million (National Bureau of Statistics of the People's Republic of China, 2011b), most of whom are young migrant workers (mostly male, mean age = 27.3 years) who lack higher education, training opportunities and social resources (Li, Song, Qi, Tang, & Qin, 2010). Floating fathers, frequently with working wives, leave behind a growing number of "skipped gen-eration families" (隔代家庭) consisting of grandparents and children. This phenomenon is especially apparent in rural areas, where the number of skipped generation families has quadrupled over the last few decades, from 0.5% of the population in 1990 to 2.4% in 2000 (Wang, 2006). Paternal absence as a result of migration is often accompanied by other pathogenic factors, including economic hardship, limited parental education, mental

Figure 2.2 Three-year-old Qinqin, left behind in a rural home by working par-ents, is spending an early spring day with her grandmother. Guojia Village, Anren County, Hunan Province, March 30, 2011. Photo courtesy of China News Service.

stress, and marital instability, and this situation has fostered concern among both researchers and policy makers.

Reminders for researchers

The complicated social reality discussed above has increased the diversity of the Chinese population substantially and complicated the task of scholars who explore Chinese fatherhood. Although public policies affect private life, social policies – like cultural notions – are not the only determinant of individual behaviour, which is also influenced by practicalities. This is especially true in developing countries like China, where the struggle for survival often trumps the wishes of policy makers. To understand Chinese fatherhood, therefore, researchers need to study the actual behaviour of Chinese fathers, and not only government documents.

Summary

It is important to understand the cultural roots and social contexts in which Chinese fatherhood is articulated, although their implications are neither simple nor straightforward. The traditional Chinese fathering style is considered to be a product of Confucian, Taoist and Buddhist thought, with the ideal father being a responsible but affectively distant disciplinarian and role model. However, it is difficult to describe Chinese fatherhood generally because Chinese culture is so diverse and dynamic. Contemporary social contexts also shape Chinese fathering. Family planning policies, gender roles and socioeconomic development contribute to differences in paternal behaviours across regions and classes. Practicalities such as the availability of social resources are at least as important as cultural values and public policies in shaping Chinese paternal behaviour.

Review of Fathering Research

Overview of research on Chinese fatherhood

The scholarly analysis of Chinese fathers dates back to the early 1980s, soon after the renaissance of research on fatherhood in the West. Early reviews by Ho (1987, 1989), for instance, examined the influence of traditional Chinese culture on fathering and depicted Chinese fathers as authoritarian and distant. Further research followed, with some scholars emphasizing Western views of fatherhood (e.g. Wang, 2005) and others focusing especially on Chinese fathers. In fact, more articles about fathering were published in China after 2000 (217 by 2008) than between 1975 and 2000 (only 90 articles; Shwalb et al., 2010). Reliable and valid empirical evidence about Chinese fatherhood remains scarce however. A search within China Academic Journals Full-Text Database, the most comprehensive academic database in Mainland China, reveals that the majority of fathering articles published between 2005 and 2010 were journalistic in nature, with very few empirical studies.

Paternal involvement

Several researchers have sought to measure paternal involvement in different subgroups, and have concluded that fathers across different Chinese societies want to be more engaged than in previous generations (a trend notable throughout the chapters of this volume). In the early 1980s, Ho and Kang (1984) noted that fathers in Hong Kong were more involved than their fathers had been, in a variety of childcare tasks such as feeding and changing diapers. Liu (1995) later reported even greater shifts in the reported behaviour of fathers in Shanghai: 83.6% of modern fathers, compared to 61.8% from their fathers' generation, thought that men should help take care of the baby. Meanwhile, 87% of these fathers, compared to 60.4% from the grandparental generation, had actually helped with childcare tasks. A detailed breakdown of childcare tasks also demonstrated that fathers of the younger generation were more likely than their predecessors to pick up children from school or to comfort distressed children (Xu & Zhang, 2008). Similarly, surveys in Taiwan indicated that while 32% of the Taiwanese fathers spent three or more hours daily with their children in 1998; 50% did so in 2002 (Wu, 2006).

Despite the preceding evidence of increases in paternal involvement, research studies have consistently shown that Chinese fathers still do less childcare than mothers. For example, Jankowiak (2010) remarked on his long-term ethnographic observations in Hohhot, a large multi-ethnic (80% Han) city in northern China, that mothers were still the main caregivers both at home and in public. Chinese fathers, even those self-identified as "modern" and involved, attended only occasionally to their children. A closer examination of parental contributions to childcare showed that Chinese mothers in Hong Kong "feed, smile at, vocalize to and engage in object play" with infants more than fathers do (Sun & Roopnarine, 1996, p. 121). More recent surveys indicate that even in Shanghai, where men are reportedly more involved in domestic labour, 93% of 1,921 married men and women identified mothers as the major caregivers in their families (Xu, 2004). Similarly, interviews with five dual-earner Taiwanese families showed that mothers provided more childcare than did fathers (Wang & Yu, 1997). Nearly 50% of the fathers in another Taiwanese sample, compared to more than 80% of the mothers, spent more than three hours daily with their children (Wu, 2006). Paternal involvement in Chinese families is also intermittent and depends on the will or mood of the father (Wang & Yu, 1997), with a discrepancy between motivation and actual involvement (Mo, 1997, cited in Huang & Wang, 2007).

A few studies have also suggested that paternal involvement depends on the children's ages. Jankowiak's (2010) observational study suggested that Chinese fathers were neither interested in nor competent with infants and children under three years of age. When their children started to walk and talk, however, fathers reportedly became more actively involved and expressed more satisfaction with their roles. Primary school enrollment (6 or 7 years of age), which coincides with the "age of reason," seems to mark another transition for fathering behaviour. It is around this age that Chinese fathers start to become formally involved in their children's education, because fathers are considered responsible for teaching and educating children. In Shanghai, for example, 53% of the fathers in a large social survey ($n = 1,921$) took primary responsibility to help with schoolwork, whereas only 14% were in charge of childcare chores (Xu, 2004).

Parenting styles

Chinese researchers also began to study parenting styles as measures of this construct became popular in the West (Shwalb et al., 2010). Differentiation between maternal and paternal behaviour could be anticipated based on traditional gender roles, but empirical findings have been mixed. The "strict father, affectionate mother" pattern was evident in some studies, including early anthropological observations by Wolf (1978), who depicted Chinese fathers as the primary disciplinarians. Similarly, Berndt and his colleagues (1993) reported that fathers in Mainland China, Hong Kong, and Taiwan were perceived as less warm than mothers by sons and daughters. Shek (1998, 2000) also found that adolescents from Hong Kong rated their fathers as less responsive, less demanding and less concerned, but also harsher than mothers. A more recent report suggests that fathers in areas of Greater China have maintained their patriarchal authority by refraining from emotional support for children as disciplinarians (DESA, 2011). By contrast, Lin and Fu (1990) found no differences between maternal and paternal behaviour in Taiwanese or immigrant Chinese families in the United States, and neither did Chuang and Su (2009) who studied Mainland Chinese and immigrant Chinese parents with toddlers. These contradictory findings may reflect differences in sampling and methods.

Despite these inconsistent findings, affectionate distance has been discussed by observers of Chinese fathering. For example, emotional suppression by traditional Chinese fathers was noted in early observational studies, as we noted earlier. As Wolf (1978, p. 225) remarked about her field study in northern Taiwan, "Taiwanese fathers say that it is only from this aloof distance that they can engender in their sons the proper behaviour of a good adult ... this remoteness also builds the supports necessary to maintain the senior male's position of authority over his adult sons" (p. 225). Similarly, following his observations in northern China, Jankowiak (2010, p. 347) noted that "... Chinese fathers ... did not strive to develop a warm emotionally charged parent–child relationship" although they "felt a warm, deep sentiment toward their children." Some evidence suggests that such emotional suppression may still persist, as evidenced by a study of 892 families in suburban areas around Shanghai which showed that fathers in these families still report low levels of communication and emotional support (Xu & Zhang, 2008).

Like paternal involvement, paternal affection changes as children attain the age of reason, when fathers become even more focused on discipline and less affectionate. Wolf (1978) further observed that father–child interaction: "... becomes more and more formal and their conversation deteriorates into paternal lectures, the father's dignity becomes more impressive and more impregnable" (p. 225). Longitudinal studies tracking developmental changes in fathering behaviour are rare, but Xu,

Figure 2.3 The life of left-behind seniors and children as a result of urbanization related immigration has become a major issue in rural China, as recognized by the Chinese government. Photograph taken November 13, 2007 with unspecified location, presumably Hunan Province. Photo courtesy of China News Service.

Ji and Zhang's (2006) cross-sectional survey confirmed that fathers of school-aged children were stricter than fathers of preschoolers. Other factors associated with variations in fathering styles include socioeconomic status (Yang, She, & Zhang, 2005), gender roles (Xu et al., 2006) and the child's gender (Chuang & Su, 2009; Shek, 1998; Sun & Roopnarine, 1996; Yang et al., 2005). In general, better educated fathers and fathers who have less rigid attitudes about gender roles appear to be more affectionate.

Paternal influences on child development

Paternal influences on different aspects of child development have also attracted the attention of researchers worldwide. A chapter on East Asian fatherhood (Shwalb et al., 2010), for example, provided a comprehensive summary of research on this topic, and concluded that Chinese fathers have a role in the cognitive development, socio-emotional development, and mental health of their children.

Cognitive development and academic performance

As teachers and disciplinarians, Chinese fathers might be expected to affect their children's cognitive development and school performance. For example, Xu and Zhang's (2008) survey in urban and suburban areas around Shanghai revealed positive associations between paternal presence, father–child relationships and children's academic performance (e.g., interest in learning, diligence, school achievement) such that children with more involved fathers outperformed their peers both at home and at school. Other researchers pointed out that fathers may be more influential than mothers in this domain (Fung, 2006; Zeng, Lu, Zou, Dong, & Chen, 1997). It is not yet clear, however, whether and how different fathering styles affect children's cognitive development, although studies in the West suggest that warm, supportive fathering styles promote academic performance. Indeed, Chen, Liu, and Li (2000)'s study of 258 12-year-old children and Zeng et al.'s (1997) study of 304 second-grade pupils both suggested that paternal warmth, or authoritative fathering style, is positively correlated with better academic performance by children, whereas paternal strictness is associated with deficient learning. Fung (2006), meanwhile, found that the children of warm, loving fathers and mothers performed better academically.

Socio-emotional development

There is increasing interest in comparing Chinese paternal and maternal influences on socio-emotional development. As in Xu and Zhang's (2008) survey of 1,752 parents in rural and urban areas of Shanghai and Hu et al.'s (2009) study of 351 college students in Tianjin, Zeng et al. (1997) reported that paternal behaviour had a greater impact than maternal behaviour on children's social skills. With regard to specific fathering behaviours, most studies show that warm, authoritative fathering is associated with better socio-emotional outcomes. In a longitudinal study involving 4- to 7-year-olds ($n = 54$), Chen, Zhang, Yin, Cheng, and Wang (2004) reported that self-rated paternal control and rejection predicted children's pro-social behaviour at school. In particular, children of controlling and reject-ing fathers were less pro-social than children with supportive fathers. Likewise, an observational study of 65 7-year-olds in Shanghai showed that paternal nurturance was related to cooperative peer play. Specifically, the more fathers encouraged their children's achievement and fostered their independence, the more socially competent and active their children were (Li et al., 2004). Elsewhere, Hu and colleagues (2009) reported that warm, understanding parents tended to have children who were more empathic in early adulthood.

Other studies have stressed the significance of Chinese paternal con-trol. For example, Zeng et al. (1997) found a positive association between paternal strictness and the frequency with which 304 primary school children were listed as their peers' favourite classmates. Similarly, Chen, Liu, and Li (2000) reported that paternal indulgence (excessive paternal warmth) could lead to maladjustment at school. It is also worth noting that, although paternal strictness is positively associated with social com-petence and popularity, it is negatively associated with shyness (Zeng et al., 1997), a counterintuitive result which reflects different social expec-tations in Eastern and Western cultures. While shyness is sometimes treated as an internalizing problem in Western societies, it is accepted, if not encouraged, as a sign of self-inhibition and maturity in Chinese cul-tures where it is thus compatible with adequate peer social skills (Chen, Rubin, & Sun, 1992).

Taken together, these correlational studies suggest several ways that Chinese fathers may affect their children's social competence at different developmental stages, although differences between samples and meas-ures limit the cohesiveness of the findings.

Mental health and problem behaviours

Chinese fathers also reportedly affect their children's mental health, as dem-onstrated in research on social inequality and family welfare using locally validated clinical diagnostic tools. Chen (2007) found that children whose fathers migrated to work were more inhibited, anxious, and depressed than those living with their fathers. Unfortunately, this study did not control for possibly confounding socioeconomic factors which might have affected fathers' work patterns in the first place. Specifically, fathers from impover-ished families may be more inclined to seek work away from home, making it hard to know whether socioeconomic factors or father absence (or both) affected the children. Other studies have examined the link between fathering styles and children's mental pathologies. Lu, Chen, Wang, and Chen (2003) used a cross-lagged longitudinal design to explore the associations between Q-sort assessed parental behaviour and 2- to 4-year-old children's reported problem behaviour. Here, externalizing behavioural problems were associated with paternal punishment at both time points, while paternal punitiveness was stable over time. In a study of 283 third- to sixth-graders (9- to 12-year-olds), for example, Sun, Lu, and Dong (1998) reported that punitive, overprotective fathers and mothers tended to have highly anxious children, while loving, supportive and trusting parenting styles were negatively associated with the children's anxiety levels. Similarly, the behaviour problems of 652 Chinese 6- to 11-year-olds were closely related to self-reported paternal punitiveness, denial, lack of warmth, and lack of understanding (Zou, Liu, & Zou, 2007).

Further, Zhao's (2006) meta-analysis of 27 articles published between 1996 and 2005 on parenting styles and Chinese children's behaviour problems showed that paternal punishment was positively correlated with externalized problems in high school students while paternal interference was associated with internalizing problems. Meanwhile, paternal warmth and understanding were correlated negatively with internalized problems in primary school students and adolescents. Hao and Li (2008) found associations between paternal rejection, denial and overprotection and a variety of symptoms such as obsessive-compulsive behaviours, interpersonal sensitivity, depression, phobia, paranoia and psychosis in a study of 1,756 senior high school students. Together, these correlational studies suggest that there is an association between warm, non-punitive fathering and desirable mental health outcomes for Chinese children, adolescents and young adults, whereas paternal overprotection and strictness remain risk factors, especially for older offspring (Ma, 2005; Mao, Han, Liu, Wang, & Pan, 2006; Zeng, Wang, & Zhu, 2008).

Fathers' behaviour may also affect the behaviour problems of sons and daughters differently. In their study of 4- to 7-year-olds' problem behaviour at school, Chen et al. (2004) found that paternal indulgence, overprotection and rejection were more strongly associated with boys' than girls' behaviour problems. This association contrasted with the findings of Yuan, Zhao, and Zhang (2009), who reported that the involvement of 1,022 fathers in Guangzhou was related to behaviour problems of primary school-aged girls, but not boys.

Images of father–child relations

A few researchers have compared children's images of Chinese father–child and mother–child relationships. For example, Yu and Zhou (2002) reported that children were "better attached" to their mothers than to their fathers. Similarly, adolescents in 14 Chinese cities reported feeling closer to their mothers than to their fathers (Feng, 2002). Focus groups involving Taiwanese youth revealed that Taiwanese fathers and sons had more distant relations than fathers and daughters (Chiu, 2005), and a study of 506 adolescent Taiwanese girls identified a "longing-for-father's-love complex" defined by attitudes, feelings and desires associated with extended suppression of strong desires for the father's love (Yeh, Lin, Wang, & Lin, 2006). Taiwanese girls who suppressed their yearning for paternal affection reported more psychosomatic symptoms, more social difficulties, and poorer mental health.

Other research has emphasized more positive images of father–child relations. For example, college students participating in focus groups had more positive perceptions of their fathers than early adolescents (Chiu, 2005, 2009), perhaps because they were better able to appreciate the affection that their fathers often did not express openly. Using a more quantitative approach, Zhang (2009) found that 423 Mainland Chinese adolescents were satisfied with their fathers on four dimensions: fathers' attitudes toward education, personality, competence, and level of modernity. They rated their fathers as competent, reliable, frank, tolerant, and brave, but also stubborn, inflexible, non-creative, proud, and distant at the same time.

Commentary on the research literature

An increasing number of empirical studies concerned with many aspects of fatherhood have been conducted in diverse Chinese cultures, and some consistent findings have emerged. For example, it is clear that that paternal warmth and support are associated with positive aspects of child development, but also that fathers tend not to be involved in nurturant childcare. However, like their counterparts in many other societies (as described in most of the chapters of this volume), contemporary Chinese fathers face social pressures to become more closely involved in their children's lives. As also noted in many countries worldwide, Chinese fathers also play the roles of employee and are the subjects of social policy, and the demands of their various roles affect paternal behaviour and their children's development.

Considerable efforts have been made by scholars, especially in Taiwan, to capture the defining characteristics of Chinese fatherhood and father–child relationships, often using rich qualitative data in studies informed by extensive observations (e.g., Tu, 2004), while Chiu's (2009) focus group interviews explored the perceptions of children in several age groups. Such research may provide a useful foundation for future indigenous studies of Chinese fatherhood, especially on subjective experiences of father–child relations and perceptions of fathers.

However, in other areas of research the data are less consistent. It is not yet clear, for instance, whether Chinese fathers and mothers approach parenting differently, or whether Chinese fathers treat sons and daughters differently. More fundamentally, it is unclear what is "Chinese" about fathering, or whether the "traditional Chinese father" still exists. These doubts reflect conceptual weaknesses in the research on Chinese fatherhood. Influential English-language works on fatherhood (e.g., Lamb, 1975, 2010; Doherty, Kouneski, & Erickson, 1998; Paquette, 2004; Tamis-LeMonda, 2004) have rarely been considered by the Chinese, possibly because of language barriers and lack of access to academic resources. This is especially true in Mainland China, where research findings tend not to be well summarized or disseminated. Many studies are student projects and psychology and the other social sciences are still not yet well developed in China. In addition, the specific components of the Chinese culture that influence paternal behaviour and family relations have yet to be disentangled. Although further exploration is still needed to grasp the essence of Chinese fatherhood, the widespread belief that Chinese fathers are unique or significantly different from their counterparts in other cultures is not well supported by research. This discrepancy between perceptions and the true nature of Chinese fathers makes clear that there is a need for inter-cultural and intra-cultural comparative research. Most of the existing research is descriptive and correlational in nature, and while policy-related questions (e.g., paternal leave) have started to attract attention from academics, there has been little intervention research. This may be because research on mental health has a low priority in contemporary China.

Sampling is problematic in many studies. It is difficult to obtain representative samples of Chinese fathers and families for a number of reasons, including the large and diverse population size and the mobile nature of contemporary Chinese life. Political segregation of certain sub-groups such as that between Mainland China and Taiwan also limits opportunities for sampling across groups, while the fathers' roles as primary wage-earners and managers of external familial affairs make them less accessible at home, where data collection usually takes place. Attempts have been made to obtain representative samples by expanding sample sizes, recruiting across geographic regions and socioeconomic sectors, and by collaborating with researchers from different sub-groups. An example of the latter was Berndt et al.'s (1993) research collaboration which involved matched large samples from Mainland China, Taiwan and Hong Kong, and provided convincing results that took into consideration variations between sub-groups. Meanwhile, Liu's (1995) replication in Shanghai of

Ho and Kang's (1984) Hong Kong study helped us to understand the similarities and differences between fathers in these two locations. Because such comparative studies are rare, within-culture variation has received little attention. Finally, the scarcity of indigenous measures (Zhang, Chen, Zhang, Zhou, & Wu, 2008, was a rare exception) raises questions about the cultural equivalence of measures introduced from other cultures.

Conclusions and Predictions for the Future

Fathering, as is shown in every chapter of this volume, involves behaviours that are embedded in multiple, complex, social, cultural and familial contexts, and is thus very difficult to explore. It is particularly difficult to study Chinese fatherhood because multi-millennial historical influences clash and intertwine with rapid contemporary social influences. Due to the theoretical and methodological weaknesses discussed above, and which again characterizes research in many cultures, findings must be interpreted carefully and conclusions drawn with great caution.

Researchers have been making great efforts to understanding the role of the father as the ultimate authority figure in traditional Chinese culture, by reviewing relevant classic texts (Ho, 1987; Hwang, 2001) and by examining related modern social phenomena such as the rural/urban contrast (Yang et al., 2005). Discussions of Chinese fathers are still fragmentary and unsystematic, however, and it is unclear what is unique about Chinese fathering. Although historical documents and popular proverbs help characterize Chinese fathers, the specific influences of culture are still undefined.

Several researchers have studied paternal involvement, parenting styles, father–child relations and perceptions of fathers in different Chinese subgroups, and an array of hypotheses about Chinese fathers have been tested, derived from research in other cultures and core Confucian beliefs. Findings suggest both universality and cultural specificity. Chinese fathers influence their children just as their counterparts do in most other cultures. They affect many aspects of their children's development and are probably now being drawn, like men around the world, to more warm and nurturant engagement. Although such a trend has not been well documented (Liu, 1995; Xu & Zhang, 2008), gradual changes are likely to reflect the influence of Western culture by way of media and entertainment that have entered the Chinese market over recent decades. An example of this is the 1985–1992 American television series *Growing Pains*, which featured a warm, understanding father and appeared on Chinese television as recently as 2005. Changes in family structure and gender roles may also have been influential. Growing female employment and the decline of multi-generational families have also made it necessary for fathers to become more involved in their children's care and rearing.

On the other hand, cultural factors, governmental policies and regional development all affect paternal behaviour and family relations in Chinese culture. Chinese fathers are implicitly encouraged by Confucian ideology to behave as stern educators and role models rather than as their children's caregivers or playmates. Although many contemporary Chinese fathers are becoming more involved in childcare, their availability depends on their employment status, social resources, and social policies (e.g., paternal leave), all of which vary greatly across regions and ethnicities. In Mainland China, for instance, family-planning policies might have made children especially precious to their parents, which may foster more rapid changes than in Taiwan or Hong Kong.

The future of Chinese fatherhood

We have surveyed the literature on Chinese fatherhood, but this review was far from exhaustive. Still in its infancy, research on Chinese fatherhood should be complemented by interdisciplinary discussion and cross-regional collaborations between different societies within Chinese culture. Drawing on conceptualizations of the Chinese culture, representative sampling and validated measurements, the influence of other understudied factors on paternal behaviour, including paternal personality, education, cultural identity, and family structure, would help elucidate the diversity of Chinese fatherhood. While most researchers have focused on child development, future studies should also explore the development and subjective experiences of Chinese fathers. In an exemplary study of 872 Shanghai fathers' perceptions and experiences, Xu and Zhang (2009) found that Shanghai fathers reported overwhelmingly positive experiences, emphasizing pride and excitement about having children, and happiness (as also expressed by Qiu in our opening Case Story) regarding their children's development and progress. Fathers, especially those from suburban backgrounds, also remarked on the positive ways in which fatherhood had affected their own development. Similar studies of fathers from other regions and backgrounds could contribute greatly to our understanding of intra-cultural variations in fathering attitudes and experiences. A wider range of ethnic minorities within Chinese culture should be studied as should new family forms (e.g., single-parent families, adoptive families, families with floating fathers). The floating fathers, both those who take their children with them and those who leave their families behind, should be of particular interest to policy makers and researchers concerned with social equality. Researchers should, for instance, explore how paternal identity affects decisions about where men work and how fathers feel about parenting from afar. With respect to floating fathers working away from home, the influence of paternal absence on child development, on father–child relationships and on between-parent coordination should be investigated. Such issues could also be studied in comparison to fathers who migrate across borders, who have been investigated more widely and intensively (DESA, 2011). Finally, as our knowledge about Chinese fathers becomes more robust, research data might be used to guide family intervention programs and social policies.

Summary

This chapter summarized the research literature on fathers in Chinese culture. It described cultural traditions and contemporary socioeconomic situations, and reviewed empirical studies. We also speculated about the ways in which Chinese fathers might differ from those in other cultures and how their attitudes and behaviour might be complicated by current circumstances.

The chapter reviewed many empirical studies that utilized samples from various Chinese societies and regions. These studies suggested that Chinese fathers resembled fathers from other cultural backgrounds in the ways they influence various aspects of child development, and that social attitudes towards fathers are in a process of transition. Modern Chinese fathers tend to be more involved than those in previous generations, although like their predecessors they tend to focus on responsibility for academic issues. Researchers have attempted to explore intra-cultural variations in fathering across socio-economic classes and generations, but have not systematically compared the behaviour of fathers among different Chinese societies.

Informed by the results of past research, we also speculated about the future of research on Chinese fatherhood, which may involve a clearer and more inclusive conceptualization of Chinese fatherhood and further research on particular social groups, including "the floating population" of migrant fathers.

References

90m Chinese growing up as only children. (2007, January 23). _Xinhua Net._ Retrieved from: http://news.xinhuanet.com/edu/2007–01/23/content_5642765.htm

Berndt, T. J., Cheung, P. C., Lau, S., Hau, K.-T., & Lew, W. J. F. (1993). Perceptions of parenting in Mainland China, Taiwan, and Hong Kong: Sex differences and societal differences. _Developmental Psychology, 29_(1), 156–164.

Chao, R. K. (1994). Beyond parental control and authoritarian parenting style: Understanding Chinese parenting through the cultural notion of training. _Child Development, 65_(4), 1111–1119.

Chen, X. (2007). _The research on left-behind children's academic achievement, self-esteem and personality under father absence_ [Abstract] (Unpublished master's thesis, Northwest Normal University, Lanzhou, Gansu, China). Retrieved from http://epub.cnki.net/grid2008/detail.aspx?QueryID=102&CurRec=1

Chen, X., Liu, M., & Li, D. (2000). Parental warmth, control, and indulgence and their relations to adjustment in Chinese children: A longitudinal study. *Journal of Family Psychology, 14*(3), 401–419.

Chen, X., Rubin, K. H., & Sun, Y. (1992). Social reputation and peer relationship in Chinese and Canadian children: A cross-cultural study. *Child Development, 63,* 1336–1343.

Chen, H., Zhang, H., Yin, J., Cheng, X., & Wang, M. (2004). Father's rearing attitude and its prediction for 4–7 years old children's problem behaviors and school adjustment. *Psychological Science, 27*(5), 1041–1045.

Chiu, J. (2005). Father image: How college students perceive their fathers? *Bulletin of National Ping-Tung Teachers College, 22,* 291–330.

Chiu, J. (2009). Father image: The perspectives of students from junior high through college: A comparison study. *Bulletin of Educational Research, 43*(2), 29–54.

Chuang, S. S., & Su, Y. (2009). Says who? Decision making and conflicts among Chinese-Canadian and Mainland Chinese parents of young children. *Sex Roles, 60,* 523–536.

Doherty, W. J., Kouneski, E. F., & Erickson, M. F. (1998). Responsible fathering: An overview and conceptual framework. *Journal of Marriage and Family, 60*(2), 277–292.

Feng, X. (2002). Urban high school students' images of their relationships with parents. *Youth Studies, 21,* 36–40.

Fung, H. (2006). Affect and early moral socialization: Indigenous research from Taiwan. In U. Kim, K.-S. Yang, & K.-K. Huang. (Eds.), *Indigenous and cultural psychology: Understanding people in context* (pp. 175–196). New York, NJ: Springer Science + Business Media.

Guo, Z., Chen, J., Xie, P., Zhang, D., & Lin, A. (2009). *Shijie huashang baogao* [2008 World Chinese Entrepreneurs Development Report]. Retrieved on May 9, 2012, from Jinan University website: http://aocs.jnu.edu.cn/upfile/200910202005678.pdf (in Chinese).

Hao, Y., & Li, J. (2008). The impact of urban/rural parental rearing pattern on the mental health of senior high school students of Xi'an. *China Journal of Health Psychology, 16*(2), 201–203.

Hausmann, R., Tyson, L. D., & Zahidi, S. (2010). *Global Gender Gap Report 2010.* Geneva, Switzerland: World Economic Forum. Retrieved from: http://www.weforum.org/reports/global-gender-gap-report-2010?fo=1

Ho, D. Y. F. (1987). Fatherhood in Chinese culture. In M. E. Lamb (Ed.), *The father's role: Cross-cultural perspectives* (pp. 227–246). Hillsdale, NJ: Lawrence Erlbaum Associates.

Ho, D. Y. F. (1989). Continuity and variation in Chinese patterns of socialization. *Journal of Marriage and Family, 51*(1), 149–163.

Ho, D. Y. F., & Kang, T. K. (1984). Intergenerational comparisons of child-rearing practices and attitudes in Hong Kong. *Developmental Psychology, 20*(6), 1004–1016.

Hu, W., Gao, J., Kang, T., Wu, B., Shi, K., Wang, X., & Wen, Z. (2009, September). Research on the relationship and influencing factors between university students' empathy and parental rearing patterns. *China Journal of Health Psychology,* 1050–1055.

Huang, I., & Wang, K. (2007). Nanxing canyu qinzhi zhi xianxingjiegou moshi fenxi [Linear analyses of involvement pattern of men's parental involvement]. Paper presented at *Meeting of Taiwanese Feminist Scholars Association and National Kao Hsiung Normal University 40th Anniversary*, Kao Hsiung, Taiwan (in Chinese).

Hwang, K.-K. (2001). The deep structure of Confucianism: A social psychological approach. *Asian Philosophy, 11*(3), 179–204.

Information Office, State Council of People's Republic of China. (1995). *Family Planning in China*. Retrieved from: www.china.org.cn/e-white/familyplanning/

Institute of Social Science Survey, Peking University. (2010). *Chinese Family Dynamics 2010*. Beijing, China: Peking University Press.

Jankowiak, W. (2010). Father and child relations in urban China. In B. S. Hewlett (Ed.), *Parent–youth relations* (Vol. 1, pp. 345–363). New Brunswick, NJ: Aldine Transaction.

Lamb, M. E. (1975). Fathers: Forgotten contributors to child development. *Human Development, 18*, 245–266.

Lamb, M. E. (Ed.). (2010). *The role of father in child development* (5th ed.). Hoboken, NJ: Wiley.

Li, D., Cui, L., Cen, G., Zhou, J., & Chen, X. (2004). Peer interaction of children aged 6–8 and its relation to paternal nurturing styles. *Psychological Science, 27*(4), 803–806.

Li, B., Song, Y., Qi, J., Tang, D., & Qin, M. (2010). Current living situation of migrant population in China: A pilot survey of migrant population in five major cities. *Population Research* (January), 6–18.

Lin, C.-Y. C., & Fu, V. R. (1990). Comparison of childrearing practices among Chinese, immigrant Chinese and Caucasian American parents [2nd Special Issue on Minority Children]. *Child Development, 61*(April), 429–433.

Liu, J. (1995). An intergenerational comparison of paternal child-rearing attitudes and ideas in Shanghai. *Psychological Science, 4*, 211–215, 255.

Lu, Q., Chen, H., Wang, L., & Chen, X. (2003). Parents' child-rearing attitude and children's problem behaviors at two and four years of age. *Acta Psychologica Sinica, 35*(1), 89–92.

Ma, W. (2005). Relationship of parental rearing styles and the correlative factors with the mental health of medical students. *Chinese Journal of Clinical Rehabilitation, 11*, 226–227.

Ma, J. (2011). *Diliuci quanguo renkoupucha zhuyao shuju fabu* [Press Release on Major Figures of the 2010 National Population Census]. Retrieved May 9, 2012, from National Bureau of Statistics of the People's Republic of China website (in Chinese): http://www.stats.gov.cn/zgrkpc/dlc/yw/t20110428_402722384.htm

Mao, X., Han, J., Liu, M., Wang, M., & Pan, F. (2006). Personality traits and parental rearing practices in adolescents' adjustment disorders. *Journal of Shandong University (Health Sciences), 44*(11), 1132–1134, 1138.

National Bureau of Statistics of the People's Republic of China. (2011a). *Major statistics on residents from Hong Kong, Macau, Taiwan and foreigners covered by 2010 population census.* Retrieved from: www.stats.gov.cn/was40/gjtjj_en_detail. jsp?channelid=1175&record=17

National Bureau of Statistics of the People's Republic of China. (2011b). *Communiqué of the National Bureau of Statistics of the People's Republic of China on major figures of the 2010 population census [1].* Retrieved from: www.stats.gov.cn/was40/ gjtjj_en_detail.jsp?channelid=1175&record=19

Overseas Chinese. (n.d.). In *Wikipedia.* Retrieved from: http://en.wikipedia.org/ wiki/Overseas_Chinese

Paquette, D. (2004). Theorizing the father–child relationship: Mechanisms and developmental outcomes. *Human Development, 47*(4), 193–219.

Shek, D. T. L. (1998). Adolescents' perception of paternal and maternal parenting styles in a Chinese cultural context. *Journal of Psychology, 132*(5), 527–537.

Shek, D. T. L. (2000). Differences between fathers and mothers in the treatment of, and relationship with, their teenage children: Perceptions of Chinese adolescents. *Adolescence, 35*(137), 135–146.

Shwalb, D. W., Nakazawa, J., Yamamoto, T., & Hyun, J.-H. (2010). Fathering in Japan, China and Korea. In M. E. Lamb (Ed.), (2010). *The role of the father in child development* (5th ed., pp. 341–387). Hoboken, NJ: Wiley.

Sun, L.-C., & Roopnarine, J. L. (1996). Mother-infant, father–infant interaction and involvement in household Taiwanese families. *Infant Behavior and Development, 19*(1), 121–129.

Sun, Y., Lu, Y., & Dong, Q. (1998). Fumu jiaoyuxingwei de jiegou ji qi yu xiaoxue ertong jiaolvqingxu de guanxi [The relationship between structure of parental behaviours and anxiety of primary school children]. *Xinlifazhan yu jiaoyu, 3,* 14–18 (in Chinese).

Survey and Research Center for China Household Finance. (2012). *Zhongguo jiating jinrong diaocha baogao jingxuan* [Highlights of China Household Finance Survey]. Retrieved May 20, 2012, from website of Southwestern University of Finance and Economics website: http://chfs.swufe.edu. cn/NewsDetails.aspx?currpage=default.aspx&pid=xwzx&sid=&id=154 (in Chinese)

Tamis-LeMonda, C. S. (2004). Conceptualizing fathers' roles: Playmates and more. *Human Development, 47*(4), 220–227.

Tang, N. M. (1992). Some psychoanalytic implications of Chinese philosophy and child-rearing practices. *Psychoanalytic Study of the Child, 47,* 371–389.

Tu, Y.-C. (2004). *A study of paternal involvement intention, involvement behaviour, involvement perception and its related factors.* (Unpublished doctoral dissertation, National Tainan Normal University, Tainan, Taiwan). Retrieved from: http://140.133.6.3/handle/987654321/5049

United Nations Secretariat, Department of Economic and Social Affairs. (2011). *Men in families and family policy in a changing world.* New York, NY: Author.

Wang, L. (2005). The history, present condition and trend of the research on fathering pattern in the Western. *Advances in Psychological Science, 13*(3), 290–297.

Wang, S.-Y., & Yu, H.-Y. (1997). Fatherhood in dual-wage family. *Journal of Feminist and Gender Studies, 8,* 115–149.

Wang, Y. (2006). *Dangdai Zhongguo Chengxiang Jiating Jiegou Biandong Bijiao* [Comparisons of changes in family structure in contemporary rural and urban China]. *Shehui, 26*(3), 118–136 (in Chinese).

Wolf, M. (1978). Child training and the Chinese family. In A. P. Wolf & E. M. Ahren (Eds.), *Studies in Chinese society* (pp. 221–243). Palo Alto, CA: Stanford University Press.

Wu, C. (2006). *A study of father involvement in elementary education.* (Unpublished master's thesis, National University of Tainan, Tainan, Taiwan). Retrieved from: http://140.133.6.46/ETD-db/ETD-search/view_etd?URN=etd-0717106–154627

Xu, A. (2004). *Nvxing de jiawu gongxian he jiating diwei, jian ping shanghai "weiqun zhangfu" "qiguanyan" de dingxing wudao* [The females' contribution to housework and their family status, with comments on the misleading steoreotype of "husband in apron" or "hen-pecked husband" in Shanghai]. Retrieved June 9, 2011, from the Chinese Sociology website: http://www.sass.org.cn/eWebEditor/UploadFile/00n/ull/20060530125357103.doc (in Chinese).

Xu, A., & Zhang, L. (2008). Rural fathers' will, acts and experience of parenting: Experienced researcher of Shanghai's suburb, *Hunan Normal University Bulletin of Social Science, 3,* 72–76.

Xu, A., & Zhang, L. (2009). Fuzhicanyu dui nanxing zishenchengzhang de jiji xiaoying [Positive influence of paternal involvement on men: Empirical evidence from Shanghai]. *Shehui Kexue Yanjiu, 3,* 123–129 (in Chinese).

Xu, Y., Ji, L., & Zhang, W. (2006). Urban fathers' involvement in children's parenting and its relationship with gender roles. *Psychological Development and Education, 3,* 35–40.

Yang, Y., She, C., & Zhang, L. (2005). A comparative study on children and adolescents' parenting styles between urban and rural China. *Journal of Shandong Normal University (Humanities and Social Sciences), 50*(6), 152–155.

Yeh, K.-H., Lin, Y.-J., Wang, W.-M. G., & Lin, C.-J. (2006). Father–daughter relationship and the complex of longing for father's love. *Journal of Education and Psychology, 29*(1), 93–119.

Yu, H., & Zhou, Z. (2002). 4–6 graders' attachments to parents and its association to peer relations. *Psychological Development and Education, 18*(4), 36–40.

Yuan, Y., Zhao, J., & Zhang, B. (2009). A study on behavior problems of children in city of Guangzhou. *Chinese Journal of Clinical Psychology, 17*(3), 359–361.

Zeng, Q., Lu, Y., Zou, H., Dong, Q., & Chen, X. (1997). *Fumu jiaoyufangshi yu ertong de xuexiao shiying* [Educational style of the parents and school adjustment of the child]. *Xinlifazhan yu jiaoyu, 2,* 46–51 (in Chinese).

Zeng, R., Wang, J., & Zhu, X. (2008). The effect of parental rearing patterns on college students' academic adjustment. *China Journal of Health Psychology, 16*(10), 1114–1117.

Zhang, F. (2009). A study on satisfaction degree on the father image by middle school students. *Journal of Taiyuan Normal University (Social Science Edition), 8*(4), 18–20.

Zhang, X., Chen, H., Zhang, G., Zhou, B., & Wu, W. (2008). Reliability and validity of Early Father–Child Relationship Scale in China. *Chinese Journal of Clinical Psychology, 16*(1), 13–14, 21.

Zhao, Y. (2006). *The relationship between fathers' rearing and internalizing problems in youth.* [Abstract] (Unpublished master's thesis, Hebei Normal University, Hebei, China). Retrieved from: http://epub.cnki.net/grid2008/detail. aspx?QueryID=8&CurRec=1

Zou, F., Liu, X., & Zou, T. (2007). Relationship between childhood behavior problems and parents' raising methods. *Chinese Journal of Child Health Care, 15*(5), 528–530.

Chapter Three

Fathering in Japan

Entering an Era of Involvement with Children

Jun Nakazawa
Chiba University, Chiba, Japan

David W. Shwalb
Southern Utah University, Cedar City, UT, USA

Case Story: Finding a Balance in Life

Masahiko Tanaka is 36 years old and is an employee of a company in Tokyo. He lives with his wife, who is also employed, and their 3-year-old son. His wife was a college classmate, and he shares the housework equally with her. Masahiko enjoyed everyday life with his wife until the time of her pregnancy. When he learned she was pregnant, he was very happy about becoming a father, but he did not realize what it would mean to be a father. Masahiko gradually came to understand about life as a parent when he attended a fathering class at the urging of his wife. In this class he learned how to support his pregnant wife and to take care of a baby. When he met his son just after the delivery, he experienced new feelings of responsibility.

As a department chief, Masahiko works very hard to achieve his sales goals despite the prolonged recession. His wife is an employee of another company, and when she took maternity leave, she asked Masahiko to also take childcare leave. But he did not take it, because he worried about problems at work during his absence, and about the difficulties he might have later when he returned to work. Instead he does the cooking and childcare on weekends, and has started to enjoy child rearing. Recently, he watched a TV program describing the activities of a non-profit group on fathering and drawing attention to the many fathers who participate actively in childcare. He is planning to attend a father–child camp program run by this group.

He thinks about the kind of father–son relationship he will have when his child gets older. For example, when he was an adolescent, Masahiko's own father was a hard worker and provider who did not have time to communicate with his son. Later on when Masahiko was a senior in college and job-hunting, his father gave him valuable advice about how to work at a company. Looking back at those days, Masahiko now hopes that he can have a closer father–son relationship that his father had with him.

Cultural and Historical Background as It Influences Fathering

Japan and China (Li & Lamb, Ch. 2, this volume) are both international powers, but each combined Western influences with its traditional culture in a unique manner. As a result, the father's role in the two East Asian cultures became distinctive long ago (Shwalb, Nakazawa, Yamamoto, & Hyun, 2010). Western involvement with Japan dates back over 500 years to missionary contacts, and several foreigners' depictions of Japanese life suggest a degree of historical continuity in child rearing and family life. For example, a Portuguese missionary named Fróis (1585/1955) wrote that "We whipped our son as a form of discipline, but do not observe any whipping in Japan. Instead, the Japanese only scold verbally." The Japanese government of the Edo Period (1603–1867) subsequently prohibited the Christian religion and closed the country to the world for over 200 years (with the exception of the Netherlands). Thunberg (1791, 1793), an embassy medical official who came to Japan from Holland in 1775, two centuries after Fróis, made the identical observation that "it is notable that nobody flogs a child in this country." A similar pattern was observed by Kojima (2001) in his analysis of the private journals of a *samurai* from the Edo Period; this warrior father reportedly raised his child in a non-coercive and affectionate manner. After Japan reopened itself to the world in the Meiji Era (1868–1912), Westerners continued to make similar descriptions of Japanese children and parents as permissive and non-coercive. For example, an American biologist (Morse, 1917) who came to Japan in 1877 reported that "… foreign writers agree with one thing, that Japan is a paradise for children. The children in this country are not only treated kindly, but they also have more freedom than children in other countries. They do not abuse this freedom and have many good experiences and a range of opportunities." Finally, Fukaya's (2008) analysis of 100 post-Meiji Era autobiographies revealed self-descriptions of fathers as childlike, weak, and lacking in self-awareness, i.e., neither strict nor strong. These observations across four centuries all indicated a consistent image of Japanese child rearing and fathering, as permissive and based on close attachments rather than on strict discipline or physical punishment.

Japanese-style Confucianism

Japanese society has blended indigenous Shinto culture with Chinese Confucianism and Buddhism. Both Shintoism and Buddhism were originally sanctioned by the Japanese emperor, and for over 1,000 years they probably had a greater impact on Japanese culture than did Confucianism. However, in the Edo Period the government established Confucianism as an official ideology of feudalistic society, and the Confucian ethical code spread across all four social classes (warriors, merchants, artisans, and farmers). After the Meiji Period, when Japan reconnected with the outside world and modernized, Confucian ideology served as a framework for education and family life until the end of World War II.

One of the main tenets of Confucianism was *kou*孝, which mandated obedience to the father and was the basis for patriarchy. The Confucian creed of *genpu jibo* (厳父慈母 strict father, affectionate mother) was also well known in China and Korea, and it encouraged fathers to maintain distance from children and to discipline children harshly. Meanwhile, mothers were said to be closer to children and to provide emotional protection and support. But as we concluded in a recent review of fathering research in East Asia (Shwalb et al., 2010), Confucianism probably always had less impact on family life in Japan than in China or Korea. In addition, Chinese Confucianism (see Li & Lamb, Ch. 2, this volume, p. 18) also stated that kindness was an essential element of fathering, and Japanese-style Confucianism came to selectively prioritize kindness over strictness. When Japan officially abolished its Confucian ideology and family laws at the end of World War II, Japanese-style child rearing based on affectionate attachment relations and permissiveness (as described above by foreign observers) became more open than ever, and strict fathering was no longer seen as the standard.

Post-World War II fathers

In 1947 a new Constitution emphasized democracy, and egalitarian ideology replaced the Confucian system of family relations that had promoted paternal detachment and patriarchy. Accordingly, the mentality of "strict father, affectionate mother" weakened. But instead of sharing democratically in child rearing, Japanese fathers in the late 1950s and 1960s concentrated on their role as company employees, contributing to the restoration of Japan as an economic power. The Japanese employment system gave priority to men's work over their family life, as seen in high rates of over-time work and *tanshinfunin* (job transfer to another city, leaving behind one's family; see Tanaka & Nakazawa, 2005). In return, the system offered economic stability in the form of company-subsidized housing and guar-anteed lifetime employment. As a result, many fathers became worka-holics and left child rearing entirely to their wives. The grandfathers of today's young fathers were of this generation, and they were the driving force behind Japan's post-war economic boom (E. A. Vogel, 1963; S. H. Vogel, 1996).

Contemporary fathers

It is now over 20 years since the Japanese economic 'bubble' burst, and the fathers of today's young fathers worked through the post-bubble era. In a study of families during the post-bubble era, Kato, Ishii-Kuntz, Makino, and Tsuchiya (2002) analyzed two cohorts (1992–1993 and 1997–1998 cohorts) of salaried employee fathers and the stay-at-home mothers of 3-year-old children. The percentage of fathers who ate dinner at home with their families and the frequency of conversations between husbands and wives both decreased between these cohorts; during this same period mothers' intrusiveness with children increased and children's social abili-ties declined. Throughout the 1990s, fathers' work conditions remained harsh, which at first had a negative impact on their involvement in family life and child rearing. This perpetuated for another decade the primacy of mothers in the household and fathers in the provider role, despite attitude shifts toward egalitarian roles.

Today's young fathers (including our Case Story father, Masahiko Tanaka) grew up in the 1980s and 1990s, and, perhaps because of a lack of contact with their own fathers, many young fathers now believe that a sta-ble and intimate family bond is even more important than economic suc-cess. This attitudinal shift away from a gender-based division of labor was reflected in government national survey data that presented men's and women's *disagreement* with the statement, "Husbands should work out-side the home, while wives should take on domestic duties" (see Figure 3.1). This trend may have reflected both a gradual societal acceptance of gender equality and recognition of an increase in maternal employment in Japanese society. However, it is only in the current generation that incremental increases in actual paternal *behavior* became clearly observ-able, preceded for two decades by attitudinal changes. These data also reveal that about half of men and women still favor a traditional division of labor.

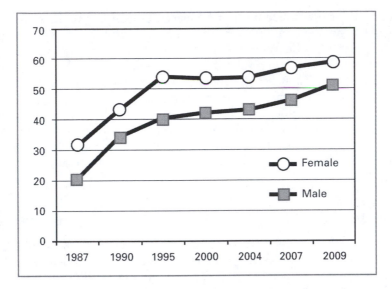

Figure 3.1 Percent disagreement with statement: "Husbands should work outside the home while wives should take on domestic duties." Data from "Real conditions of working women" (Ministry of Health, Labor and Welfare, 1997), and "Public survey about gender equality in society" (Cabinet Office, 2002, 2004, 2007, 2009). Figure created by and courtesy of Jun Nakazawa.

The low birthrate

Another major reason for changes in Japanese child rearing attitudes and behavior has been a declining low birth rate. In 1989, the Japanese Population Survey Report showed that Japan's total fertility rate was 1.57, which was even lower than the previous record low of 1.58 in 1966. In 1966, many Japanese had avoided pregnancy because of an astrological superstition that women born that year would grow up to become highly aggressive (Hara & Minagawa, 1996). The new record rate of 1989 was labeled the "1.57 Shock," and the rate has declined steadily since then. For example, in 1949 there were 2.7 million births compared to only 1.09 million in 2008. The fertility rate (births/woman) in 2010 in Japan was 1.20 while comparative rates were 1.54 in China, 2.06 in the U.S., and 2.56 worldwide (cf. Table 1.1, this volume, p. 5). This low fertility rate has caused chronic labor shortages, and as a result mothers are expected to work despite a lack of adequate daycare resources. Women's increased activity outside the home elevated the expectations for fathers to share in childcare and housework, while modern conveniences have simplified housekeeping and most couples only raise one or two children.

It is also possible that the low birthrate induces parents to be overprotective of their children, a phenomenon we have also noted in Chinese and Korean families (Shwalb et al., 2010). Nowadays, many Japanese fathers appear to be more involved with their children than were their fathers or grandfathers, and they are encouraged by professionals from the fields of obstetrics, pediatrics, and developmental psychology who publicly emphasize the importance of the paternal role. In the current era of economic instability, national surveys of Japanese fathers indicate that while they continue to work hard they also are becoming more active with their children in play, feeding, bathing, and putting children to bed (National Institute of Population and Social Security Research, 2008).

Review of Fathering Research in Japan

Fathering research in the field of developmental psychology in Japan started in the late 1970s, spurred by the publication of Japanese translations of books by Lamb (1976) and Lynn (1978). Over the years numerous Japanese books on fathering have appeared (e.g., Kashiwagi, 1993; Makino, Nakano, & Kashiwagi, 1996), and over 1,600 articles on fathering were published in Japan between 1975 and 2008 (Shwalb et al., 2010). Most of these publications are accessible only to readers of Japanese. Comparisons of our previous reviews of research on Japanese fathering (Shwalb, Imaizumi, & Nakazawa, 1987; Shwalb, Nakazawa, Yamamoto, & Hyun, 2004; Shwalb et al., 2010) indicate a steadily growing interest in the father's role among both scholars and the general public. The research selected for review here is organized to represent several of the topics most often addressed by Japanese fathering researchers.

Methodological advances

Shwalb et al. (1987) cited no behavioral studies on Japanese fathering, but in recent years there have been several innovative investigations. As in most of the societies included in this volume, questionnaire surveys are still the typical way to collect data about and from Japanese fathers. However, experimental and observational studies with direct measures of fathers' behavior are beginning to emerge, as in the following examples.

Experimental studies: Fathers' perceptions of baby crying

Kamiya (2002) asked unmarried male students, childless men in the first year of marriage, expectant fathers (during the wife's first pregnancy), and fathers of infants and preschool-age children to rate the crying of a baby. The students rated the crying most negatively. In comparisons among the four groups, Kamiya noted that the less motivated or experienced men were with regard to child rearing, the more negatively they reacted to babies' cries. Esposito, Nakazawa, Venuti, and Bornstein (2012) compared adult males and females (25–35 years old, in groups with or without children) for their ratings of the distress they felt when hearing the cries of normal and autistic babies. There were no differences in estimating distress between males and females, or between adults with/without children. My own subsequent analysis revealed that in Japan, while there were no differences in estimating the age of crying babies among the female sub-samples, fathers were more accurate than non-fathers in estimating the ages of babies. We can infer from these data that fathers' experiences with their babies may help them understand the relationship between age and babies' crying patterns. That is, the experience of being a father altered Japanese men's perceptions of babies.

Observational studies: Father–child interactions

Observational studies are also becoming more common in the Japanese fathering literature. For example, Fukuda (2003) observed fathers and mothers as they encouraged their 4- to 5-year-old children to eat. Fathers in her study were less assertive than mothers in urging children to eat. She also found that the younger the children, the harder both fathers and mothers tried to get their children to eat, which promoted a negative reaction in many children. In a second example of observational research, Nakazawa (2011) analyzed the behavior of father–mother–child triads as they constructed puzzles with blocks. A sub-sample of fathers were members of a non-profit organization (NPO) called "Fathering Japan" (see discussion on p. 55) and were active participants in child rearing. When these men were compared with fathers who were not associated with the NPO, men in the Fathering Japan group expressed more encouragement, praise, and positive emotion toward their children than the non-NPO fathers. In addition, during clean-up time after the puzzle task, the Fathering Japan men and their wives supported the child's clean-up behavior together. These behavioral data suggest that fathers belonging to a group that promotes active fathering interacted with their children and wives in ways that were more positive and collaborative, although men who are already active fathers may also choose to join Fathering Japan.

The father's roles

As indicated under "Cultural/Historical Background," the Japanese father's role reflects both historical continuity and change. An example of a study comparing the relative importance of men's roles was Onodera's (2003) investigation of the roles of husband, worker, and member of society, as rank-ordered on a questionnaire. She compared men's roles at three times: when their wives were 7–8 months pregnant, and when their children were 2 and 3 years old. Across these periods of time, the value of men's role as a member of society increased, that of the husband role decreased, and the ranking of the paternal role did not change (fathers reported the relative weights they assigned to their roles as husband, worker, and member of society) by the time children became 3 years old. This trend reflects the fact that in Japan the family system changes with the birth of a child from a system centered on husband–wife relations, to a system centered on parent–child relations. When they become parents, the husband–wife relationship transforms into a father–mother relationship. This is different from the norm in some Western cultures, where the husband–wife relationship remains at the core of family relations. In the child-centered Japanese family system, fathers become more aware (compared with prior to the child's birth) that the purpose of their role as wage earners and members of society is to provide for family life. In addition, traditional Japanese affection-based child rearing may be a historical antecedent of child-centered family life.

Factors related to the father's participation in child rearing

Several researchers have investigated factors that support or inhibit paternal involvement. For example, Morishita (2006) conducted a questionnaire survey of fathers of preschoolers (mean age = 36.5 years; $N = 381$) and found through path analysis that many factors affected men's participation in child rearing. These factors included the husband–wife relationship, children's behavior toward the father, the father's acceptance of his paternal role, gender roles, and acceptance by co-workers of time dedicated to child rearing. In turn, the father's participation in child rearing affected the development of his thinking about fathering, in terms of love for the family, responsibility, open-mindedness, and a new perspective on both the past and future. Morishita concluded that fathers' participation in childcare was related to harmonious husband–wife relations, men's adaptability, and a pro-childcare atmosphere at work, and that men who more actively participated in child care developed a more engaged attitude toward fathering.

Early contact with one's child is another factor that is related to Japanese paternal involvement. In Japan, one common context of childbirth is called *satogaeri shussan*, or delivery in the mother's parents' hometown, irrespective of the distance between homes. Following this tradition, the mother benefits from the presence and support of her parents and relatives, but not from that of her husband (who continues at work), and she can be relieved of some of her anxiety prior to delivery. However, the father in this scenario loses the opportunity for early contact with his newborn child. Kimura et al. (2003) examined 657 pairs of pregnant wives and husbands twice, before delivery and four months postpartum. There were no differences in women's feelings about being mothers, between those who delivered in their parents' hometowns or not. But the intensity of men's feelings about being a father and their participation in taking care of the baby were lessened if the wife delivered in her own parents' hometown rather than with the husband's support. This study suggested that involvement at the time of delivery and early contact with the baby may affect fathers' subsequent attitudes and behavior.

Other studies have shown that fathers are influenced by the behavior of their own fathers and by their wives. For example, Aoki (2009) examined the effects of collaborative child rearing on two-income parents of children aged 3–5 years. Her regression analysis showed that collaborative child rearing affected the mother's expectations for co-parenting and father/mother dialogues about child rearing, and on the level and positive quality of the father's role. In addition, a pro-fathering atmosphere of support from the workplace influenced the degree of collaborative child rearing by these fathers and mothers. In relation to another age group, Hirata (2003) asked 412 fathers of middle-school students about their participation in child rearing, their degree of collaboration with their wives in child rearing, and about their own fathers' interactions with them when they were in middle school. Fathers who participated more in child rearing had higher scores for interactions with their own fathers as adolescents, and for collaboration with their wives.

Together, these studies indicate that not only Japanese men's work situation and work hours, but also their early contact experiences with infants, collaboration with wives, views of children, wives' expectations, and experiences with their own fathers, may have a cumulative positive influence on fathers' involvement with child rearing.

The father's influence on child development

Although many of the following studies on fathers' influences were correlational in design, they consistently reveal associations between paternal behavior and aspects of child development, from infancy through adolescence.

Cognitive development

Despite the cultural value placed on education and learning (Azuma, 1996), there have been few research studies on the influence of Japanese fathers on children's cognitive development. In one notable study, Tsuchiya, Iinaga, Kato, and Kazui (1996) examined paternal influences by relating fathers' behavior to the abilities of their 3½-year-old children. Fathers' self-reported level of participation in playing with children was correlated with children's level of language development. Tsuchiya et al. also related the father's participation in child rearing to his degree of flexibility during interactions with the child. Examples of flexibility included empathy for the child, playing at the child's level, being non-restrictive, and using a variety of discipline strategies. Fathers' flexibility with children was positively correlated with children's verbal abilities (comprehension, verbal fluency, and verbalization of images), and cognitive and behavioral abilities (goal-oriented behavior, role-taking, and pretend behavior).

Social development

The impact of Japanese fathers on children's social development has been studied more often than their influence on cognitive development. For example, Kato, Ishii-Kuntz, Makino, and Tsuchiya (2002) investigated the connections between how often fathers ate dinner with the family, frequency of conversations between husband and wife, and the father's time spent in child rearing, with children's social abilities as observed at 3 years of age. Their path analysis showed that frequency of meals together had no effect, but that frequency of conversations between husband and wife predicted the participation of fathers in child rearing, which in turn had a positive effect on children's social skills.

In a related study, Kato and Kondo (2007) observed father–child and mother–child play interactions with 3-year-olds. They rated both fathers' and mothers' behavior on three dimensions: structure/limit setting, respect for the child's autonomy, and sensitivity. Based on these ratings, they classified fathers and mothers into four categories: High (high scores on all three dimensions), Limited High (high only on structure/limit setting), Limited Low (low only on structure/limit setting), and Low (low scores on all three dimensions). Comparing fathers' attitudes as reported on a questionnaire, the Low type fathers were lower in flexibility of child rearing attitudes and in commitment to child rearing. When they reached the age of 3½ years, children of Low fathers and of Limited High mothers showed the least emotional regulation during conflicts with peers. These data indicated that fathers' sensitivity and flexibility in child rearing, and structural support for children's play, were all associated with young children's social and emotional development.

Motor development

In a rare study of fathering in relation to motor development, Nakazawa (2011) assessed the development of 2- to 3-year-old children using the Bayley-III Scales. His participants were children of active members of the Fathering Japan NPO, in comparison with non-member 'control' fathers. Children of the active fathering group members had higher scores for gross motor development than children of control group fathers. Fathering Japan members interacted more actively with their children, and while we cannot claim that their interactions had a causal effect on motor development, further research on fathering in relation to children's physical development is warranted.

Peer relations and academic aspirations

Ishii-Kuntz (2007) asked fathers about their child rearing behavior (i.e., talk, play, eating with child, discipline, and support of child's homework). She asked the men's 10- to 15-year-old children about their peer relations (number of friends, estimate of their competence in peer relations, anxiety for friends), self-esteem, academic orientation (enjoyment of school studies, motivation to learn new things), and work orientation (clear job plans). Her multiple regression analysis showed that children whose fathers played and ate with them had more positive peer relations and self-esteem. In addition, fathers' academic attainment related positively to children's peer relations and academic orientations. For boys, fathers' academic attainments also were related to sons' positive self-esteem and clearer job orientation. It was notable that fathers' academic background (which reflected social, economic and cultural traits) was associated with children's psychological health. Perhaps men's higher academic attainment exposed children to academic-oriented values and child rearing, which may be predictive of children's subsequent economic stability and academic success.

Internalizing and externalizing problem behavior

Common internalizing disorders in Japan include school non-attendance (or refusal), withdrawal, and shutting-in (*hikikomori*: youth who are emotionally incapable of leaving their rooms for work or school). Igarashi and Hagiwara (2004) found that school non-attendance by middle-school girls was positively correlated with a distrustful/refusal type of attachment to fathers in early childhood; boys had the same pattern in relation to their mothers. They inferred from these data that, since middle-school students are sexually mature, school refusal may have been based on feelings of rebellion, denial, and avoidance toward opposite sex parents. In a related study, Hanashima (2007) compared normal university male students with *hikikomori* shut-in males who had refused social interactions for at least 6 months by age 21, in terms of their fathers' personality, relationships with their fathers, and relationships between the father and other family members. The personalities of fathers of *hikikomori* males were reported as more strict, less flexible, and less intimate (i.e., respectful, trusting, understanding, loving, or directly interactive), compared with fathers of normal students. Correlations also showed that youths' duration as *hikikomori* was longer when their fathers were strict, inflexible, and less intimate, interactive, respectful or trusting.

In a study of externalizing behavior, Nakamichi and Nakazawa (2003) examined the relationship between fathers' behavior and the aggressive behavior of young children (mean age = 5.2 years). There was no association between children's aggression and mothers' attitudes, but children's aggressive behavior was stronger when their fathers' style was authoritarian than when it was either authoritative or permissive. Examining a different age group, Obokata and Muto (2005) focused on the delinquent behavior of middle-school children. They noted that children who had intimate father–child relationships were more resistant toward peer pressure (e.g., "If my friends perform a delinquent act, I do not do it"). Both of these correlational studies suggested that father–child relations may have a bearing on children's problem behavior.

Social Policy Issues Related to Fathering

We have seen that Japanese fathers may have various influences on children, and that the relative importance of fathers' different roles has changed across generations. Social policies relevant to Japanese fathering have mainly focused on measures that would increase fathers' involvement in child rearing.

As noted earlier, following the 1.57 Shock of 1989, the Japanese fertility rate continued to decline. There were many reasons for this decline, including a tendency to marry later, increases in the numbers of unmarried people, insufficient support of fathering from employers, and the psychological, physical, and economic burdens of child rearing (Ministry of Health, Labor and Welfare, 1994). Since the 1.57 Shock, the Japanese government has implemented various policies and programs to promote child rearing and fathering. The following outlines these measures and their impact.

1. Angel Plan, 1995–1999 (Ministry of Health, Labor and Welfare, 1994). This policy supported motherhood through an expansion of the capacities of childcare centers for 0- to 2-year-old children, extension of the hours per day of daycare, and promotion of a system of after-school care for primary school children. However, these measures did not stem the decline of the birth rate. Although the original Angel Plan was not directed at fathers, it became apparent over the ensuing decade that it was also necessary to address the problem of men's work hours. Policy makers became aware that the Angel Plan would not have a positive effect on women or children unless men were given more time to support their wives' efforts and more time to contribute to child rearing. Subsequent policies, therefore, focused increasingly on fathers.

2. New Angel Plan, 2000–2004 (Ministry of Health, Labor and Welfare, 1999). This policy extended public childcare services, constructed community child rearing centers, and included other labor and education measures. It marked the advent of the first Japanese national fathering policy. The stated goal of the plan was to create a work environment that fostered a balance between work and child rearing. It encouraged paternal childcare leave, expanded payments to men who took leave from 25% of their regular salary to 40%, and subsidized the hiring of workers to cover for men who took childcare leave. Specifically, it sought to change gender roles and to reform a corporate culture that had prioritized work over family life.

However, very few males took advantage of the childcare leave program, and while Japan failed to stop the drop in the birth rate there was also little change overall in the corporate environment. Japanese government therefore decided to promote a policy to change the way that people think about work.

3. Support Plans for Children and Child Rearing, 2005–2009 (Ministry of Health, Labor and Welfare, 2004). This policy tried to reformulate the work environment so that both male and female employees could fulfill child rearing responsibilities. It extended the child rearing policy of incentives that previously focused on early childhood, to a policy relevant to infants, children, and adolescents, and reviewed the ways in which companies supported or discouraged active fathering. Accordingly, the national government set the following goals with regard to work: within 5 years 10% of eligible men and 80% of eligible women would take paid childcare leave; adoption by 25% of companies of a system to reduce work hours of businesses until workers' children enter school, to give fathers time to interact with their children; finally, fathers' child rearing time was to become equal to that in Western countries. Unfortunately, as Japan continued to undergo a prolonged economic recession and global economic crisis, it did not achieve any of these goals (Cabinet Office, 2010). Specifically, the Cabinet Office reported that strong majorities in a 2008 national sample of mothers and fathers responded negatively when asked if Japan was a society where men were actively engaged with their children at home (61.8% negative), where men could feel at ease taking paternal leave (71.3% negative), or where there were adequate programs to foster paternal involvement (59.2% negative). The authors of this White Paper concluded that "progress was gradual and the goals were not achieved."

4. Children and Child Rearing Vision, 2010–2014 (Ministry of Health, Labor and Welfare, 2010). Current ongoing measures focus on support for children and child rearing, with the goal (as in previous policies) of a balance between family life and work. This approach marked an ideological shift from family responsibility toward societal responsibility for child rearing. As part of the latest fathering policy, a child rearing allowance is provided for single-parent fathers; such a benefit previously had been only offered to single-parent mothers. It emphasizes promotion of fathers' participation in child rearing by the following means: encouragement of employers to extend the duration of childcare leave for both fathers and mothers; dissemination of educational material about fathering and men's experiences with childcare leave; and promotion of a change in the priority placed on housework and child rearing by fathers. The Japanese government set the year 2014 as the target for the following goals: a decrease in the percentage of companies whose workers work more than 60 hours weekly, from 10% to 5%; increase in the percentage of fathers who take childcare leave from 1.23% in 2010 to 10%; and an increase in the amount of time fathers (with children under age 6) spend daily in child rearing or housework, from 60 minutes in 2010 to 150 minutes.

Through these initiatives, the national Japanese government has promoted policies for two decades (with limited success) to establish a balance between work and family life, and to support an increase in fathers' participation in child rearing and household work. Although harsh economic conditions have slowed the spread of paternal leave, fathers' interest in becoming more involved at home and their motivation to attend child rearing classes have increased dramatically.

Non-profit organizations and fathering classes

Among the pro-fathering NPOs the most prominent are *"Ikujiren*: Let's have time for child rearing by both men and women!" founded in 1980 (www.eqg.org/index-e.html), and Fathering Japan, founded in 2006 (www.fathering.jp/english/index.html). These groups organize fathering classes and other public events, and advocate new fathering policies. Figure 3.2 is an image from the home page of Fathering Japan. On the home page of the English-language version of "Fathering Japan" is the following statement:

> More and more men today are starting to realize how rewarding it can be to spend time with their children. While it takes courage to create a balance between work and family, we reckon that these men understand the true definition of "Fathering." Unfortunately, here in Japan, corporates and the older generation who are still in control of most of them have been much slower to change. How on

earth can you expect to find "work life balance"
when you are trapped between a rock (your company asking you to work longer and longer hours)
and a hard place (your wife who wants you to take
a role in your children's upbringing)? ... Our aim at
Fathering Japan is to promote understanding and
acceptance for Dads who want to play an active role
in their children's lives. ... We believe that through
this we can ultimately influence the corporate mind,
contribute to society and create a happier, healthier
and more balanced future generation.

(http://www.fathering.jp/english/
business.html)

In one notable study of fathering classes, Yoshioka (2009) analyzed the
narratives of fathers at several classes sponsored by local governments.
In a typical class, one presenter talked for about 30 minutes, followed by
free discussion among the participants. The emphasis on discussion provided men with opportunities to hear about child rearing in other families, an understanding of mothers' experiences and isolation as caregivers,
and insights into the work situations of other fathers. Generally these
classes also appear to promote mutual understanding among fathers and
between fathers and mothers.

Figure 3.2 Image adapted from home page of Fathering Japan (retrieved August
1, 2011 at www.fathering.jp). The white lettering on the photo reads "It's fun to be
a Dad!" in Japanese. The English version of this website is www.fathering.jp/eng-
lish/. Photo courtesy of Fathering Japan.

The new Japanese father

New types of Japanese fathers are emerging, for example those who take childcare leave (exemplified by the following two studies) or who are stay-at-home fathers. Kikuchi and Kashiwagi (2007) interviewed a sample of fathers who took childcare leave and compared them with fathers who did not take leave. The fathers who did not take leave had a more passive form of child rearing, i.e., active only in response to the mother's requests. In contrast, fathers who took childcare leave had a higher concern for child rearing, a stronger consciousness of gender equality, and a more active approach to child rearing and housework. However, these new Japanese fathers also worried about the routinized nature of child rearing, felt isolated from society, and reported boredom and stress from being alone with their children all the time. Men who took childcare leave for more than two months felt especially isolated. In a unique qualitative study of stay-at-home fathers, Yagi (2009) interviewed seven men and found that they experienced conflicts because they lost a sense of social and personal relationships, lost their pride as men, found housework boring, and lived in isolation from society. On the other hand, the stay-at-home fathers in Yagi's sample also reported that they had gained a perspective on the lives of stay-at-home mothers, a new awareness of their potential as active fathers, and recognition of the importance of time with the family. These two interview studies of new-style fathers showed that Japanese fathers indeed have the ability to do housework and child rearing, and that men can find these activities both meaningful and challenging. They also showed that active fathers have emotions such as loneliness and anxiety, which are experienced more commonly at home by mothers.

Sub-Cultural Variations in Fathering: Japanese-Brazilians and Korean Residents

Beginning in 1908, many Japanese immigrated to Brazil (anti-immigrant policies in that generation had discouraged immigration to the U.S.), and there are now over 1.5 million of Japanese descent living in Brazil. Many succeeded abroad in the fields of law, politics, and academics. However, at the time of the Brazilian economic crisis in the 1980s, descendants of these Japanese-Brazilians returned to Japan to seek employment. As a result, the 1990 regulations for Japanese Immigration Control and Refugee Recognition were amended to relax job restrictions for foreigners of Japanese descent. Now in an era of chronic labor shortage, almost 300,000 Brazilians live in Japan (approximately one-third of these are in the labor force). They are not considered immigrants, but rather they are treated as temporary residents who plan to return to Brazil in the future. Thus, many of them do not want to learn Japanese or assimilate into Japanese society and culture, which unfortunately often limits their employment to unskilled and part-time work. Their children can attend public schools in Japan, but since they have weak Japanese abilities and education in Japan is not compulsory for Brazilians, many of these children drop out of school. In Japanese schools they can learn the Japanese language, but their native Portuguese language ability may decline. Some of these children become interpreters for their parents who cannot understand Japanese, which changes their status in the family and confuses parent–child relations (Nakura, Nakazawa, & Yamamoto, 2001).

Tanibuchi (2009) conducted a questionnaire survey of Japanese-Brazilian parents and their 5th–9th grade children, in comparison to a native Japanese sample. According to children's reports, Japanese-Brazilian parents had greater levels of achievement motivation and overprotection for their children than did native Japanese parents. Japanese-Brazilian parents also reported that they had higher aspirations for the education of their children, and a closer emotional relationship with children. Japanese-Brazilian children who felt accepted by their parents reportedly understood their school subjects better and had a stronger interest in their studies. However, Japanese-Brazilian children who perceived their parents as intrusive or strict reported less school absence.

Recently, Brazilian schools were founded in Japan whereby Brazilian teachers teach Japanese-Brazilian children using Brazilian textbooks. In 2010, there were 83 Brazilian schools and over 6,000 Brazilian children attended these schools. Kondo et al. (2010) assessed 4- to 10-year-old Japanese-Brazilian children at these schools. His multiple logistic regression analysis showed that conduct disorders were more common among 8- to 10-year-old boys who had absent fathers and did not speak with teachers. Kondo et al. concluded that the main cause of conduct disorder among Japanese-Brazilian children was father absence. This absence occurred because fathers worked elsewhere in Japan or in Brazil, or was due to divorce, father–mother conflict, or the father's death.

There has also been a long history of Koreans and Chinese living in Japan; for example, more than 600,000 people of Korean descent live in Japan. Hiruta, Cho, and Nishino (2005) conducted a comparative study of Japanese fathers (mean age = 36.0 years) and fathers who were Korean residents of Japan (2nd and 3rd generation; mean age = 38.8 years). They noted that more Korean residents than Japanese fathers agreed with the statement "It is important for masculinity or femininity to be a big part of a person." In addition, 47% of 2nd generation Korean residents in Japan, and 39% of 3rd generation Korean resident fathers, reported that they respected their own fathers, compared with only 18% of Japanese fathers. Hiruta et al. also noted that the Korean resident fathers reported a stronger sense of filial piety and adherence to Confucian-style gender roles than Japanese fathers in their sample. In addition, almost 6,000 native speakers of Chinese now attend Japanese public schools, but to our knowledge there has been no fathering research on this population. Brazilian children and families, in contrast, have gained more public attention recently, and have been the subject of more systematic research because of their larger cultural differences from mainstream Japanese.

Contemporary Social/Economic Conditions That Impact Japanese Fathering

As noted earlier, the Japanese economy has been in poor condition almost continuously since 1991. A recession extended across what is now called the 'lost decade,' and while conditions had begun to improve a few years ago, the economy faltered again in the worldwide economic collapse of 2008. Over this long period, Japanese work conditions changed drastically. For example, workers no longer have a guarantee of lifetime employment or seniority-based pay, and there have been layoffs of regular employees and increases in substitute part-time employees. Japanese fathers today thus face their work and child rearing responsibilities in times of unstable employment and declining income (Takahashi, 2008). In the past, a good academic background ensured men stable and favorable employment, but nowadays a good academic background does not guarantee a good and secure life. In our opinion, chronic recession and an unstable work environment are likely to create class differences in a society where once almost all Japanese belonged to the middle class (Vogel, 1996; see later discussion under "Speculation and Predictions").

Discussion

Fathering research

Shwalb, Imaizumi, and Nakazawa (1987) criticized early Japanese fathering research because it was lacking in four areas: (1) experimental and observational studies, (2) direct assessments of fathers, (3) studies of father–child attachment, effects of fathers on children's gender roles, and effects of fathers on child psychopathology, and (4) research on how males becomes fathers, how fathers develop, or on changes in husband–wife and father–child relations over time. Twenty-five years later, we may conclude that fathering research has improved in depth and breadth as a reflection of the increased overall quality of scholarship in the field of Japanese developmental psychology (Shwalb, Nakazawa, & Shwalb, 2005).

In terms of research methodology, there are still few behavioral, experimental, or observational studies of contemporary Japanese fathering. Most published reports are still based on self-report questionnaire surveys (e.g., Shwalb, Kawai, Shoji, & Tsunetsugu, 1997). However, as we noted earlier, the quality of research (objective methods and sophisticated data analysis) have improved during the past generation. In addition, there is now a growing interest in qualitative research which provides more fine-grain analysis of fathers' child rearing, household work, and husband–wife relations than appeared in past quantitative studies.

Increasingly, Japanese fathering data is collected directly from fathers. In the past, fathers were often reluctant to participate in research. But because men's participation to child rearing is now considered natural, today's researchers have much better access to and cooperation from fathers. In two of the content areas we highlighted in 1987, there is now more and better research: the father's role in the development of child psychopathology, and studies about men's development as fathers. However, there are still very few studies of father–child attachment or the fathers' influence on children's gender roles. There have been several studies on the transition to fatherhood (see Shwalb et al., 2010 for a review), but the issues of age-related changes in husband–wife and father–child relations over time both continue to be neglected by Japanese researchers. Overall, the literature on Japanese fathering has matured since our first critique in 1987, and fathering is now a mainstream topic among scholars who study Japanese families and child development.

Today's Japanese fathers

Under the Confucian code of "strict father, affectionate mother" and during the period of economic growth after World War II, gender-based division of labor between salaried work and domestic tasks appeared to be normative. As a result, Japanese fathers were not very active in child rearing. But the influence of the Confucian moral code, which coexisted with traditionally permissive and affect-based parenting, has faded in recent decades. Changes in values for work triggered by chronic recession, the high value placed on each child in a society with an extremely low birth rate, and the social acceptability of gender equality all motivate today's Japanese fathers to participate in child rearing. Campaigns by the Japanese government started in 1999, as shown in a poster of a celebrity father with the caption "A man who is not involved in child rearing is not really a father" (Figure 3.3) have had a strong influence on fathers' attitudes toward child rearing, so that active fathering is more appealing and natural to young fathers today. Our opening Case Story of Masahiko Tanaka was emblematic of an active father in a small dual-career family.

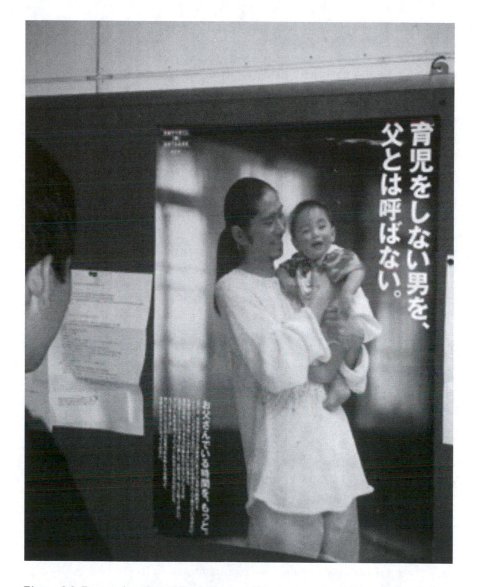

Figure 3.3 Poster distributed by Japanese Government in 1999, reading "A man who is not involved in child rearing is not really a father" and subtitled, "Let's make more time for fathering." Photo courtesy of Keito Nakamichi.

He represents the direction of the current generation of young fathers, which is beginning to translate late 20th-century pro-fathering attitudes into actual involvement.

An interview study on the effects of fathers' participation in father-ing classes showed that fathers who take classes evaluated their activities positively, because the activities gave them the opportunity to understand other fathers and to reflect on their behavior and attitudes (Nakazawa, 2011). However, as is often the case in Japanese fathering research, the direction of causality was not clear from these data. Nevertheless, the growing involvement of young Japanese fathers in childcare and house-hold work marks a change from previous generations. Today, fathers who perform childcare actively are viewed as cutting edge and are called by the flattering nickname of *iku-men* (men who 'do' child rearing), and the Japanese government endorses this movement (see a description of this movement at http://ikumen-project.jp/index.html). How do these active young fathers behave when their children go through middle childhood and adolescence? Research is lacking on fathers of these age groups, but if men continue to be active with their older children, they may help to prevent children's later psychological and adaptive problems. Japanese fathers are still changing gradually, but the change is unmistakable. What may be unique about the situation in Japan is the combination of influ-ences that have led to increased involvement. Specifically, chronically depressed economic growth may have given fathers more time to become active at home, and to finally behave in accordance with attitudes which had favored active fathering for well over a decade. On the other hand, the results of the Cabinet Office (2010) study (p. 54, this chapter) indicate that Japanese fathers and mothers alike are still dissatisfied with the current levels and pace of change.

Speculation and Predictions for the Future of Japanese Fathering

On March 11, 2011, a wide area of eastern Japan was struck by a huge earthquake and *tsunami*. Beyond the impact of an ongoing economic reces-sion, this unprecedented disaster is likely to intensify and prolong Japan's economic slowdown. These economic conditions will bring about a wid-ening income gap, and lower class fathers may lack the resources of time, money, and psychological comfort to provide to their children. This dep-rivation may result in a new impediment to participation in child rearing, or even in changes in fathering behavior in the direction of neglectful or authoritarian styles. On the other hand, fathers who have better resources may continue to build a pro-fathering ethos and adopt authoritative rear-ing strategies. They may be more likely to provide cognitive and eco-nomic support for children's studies at home and school, which still tends to predict a favorable academic and economic future for their children.

If these predictions prove to be accurate, the future may see a polarization of father–child relations in Japan between active and uninvolved fathers linked to income disparities, whereas fathering in the past was probably more homogeneous.

As the Japanese population continues to age, we expect that children will be treated as protectively as in the current generation, or even more so. We also predict that fathers' participation in child rearing will generally increase into the future. A low birth rate and stagnant economy require the labor power of women, and the two-income families in which fathers perform domestic work and child rearing will increasingly be the norm.

Finally, its low birth rate and economic globalization may lead Japan to rely more on foreign workers. Cultural conflicts and parent–child conflicts, as seen in the case of Brazilian families, may also become a bigger problem as Japan increasingly absorbs foreign families. In this context, and in light of our prediction of growing social class distinctions, the question of "What are Japanese fathers like?" will become more difficult to answer in the future than it was 25 years ago, when we thought of Japanese fathers as one population.

Summary

Japanese traditional childcare has historically been based on close parent–child attachments and a permissive child rearing style. The influence of the Confucian ethical code ("strict father, affectionate mother") weakened in the post-World War II era, when fathers bore the heavy burden of reviving the Japanese economy and had little time to interact with their children. A long economic recession from the 1990s has brought about an unstable work environment, and this situation demands that fathers continue to work hard. At the same time, close family relations have become more important to most men than single-minded economic success, and the economic slowdown has freed men's time to become more active at home.

Compared with 25 years ago, empirical Japanese psychological research on fathers has increased in quality and quantity. At the same time, the Japanese government has promoted new policies designed to increase the father's participation in child rearing, with only limited success. Public initiatives have received powerful support from NPOs, which organize fathering classes and advocate pro-fathering policies.

Economic forces continue to have a powerful impact on fathering. For example, Japanese fathers live in an era in which the stable post-war employment system has collapsed and a performance-based pay system has been introduced. Under these conditions, economic and academic gaps tend to be widening, which may have an effect on some fathers' ability to provide for their children.

Overall, young Japanese fathers are more likely to participate in childcare than did fathers in the 20th century. We predicted that the trend toward active fathering in Japan will continue in future generations.

Acknowledgments

This chapter was written with the support of the Grant-in Aid for Scientific Research of the Japanese Society for the Promotion of Science #22530694 for JN and the Psychology Department of Southern Utah University for DWS. We dedicate this chapter to Shirou and Kikue Nakazawa, and to the memory of Masaya Miyake and Kichiro Tanaka.

References

Aoki, S. (2009). Determinants of co-parenting in dual-earner couples with 3- to 6-year old children: Child care coordination, sharing and planning. *The Japanese Journal of Developmental Psychology, 20,* 382–392.

Azuma, H. (1996). Cross-national research on child development: The Hess-Azuma collaboration in retrospect. In D. Shwalb & B. Shwalb (Eds.), *Japanese child rearing: Two generations of scholarship* (pp. 220–240). New York, NY: Guilford Press.

Cabinet Office. (2002). *Public survey about gender equality society.* Retrieved from http://www8.cao.go.jp/survey/h14/h14-danjo/index.html

Cabinet Office. (2004). *Public survey about gender equality society.*Retrieved from http://www8.cao.go.jp/survey/h16/h16-danjo/index.html

Cabinet Office. (2007). *Public survey about gender equality society.* Retrieved from http://www8.cao.go.jp/survey/h19/h19-danjyo/index.html

Cabinet Office. (2009). *Public survey about gender equality society.* Retrieved from http://www8.cao.go.jp/survey/h21/h21-danjo/index.html

Cabinet Office. (2010). *White paper on children and child rearing.* Tokyo, Japan: Cabinet Office.

Esposito, G., Nakazawa, J., Venuti, P., & Bornstein, M. H. (2012). Perceptions of distress in young children with autism compared to typically developing children: A cultural comparison between Japan and Italy. *Research in Developmental Disabilities, 33,* 1059–1067.

Fróis, L. D. (1955). *Kulturgegensätze Europa-Japan* (J. F. Schütte, Ed.). Tokyo, Japan: Sophia University. (Original work published 1585)

Fukuda, K. (2003). The relationship between parents' prompting of children to eat and children's emotions: A family systems view. *The Japanese Journal of Developmental Psychology, 14,* 161–171.

Fukaya, M. (2008). *Fathers: Way of life from one hundred cases.* Tokyo, Japan: Chuokoron.

Hanashima, H. (2007). The father–son relationships as seen from Hikikomori males and their fathers. *Japanese Journal of Family Psychology, 21,* 77–94.

Hara, H., & Minagawa, M. (1996). From productive dependents to precious guests: Historical changes in Japanese children. In D. Shwalb & B. Shwalb (Eds.),

Japanese child rearing: Two generations of scholarship (pp. 9–30). New York, NY: Guilford Press.

Hirata, H. (2003). Fathers' behaviors relating to their children in early adolescence. *Japanese Journal of Family Psychology, 17,* 35–54.

Hiruta, Y., Cho, Y., & Nishino, E. (2005). A study of contemporary child care and the family life of fathers: A comparative survey of Japanese and Korean residents-in-Japan in the Osaka area. *Japanese Journal of Human Sciences of Health and Social Services, 11,* 65–77.

Igarashi, T., & Hagiwara, H. (2004). Junior high school students' tendency toward non-attendance at school and attachment in early childhood. *Japanese Journal of Educational Psychology, 52,* 264–276.

Ishii-Kuntz, M. (2007). Fathers' effects on their adolescent children's development: How do fathers affect children's social development? In H. Mimizuka & K. Makino (Eds.), *Academic achievement and crisis of transition* (pp. 125–142). Tokyo, Japan: Kaneko Shobo.

Kamiya, T. (2002). Paternal cognition of infant crying. *The Japanese Journal of Developmental Psychology, 13,* 284–294.

Kashiwagi, K. (1993). *The developmental psychology of fathers.* Tokyo, Japan: Kawashima Shoten.

Kato, K., Ishii-Kuntz, M., Makino, K., & Tsuchiya, M. (2002). The impact of parental involvement and maternal childcare anxiety on sociability of three-year-olds: A two-cohort comparison. *The Japanese Journal of Developmental Psychology, 13,* 30–41.

Kato, K., & Kondo, K. (2007). A comparison between fathers and mothers in a play situation with three-year olds. *The Japanese Journal of Developmental Psychology, 18,* 35–44.

Kikuchi, F., & Kashiwagi, K. (2007). Fathers' child rearing: Fathers who took childcare leave. *Journal of the Faculty of Human Studies, Bunkyo Gakuin University, 9,* 189–207.

Kimura, K., Tamura, T., Kuramochi, K., Nakazawa, C., Kishida, Y., Oikawa, Y., Aramaki, M., Morita, C., & Izumi, H. (2003). A comparison of marital relationships of couples who had their first childbirth, in relation to perinatal visits to the family of origin. *Bulletin of Tokyo Gakugei University. Section 6 , Technology, Home Economics and Environmental Education, 55,* 123–131.

Kojima, H. (2001). *Development and mind and culture.* Tokyo, Japan: Yuhikaku.

Kondo, S., Otsuka, K., Sawaguchi, G. T., Honda, E. T., Nakamura, Y., & Kato, S. (2010). Mental health status of Japanese-Brazilian children at Brazilian schools in Japan. *Asia-Pacific Psychiatry, 2,* 92–98.

Lamb, M. E. (1976). *The role of the father in child development.* New York, NY: Wiley.

Lynn, D. B. (1978). *The father: His role in child development.* Monterey, CA: Brooks/ Cole.

Makino, K., Nakano, Y., & Kashiwagi, K. (1996). *Child development and the role of the father.* Kyoto, Japan: Minerva Shobo.

Ministry of Health, Labor and Welfare. (1994). *Basic directions for future child rearing support measures (Angel Plan).* Retrieved from http://www.mhlw.go.jp/ bunya/kodomo/angelplan.html

Ministry of Health, Labor and Welfare. (1997). *Survey of actual conditions of working women*. Retrieved from http://wwwhakusyo.mhlw.go.jp/wpdocs/hpwj199701/b0000.html

Ministry of Health, Labor and Welfare. (1999). *Concrete plan to implement priority measures for the declining birth rate (New Angel Plan)*. Retrieved from http://www1.mhlw.go.jp/topics/syousika/tp0816-3_18.html

Ministry of Health, Labor and Welfare. (2004). *Support plans for children and child rearing*. Retrieved from http://www.mhlw.go.jp/houdou/2004/12/h1224-4.html

Ministry of Health, Labor and Welfare. (2010). *Vision for children and child-rearing*. Retrieved from http://www.mhlw.go.jp/bunya/kodomo/pdf/vision-zen-bun.pdf

Morishita,Y. (2006). The effect of becoming fathers on men's development. *The Japanese Journal of Developmental Psychology, 17*, 182–192.

Morse, E. S. (1917). *Japan day by day*. Boston, MA: Houghton Mifflin.

Nakamichi, K., & Nakazawa, J. (2003). Maternal/paternal child rearing style and young children's aggressive behavior. *Chiba University Faculty of Education Bulletin, 51*, 173–179.

Nakazawa, J. (2011). *Factors of father's child rearing*. Report of the Foundation of Children's Future.

Nakura, K., Nakazawa, J., & Yamamoto, T. (2001). Multicultural early childhood education in Japan: Practice of Oizumi, Gunma [Report of symposium organized by International Relations Committee, Japan Society of Research on Early Childhood Care and Education]. *Research on Early Childhood Care and Education in Japan, 39*, 279–286.

National Institute of Population and Social Security Research. (2008). *The 4th national survey on the family in Japan*. Tokyo. Japan: National Institute of Population and Social Security Research.

Obokata, A., & Muto, T. (2005). Regulatory and preventive factors for mild delinquency of junior high school students: Child-parent relationships, peer relationships, and self-control. *The Japanese Journal of Developmental Psychology, 16*, 286–299.

Onodera, A. (2003). Changes in self-concept in the transition to parenthood. *The Japanese Journal of Developmental Psychology, 14*, 180–190.

Shwalb, D. W., Imaizumi, N., & Nakazawa, J. (1987). The modern Japanese father: Roles and problems in a changing society. In M. E. Lamb (Ed.), *The father's role: Cross-cultural perspectives* (pp. 247–269). Hillsdale, NJ: Lawrence Erlbaum Associates.

Shwalb, D. W., Kawai, H., Shoji, J., & Tsunetsugu, K. (1997). The middle class Japanese father: A survey of parents of preschoolers. *Journal of Applied Developmental Psychology, 18*, 497–511.

Shwalb, D. W., Nakazawa, J., & Shwalb, B. J. (Eds.). (2005). *Applied developmental psychology: Theory, practice, and research from Japan*. Charlotte, NC: Information Age Publishing.

Shwalb, D. W., Nakazawa, J., Yamamoto, T., & Hyun, J.-H. (2004). Fathering in Japanese, Chinese and Korean cultures: A review of the research literature. In

M. E. Lamb (Ed.), *The role of the father in child development* (4th ed., pp. 146–181). Hoboken, NJ: Wiley.

Shwalb, D. W., Nakazawa, J., Yamamoto, T., & Hyun, J.-H. (2010). Fathering in Japan, China, and Korea: Changing context, images, and roles. In M. E. Lamb (Ed.) *The role of the father in child development* (5th ed., pp. 341–387). Hoboken, NJ: Wiley.

Takahashi, M. (2008). Difficulties of unemployed middle-aged men in their company and social connections. *The Japanese Journal of Developmental Psychology, 19*, 132–143.

Tanaka, Y., & Nakazawa, J. (2005). Job-related temporary father absence (*tanshin-funin*) and child development. In D. Shwalb, J. Nakazawa, & B. Shwalb (Eds.), *Applied developmental psychology: Theory, practice, and research from Japan* (pp. 241–260). Charlotte, NC: Information Age.

Thunberg, C. P. (1791, 1793). *Resa uti Europa, Afrika, Asia, förrättad åren 1770–1779* [Travels in Europe, Africa and Asia made between the years 1770 and 1779].

Tanibuchi, S. (2009). A research of school adaptation, parent–child relationship and community participation among Japanese-Brazilian living in Japan: Comparative study with Japanese. *Bulletin of the Graduate School of Education, Hiroshima University. Part III, Education and Human Science, 58*, 183–192.

Tsuchiya, M., Iinaga, K., Kato, K., & Kazui, M. (1996). Father's flexibility of child rearing behavior and development of their children. In K. Makino, Y. Nakano, & K. Kashiwagi (Eds.), *Child development and the role of the father* (pp. 159–171). Kyoto, Japan: Minerva Shobo.

Vogel, E. A. (1963). *Japan's new middle class.* Berkeley, CA: University of California Press.

Vogel, S. H. (1996). Urban middle-class Japanese family life, 1958–1996: A personal and evolving perspective. In D. Shwalb & B. Shwalb (Eds.), *Japanese child rearing: Two generations of scholarship* (pp. 177–207). New York, NY: Guilford Press.

Yagi, T. (2009). Being a househusband as an alternative lifestyle of the family: A qualitative study on the consciousness of house husbands. *Annals of Family Studies, 34*, 91–108.

Yoshioka, A. (2009). Learning process and change of parenting consciousness at the father's study program. *Bulletin of Faculty of Education, Hokkaido University, 107*, 179–193.

Chapter Four

The Father's Role in the Indian Family

A Story That Must Be Told

Nandita Chaudhary
University of Delhi, Delhi, India

Case Story: Chandan's Devotion to His Family

Chandan was a young boy when his family was torn from their home in Lahore (now in Pakistan), where his father worked as a sheet metal worker in a factory. The 1947 partition of India and Pakistan was violent, and had taken its toll on thousands of families on both sides of the new border. Chandan's family was among the thousands of Punjabi Hindus who fled for their lives. His father was determined to protect his family and worked very hard after settling in a small town, north of Delhi. Chandan grew up in harsh circumstances, shielded by strong family ties. Soon after completing high school, he decided to quit study and set up a small enterprise, charging batteries in the local marketplace. With his unfailing dedication, the business expanded to include several locations. The family continued to be extremely cohesive and supportive of each other. Chandan married and the couple had three children. He was determined to educate his children well, something he had missed in his life. Today all three of his children are engineers.

Now as his children enter adulthood, Chandan is passionate, forceful, autocratic, and conservative in matters he considers his responsibility. He is intolerant of modernity and liberalism where family relationships are concerned, and is often angry and even unmanageable when things don't go his way. Chandan's conviction is guided by his devotion towards the family, something so sacred that it cannot be derailed by anyone. His son's recent affections and desire to marry is a current crisis for the family. What he sees as his son's momentary lapse of reason cannot be allowed to jeopardise Chandan's world. Apart from his disagreement with the concept of love before marriage, the fact that this young woman is from a different ethnic community is an additional impediment. Chandan feels that children owe it to the family to marry someone chosen through the time-tested process of family arrangement and that his honour, his word, and his world would be crushed if such a thing came to pass. In a moment of dramatic despair, he ordered his son to declare him (Chandan) dead in writing if he insisted on marrying this woman. He has cried, yelled, and thrown things around the house, deeply traumatising his children and wife over this issue. Chandan is driven by a passionate belief in his role and responsibility as a father. He truly believes in what he is doing and as I write this Case Story it has been two years since the son proposed to his girlfriend, whom he says he cannot marry unless his father is in agreement. His father's reaction was not unexpected, but the young man was confident of his capacity to persuade him, and that confidence is now weakening. He feels incapable of going ahead with the marriage if his father does not concede, on account of the sacrifices that his father has made for the family. But he is also determined to marry ...

Postscript to Case Story

Just prior to the publication of this book, the couple was finally married in a traditional wedding ceremony. In this story, the young man did not display direct disrespect or confront the father, but showed steadfast determination. The young couple now lives close to Chandan's home and travels every weekend for family visits to maintain the togetherness so desired by the father.

> A professor is the equivalent of ten teachers,
> A father is equal to a hundred professors,
> A mother exceeds a thousand fathers in honour.
> (Raghavan, 2010)

The concept of a nation predisposes people to assume internal consistency in the ways in which its citizens think. In fact, whatever social group we encounter, the label that it carries prompts the assumption of at least some degree of homogeneity. The human mind does not necessarily need a reason to string together particular constructions of the world, and the narrative self makes us who we are, as is the case when collective identities are seen as grand narratives about groups of people (Berreby, 2005). By adopting a 'wide angle lens' on occasion and also by zooming in on individual lives, we are able to arrive at reasonable descriptions. This chapter has been written with this two-focus approach, drawing inferences from both individual cases and from the study of collectives.

Cultural/Historical Background as It Influences Fathering

Given the sheer size of its people, India includes several large sub-cultural communities within and outside of its borders. In an example of the latter, there are Indian communities thriving, economically, socially and politically in various parts of the world who identify very passionately as being Indian. Further, the nation of India and its people are divided by regional, linguistic, religious, caste, ethnicity, and geographical divergences that are mindboggling to apprehend. I have often argued that Indian society is a complex coexistence of all critical phases of human society, from the hunter-gatherer, to early domestication and subsistence farming, and framed within a central political ideology as it gallops quickly towards becoming a powerful nation. Perhaps much of the potential power is derived from the size of its people, rather than from other important developments taking place within its boundaries. Even in the huge metropolitan cities, we encounter people living on the margins of survival. Although they may have knowledge of the 21st century, their access to its inventions is only peripheral. Remote regions remain largely detached from technologically driven lives and the monetary economy, resulting in a phenomenon that I call 'multi-chronicity,' a permanent multiplicity in terms of social history.

When speaking of Indian-ness, I do not imply a uniform, monolithic structure of a consolidated, consistent way of living. If anything, Indian culture provides us with the exact inverse. The number of people and the diversity of languages, cultural practices, narratives and experiences make uniformity rather inconceivable. Even the past is fraught with plurality, as India "does not have one past, but many pasts" (Ramanujan, 1999, p. 187). Added to the texture of multiplicity is the fact that the past always has a constant presence in our present (Anandalakshmy, 2010). As Thapar (2000) remarked, "At certain levels there are aspects of cultural traditions in India that can be traced to roots as far back as a few thousand years, but such a continuity must not be confused with stagnation" (p. xxv). This sense of parallel histories underlying technological advancement in every sphere of life is enormously difficult to comprehend. Thus, a collective 'multi-voicedness' characterises Indian cultural reality. It is like living in a time machine which creates periods of history along its journey (Chaudhary, 2012).

It is thus impossible to express the incredible variability of Indian social life. Although distinctions based on religions and regions are marked, there is no doubt that there are several features of social life where one can find common threads. Family relationships are one such domain. There are, in fact, many Indias that one could write about. The northeast region of the country bordering China and Myanmar has several tribal communities, many of them having converted to Christianity and where daily life is guided by the Church. The union territory of Goa has a powerful Portuguese influence, whereas the French have left a lasting impression on the eastern coastal area of Pondicherry. If one attempts to portray the greatness of India's diversity, it would be impossible to present it within the confines of a single chapter. I have therefore chosen to focus on the Hindu majority as an illustration, to explain some patterns of Indian fatherhood.

Among Hindus the notion of *Ashramas*, or periods in the life of a person, is critical to understand while discussing any element of a person's life, roles or relationships. The patriarchal ideal is defined through advancing states and stages of being a child, an adolescent, a young person (*bhramcharya*), a householder (*grihasta ashrama*), an elderly person (*vanaprastha*), and finally an ascetic (*sanyasa*). This progression permits the life of any one person to go from intense closeness and collectiveness (even for survival) as a baby and child, to practice and persistence (as a young person learning the tasks of adulthood), to being an engaged partner (as a householder and member of a family), to gradually moving towards a preparation for detachment by gradually handing over the work of society to younger generations. Although this is an idealized trajectory, it remains a potent backdrop for the evaluation and appraisal of one's own and others' conduct and situation (Krishnan, 1998). As I have argued elsewhere (Chaudhary, 2007), the stereotype that Indians are a collectivistic people fails to grasp either their behaviour or ideology. Instead, complex variations exist with reference to the ways in which Indians lead their lives, depending upon context, company, and chronology. The important point that I would like to make at this juncture is that spirituality, detachment, and distance are basic to an accepted path for the Indian person.

Plurality, gender, and the Indian father

The "symbolic inheritance" of a people (Shweder, Goodnow, Hatano, LeVine, Markus, & Miller, 2006, p. 724) profoundly guides the ways in which experience is apprehended, appraised and acted upon. In India this legacy has been textured by several critical experiences from outside its borders, from the earliest invasions by land and sea. These intrusions, invasions and occupations of the country have made significant contributions to the ways in which the country and its people have evolved. Throughout its history, India has been predominantly patriarchal with a few exceptions, an ideology that received strong reinforcement during British rule from 1858 to 1947 (Uberoi, 2006). There are, however, different versions of patriarchy that have emerged over the years, alongside the survival of several matriarchal communities and other exceptions to the dominant patterns. Thus, for the majority, authority, residence, inheritance and over the years the boundaries of division of labour based on gender, have all been seriously tested, and what emerges is a "plurality of family lifestyles" rather than simple reorganisation (Oomen, 2002, p. 39). "Residence" refers to the traditional patrilocal pattern of the movement of a woman to her husband's natal home after marriage. Regarding inheritance, although the law defines sons and daughters as equal in inheritance of family property, there is a common belief that women receive movable property during their wedding and sons should be the exclusive heirs of immovable property.

Due to its vast territory, and immense diversity in social, linguistic, ecological and cultural aspects of life, generalisations become extremely contentious. "No story about India can end unambiguously" wrote Nandy (2002, p. 35) about contemporary political life. People may believe that the country is moving simply from a traditional way of living to a modern, progressive way of understanding governance and "a consolidation constitutional processes and citizenship" (p. 35). But there is actually a constant renewal of tradition, sometimes even in the most progressive and modern aspects of Indian culture. The essence of Indian relationships persists as fundamentally hierarchical and familial, with women as the central players in a predominantly patriarchal society. As a social category, gender falls far short of other guiding principles: familism, hierarchy, and sensitivity to context. Relativism and subjectivity also are pervasive in directing individual behaviour, social evaluations, and moral order.

In India, gender-typing of behaviour, roles, and relationships is distinct and takes place early in the lifespan; and there is also a greater merging of masculine and feminine images. This "lesser differentiation" is clearly visible in presentations of male and female images, divine and other. Gods are drawn with distinctly feminine features and 'superior human beings' openly discuss feminine traits openly with masculine ones. Even in prayer among Hindus, Lord Krishna is believed to be the only male, while all devotees, men and women, are female (Kakar & Kakar, 2007, p. 202).

The lives of Indian fathers are transacted under strong social constraints of family life (Seymour, 1999). This theme has emerged in the few instances of research that has tried to take a closer look at the lives of young men in Indian families and society (Derne, 1995). Young men reported several constraints on their lives and indicated a preference for the joint family because the presence of elders kept negative and self-destructive impulses under control. This preference for the joint family indicates that the presence of the 'other' is a very real and intense experience in the transaction of fatherhood. Thus, other people who are present at the time influence the father's conduct towards his children (Tuli & Chaudhary, 2010).

The patriarchal tradition and family life in India

The ancient Hindu text, *Manusmriti* (about 200 BCE) consisted of the words of a sage (Manu) in oral discourse with other sages who beseeched him to define the laws of all social classes. Regarding the relative position of males and females within a family, Manu's legendary remarks about women depicted their 'rights' as severely restricted, referring to the woman as under the supervision of a progression of men in their lives, the father, the brother and then the husband. The role of the father was thus considered central to family life.

This pre-eminence of the father is not without exception. Despite the father's revered position in the family (as was indicated in my opening quotation from the Hindu scriptures, "a father is equivalent to a hundred professors"), the place of the mother in the Hindu family remains one of dramatic and decisive goodness. If the Western family is centred around the conjugal relations between husband and wife, there is no denying that the central unit of an Indian family is the mother and son (Uberoi, 2006) as was evidenced in the study of sleeping patterns in Oriya families (Shweder, Jensen, & Goldstein, 1995). This dramatic position of the mother sustains (and is sustained by) patriarchy since she is functionally central despite the acknowledged authority of the father (Chaudhary, 2009). Several authors (Kakar, 1981; Roland, 1988; Seymour, 1999) have written about the awkwardness that the father feels when he is with his child in the company of others, especially older men. In this sense, the company decides the conduct of the father in traditional families. The fact that the father deflects expression of favour for his children adds to the glue that holds the mother and her children together. This emotional distancing of the father is one of the most visible characteristics of traditional fatherhood in India, although recent research suggests that it may be lessening among urban and educated fathers (Sriram & Kaur, 2011).

One critical task of an Indian father is the giving away of a daughter in marriage, known in Hindi as *kanyadaan* that literally means "giving away a virgin." This ritual is believed to uplift the status of a father both in spiritual and social terms, and also potentially cleanses him of any 'wrong' that he may have done in his entire life. The action of giving away a loved one who is a precious part of oneself is in itself a noteworthy act. Even in contemporary Hindu families, the *kanyadaan* ceremony is significant, serious and sentimental. In fact, a man who has not given away a daughter in marriage is believed to be somewhat incomplete in the spiritual sense (Krishnan, 1998). I propose that it is not in 'being' the father, but in 'transacting' fatherhood that a man's status is maintained, making the other family members a critical element in fulfilment of the paternal role.

The Indian family is believed to be at the heart of a person's identity, and in fact family life emerges as a very strong ideal even in the lives of young people who have lived by themselves on the street (Chaudhary, 2004). However, it is essential to note that filial solidarity of children towards their parents has always been given more importance than sibling alliances (Gore, 1978), with the least attention paid to the conjugal relationship. Thus the obligatory role of a son towards his father remains life-long and pre-dominant in a man's life, even when he himself becomes a father. In con-temporary society some transformation has taken place, especially among urban and educated men who chose their own spouses, thereby investing far more in the conjugal relationship and making changes within the dynamics of the family (Uberoi, 2003). In many cases, the family system has adapted to these changes, whereas in other instances it has caused a breakdown of relationships within or among families with a corresponding strengthen-ing of the conjugal unit (Pattanaik & Sriram, 2010). Yet, even among these exceptional families, one does find remnants of traditional beliefs and prac-tices, albeit less frequently and of lower intensity. For instance, Sriram, Dave, Khasgiwala, and Joshi (2006) found that although many men appre-ciated the changes in women's participation in public activities and careers, transformations within the domestic unit still remained unacceptable. The expectation remained for women to take primary responsibility for the care of children and other household tasks (Kapoor, 2006; Sriram et al., 2006).

Fathers and mothers are both idealised in Indian homes. Unless proved otherwise, the ideal of a father as a repository of heroic sacrifice and hard work for the family in his role as a provider is a very dramatic and sustain-ing image, while the construction of a mother is as affectionate and loving. As in all patriarchal families, the father in an Indian household is seen as the breadwinner. In the space between the stern authority of the father and the benevolence of the mother, there is a negotiability of roles that sustains the patriarchal system, because otherwise it would become too inflexible to survive. In the appraisal of social conduct, context determines its evaluation (Menon, 2003). Just as a father's conduct is determined by the company in which the transaction takes place, children's approach towards the father is also guided by ambiguity and ambivalence (Kakar & Kakar, 2007). A child has to be extremely aware of who all are present when interacting with the father, for it is not simply the dyadic relationship but the relative position-ing of the father in the surrounding social group that guides socialisation. Children begin to notice these complexities early in life (Chaudhary, 2004).

Horizontal and vertical displacement of the father's attention

In the dynamics of roles and relationships within the family related to the father, there are systematic and socially acceptable ways to actually create a separation between a father and his children, to attain the objective of maintaining an extended family system. There seem to be important cultural goals linked with these patterns. I propose here that the community deliberately encourages a father to express a distancing from his own children. Two somewhat distinct examples can be articulated: horizontal distancing and vertical distancing.

Horizontal distancing of a father's affection

The traditional father in an Indian (joint) family system is defined by distance, unending responsibility, and unquestioned authority over family members. This image is detailed by the absence of overt expression of emotions and apparent detachment (Bisht & Sinha, 1981). There are serious cultural obstacles to accurate communication feedback in the hierarchical structures of Indian families and society due to this distancing (Kakar & Kakar, 2007). This pattern has profound implications for relationships at home and the workplace particularly for men, because there is a strong expectation for employers to be benevolent patriarchs (Roland, 1988). The giving and receiving of negative feedback becomes problematic especially for people who are higher in seniority. In the family, this implies that there is much difficulty associated with negative feedback toward the father, resulting in an aura of authority. At the same time, the patriarch also has to maintain the reputation of a benevolent and generous person, or otherwise the family system would come under threat. Roland (1988) found many similar dynamics in his study of relationships at the workplace, not only among Indians living in India, but also among Indian expatriates in the U.S.

In traditional Indian society, the father's involvement with his son's life begins quite late in development, and is transacted in the shadow of the larger family to whom the father is obligated. In the case of one of my close associates, the father took responsibility for raising his older brother's offspring after the brother passed away. Since these children were already in his life back when he was married and had his own children, all 'children' in the family addressed the patriarch as *Chacha*, the kin term specifically used for father's younger brother. This choice was symbolic of the equitable disbursement of favour.

The father's effort to be fair towards others is accompanied by another theme. In traditional families, many young fathers were embarrassed to hold their young infants in the presence of elder family members, because such contact was suggestive of his sexuality in that the children were the product of his sexuality (Kakar & Kakar, 2007). This near taboo on any direct expression of certain feelings (especially affection) towards one's own children is reported by several observers as one of the most noted characteristics of Indian child rearing (Seymour, 1999; Trawick, 1990). Apparently, it seems to lead to a pronounced limitation of paternal contact with the child depending upon context and company. This feature of family life remains one of the cornerstones of socialisation (Chaudhary, 2004; 2007; Menon, 2003) and the personal and social orientations of Indians.

Taken from the inside perspective as a member of the Indian community, my interpretation of this trend is that it does not signify the absence of affection, but rather an awkwardness about conveying this emotion, especially in the company of others, intimate or otherwise. Some recent changes are observable in this regard, as urban Indian fathers have been found to be increasingly expressive, interactive, and unhesitating in expressions of affection and care of young children (Roopnarine & Suppal, 2003). Recent studies also indicate that there is a growing expectation among children and women for enhanced paternal participation (Kumari, 2008; Sriram, Karnik, & Ali, 2002). Meanwhile, a review of research in three cities in Western India reported that fathers indicated a heightened awareness of their increased involvement in the lives of their children (Saraff & Srivastava, 2008). In more traditional homes, a father usually maintains a distance from his own children in the presence of others. According to Kakar and Kakar (2007, p. 55), one of the "most poignant" observations of the Indian family is the scant time that a daughter is able to spend with her father. Although this has changed in many urban families, the interaction still remains visibly limited in most instances. In fact, mealtimes are often the only moments when young girls and women are seen to interact with their fathers in a traditional Indian family (p. 55). In a recent online news item, traditional Indian fathering was discussed:

> An elderly relative recounts an incident from his childhood. When he, then nine, and his three siblings walked into the house from school, their father was in the living room with a visitor. The introductions were done, and then the visitor asked: "In what class are they studying?" Their father was taken aback for a moment. But he soon gathered his wits and told the children, "Tell Uncle which classes you are studying in." One or two generations ago, mothers took complete responsibility of the children and household work. The kids, for their part, performed well without expecting any help from their fathers. In fact, so uninvolved were many fathers in childcare that they did not know much about their children. Not that there are no such unaware fathers today. But their numbers have dwindled.
>
> (Raj, 2010, n.p.)

This awkwardness was also linked by Kakar and Kakar (2007) to the relationship between Indian men and their mothers. The indubitable appraisal of the mother as a good person, no matter what, is a cultural given resulting in what Kakar (1981) termed a life-long "maternal enthrallment." These feelings consist of a deeply conflicted orientation of wanting to get away from the mother, combined with a dread of being separated (Kakar & Kakar, 2007). The sudden and traumatic displacement of a child from the comfort of the company of women to the harsh territory of the father was described as "catastrophic" by Carstairs (1967, p. 160) whereby comforting women are suddenly replaced by demanding men. Carstairs concluded that the outcomes of Hindu child rearing were far more pathogenic than those based on child rearing techniques used in the West. This hypothesis is no longer acceptable, due to the reorientation of developmental psychology away from psychoanalytic theory, and the emergence of cultural psychology as a discipline where conclusions about cultural differences are more cautious (Valsiner, 2007).

The traditional Indian father is believed to be a distant, benevolent and protective figure whose basic responsibility is to be socially committed rather than psychologically close to his developing children (Pandey, 2006). A great deal of effort was actually taken in Indian families to ensure that fathers did not actually invest exclusively in their own children, either in their time or resources. This was with the clear objectives of sustaining the larger family system and commitment to one's own brothers, sisters and their families. A father who is exclusively indulgent toward his own children is an awkward, even disruptive phenomenon within the larger patriarchal ideology, where commitment to family elders is of primary importance. Indulgence toward one's children is traditionally seen as harmful (Kakar & Kakar, 2007), detracting attention from the larger network whose maintenance is the responsibility of every individual, over and above one's self. As Trawick (1990) has shown, it is not the absence of love but a 'different' way of loving that characterises Indian fathering.

Regarding family interactions and childcare, for instance, there is a clear absence of the father in research records. One of the things that is responsible for this void, in addition to the absence of fathers from the lives of young children, is the fact the family and child development researchers who conduct such studies have mostly been women. This is likely to create a greater distancing by fathers during periods of data collection, due to a feeling of awkwardness in performing a familial task in the presence of an outsider.

Vertical distancing: A recursive formula for alternating generations

"*Mool se soot pyara*" ("Interest is more rewarding than capital") is a celebrated aphorism in Indian families. The underlying meaning of this saying is that while it is difficult for a father to demonstrate a positive bias towards his children, there is quite a different story across generations. The awkwardness and shame of preferential treatment, in relation to grandchildren, is completely dissolved when a man advances to the status of being a grandfather. There seems to be a life stage-related change in ease of expression of love, such that a man becomes far more affectionate with children as a grandfather than he was as a father. Thus, grandfathers play the role of affectionate patriarch toward the children of his offspring (Figure 4.1).

Display of affection in family relationships is rather oblique. It is common that display of conjugal love is discouraged since it is believed to detract from concern for other family members. Please note that I write here of the *expression* of love, not its internal experience. It is reasonable to say that affection in the Indian family skips a generation, particularly for men. Mothers' expression of love is far more acceptable, while for fathers it may be rather awkward in the presence of older members of the family, particularly in the case of multiple generation households. This distinction is seen in several studies referenced below. In contrast with fathers,

Figure 4.1 A grandfather (about age 60) supervises grandchildren (about 2 and 4 years old) in a village courtyard. This is a typical scene in rural homes. The grandfather is a farmer of lower SES. Photo courtesy of Shashi Shukla.

grandfathers are generally unhesitating in their outward expression of affection towards young children.

Review of Fathering Research

In the fields of family and cultural studies, empirical and ethnographic work in India lags far behind scholarly writing (Sharma, 2003) to the extent of being "dramatically unbalanced" (LeVine, 2003, p. xiii). Another significant pattern in the research literature is the greater focus on women's lives. The advent of gender studies as a discipline, as well as the increased investment in studies of 'women as disadvantaged' are important reasons for the far greater coverage of the lives of mothers, women and girls, compared with research on fathers, men and boys.

Pandey (2006) outlined the diversity of Indians by remarking that almost "every possible form of family and marriage systems may be found" here (p. 365). Patriarchy is a defining feature in most communities, with a few exceptions, thus clearly demarcating the division of power within the larger family system. In communities where there is co-residence of several members in the traditional joint family, typically defined as one where parents live with their adult sons, their spouses and offspring (and most common among business communities in northern India), the visible power and authority of male members is evident and filial devotion towards their parents is considered absolute. This authority is a given, and the father is believed to be an ultimate authority, and in the hierarchical organisation the paternal grandfather often is even more in control of the family than the father. But these patterns tell only one side of the story. Research and experience with family dynamics has shed light on several smaller narratives on family dynamics that question the notion of unyielding patriarchy, and even the universality of the joint family in Indian society (Uberoi, 2003). The realities of life have a way of circumventing ideology in all human associations, in powerful and sometimes invisible ways. This can be clearly encountered in ethnographic descriptions of the Indian family (Chaudhary, 2004), where reversals, exceptions and negotiations characterise the lives of ordinary people, and classification of the structure of families becomes nearly impossible.

The situation of women in India is generally similar to that in other patriarchal societies, although Chowdhury (1994) argues that their plight was even deeper under colonial rule. It was argued by feminists that British administrators, who were unable to exercise control over women in their own culture, prevailed over the Indian legal system and diminished the political and social rights of women even further. In a study of family dynamics (Tuli & Chaudhary, 2010), mothers were found characteristically to describe the father's role as rather limited in terms of time spent with the child, but also as central and intense. This suggested both gender specific and role specific patterns in child rearing. In their study, only a few mothers reported sharing the daily care of children with their husbands, and the active involvement of fathers was reported to increase as the children got older. Regardless of fathers' purported levels of involvement, mothers reported that men were undeniably important in children's lives. Even when there were problems over the father's role in his child's life, mothers in our study reported that they tried not to discuss the problems with the child, so as not to tarnish the father's image or position.

Maternal education and employment are important factors in redefining the distribution of domestic work within the family's lifecycle. In one study on urban educated Indian families (Sharma, 1990), it was found that although fathers reported significant equity in responsibility for household tasks when their wives were employed, the reports of the women indicated somewhat different perceptions of their husbands' participation. However, most studies (see also Shukla, 1987; Suppal & Roopnarine, 1999) indicate that actual paternal involvement with infant childcare, especially girls, remained quite marginal. Fathers in these studies were positive and welcoming of the baby, but the primary responsibility for childcare was the mother's. For bathing the baby, for example, men and women alike felt that the mother was 'naturally' more capable of handling the baby and even that fathers might cause an injury by their clumsy handling.

As mentioned earlier, Kakar's (1981) work focused on the restraint shown by Indian fathers, and the sudden departure of children, especially sons, from the comfort of the mother. He referred to the transition to the company of the father and other men as a 'second birth.' This milestone was traditionally considered desirable, as a transition from requiring maternal care and protection, to an apprenticeship with the father or other male family members. Kurtz (1992) contended, as supported by my own data, that prior to this transition, however, the first departure of the child from the mother actually came earlier in development, toward the care of other women in a family. Thus, Kakar's account may have omitted a critical element in the advancement of the Indian child in preparation for relationships with adults other than the mother. As Kurtz (1992) remarked, the objective of Hindu socialisation is *not* identification with one individual, as is assumed in Western family and society, but rather it is identification with the group. Failure to appreciate this cultural fact can lead to a profound misunderstanding of the Indian cultural experience and personal outcomes.

The absence of the father from studies of Indian childhood has been noted in the literature (Roopnarine & Suppal, 2003; Sriram, 2003). But while this work has focused on the contemporary Indian family and recent changes, the absence of the father from traditional childcare should not be construed as the absence of *men*. I have found in my own work

(Chaudhary, 2004) that the grandfather is a very important companion for young children, in both rural and urban households. When women of all ages are busy with domestic chores, it is a common sight to see the grandfather near the doorway of the home, keeping a young baby occupied or watching over an older child in the yard or street. The 'absence' of men is also attributable to the fact that when researchers (especially females) enter a family home, there is a silent withdrawal of the men from the scene, and this is true across social class and caste. The men of the family, if they were home, watch quietly from a distance, sometimes making their presence felt but usually not. In the instance when the researcher's attention is focused on them, men's reactions may range from extreme awkwardness to frank openness. Since much of the research on developmental psychology in India is framed within a Western paradigm (Roopnarine & Suppal, 2003), it is easy to understand how the father became isolated from the primary focus of researchers, given men's awkwardness with research procedures. The 'blind embellishment" (Roopnarine & Suppal, 2003, p. 117) of research that presumed a patriarchal tradition and the ideology of a 'distant father,' and the exclusion of other family members from research, precluded discussion of the men's role in the care of children. It is actually the presence of researchers that often causes the father to depart. Indeed it is *not* true that the father does not love his children; rather, he is unwilling and awkward about expressing this love *in the presence of others*.

Roland (1988), in comparing Japanese and Indian fathers, remarked that although they both seemed distant and preoccupied, fathers in these two societies are deeply attached to their children. If we can appreciate this element of fathering in India, we will have a better grasp of the Indian paternal role. As indicated by Suppal and Roopnarine (1999), there is a need for more innovative and strategic methods to investigate fathers' contributions to domestic work and other family tasks. For example, in a detailed observation of the care of young children in Delhi families, it was found that the father was *not* absent from the physical care, handling or holding of children, even of babies, although their involvement was much less than that of women (Roopnarine, Talukder, Jain, Joshi, & Srivastav, 1992). Their study of 54 families focused on interactions of fathers and mothers with year-old infants. They found that fathers focused more on rough play with the infants, and that infants spent more time following mothers than fathers.

Sub-Cultural Variations in Fathering

Gender relations and the great Indian divide

Regionally, there is tremendous variability in contemporary Indian gender relations. The arrangement of castes persists as an important identifying feature of social arrangements in India, despite the secularising trends of a democratic constitution that negates caste as an ascribed status. It is of historic interest, however, to note that the distance between the sexes was more characteristic of higher castes than the lower castes, where greater equality was observed between men and women. There are also regional differences in gender relations, for example, in the southern states of India there has always been more social interaction between the sexes than in the northern states (Lannoy, 1971).

Some important variations in gender relations have emerged from the investigation of rural vs. urban samples, between parents with different educational and occupational levels, and most importantly in relation to maternal employment outside the home. Dual-career nuclear families show marked changes in their beliefs about the care of children, although behavioural changes lag behind (Suppal & Roopnarine, 1999; Sharma, 1990; Shukla, 1987, Sriram, 2011). Although fathers expressed a desire to be more involved with the care of children and domestic work, actual involvement emerged only in a few cases; in one study it was the outcome of an intervention programme (Sriram & Kaur, 2011). Regarding changes in the Indian paternal role, there is research evidence to show that immigrant Indian fathers residing in the U.S. become intensely involved in daily activities after migrating (Jain & Belsky, 1997). In another study of children of Americans of Indian descent, men were more than "onlookers" in the care of their children (Roopnarine & Suppal, 2003), indicating that current circumstances can have a profound impact on the basic structure of the paternal role and relationships. These studies indicated that in the absence of a larger network of relationships where others viewed the father in action, the father in a nuclear family was much more interactive and involved with children and more participative in domestic activities. I would, however, like to mention another qualifier here: Indian families living in other parts of the developed world experience an additional factor that we have to consider. It is not simply a matter of the new conditions in which they live, and the parental ethnotheories of the new setting, but also departure from the dense social atmosphere of the Indian culture of origin the affects parental choices in childcare. What fathers move *away from* becomes as significant as what fathers move *into*. The phenomenon of the 'roving grandparents' reported by Anandalakshmy (2010) is an important example of this point, and it is important to note that fathers who were not very interactive in the care of their own children may become intensely involved with grandchildren. The profound importance of being cared for by family led to a frantic rush of parents and grandparents across distances they had never traversed, and departures they had only imagined, just so that the grandchildren could have the benefit of the care their parents had when they were young.

Social class and economic disparity

Economic inequalities remain a characteristic of Indian contemporary society, and along with regional, linguistic, caste and ethnic diversity, economic status is a critical determinant of the circumstances that define fatherhood. In the absence of comparative data from fathers in different economic settings, one study did show that fathers in poor families were far more involved in fathering and domestic activities than their middle and upper class counterparts (Jain & Belsky, 1997). Perhaps the traditions that bind families together in wealthier communities are weakened by the harsh realities of poverty where it is essential to cooperate for the sake of survival and sustenance.

Fathers in contemporary Indian society

Research on fathers in recent years has shown increased participation by fathers in the care of children (Roopnarine & Suppal, 2003), although for the researcher, men continue to remain very difficult to recruit as research participants (Chaudhary, 2004). Children and their care are still considered the primary responsibility of women in the family, although there are always exceptions to this trend when we visit family homes for our research. In such exceptional families, the father is far more forthcoming about his participation in the care of children and enthusiastic about his participation in the study. But it is not simply visibility of participation that is important to note and explain. In less urbanised townships and rural areas, the fact that most researchers in the field are women tends to decrease the active participation of the men of the family in field studies. In my opinion, this should not be taken as their absence, but more as a reminder of the social distance between the research team and the participants. In a conventional Indian family, men and women usually operate in different spaces of the home.

In revisiting the site of an earlier study of family life, Sharma (2003) found significant changes in the physical structures of the homes, new literacy and occupational profiles of the families, and a transformation of material possessions. Much of this change has been attributed by the community to the arrival of better educated spouses for the young men of the families. Sharma's (2003) research findings contradict the observations and analyses of several scholars about the undivided, indulgent and singular attention given to the child by the mother. The situation in a majority of families in Indian homes actually reveals a trend toward a wider network of relationships involved in the care of children that is not transacted as the warm, loving, and exclusive indulgence described in past studies. Instead, contemporary family life appears to be characterised by a rather comfortable, collectivist, supervised, shared and distributed care of children, in which the role of fathers (Roopnarine & Suppal, 2003) and older siblings (Sharma & Chaudhary, 2004) has gone largely unrecognised by most researchers. With increased mobility, migration, and departure from known places, there is inevitably an increase in the prevalence of nuclear families, despite persistent longer distance connections with the wider family. However, there is evidence to suggest that this change is important for the paternal role, since the involvement of fathers and closeness to their own children is found to be significantly greater in nuclear families (Roland, 1988).

Social Policy Issues Related to Fathering

Regarding laws and policies related to family life and fathering, Uberoi (2006) argued that patriarchy dominates the Indian family despite much lip service paid to the rights of women and equality. This does not imply the complete subjugation and exploitation of women, since the ideology of the family tends towards protection, obligation and affection between male and female members of a family. For example, brother–sister bonds are believed to be intense and life-long, wherein a brother is supposed to protect the interests of his sister forever. The traditional patriarchal system is meant to be protective, benevolent and complementary towards and with women, rather than to confront or subjugate women.

Contemporary Indian society has made several adaptations to global trends without foregoing its traditions in several important spheres of life. For example, Uberoi (2006) described what she called the "arranged love marriage," an innovative adaptation of the older system to the demands of increasingly educated youth. In this case, young people's romantic inclinations are accepted and transformed into arrangements between families.

One specific law related to the family was the Hindu Succession Act (1956), which made women and men equally eligible to inherit family property. However, this law also mentions the proximity of the relationship, in that preference shall be given to those heirs who are closer to the parents. This provision left room for unequal disbursements. In the case of an intestate death when a person dies without a will, the law states that property shall be equally divided among the sons, daughters, and other relevant heirs. The equal inheritance law for sons and daughters has had a great impact on gender relations in India. According to convention, women are given their share of moveable property upon their marriage in the form of dowry in most families. The sons, on the other hand, inherit the immoveable property that remains with the patrilineal family.

Regarding the custody of children, India still follows an outdated legal provision of the Guardians and Wards Act (1890), which mentions the inheritance to be given to the guardian. In the implementation of this

Act, there was a persistent bias in favour of the father. There has recently been pressure on the government to make changes to better provide for women's rights as mothers in the custody of children following divorce (Pandey, 2010).

More recently, the media have reported occasional news stories about the darker side of family life, loyalty, and togetherness. The opposition of parents to adult children's romantic involvement and inter-caste marriages are examples. However, one particular phenomenon has become essential to discussions of Indian fatherhood: the Indian father holds himself responsible for the standard of living and financial health of the family (Pandey, 2006). If the household is a joint family with co-residence of several kin, it is the men who are responsible to run the finances. Sometimes this responsibility can go too far, as in the following case of the family suicide.

> On the 9th of March, 2005, a young man and his distraught wife, residents of New Delhi, first took the lives of their two young children and then their own. The news item said that he was bankrupt and could not manage to pay back the debts that had piled up. His feeling of responsibility towards the members of his family, his wife and his two children, pushed him towards "family suicide."
>
> (Chaudhary, 2007)

In another incident (Chauhan, 2005), a father actually poisoned his 21-year-old daughter because he had gone bankrupt. The distress that such news items spreads among readers is perhaps the collective price we pay for the exaggerated importance that is placed on the father's role as breadwinner. These are indeed isolated instances of desperation, but they do reflect a sentiment that is shared by many.

Father, mother, and parent

In modern families, roles are interchangeable and fathers can perform almost every role other than in biological functions. As in other traditional cultures accelerating towards the future, Indian society is also faced with new options in the interpretation of the roles and responsibilities of fathers and mothers. There is ample evidence to suggest that many fathers in contemporary, educated Indian families are redefining their roles in the lives of their own children. For example, a father may come to the school where his young child is studying, and far more fathers today take the initiative to inform themselves and actively participate in childcare than in the past (Indu Kaura, personal communication, January 21, 2011).

Comparisons with Fathers in Other Societies

The role of the Indian father in the family seems to have some important consequences, according to psychoanalysts. As I remarked earlier, the attention of the father is always sought, and children are extremely sensitive to the possibility of preferential treatment in the family. This sensitivity finds expression in the workplace as well, which is something quite particular to Indians (Kakar & Kakar, 2007; Roland, 1988). They are deeply discerning of signals of favouritism at the workplace, although they are not against it when they are being favoured. Familism remains an extremely critical ideology, and fathers are at the head of this familism.

Educated urban fathers in today's globalized world have realized the importance of participation and visibility in the lives of their children. Yet in a cross-cultural study of families in 30 nations, Poortinga and Georgas (2006) found that the key person in families worldwide was the mother. In various accounts, she is seen as most sensitive to and emotionally connected with her children, more than the father. Although the paternal role

Figure 4.2 A father (about age 35) and son (about 2 years old) at a park in New Dehli. The father is a skilled construction worker of lower-middle SES. Photo courtesy of Shashi Shukla.

seemed to have changed somewhat, the mother remains central despite the fact that many more women are employed outside the home than ever before. Regarding the Indian father's role in the context of women's dual responsibilities, unfortunately, the findings indicate that although fathers now spend more time than previously in domestic work, their participation is perceived as minimal in most families, e.g., doing odd jobs rather than substantial work (Poortinga & Georgas, 2006). This was a significant finding because this research included samples from the most economically and technologically advanced nations where there are expectations of shared roles and responsibilities. A recent publication of the United Nations (2011) makes a similar point, that "women are still the main providers of care at home, even as they assume greater work responsibilities outside the home" (p. 1). The distance of fathers from care of children and household work is therefore not very different, across cultures, from what we find in Indian families, irrespective of social class, education, region and religion.

In the theoretical separation of 'instrumental' (related to survival) and 'expressive' (relating to cooperation and maintenance) roles within the family (Parsons, 1965), expressive activities are typically linked with mothers, who have a more active role in the family. This appears to be a near-universal tendency, although there have been some exceptions in cultural samples with different religions, affluence, and ideologies (Georgas, Berry, & Kagitcibasi, 2006). For instance, Georgas et al. noted that Muslim fathers and mothers had the highest emotional/expressive scores, followed by parents in Orthodox Protestant and Catholic countries. The financial role was the strongest among Muslim fathers, and Catholic mothers emerged as the strongest in childcare activities. Another interesting finding concerned the roles of grandparents, aunts and uncles. I mention this here because the presence of significant others who interact and participate in family roles and relationships on an everyday basis is very common for Indian families. Specifically, the expressive role was related to affluence and grandparents' participation in the family, and it was far more prominent in less affluent nations; in Indian families this tendency was highly significant (Georgas, Berry, & Kagitcibasi, 2006). This again demonstrated that the role of the Indian father is almost always transacted in the physical or ideological presence of others.

Gandhi, My Father

The name of Mahatma Gandhi is revered all over the world. In India, he is known most popularly as the 'father of the nation.' Gandhi lived in Sabarmati Ashram, which was run as a commune based on his philosophy of equality, asceticism, and community living. The rules of the *ashram* were very strict, and Gandhi became a role model for hundreds of thousands of young men and women, who were inspired to lead a life with full commitment to the service of a nation. His commitment to community living was absolute and Gandhi was harsh in his methods. One incident is exemplary in this regard. One day he began his talk at the morning assembly by describing his wife Kasturba's extraordinary character and strength. However, the audience soon realised that all was not well. Gandhi continued his lecture by taking a turn that was disastrous for Kasturba. No one in the Ashram was allowed to keep personal money, but the day before someone had given Kasturba a small sum of money that she had placed under her pillow. Gandhi continued that although his wife was of the highest of virtues, she was thus shown to be unable to abide by the rule of the *ashram*. She was asked by another member who witnessed the incident to give up the money, which she subsequently did. Gandhi did not let the incident go by without public humiliation to Kasturba for her conduct, and suggested that while she had suffered humiliation and returned the money, she had agreed to withdraw from the Ashram if there was another lapse on her part. Lastly he stated that he himself was responsible, since episodes like this emerged because of his own hidden faults (Kakar, 2004, p. 139). Gandhi's ideals were unattainable by most people, but he remained a strong influence on the lives of the people of India. One incident described by Kakar from archives from Gandhi's life depicts the story of a young man pulled away from his family towards what he believed was a larger cause. The reason I provide this extract is that it epitomises the pull of a charismatic leader, which was something that his own family found immensely threatening.

> The day after I received my BA results. ... [when] I announced (to my family) that I did not intend to appear for the provincial civil service exam remains etched in my mind to this day. Ever since I was a little boy it had been taken for granted by the family – my grandparents, uncles, aunts and cousins – and especially by my father, that I was destined for a high position in the administration of British India. ... My father was furious when I told him I intended to join MA classes in Hindi Literature. He started calling me an ungrateful wretch and threatened to turn me out of the house, before directing his wrath at my mother and accusing her of spoiling me; it was her fault that I turned out to be so wilful. He wished he had more sons to make up for the distress I was causing him.
>
> (Kakar, 2004, pp. 80, 81)

This passage highlights the silent revolution that took place within the Indian family during the time of the freedom movement. As a charismatic figure, Gandhi succeeded in drawing many young people into his movement. However, in many instances, this participation and even passionate involvement was transacted by a fundamental distancing from domestic life.

Specifically, Gandhi's relationship with his eldest son Harilal was a disaster. According to Dalal (2007), Gandhi's life as a celebrated person and 'father of the nation' made him unavailable as a father in the ordinary domestic sense. The relationship between Gandhi and his young son, Harilal, was extremely strained; when he wanted to study to be a barrister the way his father had, Gandhi did not give him permission. Being fundamentally opposed to a British way of life, Gandhi was unwilling to allow his son to pursue this life. After returning to India from South Africa, Harilal tried several times to make a life for himself, but each time he failed. Gandhi was even known to have said publicly "I was a slave to my passions when Harilal was conceived." At his father's funeral, Harilal appeared as a destitute drunkard and most people failed to even recognise him. In Dalal's book Harilal encounters life as a young man, deeply lost in the shadow of a father whose larger than life role as a freedom fighter left him no room to grow as a person. In his own autobiography, Gandhi expressed regret that he could never be as involved as he would have liked to be in the lives of his children (Gandhi, 1948).

Gandhi was exceptional, yet I have found resonance with his features in many families, especially in the pressures he faced in his role as a father. Were his pressures as a father really so different from those of Chandan in our opening Case Story, a man who *"ordered his son to declare him (Chandan) dead in writing ..."*? Gandhi surely was an example of an Indian father, if not representative of "all" Indian fathers. As mentioned earlier, Kakar and Kakar (2007, p. 20) reported that within the joint family orientation (even in nuclear families), there is a deliberate attempt by the father to underplay his relationship with his own children (especially sons) so as not to distract from the children of others, i.e., "favouritism is to be avoided to maintain harmony." The example of Gandhi is useful in this regard since he believed that India was his family, and to exemplify his fairness to others he was particularly careful about being seen as fair. This, I believe, is characteristic of Indian fathering in general. In the dynamics of this social engagement, Gandhi had to sacrifice his roles as a father and husband, in order to fulfil his devotion to India.

Speculation and Commentary

The family is very important for any individual, anywhere. Although I mentioned that the family is central to the identity of the Indian, I did not mean to imply that this is not so in other cultures. For instance, Georgas (2006) mentioned a research study in the EU on the importance of family where 95.7% people believed that the family was the most important thing in their lives. The paternal role, whether as a patriarch or partner, remains critical to the definition of the family everywhere. Research on the Indian family reveals that whether a family has a nuclear, extended or joint structure, roles and relationships within the family are shared with a wide network of people including relatives, neighbours, friends or household helpers. Grandparents have a central role to play as keepers and carriers of tradition, and have an important place in the family for that purpose, whether or not they reside with their children and grandchildren. Connections with this larger network have recently found new support through technological developments in the field of communications. The particular phenomenon of expressions of love in alternating generations illustrates the critical element of Indian men's reservation of unbridled affection for one's own progeny; such expressions might be viewed as destructive for the larger family network of relationships in which a person (especially a man) has several obligatory roles. However, it would be erroneous to take this as evidence that the traditional distant father is inherent in the dominant patriarchal tradition in India. Perhaps more than in other parts of the world, the Indian father remains rather awkward and shy, and appears more detached than he really is. I would like to end with a quote from Philip K. Dick (1978, http://deoxy.org/pkd_how2build. htm) about reality as "that which, when you stop believing in it, doesn't go away." I suppose that in our study of Indian fathers, this statement remains an important caution. Reality may change when the researcher's camera is removed.

Summary

In this chapter, I presented the dynamic transaction of 'fatherhood' against the backdrop of the history and culture of Indian families and society. The diversity and multiplicity of the Indian subcontinent renders it challenging, if not impossible, to construct a coherent prototype of an Indian father. The portrayal of Indian fathers here was based on fragments of history, literature, and scholarly writing about India and findings from research on the family. I sought not so much to represent all fathers in India, as to illustrate the dynamic transacti of Indian fatherhood. In the predominantly patriarchal communities of the Indian subcontinent, the father is a dramatic and pivotal figure for the outside world. At home, the father's role is transacted with due consideration to several key relationships in the lives of children: the mother, other women of the family, grandparents, older siblings and others who may be living with or near the family.

What an Indian father is and what he does was found to be determined not only by praxis, position and personality, but also by the constellation of significant others around him. This feature of dynamic negotiability and constant redefinition of roles and relationships relative to other people is, in my judgement, a key characteristic of family relationships and therefore fatherhood in India.

References

Anandalakshmy, S. (2010). *Through the lens of culture: Centuries of childhood and education in India*. [Monographs of Bala Mandir Research Foundation]. Chennai, India: Bala Mandir Research Foundation.

Bisht, S., & Sinha, D. (1981). Socialisation, family and psychological differentiation. In D. Sinha (Ed.), *Socialisation of the Indian child* (pp. 41–54). New Delhi, India: Concept.

Berreby, D. (2005). *Us and them: Understanding your tribal mind*. New York, NY: Little Brown & Company.

Carstairs, G. M. (1967). The *twice-born: A study of high caste Hindus*. Bloomington, IN: Indiana University Press.

Chaudhary, N. (2004). *Listening to culture: Constructing reality from everyday talk*. New Delhi, India: Sage.

Chaudhary, N. (2007). The family: Negotiating cultural values. In J. Valsiner & A. Rosa (Eds.), *The Cambridge handbook of socio-cultural psychology* (pp. 524–539). New York, NY: Cambridge University Press.

Chaudhary, N. (2009). Social dynamics in complex family contexts and its study. In J. Valsiner, P. C. M. Molenaar, M. C. D. P. Lyra, & N. Chaudhary (Eds.), *Dynamic process methodology in the social and developmental sciences* (pp. 383–404). New York, NY: Springer Books.

Chaudhary, N. (2012). Negotiating with autonomy and relatedness: Dialogical processes in everyday lives of Indians. In H. J. M. Hermans & T. Gieser (Eds.), *Handbook of dialogical self theory* (pp. 169–184). Cambridge, UK: Cambridge University Press.

Chauhan, A. (2005). Driven to despair. *Times of India*, March 14th, 2005. Retrieved April 10, 2005, from http//:timesofindia.indiatimes.com/articleshow/1050309.cms

Chowdhury, P. (1994). *The veiled women: Shifting gender equations in rural Haryana*. New Delhi, India: Oxford University Press.

Dalal, C. (2007). *Hiralal Gandhi: A life*. New Delhi, India: Orient Longman.

Derne, S. (1995). *Culture in action: Family life, emotion and male dominance in Benaras, India*. Albany, NY: State University of New York Press.

Dick, P. K. (1978). *How to build a universe that doesn't fall apart two days later*. Retrieved 2011 from http://deoxy.org/pkd_how2build.htm

Gandhi, M. K. (1948). *The story of my experiments with truth: An autobiography* (Trans. M. Desai). Washington, DC: Public Affairs Press.

Georgas, J. (2006). Families and family change. In J. Georgas, J. W. Berry, F. J. R. Van de Vijver, Ç. Kagitçibasi, & Y. H. Poortinga (Eds.), *Families across cultures: A 30 nation psychological study* (pp. 3–50). New York, NY: Cambridge University Press.

Georgas, J., Berry, J. W., Kagitçibasi, Ç., Poortinga, Y. H., & Van de Vijver, F. J. R. (2006). Synthesis: How similar and different are families across cultures? In J. Georgas, J. W. Berry, F. J. R. Van de Vijver, Ç. Kagitçibasi, & Y. H. Poortinga (Eds.), *Families across cultures: A 30 nation psychological study* (pp. 186–240). New York, NY: Cambridge University Press.

Gore, M. S. (1978). Familial change and the process of socialisation in India. In E. Anthony & C. Chiland (Eds.), *The child and his family in social change* (pp. 365–374). New York, NY: John Wiley.

Jain, A., & Belsky, J. (1997). Fathering and acculturation: Immigrant Indian families with young children. *Journal of Marriage and Family, 59*, 873–883.

Kakar, S. (1981). *The inner world: The psychoanalytic study of childhood and society in India*. New Delhi, India: Oxford University Press.

Kakar, S. (2004). *Mira and the mahatma*. New Delhi, India: Penguin.

Kakar, S., & Kakar, K. (2007). *The Indians: Portrait of a people*. New Delhi, India: Viking/Penguin.

Kapoor, S. (2006). *Alternate care for infants of employed mothers*. Unpublished doctoral dissertation of the Department of Child Development, Lady Irwin College, University of Delhi, India.

Krishnan, L. (1998). Child rearing: An Indian perspective. In A. K. Srivastava (Ed.), *Child development: An Indian perspective* (pp. 25–55). New Delhi, India: National Council for Educational Research and Training.

Kumari, A. (2008). *Father involvement: As children view it*. Unpublished master's dissertation, Department of Human Development and Family Studies, Maharaja Sayajirao University of Baroda, Baroda, India.

Kurtz, S. M. (1992). *All the mothers are one: Hindu India and the cultural reshaping of psychoanalysis*. New York, NY: Columbia University Press.

Lannoy, R. (1971). *The speaking tree*. New Delhi, India: Oxford University Press.

LeVine, R. A. (2003). Preface: A social science perspective on childhood experience in India. In D. Sharma (Ed.), *Childhood, family and sociocultural change in India* (pp. xiii–xviii). New Delhi, India: Oxford University Press.

Menon, U. (2003). Morality and context: A study of Hindu understandings. In J. Valsiner & K. J. Connolly (Eds.), *Handbook of developmental psychology* (pp. 431–448). London, UK: Sage.

Nandy, A. (2002). *Time warps: The insistent politics of silent and evasive pasts*. Delhi, India: Orient Longman.

Oomen, T. K. (2002). *Pluralism, equality and identity: Comparative studies*. New Delhi, India: Oxford University Press.

Pandey, J. (2006). India. In J. Georgas, J. W. Berry, F. J. R. Van de Vijver, Ç. Kagitçibasi, & Y. H. Poortinga (Eds.), *Families across cultures: A 30 nation psychological study* (pp. 362–369). New York, NY: Cambridge University Press.

Pandey, V. (2010). *Law ministry wants to give mothers same rights as fathers*. Saturday, May 20th, 2010. *DNA online*. Retrieved on January 23, 2011, from http://www.dnaindia.com/india/report_law-ministry-wants-to-give-mothers-same-rights-as-fathers_1386148

Parsons, T. (1965). The normal American family. In S. M. Farber (Ed.), *Man and civilisation: The family's search for survival* (pp. 34–36). New York, NY: McGraw-Hill.

Pattnaik, J., & Sriram, R. (2010). Father male involvement in care and education of children: History, trends, research, policies and programs around the world, *Childhood Education, 86* (6), 354–359.

Poortinga, Y., & Georgas, J. (2006). Family portraits from 30 countries: An overview. In J. Georgas, J. W. Berry, F. J. R. Van de Vijver, Ç. Kagitçibasi, & Y. H. Poortinga (Eds.), *Families across cultures: A 30 nation psychological study* (pp. 90–99). New York, NY: Cambridge University Press.

Raghavan, J. (2010). *The status of a mother in ancient Hindu scriptures: Empowering the girl child.* [Online]. Retrieved January 14, 2010, from http://www.indianmba.com/Faculty_Column/FC1109/fc1109.html

Raj, S. M. (2010). *How is the modern Indian father doing?* [Online]. Retrieved from http://www.sify.com/news/how-is-the-modern-indian-father-doing-news-columns-kgsrC3ifffa.html?ref=false

Ramanujan, A. K. (1999). *The collected essays of A. K. Ramanujan* (V. Dharwadkar, Ed.). New Delhi, India: Oxford University Press.

Roland, A. (1988). *In search of self in India and Japan: Towards a cross cultural psychology.* Princeton, NJ: Princeton University Press.

Roopnarine, J. L., & Suppal, P. (2003). Kakar's psychoanalytic interpretation of Indian childhood: The need to emphasise the father and multiple caregivers in the socialisation equation. In D. Sharma (Ed.), *Childhood, family and sociocultural change in India* (pp. 115–137). New Delhi, India: Oxford University Press.

Roopnarine, J. L., Talukder, E., Jain, D., Joshi, P., & Srivastav, P. (1992). Characteristics of holding, patterns of play, and social behaviours between parents and infants in New Delhi, India. *Developmental Psychology, 26* (2), 867–873.

Saraff, A., & Srivastava, H. (2008). Envisioning fatherhood: Indian fathers' perceptions of an ideal father. *Population Review, 47* (1). Retrieved July 7, 2011, from http://muse.jhu.edu/journals/population_review/v047/47. 1.saraff.pdf

Seymour, S. (1999). *Women, family and child care in India.* Cambridge, UK: Cambridge University Press.

Sharma, D. (2003). Infancy and childhood in India. In D. Sharma (Ed.), *Childhood, family and sociocultural change in India* (pp. 13–47). New Delhi, India: Oxford University Press.

Sharma, N., & Chaudhary, N. (2004). From home to school. *Seminar, 546.* [Online] Retrieved January 23, 2011, from http://www.google.co.in/search?q=neerja+sharma+nandita+chaudhary+seminar&ie=utf-8&oe=utf-8&aq=t&client=firefox-a&rlz=1R1GGGL_en-GBIN334IN334

Sharma, N. (1990). Current trends in infant care: An Indian experience. *Early Child Development and Care, 50* (1), 71–79.

Shukla, A. (1987). Decision making in single and dual-career families in India. *Journal of Marriage and Family, 49,* 621–629.

Shweder, R. A., Goodnow, J. J., Hatano, G., LeVine, R. A., Markus, H. R., & Miller, P. J. (2006). In W. Damon & R. M. Lerner (Eds.), *Handbook of developmental psychology: Theoretical models of human development* (pp. 716–792). New York, NY: Wiley.

Shweder, R. A., Jensen, L. A., & Goldstein, W. M. (1995). Who sleeps by whom revisited: A method for extracting moral goods implicit in practice. In J. J. Goodnow, P. J. Miller, & F. Kessel (Eds.), *Cultural practices as contexts for development* (pp. 21–40). San Francisco, CA: Jossey-Bass.

Sriram, R. (2011). Role of fathers in children's lives: A view from urban India. *Childhood Education, 87* (3) 185–190.

Sriram, R. (2003). *Subjective experiences of fatherhood and motherhood: Realities and reflections.* Unpublished doctoral dissertation, Department of Human Development and Family Studies, Maharaja Sayajirao University of Baroda, Baroda.

Sriram, R., Dave, P., Khasgiwala, A., & Joshi, A. (2006). Women in families and households of Gujarat. In P. Dave (Ed.), *A profile of women in Gujarat* (pp. 195–218). Vadodara, India: Women's Studies Research Centre, M.S. University of Baroda.

Sriram, R., Karnik, R., & Ali, R. (2002). *Social construction of fatherhood and motherhood: A view from within families* (Research Report) [Mimeo]. Baroda, India: Maharaja Sayajirao University of Baroda, Women's Studies Research Centre.

Sriram, R., & Kaur, A. (2011). *Fathering as a process of transformation in men: Reflections of involved fathers.* Unpublished masters' dissertation. Department of Human Development and Family Studies, M. S. University of Baroda, Vadodara, Gujarat, India.

Suppal, P., & Roopnarine, J. (1999). Parental involvement in child care as a function of maternal employment in nuclear and extended families in India. *Sex Roles, 40* (9–10), 731–744.

Thapar, R. (2000). *The Penguin early history of India.* New Delhi, India: Penguin.

Trawick, M. (1990). *Notes on love in a Tamil family.* Berkeley, CA: University of California Press.

Tuli, M., & Chaudhary, N. (2010). Elective interdependence: Understanding individual agency and interpersonal relationships in Indian families. *Culture and Psychology, 16* (4), 477–496.

Uberoi, P. (2006). *Freedom and destiny: Gender, family and popular culture in India.* New Delhi, India: Oxford University Press.

Uberoi, P. (2003). The family in India: Beyond the nuclear and joint debate. In V. Das (Ed.), *The Oxford India companion to sociology and social anthropology* (pp. 1061–1103). New Delhi, India: Oxford University Press.

United Nations. (2011). *Men in families and family policy in a changing world* [Sales No E.11.IV.1]. New York, NY: UN Department of Economic and Social Affairs, Division for Social Policy and Development.

Valsiner, J. (2007). *Culture in minds and societies: Foundations of a cultural psychology.* New Delhi, India: Sage.

Chapter Five

Fathers in Muslim Families in Bangladesh and Malaysia

Ziarat Hossain

University of New Mexico, Albuquerque, NM, USA

Case Story: Munir's Respect for His Father

Munir grew up in a Muslim family in rural Bangladesh in the 1960s. He is the oldest among five siblings, with two brothers and two sisters. His father had enough income from farming to bear the expenses of Munir's college education. His brothers, however, were not very successful in school and therefore joined their father working on the farm. Likewise, his sisters had to stop going to school after completing elementary school. When each of his sisters became 16, Munir actively assisted his father in arranging marriages for them.

Munir's father took care of his own parents in the same household. The interactions in this three-generation family were cordial, and both Munir and his father consulted with the grandfather on major family matters. Munir had to find an outside job because the income from agriculture was no longer good enough to maintain the family, so in the 1980s he took the opportunity to work in a factory in the Middle East. His father did not object to this departure since they needed additional income to run the family. But when his father fell ill, as the oldest son Munir became the primary provider for the family. Several years later he met his wife, Shirin, while on vacation in Bangladesh. As Muslims they refrained from having an intimate pre-marital relationship. However, they met a few times and gained an understanding of each other's personality and expectations. Although Munir's father had in mind another girl for him to marry, he convinced his father that Shirin would be a good wife and a good daughter-in-law to take care of the family. They were married and Shirin became pregnant before Munir left for the Middle East again. As expected within the Islamic norm, Shirin dutifully took care of her in-laws and they accepted her with love and kindness. Shirin's in-laws also joined her in caring for her daughter.

Munir always missed his family and envisioned that his daughter would someday earn a graduate degree. Several years later, Munir resigned from his Middle Eastern job and returned to Bangladesh to live with his family. Now Munir is a businessman at a small firm, his wife is a school teacher, and their daughter is a college student.

This Case Story reflects the socio-cultural and religious contexts of paternal practices, roles and responsibilities in Bangladesh society. Fatherhood and family life center on marital ties, extended networks, religious customs, and a traditional division of gender roles. This scenario of paternal practices is also very common across Muslim communities throughout Asia (Ahmed & Gielen, 1998). Although the father's provisioning role remains a priority, some transitions in men's roles in contemporary Muslim families in Asian societies are also apparent. Over the past several years, I have systematically documented patterns of fathers' involvement with children in Malaysian and Bangladeshi families. While there has been research on gender roles and father–child interactions in select Asian (Manganaro & Alozie, 2011; Noor, 1999; Roopnarine, Talukder, Jain, Joshi, & Srivastav, 1992; Shwalb, Nakazawa, Yamamoto, & Hyun, 2010; Sun & Roopnarine, 1996), Caribbean (Roopnarine, 2011), African (Hewlett & Macfarlan, 2010; Nsamenang, 2010), and South American (da Cruz Benetti & Roopnarine, 2006; de Minzi, 2010) societies, all brought together in this volume, specific research on paternal involvement in Asian Muslim families is extremely limited. This chapter explores the cultural, religious, and ecological contexts of the father's role in Muslim families in Bangladesh and Malaysia.

Particularly since the 1970s, scholars have investigated the level of fathers' involvement in early childhood development, fathers' contribution to children's cognitive and social skills, and the impact of paternal involvement on children's developmental outcomes across cultural groups. Lamb (2010) and others have argued that published information on fathering, education and employment opportunities for women, personal attitudes, religious beliefs, and an overall shift in gender role ideologies have all substantially influenced fathering behavior. Others have suggested that religious beliefs are linked to parenting styles and gender roles in marital relations (Gallagher & Smith, 1999; Gunnoe, Hetherington, & Reiss, 1999). Unfortunately, empirical research and conceptualization about the father's role in the family has derived primarily from Western families, although this volume redresses the geographical imbalance of the literature. Psychological and behavioral research on fathering in non-European or non-Euro-American families is increasing (e.g., Roopnarine, Krishnakumar, & Xu, 2009; Shwalb et al., 2010; United Nations, 2011), yet we still know little about fathering behaviors in Muslim families.

With about 1.6 billion people, Muslims are the second largest religious group in the world (Pew Research Center, 2011). Although they are a very diverse population with unique ecological, language, economic, and cultural differences, Muslims are one of the most understudied and mis-understood populations in the world. Readers of this book will find the differences between Arab (Ahmed, Chapter 6) and Asian (this chapter) Muslim families revealing.

I begin this chapter with an outline of the socio-cultural framework of Bangladesh and Malaysia. For consistency, the terms Bengali and Malay will be used to refer to Muslim Bangladeshi and Malaysian families. I have combined these two cultural groups in this chapter because they share sim-ilar religious and social backgrounds, and that is where I have conducted my research. The second section will elaborate on how Islamic values and cultural tenets provide the context for fathers' role in the family. The third section discusses major findings on the father's role in Bengali and Malay families. Specifically, this section summarizes the body of knowledge about fathers' involvement in childcare and domestic labor. The fourth section offers interpretation and speculation about fathers' involvement in Bengali and Malay families. Finally, the fifth section will discuss the influ-ence of contemporary social, economic, and technological changes on the father's role in Muslim Bangladeshi and Malaysian populations.

Cultural and Historical Background as It Influences Fathering

Bangladesh

With 158 million people in an area of about 55,000 square miles in South Asia, Bangladesh has the fourth largest Muslim population (following Indonesia, Pakistan, and India), and the seventh largest national popula-tion in the world. Its per capita income of US $590 (see Table 1.1, p. 5) clearly marks it as a developing nation. Although Bangladesh is still largely an agricultural society, current estimates show that its urban population (28%) is increasing and its fertility rate (2.6%) is falling. Urbanization (mostly through rural-to-urban migration), women's education, technological and industrial development, and overseas employment (e.g., in Saudi Arabia, United Arab Emirates, Kuwait, Iraq, Malaysia, and Singapore) all contrib-ute immensely to its modernization. The Bangladeshi lifestyle is largely related to the ecology of the fertile plains where rice planting and fish-ing are central to village survival. About 98% of the people of Bangladesh are Bengalis, but there are also tribal populations (e.g., Chakma, Marma, Moorang, Khashia, Tipra) located along the hills of the northern and eastern border areas. These tribes are derived from Sino-Tibetan ancestry and their social relations and family functions often differ from the Bengalis. In general, the indigenous cultural values of the country reflect a mix of Dravidian, Aryan, Persian, Arabian, Mughal, and European cultural heritages.

Islam and Hinduism are the two predominant religions in the country and the population is comprised of – Muslims (88%), Hindus (10%), and a considerable number of Buddhists (1%) and Christians (1%). Islam was introduced by Arab traders and Persian saints (e.g., Shah Jalal) in the 13th century. Many low-income and lower caste Hindus found the new casteless religion as a way to freedom from the caste system. Most Bangladeshi tribal people are Buddhists, Hindus, Christians, and Animists. Cultural and religious festivals strengthen social ties among family and community members across these religious groups, because they bring together people from all walks of life on a regular basis. Consequently, members of Bangladeshi Muslim and non-Muslim families share common cultural beliefs in areas such as arranging feasts and gifts for a wedding, naming infants (*namakaran*), and caring for elderly parents.

The family system in Bangladesh is most often one of three major configurations – joint, extended, and nuclear – which are all very common family structures across other South Asian countries (Roopnarine & Hossain, 1992). The traditional joint family system still remains the core context for socialization and other family functioning in Bangladesh. It typically consists of three or more generations who share a common living compound and pool their economic resources. The extended family is comprised of several nuclear families that reside together in the same household but maintain separate eating/cooking arrangements and may not pool resources. All members of a family are part of a *samaj* (typically a kin-based greater neighborhood entity) and must abide by its social and religious regulations. The central focus of social life in Bangladesh society is the family and its extended network. An individual is a member of a family group that is identified by its physical residence (locally called *bari*) or family title/lineage (locally known as *bangsha*). In-laws (e.g., daughters-in-law) also become permanent members of the family since married sons often reside in their parents' households.

Traditional social mores clearly suggest that marriages are typically negotiated between families. In line with Islamic values (*adat*), marriage is considered a legal union between a husband and a wife, while co-habitation, same-sex relationships, and pre-marital sexuality are prohibited. Muslim Bangladeshis enjoy close marital ties, and family members and other relatives actively participate in familial practices and customs. Although divorce is by law an acceptable form of marital dissolution, it is strongly frowned upon by society. Sex-segregated socialization, especially

Figure 5.1 A Bengali father, 45, is holding his school-age son in a Rayerbazar slum family in Dhaka, Bangladesh. A slum household in urban Dhaka generally consists of one room that is used as both a bedroom and living room. Household items are organized and kept along the walls of the room. Physical contacts (e.g., touching, holding, sitting on lap) are a major type of father–child interactions in Bengali culture. Photo courtesy of Ziarat Hossain.

for adults, is common and the *purdha* (veil and/or modest dress to cover the body) for women is expected. Because of modernization, the nuclear family form is growing in contemporary Bangladeshi society, especially in urban areas. However, it is very common for a nuclear family to house one or more relatives for a long period of time. Although the formation of the nuclear family may suggest a shift in structural organization from the traditional joint family system, people in most Bangladesh households maintain an interconnected family identity whereby collective well-being is valued over individualism and family boundaries remain very flexible (Hossain & Skurky, 2005).

Malaysia

Compared with Bangladesh, Malaysia is a sparsely populated Southeast Asian country with over 28 million people in an area of 127,320 square miles. Its landmass consists of two major geographical areas. Western Malaysia (*Tanah Melayu*) is known as Peninsular Malaysia as it lies on the Malay Peninsula, and it borders with Thailand and Singapore. East Malaysia is known as Malaysian Borneo as it is situated on the island of Borneo. Malaysian Borneo includes the states of Sabah and Sarawak and borders with Indonesia and Brunei, and is also home to the Kadazan ethnic population which is discussed later under "Fathers' Involvement: Empirical Studies." Its very rapid modernization is reflected in remarkable growth in the economic, technological, and industrial sectors. With a current per capita GNP of about U.S. $7,230, Malaysia is a relatively affluent nation within the Asian region. The overall population of Malaysia consists of Malay (58%), Chinese (24%), Indian (8%), and indigenous groups (10%, e.g., Batek, Orang Asli). The Malays and the indigenous populations are commonly known as *Bhumiputras*, or 'sons of the soil' (Kumaraswamy & Othman, 2011; Ng, 1998). Whereas Malays are Muslims, Chinese are either Buddhists or Christians, and Indians are Hindus. Each group has its own predominant religion, culture, and language. Overall, more than 60% of the country's population is Muslim. Regardless of ethnic or religious differences, a Malaysian family is typically defined as a marital union or registration between a man and a woman, including their children and extended family members (Saad, 2001). However, trends toward nuclear families, women's education and participation in the paid labor force, female-headed households, and smaller family size increasingly characterize contemporary Malaysian families.

The evolution of Islamic culture and family values in the Malay Peninsula has a long history. For thousands of years, Malays were primarily animists and believed in the existence of spirits. It is estimated that about 1,700 years ago, Indian traders introduced Hinduism and Buddhism to the Malays. Subsequently, Indian Muslims, Chinese Muslims, and Arab traders brought Islam to the Malays from around the 12th century. Since then Islamic values took root and became an integral part of Malay families and culture. Almost all contemporary Malays are Muslims and Islamic identity has become a key aspect of Malay cultural and ethnic identity (Von der Mehden, 1987). Attracted by Islamic and sociocultural ties, Indonesian and Bangladeshi migrant workers have recently taken jobs in the booming Malaysian labor market. Indonesians now comprise the largest migrant worker population in Malaysia, followed by Bangladeshis. The migration of Bangladeshis to Malaysia began in the early 1990s, and currently about 300,000 Bangladeshis work in Malaysia. Some of them have made Malaysia their new home through employment and marriage (Ahsan Ullah, 2007).

The Malaysian Muslim (Malay) family system is heavily influenced by Islamic customs and practices locally called *adat* (Kling, 1995). Specifically, patrilineal hierarchy, kinship networks, and flexible family boundaries exert a strong influence on Malay family functioning and gender roles. It is commonly argued that hegemonic belief structures about masculinity also influence the father's role in Muslim Malaysian families (Noor, 1999). In line with this hegemonic belief, the father acts as the family patriarch and the mother must practice domesticity, purity, and a submissive role in the family. In addition, the father or grandfather enjoys the roles of authority figure and decision-maker in the family. Although the traditional norm of a joint family system and polygyny are practiced in the villages (*kampung*), such practices are far less common in contemporary urban families. The father is the head of the household and is expected to socialize his children according to Islamic and other socially acceptable values, i.e., respect, shyness, and loyalty. The primary function of Malay fathers is to provide for children and the family.

Islamic ideology

Anecdotal evidence suggests that Muslim fathers in Bangladesh and Malaysia often subscribe to traditional Islamic beliefs and values about gender roles in the family. The relevant Islamic values in both countries are commonly known as *adat*. According to *adat*, a Muslim father is responsible for caring, protecting, and providing for his family and children. Fathers are also empowered to give their daughters away in marriage. Although such a custom signifies the broad authority and power men hold over other family members, the fathering role is often performed within the context of the extended family network. Therefore, the norm of multiple caregivers becomes a characteristic particular to Muslim societies where other adults are expected to aid the father in caring for his children and family (see Chaudhary, Chapter 4, this volume, for a rather similar description of Hindu ideology pertaining to the father's role).

In their parental roles, Muslims often follow the instructions articulated in the Qur'an. The overall message of various Quranic verses underscores the importance of involved parenting, equal treatment of both male and female children, high priority given to children's education and welfare, and harmonious parent–child interactions (Chaudhry, 2009). Muslim parenting is both a spiritual attribute and a biological link with the child. This statement signifies that parenthood is construed within a valid marriage between a consenting woman and man, i.e., parents are two opposite sex individuals who are legally married. Unlike the current practice in the West, the role of adoptive parent does not exist in Islamic practice, especially in relation to inheritance. The prohibition against adoptive parents underscores the importance of the paternal descent and the genealogy of the child (Kabir & az-Zubair, 2007). Therefore, men in Muslim families become fathers through genetic linkage only. However, a woman may become the adoptive mother of a non-biological child by breast-feeding the child from infancy.

The Qur'an instructs that the father must respect the life of his child, which usually starts at the beginning of the second trimester after conception. From this perspective, the father must respect his child's rights to paternal affection, protection, and care. It is therefore the father's moral and spiritual obligation to raise his children. The 'life perspective' was also a movement away from the incidence of infanticide by some Arabs in the years that predated the Prophet Mohammad. Many Arabs used to practice infanticide on daughters, for reasons such as lack of economic resources or fear of disgraceful conduct (e.g., premarital sex) committed by their daughters. But Islamic values and the Prophet's messages do not condone such tribal practices as killing female children; rather they call for the protection of the child's life and rights.

Muslim parents attempt to follow the example of what their Prophet Mohammad professed or did in relation to his own children. This information is presented in various books written by the Prophet's closest followers. The sayings of the Prophet are typically known as *Hadith* (e.g., *al-Bukhari*). As a father, the Prophet demonstrated wisdom, compassion, and warmth toward his children. He inquired about his children's welfare as soon as he arrived home, enjoyed meals with them, engaged in play activities with them, and taught and encouraged his daughter Fatimah to learn and provide community leadership. The Prophet Mohammad also actively took part in collaborative decisions to arrange marriages for his daughters, and acted as a councilor for his daughters and their husbands. He freed slaves, believed in equal justice for all and equal rights between men and women, practiced judicious leadership, and preached human solidarity. Finally, he tried to inculcate these values in his children, and expected that Muslim fathers would provide spiritual, social, and moral guidance to their children. These Islamic beliefs and teachings all have implications for Muslim fathering, and go hand in hand with what contemporary psychologists term commitment to children's well-being as "new fathers" (Lamb, 2004). Muslims believe that Islam is a complete code of life, and therefore it is often difficult to separate Islamic values from the overall cultural and social mores of Muslim societies. It is expected that the sociocultural norms of a Muslim community conform to Islamic values, and that they define the context and content of fathering practices.

Review of Fathering Research

Assessments of parental involvement in families with various social-organizational patterns (e.g., kinship systems, multiple caregiving/communal care) and strong cultural norms and religious beliefs (*adat* in Bengali and Malay families, *rukhun* and *hormat* in Javanese culture; Keats, 2000) all support the notion that mothers are the primary caregivers of young children in Asian Muslim families. In fact, with respect to levels of involvement, mothers also far exceed fathers in primary care in different groups of non-Muslim Asian families (Lee, 2002; Roopnarine & Suppal, 2000; Shwalb et al., 2010). Fathers in contemporary Bangladeshi and Malaysian Muslim families therefore appear to be similar to fathers throughout Asia.

Bangladesh

Research findings on fathers' behaviors and roles in Bangladeshi Muslim or Bengali families are quite limited. Findings from a recent study suggested that middle-class Bangladeshi fathers spent less than four hours per week with their children on one-on-one interactions such as playing, reading, or talking (Jesmin & Seward, 2011). They further reported that mothers' estimates of fathers' involvement in these activities were slightly higher than fathers' estimate of their own involvement. Data from my own preliminary investigations of paternal involvement with school-age children suggested that mothers in both rural and urban families spent more time in children's care and assisting children in academic work than fathers. Whereas rural fathers spent 43% as much time as mothers did in children's care and academic work each week, urban fathers spent about 59% as much time as did mothers. Rural mothers spent more time with their sons than with daughters, but fathers' involvement was similar with their sons and daughters. Likewise, urban fathers showed similar levels of involvement with their sons and daughters, although they spent more time with both genders than their rural counterparts. Further analyses revealed that rural fathers spent 21.8 hours/week with their school-age children, compared with 57.28 hours/week among urban fathers. Two major patterns of paternal involvement emerge from these findings: (1) fathers in both rural and urban samples reported spending a similar amount of time with their sons and daughters; and (2) urban fathers spend more time with children than rural fathers (see Table 5.1).

These findings reflect ongoing changes in the socioeconomic context of Bengali family life. As I have indicated earlier, Bangladesh is a developing nation with notable growth in the economic, technological, and industrial sectors. Specifically, the fast pace of modernization is creating a demand for skilled and college-educated workers. This demand has put pressure on the government and other social organizations to create more employment opportunities, especially for women, and it also encourages fathers to take an active interest in caring for and educating both male and female children. Fathers in Bengali families may follow the Islamic norm

Table 5.1 Fathers' Reported Hours Spent Each Week in Children's Care and Academic Work in Rural and Urban Families in Bangladesh ($N = 82$)

Involvement Tasks	Rural Fathers ($N = 41$)				Urban Fathers ($N = 41$)			
	With Sons		With Daughters		With Sons		With Daughters	
	M	SD	M	SD	M	SD	M	SD
Basic Care	4.19	6.30	3.08	3.70	15.12	17.25	10.41	8.20
Care on Demand	0.73	0.82	0.54	0.66	2.28	2.28	1.82	1.19
Home Academic	7.61	6.90	5.32	6.85	10.52	11.12	13.68	22.24
School Academic	0.27	0.70	0.06	0.09	0.90	1.09	2.55	7.47

of providing equal resources for the development and education of their sons and daughters. As a result, females have succeeded at all academic levels and in their employment, on a par with the achievements of males. The rural–urban difference in paternal investment in children is explained by the extent to which fathers have access to support systems. Specifically, rural fathers still have easy access to other adult family members who are readily available to care for children. It is a common practice for grandparents, uncles, aunts, older siblings, other relatives, and neighbors to help rural fathers take care of their children. In contrast, urban fathers have limited access to extended family support, and therefore must spend more time themselves to help children with homework and to care for their children. In addition, urban fathers have more formal education and therefore may be able to offer more help with their children's academic pursuits than can rural fathers.

In sum, while mothers remain the primary caregivers for their children in Bengali Muslim families, there is a greater disparity between maternal and paternal involvement in rural families than in urban families. Fathers in urban families reportedly spend significantly more time than fathers in rural families in children's care and helping their children with their school work. Fathers in both rural and urban families appear to invest equally in their sons and daughters. Compared to Jesmin and Seward's (2011) findings on urban fathers' involvement with their children, both urban and rural fathers in my samples appear to be highly involved. However, paternal behavior of my samples can be considered a moderate level of involvement when compared to fathers' involvement in other cultural groups such as Navajo Native Americans in the U.S. (Hossain & Anziano, 2008).

Malaysia

Historical accounts indicate that Malay men and women in pre-colonial Malaysia worked together in subsistence agriculture. They also cooperated with childcare and other family chores (Noor, 1999). With colonization and the introduction of a mercantile economy, Malay men began to work for wages while women stayed home to take care of children and perform other household duties. The growing industrialization of Malaysia since the 1970s has provided opportunities for both husbands and wives to work in paid employment outside of the home. In spite of such changes, women in contemporary Malay families still assume major responsibility for children at home even while gainfully employed (Noor, 1999).

Empirical research on father–child and parent–child relations in Malay families is sparse. In an analysis of data from a combined sample of Malay and Chinese professional families residing in Peninsular Malaysia, Noor

(1999) found that husbands spent about 71% as much time as did wives in childcare and other domestic labor. Other researchers focused exclusively on Chinese Malaysian families in Malaysian Borneo (Roopnarine, Lu, & Ahmeduzzaman, 1989), and observed that fathers were significantly less involved in feeding, changing, and putting the baby to bed, compared with mothers. Additional findings from an anthropological perspective suggested that fathers and mothers in indigenous Batek families in Peninsular Malaysia were equally involved in bathing, cuddling, holding, and cooking for infants (Endicott, 1992), and that Batek mothers and fathers provided similar treatment for their male and female children. These three lines of research present us with an inconsistent pattern of Malaysian paternal investment in childcare and other domestic chores.

Data from my own research on maternal and paternal perceptions of their levels of involvement and amounts of time spent in childcare in rural Malay families showed that mothers were more involved than were fathers in bedtime routines, physical care, feeding, soothing, singing, and playing with their infants (Hossain, Roopnarine, Masud, Muhamed, Baharudin, Abdullah, & Juhari, 2005). Among these activities, the highest level of fathers' involvement was in play with their infants. Further analyses showed that fathers in both rural and urban families followed a similar pattern of involvement in these childcare tasks, with a few individual exceptions. Urban fathers were reportedly more involved in bedtime routines and physical care than were their rural counterparts. In their perceptions of time use, fathers in both rural and urban families reported that they spent far less time than mothers each day cleaning, feeding, and playing with their young children (see Table 5.2). In my samples, rural mothers and fathers (11.91 vs. 4.16 hours) spent more time in caregiving compared with urban mothers and fathers (4.41 vs. 2.56 hours). In sum, rural fathers on average spent 56% as much time playing with infants, 18% as much time cleaning infants, and 22% as much time feeding infants as did mothers. Urban fathers in the same sample on average spent 69% as much time playing with infants, 20% as much time cleaning infants, and 32% as much time feeding infants as mothers did. Although rural parents spent more time in childcare than urban parents (16.07 vs. 6.97 hours), fathers and mothers in rural families were far less egalitarian than fathers and mothers in urban families. These findings indicate that rural Malays still adhere more to a traditional division of childcare responsibility in the family more than do their urban counterparts.

Without identifying participants by their religious affiliations, other scholars (Rosnah, 1999; Sather, 1978) conducted research on men's and women's relative involvement with children in ethnic Kadazan families in Malaysian Borneo. Their overall findings suggested that Kadazan fathers had very limited time to be involved with their children because they

Table 5.2 Fathers' and Mothers' Reported Hours Spent Daily in Children's Care in Malay (Rural and Urban) and Kadazan Families in Malaysia (N = 282)

| | Rural Families (N = 100) | | | | Urban Families (N = 100) | | | | Kadazan Families (N = 82) | | | |
| | Father | | Mother | | Father | | Mother | | Father | | Mother | |
	M	SD	M	SD	M	SD	M	SD	M	SD	M	SD
Feeding	0.76	0.97	3.49	2.33	0.24	0.25	0.74	0.81	1.48	1.27	3.40	1.25
Cleaning	0.63	0.96	3.50	2.33	0.09	0.13	0.46	0.55	1.67	1.61	3.37	1.63
Playing	2.77	1.36	4.92	1.95	2.23	1.82	3.21	3.15	2.93	1.90	4.41	1.97

often worked long hours outside of the home. Kadazan wives assumed a greater role in caring for children and establishing stronger family relationships than did husbands (Sather, 1978). Although Kadazan fathers were found to play an important role as parents, mothers showed more affection, love, and concern for their children than did fathers (Rosnah, 1999). My own research on Kadazan fathers, many of whom are Muslims, suggested that whereas mothers exceeded fathers in the amount of time they spent cleaning, feeding, and playing with infants (11.2 vs. 6.1 hours), both mothers and fathers reported that they spent more time playing than cleaning or feeding infants each day (Hossain, Roopnarine, Ismail, Hashmi, & Sombuling, 2007; Table 5.2). Finally, Kadazan fathers reported similar levels of involvement with their infant sons and daughters.

Overall, Malay fathers in both rural and urban families reportedly spend more time playing than feeding or cleaning their infants. According to my Malay data, rural fathers were less egalitarian than their urban counterparts. Fathers in my samples were also less egalitarian than fathers in urban Chinese and urban Malay families (Noor, 1999) or indigenous Batek families in Malaysia (Endicott, 1992). The pattern of fathers' involvement with young children in Kadazan and Peninsular Malay families was somewhat similar. However, Kadazan fathers were more involved than Malay fathers in both rural and urban families (Hossain et al., 2005). On the other hand, urban fathers in Bengali families were more involved with

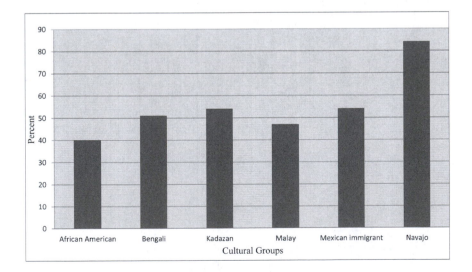

Figure 5.2 Fathers' involvement with children relative to mothers'.

their school-age children's care and school education than fathers in rural families. Like Malay and Kadazan fathers, Bengali fathers also invested a similar amount of time with their sons and daughters. Compared with my data on fathers' involvement in early caregiving among other cultural groups (e.g., African American, Navajos, Mexican immigrants in the U.S.), fathers' involvement in Kadazan and Bengali families appears to be at a moderate level. Fathers' involvement in Malay families can be termed modest, i.e., less than a moderate level (see Figure 5.2).

Fathers' Involvement: Interpretation and Speculation

Generally speaking, the high degree of differentiation between paternal and maternal involvement in primary childcare tasks in Malay families may be related to the patriarchal nature of Southeast Asian families (Kling, 1995; Roopnarine et al., 1989). In these societies, a father's role in the family is often linked to his authority and bread winning capability. Does *adat* (Islamic belief structure) stress the importance of men in economic activities vs. women in care giving? The answer to this question is open to interpretation. Whereas a conservative Muslim man may interpret his role along traditional gender lines, a progressive Muslim man may believe in egalitarian gender roles in the family (Khalid & Frieze, 2004; Quah, 2008). In fact, Islamic values regarding parental practices generally side with the idea of gender equality in the family (Chaudhry, 2009). Although *adat* calls for fathers to stay involved with their children, prevailing culturally defined gender roles may also have a significant influence on fathers' involvement in childcare in the family. The interplay of religious and cultural factors, which are not mutually exclusive, may contribute to the fact that mothers are more involved than fathers in childcare and play in these Muslim families (Jawad, 1998; Rosnah, 1999; Sather, 1978).

Flexible family boundaries allow Malays, especially women from other families, to easily visit their neighbors and take part in voluntary childcare. This practice may further reaffirm the traditional care giving role of Malay mothers. The cultural and ecological contexts of hegemonic masculinity encourage mothers/women to take care of children in Malay families. Nevertheless, my data suggest that Malay fathers are modestly (lower than a moderate level) involved with their infants, and that variations in fathers' levels of involvement are within the range of paternal involvement in other cultural communities such as African Americans and Afro-Caribbeans (Hossain & Roopnarine, 1994; Roopnarine, 2011). Although rural Malays and Bateks live in close geographic proximity, gender-based division of childcare in Malay families is less egalitarian than among indigenous Batek families in Peninsular Malaysia (Endicott, 1992). The uniqueness of their family practices and belief structures may have differential influences on the nature of fathers' involvement. While traditional *adat* and patriarchy espouse the primacy of maternal involvement in childcare in Malay families, the sustainable shifting cultivation and hunter-gatherer lifestyle may foster an egalitarian parental role in Batek families. This argument underscores the importance of distinct cultural ecologies that shape fathers' and mothers' involvement in childcare (Bronfenbrenner & Morris, 1998; Mernissi, 1975). I assume that fathers' involvement with children in Indonesian families is similar to the Malays because of geographic proximity, and religious and sociocultural ties between Malaysia and Indonesia. Mothers in Indonesian Muslim families perform most childcare responsibilities and respect male authority in the family (Hooker, 1993; Williams, 1990).

The lack of differences between paternal involvement with sons and daughters in both Malay and Bengali families was in line with previous findings on early patterns of care giving obtained in a number of Asian societies, including India and Taiwan (Roopnarine et al., 1992; Sun & Roopnarine, 1996), and Malaysia (Endicott, 1992; Roopnarine et al., 1989) In my opinion, these findings do not signify that fathers in these societies treat boys and girls similarly, but that sex-differentiated treatment begins later when children are groomed to enter the wider society and learn gender-typed roles and practices in face-to-face interactions. Islamic *adat* encourages fathers to treat their young male and female children equally. Contrary to stereotypes, Muslim fathers are expected to invest similar amounts of resources in their male and female children's growth, and especially in their education. My findings supported this expectation: Bengali fathers reported spending similar amounts of time in their school-age male and female children's care and education in both rural and urban families. Fathers likewise reported similar levels of involvement with their male and female infants in Kadazan and in both rural and urban Malay families.

Malay fathers' high level of involvement in play activities suggests that the father–child bond is frequently formed through men's role of playmate with their infants. Specifically, it has been argued that in Western cultural settings stimulating bouts of play may facilitate the formation of infant–father attachments (Lamb, 2002). However, my data were interesting in that Malay mothers in both rural and urban samples reported spending more time than fathers at play with infants, and more time at play than feeding and cleaning infants. These observations do not fully support what I would call a "father-availability-in-play hypothesis." It perhaps means that within Malay and Kadazan cultures, both parents appear to be play partners, not just fathers. I have speculated elsewhere that given the traditional cultural context of Muslim Malay society, mothers are more heavily involved than fathers in all aspects of childcare, and their greater involvement in play may be an artifact of this tendency (Hossain et al., 2005).

Levels of paternal and maternal involvement in Bengali families are heavily influenced by several factors, including patriarchal hierarchy, an extended family network, religious beliefs, and flexible family boundaries. It is common for parents and other relatives to invoke religious value systems to socialize children to take on personal, family and social roles and responsibilities. In line with Islamic *adat*, fathers are expected to provide, protect, and make decisions for the family, and are expected to give their daughters away in marriage. Mothers are responsible for the care of the children, other family members, and almost all household chores. A woman's status may improve in the family and in society when she becomes a mother, especially if the child is a boy. Because of the primacy of male status in the family and the practice of a dowry system, the birth of a male child is usually a welcome blessing for the family. An argument can be made that this latter belief is transcultural as it is practiced across religious groups (e.g., Muslim, Hindu, Buddhist) throughout South Asia. Mothers are expected to invest heavily in the daily care and socialization of young children, and to sustain strong family bonds.

Whereas Islamic *adat* and the Prophet Mohammad's practices encourage Muslim fathers to be involved with their children, my data indicate that fathers are moderately involved with their children in Kadazan families, and only modestly involved in Bengali and Malay families. I suspect that there are other cultural and ecological factors that influence fathers' involvement with children in Muslim families in Asia. Historical evidence suggests that Muslim and non-Muslim families in Bangladesh and Malaysia had similar ecological and cultural roots before they came in contact with European colonization and Islamic values. The father's role in these two cultural groups has been shaped by multiple forces such as animistic beliefs, *Sanatan* (Hindu) ideology, Buddhist views, Christian missionary activities, and Islamic values. The ecological context of subsistence agriculture in tropical climates probably encouraged egalitarian gender roles in early South and Southeast Asian societies (Endicott & Endicott, 2008; Hewlett & Macfarlan, 2010). However, the *Laws of Manu* in Hinduism, Christianity, and the impact of modernism via European colonialism all contributed to a division in gender roles between men and women.

At the same time, the *Laws of Manu* awarded men power, patriarchy, and social prestige. Likewise, Christianity and modernization uphold the privileged status of men in society. Whereas men under these influences are expected to be moral guides and economic providers, women are expected to perform care giving roles in the family. From this historical perspective, the modest level of fathers' involvement in childcare in Bengali, Malay, and Kadazan families is not surprising. Although Islamic ideals call for involved fathering, pre-Islamic tribal cultural beliefs, which advocated high levels of maternal investment in childcare, remain a strong force in Malay and Bengali families. These types of pre-Islamic tribal values are even more pronounced in Pakistani Muslim families. In terms of gender roles in Pakistani families, Muslim men hold more conservative attitudes regarding women's rights than do Muslim women (Khalid & Frieze, 2004). According to this view, women's roles have traditionally been limited to procreation, care giving, and other domestic chores. Similarly, men in conservative Muslim communities including Pakistan subscribe to a pre-Islamic tribal tradition of men's protective role and even honor killing. These views sharply deviate from the Islamic message of egalitarianism between men and women and in favor of the emancipation of women (Smith, 1987).

My informal and personal observations of father–child interactions in Malay and Bengali families sometimes contradict my empirical data. For example, during field work in Selangor, Terengganu, Kelantan, and Sabah in Malaysia and Dhaka in Bangladesh, I observed that fathers held their babies when they shopped, visited relatives or neighbors, or went fishing. They also kept their young children within sight when they worked in their rice fields, or while they ploughed land and harvested crops. At meal time, the fathers I observed often took some fish or meat from their own plates and put them on children's plates so that their children could have more. This behavior symbolized to me fathers' warm and caring attitudes toward their children's welfare. Such father–child interactions suggested that fathers are involved in both Malay and Bengali Muslim families. The Case Story from Bangladesh at the beginning of this chapter also supported this assertion. Munir resigned his job in the Middle East and returned home to invest in his daughter's care and growth. Furthermore, grandparents, older siblings, aunts, uncles, and other relatives or neighbors were constantly and easily available to provide childcare for his family. I believe that the complexity of the child rearing networks and variables discussed throughout this chapter (and the entire volume) demand that we need to move away from simple binary sources of data (i.e., paternal vs. maternal data) on fathers' involvement in Asian Muslim families. Rather, we must examine fathers' involvement with their children in the contexts of alternative ecological and multiple care models. My personal observations call for a reevaluation of the use of existing research and theoretical paradigms to assess paternal involvement in Asian Muslim families.

Although I have discussed fathers' involvement in Muslim families, I did not use any direct measures of Islamic values to relate to my outcome variables such as fathers' involvement. It may be useful in future

Figure 5.3 A Malay father, 42, is celebrating his young son's graduation with his family at a preschool in Kuala Lumpur, Malaysia. Contemporary Malays highly value children's educational success at all school levels. Although this Malay father and his children are comfortable in Western dress, the Malay mother still prefers the traditional Malaysian dress. Photo courtesy of Shamsuddin Ahmed.

research to focus on how levels of religiosity impact fathers' involvement in Muslim families. Muslim communities are diverse and we often group them as conservative, moderate, or liberal (Haq, 1996). Therefore, it is important to account for diverse historical experiences, economic practices, political events, and personal attitudes toward gender roles, when we assess the father's role in Muslim families. Another limitation of the literature is that in the absence of assessments of multiple factors that influence Bengali or Malay fathers' involvement in the family (e.g., family functioning and processes, belief systems, and supports for parenting), it is difficult to assess what drives paternal involvement in Bangladesh or Malaysia. Further, it is difficult to grasp the meaning behind fathers' levels of involvement in caring for children compared with fathers in non-Muslim families. In other words, my empirical findings across Bengali and Malay families have limited generalizability, due to sampling, methodological, and conceptual issues.

Contemporary Social/Economic Conditions That Impact Fathering, and Technological Changes

Traditional gender roles and fathering in both Bangladesh and Malaysia have been affected by Westernization. In particular, modernization of agriculture, increased population mobility, access to transportation and infrastructure, women's education, information technology, and global trade markets are reshaping the labor force and family structures of Muslim communities in these two countries. Specifically, the infusion of Western values and modern economic practices may lead to less differentiated gender roles in Asian Muslim societies. Such an impact is already highly pronounced among young and urban Malays (and Bengalis) who demonstrate a complex and unique form of gender role identity as they internalize Western values of democracy and individual choice (Edwards & Roces, 2000; Endicott & Endicott, 2008; Sen & Stivens, 1998). It is logical to assume that socioeconomic changes will offer more opportunities for Muslim women to become wage earners, exercise decision making power in personal and family matters, and experience greater equality in childcare and other domestic chores. I also expect that these changes will enable mothers to share some childcare and domestic chores with their husbands. A new question then arises: do these changes offer Asian Muslim women the option of an egalitarian gender role, or do the changes enable or require them to perform both wage earner and childcare roles as has been reported in Western families (Hochschild, 2003)? This is a legitimate question to debate as domestic labor is still gender-typed in much of the Western world (Coltrane, 2000; Kroska, 2003). For example, in many families where wives make more money than their husbands, women still end up taking most of the responsibility for childcare (Mannino & Deutsch, 2007). Likewise, the limited evidence available suggests that many women in contemporary Asian Muslim families assume major responsibility for care of children at home, even when they are employed outside the home (Hossain et al., 2005; Noor, 1999; Quah, 2008).

Undoubtedly, contemporary family life and fathering in Bangladesh have been affected by socioeconomic and technological changes. The impact of modernization, and more recently globalization, on Bangladeshi families has been highly visible, especially after it became an independent nation in 1971. Agricultural laborers, landless farmers, and college graduates from the countryside have all sought employment in service sectors and urban industrial complexes. For example, millions of under-educated young women and men have been employed in export-oriented garment factories since the 1990s. Meanwhile, thousands of both skilled and unskilled men and women have emigrated to find employment (as in the Case Story of Munir), especially in the Middle East and other Asian countries. This latter situation has strengthened fathers' provisioning role in the family. However, dislocated fathers are not able to participate in direct care interactions with their children when employment takes them away from the family for years at a time.

In Muslim societies like Bangladesh and Malaysia, formal education is accessible to female students and a coeducational system is very common. Falling rates of birth and infant mortality and increasing life expectancy suggest an improvement in the health sector. Women succeed in securing jobs in virtually all sectors including management, administrative, and political leadership positions. Western-style romantic love, companionship, and dating are increasingly common in the young generation. Indeed, all these changes will help to redefine traditional notions of institutional families, family composition, gender relations, and the overall ideology toward family and society in contemporary Muslim communities. I expect that empowered wives will soon be in a position to negotiate for an equal distribution of household labor and childcare in the family.

As indicated earlier, Western values of equality between men and women and involved fathering are congruent with Islamic *adat*. This argument was echoed in a recent study of gender roles which showed that younger, urban educated, and non-Pashtun women in Afghanistan believed in the compatibility of Western democracy and Islam (Manganaro & Alozie, 2011). This leads to another question: why do women in many Muslim societies appear to play subservient roles while Muslim fathers seem to play strong patriarchal roles in the family? These tendencies are perhaps due to the fact that the interpretation of Islamic ideals regarding gender roles has been pre-empted by very conservative and less scholarly clerics (Hassan, 2002; Khalid & Frieze, 2004). These clerics are often aided by corrupt, inept, uncouth, anti-intellectual, and pseudo-democratic political leaders. Therefore, unequal distribution of

domestic labor and treatment of women as inferior are more of a function of male-oriented cultural norms rather than Islamic *adat* itself (Jawad,
1998; Mernissi, 1975). In addition, the negative impact of colonial exploitation, poverty, and unequal and/or lack of access to resources created a
biased social system that perpetuated patriarchy in Muslim societies and
gave a bad name to Westernization. This may make it socially desirable
for fathers, in response to questions from researchers, to down play their
involvement with children. Contemporary Muslim societies are in a transition toward the rediscovery of the Islamic ideals of involved and shared
parenting. In a globalizing world, the wave of Western democratic process may accelerate this trend by creating mass awareness against ultra-
conservative beliefs and corrupt political institutions in Muslim societies
(see Ahmed, Ch. 6, this volume). Psychological research will enlighten
us on all these issues, as we begin to accurately observe active fathers in
Muslim families.

I expect that traditional cultural norms of fathering and parenting
in Bangladesh and Malaysia will come under the increased influence of
Western ideologies. As a result, late marriages (especially for women),
women's educational attainment and employment outside of the home,
and increasing divorce rates will increasingly be accepted by Muslim families in these two countries. At the same time, true Islamic *adat* regarding
parental practices has the potential to work side by side with Western
values of shared parenting in Muslim communities. It is difficult, based
on current limited research data, to know how modernization and other
socioeconomic forces have affected fathers' and mothers' attitudes toward
involvement in childcare and domestic labor in South and Southeast Asian
Muslim families.

Implications for Research and Policy

Most Muslims reside in Asian and African countries that have experienced centuries of colonial exploitation with devastating effects on their
societies. Poverty, desperation, illiteracy, unemployment, corruption,
wealth disparities, and a lack of democratic governance have consistently
undermined the strength of their cultural and religious values with regard
to parenting (United Nations, 2011). In particular, we tend either to know
very little about fathers' contribution to child development in Muslim
families, or to have a distorted picture of the father's role. More research
is therefore needed to better understand fathers' behavior in Muslim communities, especially in Asian societies. Future systematic research should
focus on the following areas: (1) the extent to which Islamic values affect
fathers' roles and responsibilities in the family; (2) how the interplay
between cultural norms and Islamic gender role ideology provide the con-

text for fathering; (3) how fathers' involvement with children is influenced by fathers' mental and physical health under depressed socioeconomic conditions; and (4) how support variables and the context of multiple care providers influence fathers' involvement with children.

Cross-cultural data suggest that contemporary Western fathers have changed their attitudes toward traditional gender roles and are becoming more involved in childcare (Lamb, 2010). In this era of increasing modernization and evolving family patterns in Bangladesh and Malaysia, the observations outlined in this chapter should be of interest to national children's or women's organizations. Information from research might also be of value to government policy makers, to redress gender disparities in domestic labor and care giving practices in the family. The data suggest the need for national policies and programs (e.g., fatherhood support groups and early childhood education programs) that create opportunities for fathers to become more involved in the family. The availability of formal support systems will undoubtedly encourage fathers to utilize existing resources (Bangladesh Paternal Leave Policy Act of 2010; National Population and Family Development Board Malaysia – NPFDB) and to become more involved in their children's social, emotional, and cognitive outcomes. Finally, research findings have the potential to strengthen the early childhood development and fathering components of various NGOs (e.g., Manusher Jonno Foundation Bangladesh) and donor agencies (e.g., OXFAM), especially in Bangladesh.

Summary

This chapter builds on prior attempts to understand fathering and gender role practices in South and Southeast Asian families. Unlike a number of past assessments that concentrated mainly on paternal involvement in urban, indigenous, and mixed religious/cultural Asian families (e.g., Endicott, 1992; Noor, 1999; Sen & Stivens, 1998), this chapter focused on urban and rural Bengali and Malay Muslim families with children, in which Islamic beliefs may have a strong grip on gender roles despite economic and technological modernization. My primary goal was to discuss the degree to which fathers and mothers were involved with their children in rural and urban Bengali and Malay Muslim families, and also to focus on whether fathers' involvement with children varied by rural–urban residence or the child's gender. According to the data, mothers remain the primary care providers in both rural and urban Bengali and Malay families. Fathers in urban Bengali families reported that they spent more time with children than did their counterparts in Malaysia. Fathers and mothers in both Malay and Bengali families were equally involved with their male and female children. Although fathers spent more time playing with than feeding or cleaning infants, mothers spent more time playing with infants than did fathers in Malay families. Whereas the overall evidence portrayed fathers as moderately involved with their children in both Bengali and Malay families, my field observations suggested that fathers in both groups were highly involved with their children. This latter observation was in line with Islamic values that call for involved fathering in Muslim families. It is also apparent that Westernization is compatible with Islamic ideology in support of reinvigorating involved fathering in these two cultural groups.

References

Ahmed, R. A., & Gielen, U. P. (Eds.). (1998). *Psychology in the Arab countries*. Cairo, Egypt: Menoufia University Press.

Ahsan Ullah, A. K. M. (2007). *Rationalizing migration: Bangladeshi immigrant workers in Hong Kong and Malaysia* (unpublished doctoral dissertation). City University of Hong Kong.

Bronfenbrenner, U., & Morris, P. (1998). The ecology of developmental processes. In W. Damon & R. Lerner (Eds.), *Handbook of child psychology: Vol. 1. Theoretical models of human development* (pp. 993–1028). New York, NY: John Wiley.

Chaudhry, M. H. (2009). *A code of the teachings of Al-Qur'an*.Delhi, India: Adam Publishers.

Coltrane, S. (2000). Research on household labor: Modeling and measuring the social embeddedness of routine family work. *Journal of Marriage and the Family, 62*, 1208–1233.

da Cruz Benetti, P. S., & Roopnarine, J. L. (2006). Paternal involvement with school-aged children in Brazilian families: Associations with childhood competence. *Sex Roles, 55*, 669–678.

de Minzi, M. C. R. (2010). Gender and cultural patterns of mothers' and fathers' attachment and links with children's self-competence, depression and loneliness in middle and late childhood. *Early Child Development and Care, 180*, 193–209.

Edwards, L. P., & Roces, M. (2000). *Women in Asia: Tradition, modernity, and globalisation*. Ann Arbor, MI: University of Michigan Press.

Endicott, K. M. (1992). Fathering in an egalitarian society. In B. S. Hewlett (Ed.), *Father–child relations: Cultural and biosocial context: Foundations of human behavior* (pp. 281–295). Hawthorne, NY: Aldine de Gruyter.

Endicott, K. M., & Endicott, K. L. (2008). *The headman was a woman: The gender egalitarian Batek of Malaysia*. Long Grove, IL: Waveland Press.

Gallagher, S. K., & Smith, C. (1999). Symbolic traditionalism and pragmatic egalitarianism: Contemporary evangelicals, families, and gender. *Gender and Society, 13*, 211–233.

Gunnoe, L. M., Hetherington, E. M., & Reiss, D. (1999). Parental religiosity, parenting style, and adolescent social responsibility. *The Journal of Early Adolescence, 19*, 199–225.

Hassan, R. (2002). *Faithless: Muslim conceptions of Islam and society*. Oxford, UK: Oxford University Press.

Haq, F. (1996). Women, Islam, and the state in Pakistan. *The Muslim World, 85*, 158–175.

Hewlett, B. S., & Macfarlan, S. J. (2010). Fathers' role in hunter-gatherer and other small-scale cultures. In M. E. Lamb (Ed.), *The role of father in child development* (5th ed., pp. 413–434). New York, NY: Wiley.

Hochschild, A. R. (2003). *The second shift*. New York, NY: Penguin Books.

Hooker, V. M. (1993). *Culture and society in new order Indonesia*. Kuala Lumpur, Malaysia: Oxford University Press.

Hossain, Z., & Anziano, M. C. (2008). Mothers' and fathers' involvement with school-age children's care and academic activities in Navajo Indian families. *Cultural Diversity and Ethnic Minority Psychology, 14*, 109–117.

Hossain, Z., & Roopnarine, J. L. (1994). African American fathers' involvement with infants: Relationship to their functioning style, support, education, and income. *Infant Behavior and Development, 17*, 175–184.

Hossain, Z., Roopnarine, J. L., Ismail, R., Hashmi, S. I., & Sombuling, A. (2007). Fathers' and mothers' reports of involvement in caring for infants in Kadazan families in Sabah, Malaysia. *Fathering, 5*, 58–78.

Hossain, Z., Roopnarine, J. L., Masud, J., Muhamed, A. A., Baharudin, R., Abdullah, R., & Juhari, R. (2005). Mothers' and fathers' childcare involvement with young children in rural families in Malaysia. *International Journal of Psychology, 40*, 385–394.

Hossain, Z., & Skurky, T.(2005). *The sense of collectivism and individualism in Malaysian families: An exploratory study*. Paper presented at the 34th Annual Meeting of the Society for Cross-Cultural Research, Santa Fe, NM, February 23–27.

Jawad, H. A. (1998). *The rights of women in Islam: An authentic approach*. New York, NY: St. Martin's Press.

Jesmin, S. S., & Seward, R. R. (2011). Parental leave and fathers' involvement with children in Bangladesh: A comparison with United States. *Journal of Comparative Family Studies, 42*, 95–112.

Kabir, M., & Az-Zubair, B. (2007). Who is a parent? Parenthood in Islamic ethics. *Journal of Medical Ethics, 33*, 605–609.

Keats, D. (2000). Cross-cultural studies in child development in Asian contexts. *Cross-Cultural Research, 34*, 339–350.

Khalid, R., & Frieze, I. H. (2004). Measuring perceptions of gender roles: The IAWS for Pakistanis and U.S. immigrant populations. *Sex Roles, 51*, 293–299.

Kling, Z. (1995). The Malay family: Beliefs and realities. *Journal of Comparative Family Studies, 26*, 43–66.

Kroska, A. (2003). Investigating gender differences in the meaning of household chores and childcare. *Journal of Marriage and the Family, 65*, 456–473.

Kumaraswamy, N., & Othman, A. (2011). Corporal punishment study: A case in Malaysia. *Psychology, 2*, 24–28.

Lamb, M. E. (2002). Father-infant attachments and their impact on child development. In C. S. Tamis-LeMonda & N. J. Cabrera (Eds.), *Handbook of father involvement: Multi disciplinary perspectives* (pp. 93–118). Mahwah, NJ: Lawrence Erlbaum.

Lamb, M. E. (Ed.). (2004). *The role of father in child development* (4th ed.). New York, NY: Wiley.

Lamb, M. E. (Ed.). (2010). *The role of father in child development* (5th ed.). New York, NY: Wiley.

Lee, W. (2002). Gender ideology and the domestic division of labor in middle class Chinese families in Hong Kong. *Gender, Place, and Culture, 9*, 245–260.

Manganaro, L. L., & Alozie, N. O. (2011). Gender role attitudes: Who supports expanded rights for women in Afghanistan? *Sex Roles, 64*, 516–529.

Mannino, C., & Deutsch, F. (2007). Changing the division of household labor: A negotiated process between partners. *Sex Roles, 56*, 309–324.

Mernissi, F. (1975). *Beyond the veil*. New York, NY: Schenkman.

Ng, K. S. (1998). Family therapy in Malaysia: An update. *Contemporary Family Therapy, 20*, 37–45.

Noor, N. (1999). Roles and women's well-being: Some preliminary findings from Malaysia. *Sex Roles, 41*, 123–145.

Nsamenang, A. B. (2010). Fathers, families, and children's well-becoming in Africa. In M. E. Lamb (Ed.), *The role of father in child development* (5th ed., pp. 388–412). New York, NY: Wiley.

Pew Research Center. (2011). The future of the global Muslim population: Projection for 2010–2030. *The Pew Forum*, January 27, 2011. htpp://www.pew-forum.org/The-Future-of-the-Global-Muslim-Population.aspx?print=true. Accessed January 27, 2011.

Quah, S. R. (2008). *Families in Asia*. London, UK: Routledge.

Roopnarine, J. L. (2011). Fathers in Caribbean cultural communities. In D. W. Shwalb, B. Shwalb, & M. E. Lamb (Eds.), *The father's role: Cross-cultural perspectives*. New York, NY: Routledge.

Roopnarine, J., & Gielen, U. (Eds.). (2004). *Families in global perspective*. Boston, MA: Allyn & Bacon.

Roopnarine, J. L., & Hossain, Z. (1992). Parent-child interactions in urban Indian families in New Delhi: Are they changing? In J. L. Roopnarine & D. B. Carter (Eds.), *Parent-child socialization in diverse cultures* (pp. 1–16). Norwood, NJ: Ablex.

Roopnarine, J. L., Krishnakumar, A., & Xu, YiLi (2009). Beliefs about mothers' and fathers' roles and the division of child care and household labor in Indo-Caribbean immigrants with young children. *Cultural Diversity and Ethnic Minority Psychology, 15*, 173–182.

Roopnarine, J. L., Lu, M., & Ahmeduzzaman, M. (1989). Parental reports of early patterns of caregiving, play and discipline in India and Malaysia. *Early Child Development and Care, 50*, 109–120.

Roopnarine, J. L., & Suppal, P. (2000). Kakar's psychoanalytic interpretation of Indian childhood: The need to emphasize the father and multiple caregivers in the socialization equation. *International Journal of Group Tensions, 29*, 349–370.

Roopnarine, J. L., Talukder, E., Jain, D., Joshi, P., & Srivastav, P. (1992). Personal well-being, kinship tie, and mother-infant and father-infant interactions in single-wage and dual-wage families in New Delhi, India. *Journal of Marriage and the Family, 54*, 293–301.

Rosnah, I. (1999). *Family quality of Kadazandusun*. Kota Kinabalu, Sabah: Universiti Malaysia Sabah.

Saad, F. (2001, October). *The family in the 21st century: Country perspectives: Malaysia*. Paper presented at the International Family Conference, Kuala Lumpur, Malaysia.

Sather, C. (1978). The societies of Borneo explorations in the theory of cognatic social structure. *American Anthropological Association*, special publication No. 6, Washington, 40–46.

Sen, K., & Stivens, M. (Eds.). (1998). *Gender and power in affluent Asia*. London, UK: Routledge.

Shwalb, D. W., Nakawaza, J., Yamamoto, T., & Hyun, Jung-Hwan (2010). Fathering in Japan, China, and Korea: Changing contexts, images, and roles. In M. E. Lamb (Ed.), *The role of the father in child development* (pp. 341–387). Hoboken, NJ: Wiley.

Smith, J. I. (1987). Islam. In A. Sharma (Ed.), *Women in world religions* (pp. 235–250). Albany, NY: SUNY Press.

Sun, L. C., & Roopnarine, J. L. (1996). Mother–infant, father–infant interaction and involvement in childcare and household labor among Taiwanese families. *Infant Behavior & Development, 19*, 121–129.

United Nations. (2011). *Men in families and family policy in a changing world* [Sales No E.11.IV.1]. New York, NY: UN Department of Economic and Social Affairs, Division for Social Policy and Development.

von der Mehden, F. R. (1987). Malaysia: Islam and multiethnic politics. In J. L. Esposito (Ed.), *Islam in Asia: Religion, politics, and society* (pp. 177–201). New York, NY: Oxford University Press.

Williams, L. B. (1990). Marriage and decision-making: Intergenerational dynamics in Indonesia. *Journal of Comparative Family Studies, 21*, 55–66.

Chapter Six

The Father's Role in the Arab World

Cultural Perspectives

Ramadan A. Ahmed
Kuwait University, Kuwait City, Kuwait

Case Story: Ahmed's Dream

Ahmed Ali was once an illiterate Egyptian man who worked as an unskilled laborer. The son of a farmer, he had three brothers and two sisters, and dreamed as a little boy of going to school with his friends. But his family could not afford to send him even to primary school because they were very poor. He worked in his youth outside the home to help support his family. Ahmed married at age 21 after obtaining a semi-skilled job as a construction supervisor. His wife had dropped out of school at age 10 and was also from a poor family.

During the next ten years, Ahmed became the father of three boys and one girl. But he never forgot his childhood dream of getting an education. His wife (who was semi-literate) encouraged him to dream, but she had no resources and could do nothing to enable him to go to school. For years this presented him with a dilemma, because he felt ashamed of his illiteracy and desperately wanted an education. But he was compelled to fulfill his duty to raise and educate his children in the best possible way. As a father, Ahmed helped his wife with childcare and to a small extent with household chores. Truly he had no choice but to put off his lifelong dream, and sacrificed everything for the sake of his four children's education. The children all enrolled in good schools, and Ahmed provided them with everything possible to help them achieve a good education.

One by one, his children entered college and graduated with degrees in business, engineering, law, and education. Now Ahmed began again to believe that his hope for his own education could finally be realized. But at the same time, the four children began their careers and thought about marriage. Like most other Arab fathers he knew, Ahmed felt that he still had an obligation toward his children (especially his daughter) to help them prepare financially for the costs of marriage. So he used all his life savings to help his four children pay for dowry (*mahr*) and marriage gifts that were required by tradition, and set them up with furnished flats in which to begin their married lives. Ahmed thought to himself, "My dream can wait." The children all married. Finally, at the age of 50, Ahmed the father enrolled himself at a private elementary school and reduced his work hours so that he could study. Today, Ahmed has six grandchildren who all live in his neighborhood, and he is a student at the Faculty of Law at Cairo University. He hopes to graduate next year at the age of 60 and to practice courtroom law.

This story reflects four themes associated with Arab fatherhood: altruism, obligation, commitment, and responsibility. The Prophet Muhammad also addressed these themes in his teachings, as follows: "You all are guardians, and each guardian is responsible for the people the guardian cares for." The Case Story also demonstrated Ahmed's determination to achieve life goals, his strong will, and feelings of shame about illiteracy (a problem that remains all too common in the Arab world). A final theme of the story was that illiterate Arab people strive harder than anybody to educate their children.

Cultural and Historical Background as It Influences Fathering

The Arab world is defined as Arabic-speaking peoples and has a population of about 320 million people. It consists of 22 countries and stretches from the Atlantic Ocean to Central Asia, from the Black Sea to the Mediterranean Seas, and to the Horn of Africa. Our map (Figure 6.1) reflects the fact that this chapter only summarizes research data from eleven countries, with the number of articles cited from each in parentheses as follows: Egypt (67), Saudi Arabia (11), Kuwait (7), Jordan (5), Tunisia (2), Yemen (2), United Arab Emirates [UAE] (2), Bahrain (1), Qatar (1), Sudan (1), and Syria (1). The Arab region is also a vast realm of enormous historical and cultural complexity, situated at the crossroads of Europe, Asia, and Africa. In fact, it was on the Mesopotamian Plain between the Tigris and Euphrates rivers, and on the banks of the Egyptian Nile, that the very earliest civilizations began over 7,000 years ago (Ahmed, 2010).

There are compelling variations on most demographic measures within the Arab world. For example, per capita income varies dramati-

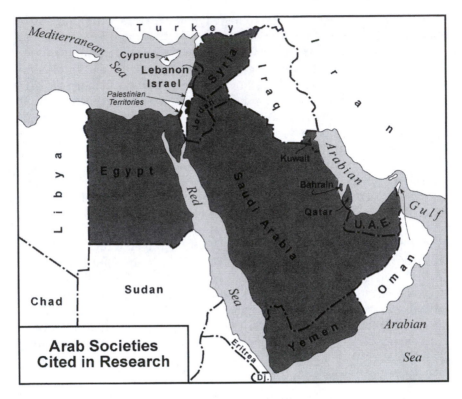

Figure 6.1 Map of Arab societies, courtesy of Paul R. Larson.

cally. Data for 2005 showed that Qatar, the United Arab Emirates (UAE), and Kuwait had among the highest income levels in the world, while Mauritania, Djibouti, Yemen, and the Sudan were among the poorest societies (*Al-Qabas*, November 30, 2007). There is also a wide range of rates of illiteracy among Arab societies. For example, in a wealthy nation like Kuwait illiteracy is only 5.4%, whereas in Egypt it is 29%, with even higher percentages among rural and female sub-populations. In countries such as the Sudan, Somalia, Mauritania, Djibouti, and Comoros, illiteracy rates exceed 80%. Because social and economic conditions impact the family, these disparities inevitably affect the father's role. Indeed, despite the stereotypical image of Arab fathers as authoritarian and controlling figures, there is diversity in the Arab world in relation to economic, social, cultural, and political circumstances. Accordingly, I would expect differences between Arab countries in fathering behavior and in the socialization process. For example, my own experiences and informal observations indicate that urban, high-SES, highly educated fathers, fathers from wealthy Arab countries (e.g., oil-producing nations), and fathers from more liberated and democratic countries (e.g., Lebanon) have more liberal and authoritative attitudes toward their offspring. Although the Islamic religion (predominant in most Arab societies) is critically important in Arab life, I believe that the research data cited in this chapter are more a product of a father's nationality (characterized by economic, social, and cultural circumstances) than of his religion.

The changing cultural context of Arab families

Arab families today face a variety of challenges that influence the role of the father (Ahmed, 2005b). In my view, the following are the three most important current challenges to families and fathers.

1. The Arab family is no longer the only agent of socialization that it was in the past. Many other institutions, including schools, media, sports

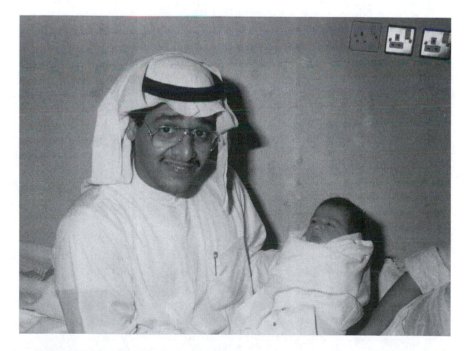

Figure 6.2 A 36-year-old Kuwaiti and father of four, with his newborn son. This man later became a prominent businessman and the boy now attends an English secondary school in Kuwait. The father will pay for the university education of all his children. Photo courtesy of Ramadan A. Ahmed.

clubs, and social and cultural associations, have become important sources of socialization. However, these agents often do not work consistently in synchrony with the goals and values of families. As a result, families (especially fathers) now take a reactive stance as they respond to or correct ideas and behaviors acquired by children from other sources (e.g., religious dogma), instead of actively promoting their own ideas and goals.

2. Many current Arab fathers (and to a lesser extent, mothers) lack the parenting skills necessary to raise children in a healthy and positive way. For example, childrearing has become increasingly difficult for mothers in Arab families, because of the growing number of absent fathers. A trend toward the concentration of responsibility in Arab mothers/wives is apparent, for example, in the growing percentage of Egyptian families headed alone by mothers, which reached 28% in 2005 (Ahmed, 2005b). It is near impossible for fathers to develop healthy parenting skills and to contribute positively to child development when so many of them now must live apart from their families.

3. Many contemporary Arab families suffer from a severe imbalance between their income and expenditures. Such severe economic stress negatively affects the socialization role of the family and strains the father's role.

The Arab family as a system

Despite upheavals in Arab families, Sanders' analysis (1986) showed that Arab families typically provided the basic context for child development and lifespan development. At every age, one's first loyalty was to the family, which was the source of one's reputation, well-being, and socioeconomic status. Family members also exerted considerable influence on the individual's education, employment, and material property. Men traditionally were the authorities within the Arab families, and according to Sanders,

> From an early age, children are taught that males are inherently superior to females. Respect for masculine authority and seniority is stressed, and children are expected to show proper deference to their elders. The questioning of decisions or judgments made by superiors is considered neither permissible nor proper. The father – characterized as stern, severe, and authoritarian – is held in awe and respect.
>
> (Sanders, 1986, p. 459)

Another group of scholars viewed the Arab family from the perspective of Minuchin's Systematic Theory (Simadi, Fatayer, & Athamneh, 2003). According to this approach the family was a social system, and there were three types of families: enmeshed (entangled), disengaged, and clear. The first two types tend to have negative impacts on their members, while the latter type tended to have a positive impact. Simadi et al.'s (2003) analysis indicated that enmeshed families (one of the less healthy types) were predominant in most Arab communities. They described the following characteristics of the enmeshed family, which I would attribute generally to Arab families:

> Absence of internal borders between the members … the whole family has lost its borders with the extended and neighboring families. Functionally, the individuals of the family are in a state of confrontation with each other. For example, each member knows the feelings and thoughts of others. In other words, there is no privacy for each individual member. At the same time, there is a confrontation between the subsystems of the family, such as the children's involvement in their parents' issues …
> (Simadi et al., 2003, p. 471)

Like fathers in other parts of the world, many fathers in the Arab world traditionally preferred to have sons, although this tradition may not be based in Islamic teachings (see Hossain, Ch. 5, this volume, for a discussion of Quranic teachings on gender roles). This preference was illustrated by the proverb that "a man with a son is immortal, whereas a girl is brought up to contribute to someone else's family tree." As my review of the research literature will show, perceptions of fathers and the possible influences of fathers appear to be different for boys and girls. One Egyptian study (Abdel-Salam, 2005) served as an example of how family relations can be related to child gender. Specifically, Abdel-Salam's results showed that female adolescents' communication with mothers was deeper and more effective than their communication with fathers. Conversely, boys reported more efficient and in-depth communication with fathers.

Power and prestige in the family

In a recent study, Ibrahim (2010) assessed children's perceptions of paternal vs. maternal power and prestige, in relation to children's psychological adjustment and conduct problems, in a sample of 10- to 11-year-old Kuwaiti children ($N = 151$). Her results showed that 52% of Kuwaiti girls saw their mothers as more powerful than fathers, but 60% of boys saw their fathers as more powerful. In addition, 61% of boys and 53% of girls believed their fathers were more prestigious than their mothers. Those children who believed the father had more power than the mother tended to self-report better psychological adjustment than children who believed their mothers had more power. Ibrahim's research and analysis of family dynamics suggested that while some Arab fathers may be powerful authorities in the family, about half of the children perceived the mother as the more prestigious and powerful figure, and children's psychological adjustment was associated with the father's role.

Review of Fathering Research

Most research on Arab fathers has been from a psychological perspective, focusing on two main topics: images of fathers and the father's influence on child development. A search of the literature revealed that many authors had conducted only a single study on Arab fathering, and that few scholars established ongoing or integrated lines of research. In addition, most studies compared fathers to mothers and very few focused primarily on fathers. Research appears most often to be descriptive and correlational, and although it may help us to chart future studies of Arab fathers, research has seldom provided causal explanations or answered general questions about the role of the Arab father. In addition, because most studies reported below took place in only eight of 22 Arab countries, it is difficult to generalize these data to portray "the Arab father."

Children's perceptions and images of fathers

Ahmed (2008) reviewed over 30 studies which had utilized Rohner's Parental Acceptance-Rejection Questionnaire (PARQ) on Arab males and females, across several age groups and Arab countries. These studies consistently showed that younger participants, compared with older ones, perceived their parents as more accepting, less aggressive, less neglecting, and less rejecting. In general, males tended more than females to perceive their parents (especially fathers) as less accepting, more aggressive, more neglecting, and more rejecting. In other words, as children get older their fathers' image becomes milder, and the general image of fathers is harsher in the eyes of boys than girls. In the same context, Ali (1992) studied perceptions of parental treatment in relation to depression, in a sample of Egyptian adolescents (aged 16–18 years), using Rohner's PARQ and a locally devised depression scale. Ali found a positive correlation between perceptions of parents' rejection and children's depression. In addition, Ali showed that while there was no significant difference between boys' and girls' perceptions of paternal vs. maternal acceptance, male adolescents tended to perceive their fathers as more aggressive, neglectful, and reject-ing than did females. In a related study, Ismaeel (2001) focused on child abuse and personality dispositions, and showed that Saudi adolescents (aged 11–14) who experienced abuse by fathers tended to self-report more negative personality traits on Rohner's PAQ (Personality Assessment Questionnaire). Ismaeel also found that Saudi males reported more abuse by their fathers than did female adolescents. Together these three studies depicted a strict Arab father, particularly with their sons, and suggested possible negative effects of severe father–child relations.

This theme of negative associations between fathers' behavior and children's psychological condition also appeared in a study by Abdel-Kader (2000). He investigated the relationship between perceptions of the father's parenting style among urban and rural Egyptian secondary school students, and students' levels of assertiveness, submissiveness and hostility. His results showed a positive correlation between students' per-ceptions of fathers' neglectful or authoritarian style and both submissive-ness and hostility among the adolescents. On the other hand, Abdel-Kader (2000) found positive associations between fathering style and healthy child outcome measures. Specifically, he noted a correlation between stu-dents' perceptions of fathers' democratic style and adolescents' levels of assertiveness, which suggested a relationship between fathering and chil-dren's adjustment. Similarly, an Egyptian study (Zaid, 1999) showed a positive relationship between children's social development and healthy treatment of 11- to 14-year-old male and female children by fathers and mothers. However, this correlation was only found for perceptions of fathers by boys and for perceptions of mothers by girls.

A different pattern of correlations were apparent in a Saudi study (Al-Nefie, 1997), which investigated the relationship between parenting styles and locus of control in a sample of male and female university students (aged 19–32). These data revealed that while the mother's parenting style correlated positively with students' external locus of control, the father's parenting style correlated positively with students' internal locus of con-trol. Integrating this set of studies from several countries which correlated images of fathers and mothers with psychological measures of children, we can see that the correlations were different for perceptions of mothers and fathers, and between boys and girls, and that fathering behavior was associated with both positive and negative aspects of child and adolescent development (Ahmed & Gielen, 2008).

Authority image

Safwat and El-Dousseki (1993) summarized the results of four studies from Egypt and other Arab countries which focused on images of authority and children's relationships with authority figures. One of these studies was conducted by Abdel-Ghany (1983), and revealed that the image of the father as an authority correlated positively with children's reports of obedience to the father and lower levels of self-control. Abdel-Ghany also found a positive correlation between children's perceptions of father rejection and negative attitudes toward authorities. This latter finding was similar to Ibrahim's (1993) data, which showed that female high-school students had more rebellious tendencies toward fathers than toward mothers. Ibrahim also uncovered more rebellious tendencies among high-school students than middle-school students. In sum, studies of images of fathers as authority figures produced the same patterns of images as in the research on images of parenting styles. That is, rebellious attitudes seemed to be more pronounced among older than younger participants, and boys and girls had different attitudes toward the father as an authority.

The father's image and children's characteristics

A number of Arab studies have correlated children's images of their fathers with children's characteristics (Allam 1993; Abou-el-Kheir, 1998; and Hamza 2002, in Egypt; and Abdouh, 2000, in Saudi Arabia). In the earliest of these studies, Allam (1993) investigated the relationship between perceptions of prison inmate fathers' images and children's behavior, and his results suggested that these children had a negative image of their fathers and a tendency to depend completely on their mothers. In a 1998 study, Abou-el-Kheir examined the correlation between perceptions of father figures and self-esteem among 285 male and female university students, using the Rosenberg Self-Esteem Scale, Rohner's Parenting Styles Questionnaire, and other interview and test measures. Abou-el-Kheir found that while male children perceived their fathers as more accepting, females perceived their fathers as more controlling, hostile, inconsistent in control of aggression, and inclined to use physical or corporal punishment. He emphasized the positive correlation between children's perception of the father as accepting and positive self-esteem, but only for male students. Finally, Abou-el-Kheir reported a negative correlation between children's self-esteem and perceptions of the father as punitive or inconsistent. These data indicated, as in several other studies mentioned previously, that associations between fathers' behavior and children's psychological status differed for sons and daughters, and were both positive and negative. In a related study, Hamza (2002) also found a positive correlation between a favorable father image and children's self-esteem, in a sample of Egyptian high school students. As in other studies of paternal images, Hamza noted that female students tended more than male students to perceive their fathers as accepting and warm. Overall, while perceptions of fathers seem to depend on the age and gender of children, these perceptions and their correlations with measures of children were both favorable and unfavorable.

Summary

The fact that studies of perceptions of fathers focused on parenting styles reflect that (1) the position of authority figure is an important part of the Arab father's role, and (2) many research studies on Arab fathers utilized measures of parenting style based on PARTheory [Perception of Acceptance/Rejection Theory] (introduced in Ch. 1, p. 9). These correlational data suggest that images of Arab fathers depend on the child's gender and age, and that his image has both positive and negative features. Likewise, the next section shows that Arab fathers may have both negative and positive effects on their children.

Paternal influences

Adjustment

One study in Saudi Arabia (Morsy, 1986) focused on the adjustment problems of adolescents and young adults, in relation to perceptions of their parental treatment during childhood. Morsy showed that perceived parental rejection correlated positively with adolescent adjustment problems. More specifically, while perceived paternal rejection correlated with adolescents' maladjustment in the home context, perceived rejection by the mother correlated with her children's health as well as social, emotional, and general maladjustment. That is, correlations between adjustment and perceptions of fathering style were more specific to the home setting, while those for mothering style were more general. A more recent study (Ahmed, Rohner, & Carrasco, 2012) explored the contributions of acceptance by mothers, fathers, siblings, best friends, and teachers to psychological adjustment among 249 Kuwaiti male and female adolescents. Their results showed that while only perceived acceptance by siblings, best friends, and fathers (in that order) accounted for independent portions of variance in male adolescents' psychological adjustment, the most important influence on girls' adjustment was the father's acceptance, followed by perceived acceptance by siblings and teachers. These findings revealed similarities between children's perceptions of fathers and their perceptions of other attachment figures, and also showed that acceptance by the father was of particular importance to girls.

Cognitive development

Very few Arab research projects have looked at the father's impact on children's cognitive development. Among these, Bedair (1995) found that while father's warmth and neglect correlated with lower levels of curiosity among their children, maternal warmth, non-protective style, and inconsistent style correlated with children's higher levels of curiosity. These findings were inconclusive, but clearly the patterns were different for fathers and mothers, and both parents' styles were correlated with children's levels of curiosity. Meanwhile, Al-Reguieb (1996) investigated perceptions of parental acceptance/rejection in relation to personality traits and creative abilities among 12- to 13-year-old Egyptian and Kuwaiti children. Here, father acceptance correlated positively with children's linguistic and ideational abilities, while paternal overprotection, neglect, and rejection correlated negatively with children's creative abilities. Together these two studies associated creativity and curiosity with perceptions of acceptance by the father.

Behavioral problems

Two Arab studies have associated children's problems with perceptions of fathers' and mothers' behavior. First, Khaleefa (2003) focused on the perceptions of parental acceptance/rejection among primary school Qatari children, and other Arab children (aged 9–12) from Egypt, Jordan, Syria, Yemen, and Sudan who lived in Qatar at the time of the study. Her results showed that perceptions of fathers' or mothers' aggression, neglect, and rejection were correlated with children's emotional, behavioral, family, and educational problems. Khaleefa also observed that children from large families, compared with children from small families, perceived their fathers more as aggressive, neglecting, and rejecting. In a related study on children's problem behavior in Egypt, Abdel-Razak (2005) investigated primary and intermediate school children's perceptions of father absence in relation to students' behavioral problems. His results showed that children who were more aware of the fathers' absence tended to report more behavioral problems than children who had less awareness of father absence. In addition, Abdel-Razak noted that children from small families were more aware that the fathers performed their roles at home, and also reported fewer behavioral problems, compared to children from large families who reported more absent fathers. These two studies on problem behavior included not only different correlations between perceptions of fathers and problem behavior by boys and girls, but also suggested the impact of father absence on both perceptions and problems. Meanwhile, a Kuwaiti study investigated the impact of father–child relations on juvenile delinquency (Al-Musslem, 2001). Her data indicated that children of younger Kuwaiti fathers (under 40 years of age) and working fathers had a higher rate of delinquency than children of older or non-working fathers.

Most recently, Mansour (2011) explored parental styles as perceived by 10- to 13-year-old Bahraini children ($N = 34$), which were associated with children's behavioral problems. He administered local scales for ADHD and Connors' Inventory and Parental Styles Scales. Mansour's results revealed that children's perceptions of fathers' parenting styles (self-dependency, child abuse, strict discipline, and rejection) were associated with symptoms of ADHD, impulsive behavior, aggressive behavior, and anxiety. Unfortunately, as in the case of much of the data summarized in this chapter, Mansour's study was correlational and therefore did not address the issue of causality.

Aggressive behavior

Many research studies have focused on the relationship between parental pressure and children's aggressive behavior (El-Dousseki, 1981; Omar, 2002; and Al-Khouly, 2004, in Egypt; and Abou-Maraq, 1997, in Saudi Arabia). The earliest of these studies (El-Dousseki, 1981) reported a correlation between parents' psychological control and children's aggressive behavior and weaker personal adjustment. El-Doussekialso reported an association between extremely independent tendencies of some fathers and aggression among 6- to 12-year-old sons. Abou-Maraq's (1997) Saudi study dealt with the connection between parental pressure and 3- to 6-year-old children's aggressive behavior, in dual-income families. His analyses revealed a correlation between parental pressure and children's verbal and physical aggression, and social isolation. Fathers, compared with mothers, reported that they applied less pressure on children. In an intervention to help fathers and their aggressive children, Omar (2002) implemented a counseling program with a group of Saudi fathers and primary school children. The effects of this intervention included improvements in fathers' parenting skills, a decline in children's aggressive behavior, and improvements in children's personal and social adjustment at home and at school. Together, these studies show that Arab fathers' style was associated with children's aggression, and that interventions can improve fathers' parental skills and behaviors and by association children's behavior.

Bullying behavior

Al-Khouly (2004) studied the prediction of children's bullying/victimization as a function of unhealthy parenting styles, with a sample of 12- to 15-year-old Egyptian boys. His results showed first that the impact of unhealthy treatment by fathers decreased with children's age. The data for 12- to 13-year-olds revealed that paternal rejection and rudeness were predictive of children's bullying behavior, while fathers' behavior was not predictive of bullying at ages 14 to 15. More specifically, fathers' authoritarian, neglectful, and inconsistent treatment styles (in older participants) contributed to the prediction of victimization in children, while only paternal neglect predicted victimization among 12- to 13-year-olds. It is of course impossible to generalize from a single study in a single country, but these data suggest an association between fathering behavior and bullying/victimization.

Summary

Whether the child measure was adjustment, cognitive development, problem behavior, aggression, or bullying, we can conclude from this section that reports of Arab fathers' parenting styles were associated with both positive and negative developmental outcomes for children. In many cases these outcomes depended on the child's gender and age, and often the associations between measures of fathers' characteristics and measures of their children were different from the correlation patterns for mothers. Other than father absence, most of these studies did not evaluate aspects of the environment or contextual factors that might explain the rather consistent correlations.

Social Policy Issues Related to Fathering: Immigration

Contemporary Arab families face numerous hardships which may negatively affect the father's role. Clearly, when fathers and families experience social and economic challenges, some fathers become unable to take care of their families effectively. Specifically, the present generation of Arab fathers is often unable to fulfill its traditional fathering roles of educating their children and providing for children's needs. Perhaps the biggest change in the conditions fathers face has been the large-scale emigration of Arab fathers to different Arab countries. Estimates of this male population movement are as high as ten million, most of whom are fathers between the ages of 20 and 65. The majority of immigrants go to the six oil-producing Gulf Arab states (Saudi Arabia, Kuwait, Qatar, Bahrain, UAE, and Sultanate of Oman). A smaller number of Arabs have emigrated to the West, especially to the U.S., Canada, Australia, the UK, France, Austria, and Italy (Ahmed, 2003). This mobility has led to improvements in the socioeconomic status of many fathers and their families. But at the same time it has caused social, economic, and cultural problems, and created challenges in their host countries. Changes associated with emigration include (1) conflicts between the value systems of Arab societies, (2) a gradual decline in the family's influence on children, (3) absence of fathers/husbands, and the negative impact of such absence on children's well-being, (4) a drastic increase in the number of mothers/wives who are responsible for their families due to father absence, and (5) the inability of fathers to fulfill their normal roles for the family.

Immigrant fathers often live separated from their families, who remain in their country of origin. As a result, they are unable to supervise their children or have face-to-face contact with their children. Several Arab studies have suggested the negative effects of distant separation by fathers from their families. In fact, these factors were estimated to affect 28% of all Egyptian families (*Al-Ahram*, August 1, 2005). Several studies in Egypt, Jordan, Saudi Arabia, and Kuwait have investigated the impact of the father's mobility on families and children (Ahmed, 2003, 2005a), and also the consequences of immigration from rural villages to urban areas within the same country (Abdel-Hamid 1992). The latter within-country study showed that wives of migrant fathers and husbands increased in their responsibility for both childcare and household chores. Abdel-Hamid further observed a negative impact of separation on children's value systems and on the structure of the family, also associated with father absence due to immigration. Other correlational studies (El-Demerdash, 1976; Abou-elala, 1994; Abdalla, 1992; Abou-el-Khair, 1998) have shown that children of absent fathers were more likely to become aggressive and delinquent. They also suggest that a father's absence has a negative effect on the psychosocial adjustment of both his wife and children, and that when fathers are absent their direct influence on children weakens dramatically. In contrast, Abdel-Hamid's (1992) study showed that in families which moved together from rural to urban areas, fathers became more tolerant toward their children.

The migration of millions of Arab men to the oil-producing Gulf States has also led to considerable changes in Arab societies with regard to conceptions of women's roles and status, especially in rural areas (Ahmed, 2003). As I wrote previously,

> As a result of the absence of fathers stemming from migration, some of the family's functions, including the socialization of children, have been adversely affected. Examples of such negative consequences include increased aggression in children, children's having a poor image of their father, weak father-child relationships, and increased delinquency among the children of migrant fathers.
>
> (Ahmed, 2003, p. 315)

In relation to the family, a sociological study by Abdel-Rahman (1996) on Egyptian immigrants to Saudi Arabia reported that male immigration was associated with lower rates of polygamy compared with that among non-immigrants. In addition, mothers of infants in immigrant families were more likely to rely on nursery servants and maids than non-immigrants mothers. Finally, Abdel-Rahman reported important changes associated with immigration, in the roles of family members and especially the father. Specifically, fathers in immigrant families became increasingly preoccupied with their work, which negatively affected their roles in the family. As a result, relationships and interactions within immigrant families tend to weaken. Overall, we can observe profound effects of immigration on fathers, children, wives, and families.

How is immigration among Arab countries related to social policies and laws? In comparison with policy initiatives in other countries (see chapters on Japan, Scandinavia, and the UK, this volume) we do not have information on actual governmental initiatives to promote fathering or to ameliorate the effects of immigration on fathers and families. Rather, we may view immigration as an Arab policy issue in the sense that governments and oil-producing countries and companies promote policies that allow and encourage fathers to immigrate. Governments and companies therefore have established policies from an economic point of view, which researchers have shown to have negative effects on fathers and families from a psychological point of view. Looking toward the future, I recommend that governmental and corporate policies and priorities consider the impact of immigration on the father's role and on the condition of Arab families.

Sub-Cultural Variations in Fathering

The Arab father's roles in rural and urban areas

El-Mofty (1988) compared perceptions of parental socialization between Egypt's rural and urban areas. Her results demonstrated that encouragement of autonomy remains one of the least important outcomes to Egyptian parents, who saw autonomy as interference in their children's lives. El-Mofty's urban/rural comparisons also indicated that rural fathers interacted more with their children than did urban fathers, likely due to differences in fathers' working conditions in villages and cities. A more recent study (Hashem, 2001) found that urban Egyptian fathers were more likely to psychologically abuse their children than were rural fathers. Hashem also noted that male children (aged 9–12 years) were most likely to perceive physical and psychological abuse from both mothers and fathers, while female children were more subject to paternal neglect. Finally, the older children in his sample were more likely than younger children to

Figure 6.3 An Egyptian father and engineer (age 28). He lives with his wife (a school teacher) and son in a small flat in Giza, near Cairo. They are middle class and have delayed having more children until they can afford the expenses. Photo courtesy of Ramadan Ahmed.

report psychological abuse and neglect by their fathers. Such results often appear in Arab research studies and media reports about perceptions of fathers' behavior, and show the importance of future research to compare urban vs. rural Arab fathers, and to compare fathers with different educational backgrounds and vocational levels associated with urban/rural locations.

Contemporary Social/Economic Conditions That Impact Fathers

Father absence

Father absence was discussed in the previous section in the context of immigration and government/corporate policies, but it also exemplifies the effects of social change in Arab societies. I view father absence as an endemic and growing contemporary problem for Arab societies. Several Arab research studies have focused on correlations between father absence and child measures including the following: children's psychological and social adjustment (Mohammedian, 1996), mental abilities, hostility, and aggression (Abdalla, 1988, 1992), academic achievement (Zaid, 1983), psychological adjustment, self-concept and depression (Dousseki, 1996/1997), gender roles (Ferahat, 1997), childhood problems (Abdel-Razek, 2005), and children's hostility and depression (Al-Mahrab, 2003). Let us next examine a few of these studies.

Mohammedian (1996) observed the negative impact of the father's absence on adolescent children and wives, and similarly Zaid (1983) reported a correlation between father absence and children's problems, with personality development and academic achievement. Specifically, Zaid observed that children of absent or uninvolved fathers had significantly lower levels of academic achievement, compared with children of present or involved fathers. The findings of Abdalla (1992) in Egypt indicated that children whose fathers were absent had significantly higher levels of hostility compared with father-present children. Her results also showed that father absence correlated negatively with children's psychological and mental development, and positively with aggression. If we refer back to the previous section on social policies, the preceding three studies demonstrated the psychological risks associated with emigration and division of families in pursuit of economic goals.

The impact of divorce and father death on children

Divorce

Arab research reports (all in Egypt) have consistently suggested that divorce has a negative effect on children, and the rate of divorce in most Arab countries is increasing rapidly. In a study focused only on father absence following divorce, Abdel-Moety (2004) compared psychological problems (anger, aggression, stealing, escape from home or school, anxiety, and low achievement in school) between samples of 10- to 15-year-old children in divorced vs. non-divorced families. His results revealed that, in families of divorce, children reported significantly higher levels of psychological problems. In these families, children who lived with their fathers after divorce reported fewer psychological problems, compared with children who resided with their divorced mothers. Lastly, according to studies by Moussa (2008), children from divorced families reported higher levels of alienation and maladjustment, compared with children in non-divorced families. Children in Moussa's study who lived with their fathers after the divorce reported lower levels of self-esteem and higher levels of aggression, compared with children who stayed with their mothers. One may explain these findings in economic terms, in that Arab fathers are at an economic advantage over mothers following divorce. In addition, the different parenting styles of fathers and mothers may account for children's different reactions to the custodial parent. For example, it is reported often in Arab research that mothers have more ability to provide the children with love, warmth and kindness, while fathers tend to practice control, strictness, and authoritarian parenting. Meanwhile, custody laws differ among Arab countries, in that fathers in some countries can have custody of their children following a divorce when the children reach age 11, 13, or 15 depending on the country, and the age for paternal custody varies among countries for sons vs. daughters.

The father's death

With regard to the impact of a father's death on children's well-being, Hanin (1987) first found that while the death of a mother affected both male and female children similarly, the father's death tended to have more negative effects on boys than girls. Elsewhere, Abdel-Kader (2000) compared the psychological needs and emotional problems of samples of orphaned vs. normal children between 9 to 12 years of age. His results indicated that orphans reported higher incidences of psychological needs and emotional problems, compared with normal children. Children whose fathers died also reported higher levels of aggression and anti-social tendencies, while children whose mothers died showed significantly higher levels of anxiety, neuroticism and depression. Katami (2006) investigated a sample of working and non-working mothers' boys between 12 to 14 years of age, and her results indicated that boys whose fathers were alive reported greater depth of friendships, than boys whose fathers were dead.

As one might expect, the death of the father is a profound event in the lives of children everywhere; it is truly notable that orphans are not discussed in any other chapter of this volume. From a more comparative perspective, El-Sayed (1996) investigated the impact of father absence due to death, divorce, and working abroad, on 14- to 17-year-old boys' responses to peers' pressure to perform antisocial behavior. Her results showed that father-absent teenage boys, compared with father-present boys, were more likely to succumb to peers' pressure for antisocial behavior. In addition, boys whose fathers were absent due to death, compared with boys whose fathers were absent due to divorce or emigration, were less likely to give in to peer pressure. El-Sayed also noted that boys whose fathers were absent due to work abroad were less likely to conform than those whose fathers were divorced. Finally, when boys' fathers had been absent since before the age of 5, they were also less likely to yield to peer pressure, compared with those whose fathers were absent from the time when they were 5 to 10 years old. A more recent study by Al-Mahrab (2003) in Saudi Arabia examined the impact of father absence due to death, divorce, or imprisonment, on children's hostility and depression. Father-absent children, compared with father-present children, reported higher levels of aggressiveness and depression. Children of divorced or impris- oned fathers, compared with orphaned children, showed the highest lev- els of aggressiveness and depression. Together, El-Sayed's Egyptian and Al-Mahrab's Saudi findings indicate that the age of child and the reason for father absence must both be considered to understand the impact of father absence on Arab children. These data also suggest that a father's death, divorce, and post-divorce custody arrangements all are negatively associated with children's well-being.

Child abuse by fathers (and mothers)

Numerous Arab studies have dealt with child abuse and its connections with parents' social, psychological and demographic variables. It should be mentioned here that in Arab societies abuse often occurs in public and that rates of child abuse in the Arab countries vary widely. In some coun- tries (Iraq, Algeria, and some Arab Gulf countries in Bedouin areas) rates of child abuse are much higher than in countries like Lebanon or Egypt. Child abuse rates also tend to be much higher in rural areas, among less educated parents, and in lower SES Arab families.

Ahmed (1994, cited by Tawifeek, 2003) showed that, for Egyptian children, abuse was typically associated with family deprivation. Abused children, compared with non-abused children in his sample, were also characterized with lower levels of self-esteem and higher levels of depression. Their fathers were found to be more abusive than their mothers, especially among low-SES families. Another Egyptian study (Ismaeel & Tawifeek, 1996, cited by Tawifeek, 2003) revealed a corre- lation between child abuse and the fathers' (and mothers') degree of neuroticism, aggression/hostility, and social isolation. In a related investi- gation, Kamal (1994, cited in Tawifeek, 2003) assessed the characteristics of parents of abused Egyptian children. His data indicated that child abuse occurred more in families with lower educational levels and lower SES, and in families where fathers were alcoholics, drug addicts, or had other psychological disturbances. Similarly, Atelem (2002), in a study of 127 abused and non-abused primary school children and their par- ents, reported that fathers and mothers perceived abused children as less self-actualized or happy compared with non-abused children. These fathers of abused children also reported higher levels of job pressures, feelings of failure, and strain in marital relations, and lower levels of self-esteem or sense of personal responsibility for their children's psychosocial problems. Finally, a Yemeni study on the impact of parental abuse on juvenile delin- quency (Saeed, 2008) showed that fathers tended more than mothers to physically abuse both their delinquent and non-delinquent children.

Summary

The impact on children of father absence due to immigration, divorce, and the father's death, and the impact of fathers' abuse on children, are all current and growing areas of concern among Arab families. Although immigration by fathers to oil-producing countries benefits families financially, it has been associated with problems for children and families. Divorce and father absence are mentioned in almost every chapter of this volume, and in Arab societies they are growing problems associated generally with negative outcomes for fathers, mothers, and children. But it is further likely that in Arab societies, many of which experience violence, conflict and even war directly at a level unknown to families from most other countries represented in this volume, the untimely death of a father may be a more common occurrence than it is elsewhere.

General Comments on Research on Arab Fathers

Arab investigations of the paternal role and fathering date back to the early 1970s. Since that time, a great number of Arab studies on the father's roles and fathering have been conducted, but many of these studies have reported on master's thesis research or doctoral dissertation studies. Only a handful of studies have been carried out in countries such as Saudi Arabia, Kuwait, Jordan, Yemen, Qatar, and Bahrain, even fewer studies of fathers can be found from countries such as Syria, Lebanon, the United Arab Emirates or Algeria. To my knowledge, no fathering research has been conducted to date in Morocco, Tunisia, Sudan, Mauritania, Somalia, Djibouti, or Comoros. This severely limits generalizations that can be made from the literature reviewed here, and there are some gaping omissions in the geographic representation of the Arab world in this chapter. For example, almost 70% of the work cited in this chapter has come from Egypt, which comprises less than 30% of the overall population of the Arab world. There are also important variations among Arab societies in the cultural, social, economic, and political contexts of fathering, which I would expect to account for diversity in fathering behavior across the Arab world. One other limitation of the research literature on Arab fathers and fathering, which is also characteristic of fathering research in many cultures outside the Arab world, is that research on fathers continue to rely on measures of children's and mothers' perceptions of parental behavior rather than on direct studies of fathers.

In my opinion, at this point in history fathers in countries such as Egypt, Lebanon, and to a lesser extent in countries like Kuwait, are becoming more flexible with their roles and their children compared to fathers in countries such as Iraq, Yemen, Saudi Arabia, Libya, or the Sudan. I would also suggest that urban fathers are more flexible, compared with Bedouin (i.e., nomadic or desert dwelling) or rural Arab fathers. These and other general statements, often based on anecdotal evidence, must be understood as educated guesses to be tested in the next generation of research on Arab fathers.

Speculation and Predictions for the Future

To conclude this chapter, I will make some general observations about future prospects for the father's role in Arab societies. First, I believe that the father's roles and fatherhood in many Arab societies have changed in a negative direction over the past few decades, due to dramatic socio-cultural, economic, and political changes, on top of transformations that occurred during the second half of the twentieth century. These changes also had a negative impact on the structure of Arab families. In my view, Arab fathers face a difficult dilemma in that they want to behave according to their beliefs, but they cannot do so because of economic hardships. They also face a conflict between their traditions, beliefs, and customs, and the demands of modernization in the era of globalization. In other words, the realities of a changing new world present challenges for the Arab father's role. For example, in recent years father absence, due to the necessity of emigration to other countries by millions of Arab fathers, has weakened father–child relations. Relocation of families from rural to urban settings, and from countries such as Egypt, Sudan, Jordan, Algeria, Tunisia, and Yemen to wealthy Arab countries such as the six Arab oil-producing Gulf states, has led to significant ongoing conflicts between value systems and in the socialization practices used in immigrant families.

Looking forward, it is widely discussed and anticipated (based on my readings of Arab newspapers over the past few years) that the recent uprisings in the Arab world (the 'Arab Spring') in countries such as Tunisia, Egypt, Libya, Syria, Yemen and elsewhere have the potential to positively alter the entire process of socialization of Arab children, including the father–child relationship. There are some expectations among both professionals and the general public that Arab fathers, because of the role of young people in launching these uprisings, will become more democratic and more tolerant toward their children and more appreciative of the younger generation for its accomplishments. I should also note that the population of most Arab societies is very young, and that the large younger generation is most likely to be the source of social change. Finally, in my opinion, future generations of Arab fathers are likely to become more authoritative and more permissive with their offspring, with no differentiation or discrimination between boys and girls. Based on my years of research on Arab families and fathers, I am becoming guardedly optimistic about the future of fathering in Arab societies.

Summary

This chapter dealt with fathers and fatherhood in the Arab world. It shed light on cultural and historical background, and on the changing cultural contexts of Arab families. It also discussed the issues of power and prestige in the Arab families, which are no longer automatically ascribed to the father. A review of Arab psychological research on fathering, most of which has been conducted in Egypt, focused mainly on children's perceptions and images of fathers and authorities. A description of fathers' apparent influences on child development included the perceptions of fathers' behavior as associated with children's characteristics, adjustment, cognitive development, behavioral problems, aggression, and bullying. Social policy issues related to fathering centered mainly on the phenomenon of Arab fathers' emigration to oil-producing nations and the impact of father absence on their children and families. This review also considered father absence in relation to the impact of divorce and the father's untimely death on children. The main concern of sub-cultural variations in Arab fathering was in comparing fathers between rural vs. urban settings. Finally, the chapter examined the impact of child abuse by fathers and mothers. Although much of the chapter emphasized negative contexts and trends, I concluded that there is reason for hope in looking toward the future of Arab fathering.

References

Abdalla, J. G. (1988). *The impact of father absence in the stage of early childhood on the children's psychological and mental development.* Unpublished doctoral dissertation, Ain Shams University, Cairo, Egypt (in Arabic).

Abdalla, J. G. (1992). Hostility as a function of father absence. *Psychological Studies* (Egypt), 2 (2), 351–369.

Abdel-Ghany, S. N. (1983). *Aggressive personality and its relation with socialization.* Unpublished master's thesis, Faculty of Arts, Ain Shams University, Cairo, Egypt (in Arabic).

Abdel-Hamid, M. I. (1992). *The relation between immigration from rural to urban areas and changes in socialization of children.* Unpublished master's thesis, Ain Shams University, Cairo, Egypt (in Arabic).

Abdel-Kader, A. A. (2000). A comparative study on psychological needs and emotional problems in a sample of orphan and normal children in late childhood. *Journal of the Faculty of Education, Zagazig University* (Egypt), 34, 259–320 (in Arabic).

Abdel-Moety, H. M. (2004). Psychological problems in divorced families' children. In H. M. Abdel-Moety (Ed.), *Family climate and children's personality* (pp. 295–326), Cairo, Egypt: Dar el-Qahara (in Arabic).

Abdel-Rahman, M. E. H. (1996). *Social interaction between Egypt and Arab Gulf Arab societies: A study of culture and society.* Alexandria, Egypt: Dar el-Maarifah al-Gammeiah (in Arabic).

Abdel-Razek, E. A. M. (2005). Perception of fathers' psychological absence and children's problems. *Proceedings of the 12th Annual Conference of Counseling Centre* (pp. 263–343), Ain Shams University, Cairo, Egypt, December 25–27, 2005 (in Arabic).

Abdel-Salam, S. A. (2005). Patterns of communication with parents in relation to family adjustment and latent delinquency in male and female adolescents. *Journal of the Faculty of Education, Ain Shams University* (Egypt), *29* (Part 4), 183–256 (in Arabic).

Abdouh, A. A. E. (2000). The psychological dimensions of father's image in Heroin addicts in Saudi Arabia. *Journal of Psychology* (Egypt), *14*, 140–160 (in Arabic).

Abou-el-Kheir, M. M. S. (1998). Perceived father figure image and self-esteem among college students. *Psychological Studies* (Egypt), *8*, 419–453 (in Arabic).

Abou-elala, M. A. M. (1994). *Father absence in relation to the psychosocial adjustment of mothers (wives) and adolescent children.* Unpublished master's thesis, Institute for Higher Studies, Ain Shams University, Cairo, Egypt (in Arabic).

Abou-Maraq, J. Z. (1997). A study of parental pressures in relation to aggressive behavior in preschool children. *Education, Faculty of Education, Al-Azhar University* (Egypt), *66*, 167–195 (in Arabic).

Ahmed, R. A. (2003). Egyptian migrations. In L. L. Adler &U. P. Gielen (Eds.), *Migration, immigration and emigration in international perspective* (pp. 311–327). Westport, CT: Praeger.

Ahmed, R. A. (2005a). Manifestations of violence in Arab schools and procedures for reducing it. In F. L. Denmark, H. H. Krauss, R. W. Wesner, E. Midlarsky, & U. P. Gielen (Eds.), *Violence in schools: Cross-national and cross-cultural perspectives* (pp. 207–236), New York, NY: Springer.

Ahmed, R. A. (2005b). Egyptian families. In J. L. Roopnarine & U. P. Gielen (Eds.), *Families in global perspective* (pp. 151–168). Boston, MA: Pearson.

Ahmed, R. A. (2008). Review of Arab research on parental acceptance-rejection. *Proceedings of the 1st International Congress of the International Society for Interpersonal Acceptance and Rejection* (pp. 201–224), Istanbul, Turkey, July 3–6, 2006, Istanbul, Turkey: Turkish Psychology Association.

Ahmed, R. A. (2010). North Africa and Middle East. In M. H. Bornstein (Ed.), *Handbook of cultural developmental science* (pp. 359–381). New York, NY: Psychology Press.

Ahmed, R. A., & Gielen, U. P. (2008, July). *Age and sex differences in perception of parental acceptance-rejection in the Arab countries.* Paper presented at the 2nd International Congress of the International Society for Interpersonal Acceptance and Rejection, University of Crete, Rethymno, Crete, Greece, July 3–6, 2008.

Ahmed, R. A., Rohner, R. P., & Carrasco, M. A. (2012). Relations between psychological adjustment and perceived parental, sibling, best friend, and teacher acceptance among Kuwaiti adolescents. *Proceedings of the 3rd International Congress of the International Society for Interpersonal Acceptance and Rejection.* University of Padua, Padua, Italy, July 29–31, 2010. Manuscript submitted for publication.

Al-Ahram (2005). *An Egyptian daily newspaper.* August 1, 2005 (in Arabic).

Al-Khouly, H. A. (2004). Prediction of bullying behavior/victim through some negative parental treatments in a sample of adolescents. *Proceedings of the 11th Annual Conference of Counseling Centre* (Vol. 1, pp. 333–380), Ain Shams University, Cairo, Egypt, December 25–27, 2004 (in Arabic).

Al-Mahrab, N. Ben Ibrahim (2003). Parents' absence, hostility and depression symptoms: The impact of parents' absence, its size, forms, and reasons. *Faculty of Arts Journal, Menoufia University* (Egypt), 52, 309–362 (in Arabic).

Al-Musslem, B. Kh. (2001). The impact of parent-children relationship on juvenile delinquency: A field study. *Journal of Social Sciences* (Kuwait), 29, 71–105 (in Arabic).

Al-Nefie, A. A. (1997). The relationship between styles of parental treatment and locus of control in a sample of male and female students at Umm el-Qura University, Mecca, Saudi Arabia, *Journal of the Faculty of Education, Al-Azhar University* (Egypt), 66, 281–314 (in Arabic).

Al-Qabas (2007). *A Kuwaiti daily newspaper.* November 30, 2007 (in Arabic).

Al-Reguieb, Y. A. F. (1996). *Parental warmth and its relation to personality traits and creativity in a sample of primary school children in Kuwait and Egypt.* Unpublished doctoral dissertation, Minia University, Minia, Egypt (in Arabic).

Ali, E. A. E. (1992). *Parental acceptance/rejection and its relation to depression symptoms in adolescents.* Unpublished master's thesis, Ain Shams University, Cairo, Egypt (in Arabic).

Allam, S. Y. H. (1993). *Father's image in convicted prisoners' non-delinquent children, in relation to children' psychological structure.* Unpublished doctoral dissertation, AinShams University, Cairo, Egypt (in Arabic).

Atelem, A. A. H. (2002). Exploring personality (cognitive and non-cognitive) aspects in a sample of preschool abused children. *Journal of the Faculty of Education, Mansoura University* (Egypt), 50, 379–431 (in Arabic).

Bedair, K. (1995). Children's curiosity in relation to families' socialization styles. In K. Bedair (Ed.), *Studies and research on Egyptian childhood* (pp. 5–103). Cairo, Egypt: Alem el-Fikr (in Arabic).

Dousseki, R. M. H. (1996/7). Father deprivation in relation to university students' psychological adjustment, self-concept, and depression: A comparative study. *Journal of Psychology* (Egypt), 11, 18–49 (in Arabic).

El-Demerdash, I. (1976). *Self-concept in father-deprived children.* Unpublished master's thesis, Ain Shams University, Cairo, Egypt (in Arabic).

El-Dousseki, M. M. S. (1981). *A study of styles of parental treatment in relation to children's aggression and personal adjustment.* Unpublished master's thesis, Al-Azhar University, Egypt (in Arabic).

El-Mofty, M. A. (1988). A comparative study of socialization in Egypt's rural and urban areas. *Proceedings of the 4th Annual Conference of Psychology in Egypt* (pp. 489–522), Egyptian Association of Psychological Studies, Cairo, January 25–27,1988 (in Arabic).

El-Sayed, N. A. A. (1996). Adolescent's responses to peer's pressures to perform antisocial behavior in relation to the father's absence. *Proceedings of the 3rd Annual Conference of Counseling Centre* (Vol. 2, pp. 1056–1083), Ain Shams University, Cairo, Egypt, December 25–27, 1996 (in Arabic).

Ferahat, E. M. (1997). Father absence and its impact on the sexual role in children. *Proceedings of the 4th Annual Conference of Counseling Centre* (Vol. 2, pp. 865–908), Ain Shams University, Cairo, Egypt, December 2–4, 1997 (in Arabic).

Hamza, J. M. (2002). Father's image and self-esteem in secondary school students. *Journal of Psychology* (Egypt), *16*, 172–189 (in Arabic).

Hanin, R. A. (1987). Orphanhood and its impact on the adolescent's mood state and parental image. *Journal of Psychology* (Egypt), *1*, 38–47 (in Arabic).

Hashem, S. M. M. (2001). A study of determinants of parental child maltreatment. *Faculty of Arts Journal, Menoufia University* (Egypt), *44*, 249–307 (in Arabic).

Ibrahim, M. A. (2010, July). *Effects of parents' power and prestige on children's psychological adjustment.* Paper presented at the 3rd International Congress on Interpersonal Acceptance and Rejection, International Society for Interpersonal Acceptance and Rejection, University of Padua, Italy, July 28–31, 2010.

Ibrahim, Z. M. (1993). *Authority's image among adolescents.* Unpublished master's thesis, Faculty of Arts, Ain Shams University, Cairo, Egypt (in Arabic).

Ismaeel, A. E. M. (2001). Differences between family-deprived and non-deprived in child's abuse and personality variables among Saudi intermediate school students. *Psychological Studies* (Egypt), *11*, 266–297 (in Arabic).

Katami, N. (2006). Children's friendship of working mothers in Amman City and its relationship to some variables. *Journal of Arab Children* (Kuwait), *6*, 26–45 (in Arabic).

Khaleefa, B. M. (2003). Children's perception of parental acceptance-rejection in relation to late childhood problems in a sample of primary school male and female children in the State of Qatar. *Proceedings of the 10th Annual Conference of Counseling Centre "Counseling and Challenges of Development: The population Problem"* (Vol. 1, pp. 68–129), Counseling Centre, Ain Shams University, Cairo, Egypt, December 13, 2003 (in Arabic)

Mansour, M. E. I. (2011). Parental styles as predictors of behavioral problems among Bahraini children. *Psychological Studies* (Egypt), *21*, 99–135 (in Arabic).

Mohammedian, H. M. M. (1996). *Father absence in relation to the psychosocial adjustment of wives/mothers and adolescent children.* Unpublished master's thesis, Ain Shams University, Cairo, Egypt (in Arabic).

Morsy, K. I. (1986). The relationship between adjustment problems (AP) in adolescence and parent–child relations as perceived in childhood (PCR). *The Educational Journal* (Kuwait), *3*, 102–133 (in Arabic).

Moussa, R. A. (2008). *Psychology of the family.* Cairo, Egypt: Alam al-Kotob (in Arabic).

Omar, A. A. M. (2002). The impact of parents' counseling on reducing aggressive behavior and improving adjustment levels in abused children. *Faculty of Education Journal, Tanta University* (Egypt), *1*, 157–190 (in Arabic).

Saeed, F. H. F. (2008). The impact of child abuse on juvenile delinquency. *Journal of Arab Children* (Kuwait), *9*, 8–31 (in Arabic).

Safwat, A., & El-Dousseki, M. L. (1993). Contribution of Egyptian psychological research to the study of prejudice. *Psychological Studies* (Egypt), *3*, 429–477 (in Arabic).

Sanders, J. L. (1986). Egyptian and American university students' attitudes toward parents and family. *Journal of Social Psychology, 126,* 459–463.

Simadi, F. A., Fatayer, J. A., & Athamneh, S. (2003). The Arabian family in the light of Minuchin's Systematic Theory: An analytical approach. *Social Behavior and Personality. 31*, 467–482.

Tawifeek, T. A. (2003). The relationship between child abuse and psychosocial variables. *Journal on Arab Children* (Kuwait), *4*, 9–35 (in Arabic).

Zaid, A. M. M. (1999). *Parental treatment in relation to social development among intermediate school male and female students.* Unpublished master's thesis, Ain Shams University, Cairo, Egypt (in Arabic).

Zaid, M. (1983). Father absence and its impact on children personality development. *Al-Baheth* [The Researcher] (Lebanon), *5*, 85–91 (in Arabic).

Part Three

Africa

Chapter Seven

Fathering in Central and East Africa

Cultural and Adaptationist Perspectives in Small-Scale Societies

Hillary N. Fouts
University of Tennessee, Knoxville, TN, USA

Case Story: Fathering and Grandfathering – Care, Comfort, and Affection

Ba'win is an elderly Bofi forager Nganga (traditional healer), father, and grandfather. He has been married three times; his first and third wives are deceased and he remains with his second wife, Dekay. He had 6 children with his first wife, with only one surviving adolescent girl who now lives in a nearby community with her deceased mother's kin. He had only one child with his third wife, a 4-year-old girl who lives in another community about 20 miles away, also with her deceased mother's kin. He has had 8 children with Dekay, four of whom are living, two who died as infants, and two who were born prematurely and died at birth. Three of their children live with them, two adolescent boys and their 3-year-old daughter. Their adult daughter (early 20s) lives next door to them with her husband, who is still performing bride-service, i.e., service to in-laws.

Ba'win is considered fairly unique in this relatively egalitarian Bofi forager community for several reasons. First, he is the only nganga in his small community of approximately 300 people, and is thought to have supernatural capabilities that can both heal and harm people. Second, he is one of the last living of the older generation of his patrilineal clan, i.e., kin group of his father's lineage, in which he and his two elderly sisters remain. Many children in Ba'win's camp are named after his deceased brothers and sisters.

Ba'win has no living brothers and has encountered considerable loss in his life, experiencing the death of nine children and two wives. Even given the Bofi forager child mortality rates of approximately 41%, his loss is still considerably above average for his community. His age and experiences are apparent in his late 60s, and he talks about pain and difficulties in walking and moving. He now rarely participates in net-hunting, and occasionally goes to the forest with his wife to gather supplies for his healing practice.

On most days, Ba'win is in camp and provides healing for clients or care for his youngest child and grandchild. His youngest daughter, Kasey, is 3 years old and his grandson, Lee, is 18 months old. During one of my four-hour focal child observations of Lee, Ba'win was the primary care provider even when Lee's grandmother and aunts were present. Lee sat near or on Ba'win's lap most of the afternoon that I observed. Ba'win was not Lee's play-partner, but instead he held him when Lee climbed into his lap, and cuddled and patted Lee when he cried. They rarely spoke to each other, but Lee's attachment to Ba'win was clear. At one point in the observation a sudden rainstorm started and Lee ran straight to Ba'win rather than to his grandmother or aunt (his parents were in the forest).

Ba'win's style of fathering and grandfathering exemplified what I typically observed among Bofi and Aka forager men who were involved with their children: they spent most of their time with children just being available and provided responsive comfort, care, and affection when their children expressed need or initiated contact with them. The photos in Figures 7.1 and 7.2 depict Aka fathers in the Congo spending time in close proximity (Figure 7.1) and providing care and comfort (Figure 7.2) to their young children.

Fathers in Central and East Africa

Central and East Africa represent a very large area of sub-Saharan Africa, spanning from the Central African Republic and Republic of Congo in the West to the Eastern Coast of Africa. Central and East Africa are typically considered to be distinct regions, and within each region there is tremendous cultural and linguistic diversity. Even though this is a large and diverse area, there have been relatively few studies that focused specifically on fathers in these regions, and most studies that had fathers as a primary or secondary focus have taken place in the Central African Republic, Republic of Congo, Democratic Republic of Congo, Kenya, and Tanzania. This review of fathering therefore does not represent the entire region, nor does it depict every cultural group or context within these regions. Instead it represents the relatively small sample of cultures and contexts in which fathering has been studied.

Descriptions of fathers in Central and East Africa have appeared in various types of studies, some of which focused specifically on understanding fathering, while other descriptions of fathering were within

Figure 7.1 Aka forager father in his late 20s (center) with his 4-year-old daughter (right) and brother (left) in a semi-permanent camp in a clearing in the Congo Basin tropical rainforest (Republic of Congo). While the young girl's mother is in the forest, this father provides care and comfort to his daughter by just being available and responsive when his daughter shows need. Photo courtesy of Hillary N. Fouts.

ethnographic studies with broader foci on aspects of communities, families, and children. The majority of data on fathering in Central or East Africa come from rural areas among hunter-gatherer (a.k.a., forager), farming, and pastoral communities. Fathering in urban areas of these regions has not been extensively studied, but brief depictions of urban fathers have been included in some studies focused on urban–rural migration, HIV/AIDS orphans, and programs for families affected by HIV/AIDS (for a review, see Hosegood & Madhavan, 2010).

Fathering research in this region has usually sought to understand the nature of fatherhood from cultural and adaptationist perspectives, examining individual and cultural variation in fathers' investment and involvement with children (e.g., Harkness & Super, 1992; Hewlett, 1991; Marlowe, 1999a). "Investment" is typically defined as one's overall contribution to

Figure 7.2 Aka forager father in his mid-20s holding his 5-year-old son in a semi-permanent camp in a clearing in the Congo Basin tropical rainforest (Republic of Congo). This photo was taken after the young boy ran to his father to be comforted, after having a conflict with another child over some roasted palm nuts. The father quietly comforts his son through physical patting and holding, exemplifying the availability and responsiveness that typifies Aka fathering. Photo courtesy of Hillary N. Fouts.

children's survival and life chances or opportunities, and may include fathers' activities that lead to the accumulation of resources for their family, and various contributions to subsistence, provisioning of children, and to children's education and inheritance of wealth. "Involvement" is usually defined as fathers' direct interactions with children, including social, emotional, and caregiving-related interactions. Cultural perspectives tend to emphasize how fathering patterns are related to knowledge and practices shared by social groups, i.e., cultures. Thus, a cultural perspective assumes that language, cultural models, and foundational schema (i.e., core beliefs shared by groups; see Shore, 1996) influence patterns of fathering. In contrast, adaptationist perspectives focus on the biological, reproductive, and

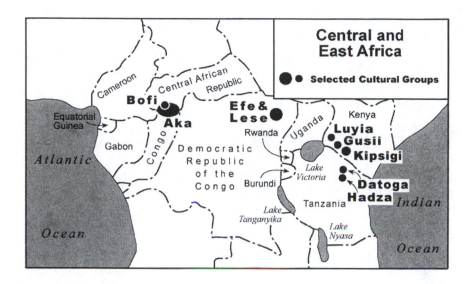

Figure 7.3 Map of Central and East Africa, courtesy of Paul R. Larson.

survival consequences of fathering as well as the biological or evolutionary bases of fathering. Adaptationist perspectives thereby assume that fathering patterns were adapted or are adapting to particular environmental conditions, such as social, economic, and demographic constraints.

Hrdy (2009) sums up patterns of human and non-human primate fathering by noting that human fathering "is extremely facultative – that is, situation-dependent and expressed only under certain conditions. This generalization holds true whether we consider provisioning or the observable intimacies between father and child" (p. 161). Thus, it is no surprise that among Central and East African fathers there is considerable inter- and intra-cultural variation in fathering. Furthermore, many scholars have recognized that foraging peoples tend to have greater father involvement than farming, pastoral, or postindustrial societies (Gray & Anderson, 2010; Hewlett, 1991; Hrdy, 2009; Marlowe, 2000). Likewise, scholars have noted generally higher rates of father involvement among foragers than other groups, and have also cited evidence that men are physiologically affected by being near or providing care to their infants, which is similar to other mammals that have substantial male-care. These two findings led to the conclusion that fathering or male-care was a significant part of the evolution of our species (e.g., Gray & Anderson, 2010; Hewlett, 1991; Hrdy, 2009). Given the presence of foraging, farming, pastoral, and urban peoples in Central and East Africa, fathering research in this region contributes not only to an understanding of the evolution of fathering, but also of adaptations that characterize fathering in various cultural and ecological contexts.

Cultural Background as It Influences Fathering in Central and East Africa

In this chapter I rely on a broad definition of culture as an integrated set of knowledge (e.g., ideology) and practices (i.e., behaviors) that are shared by social groups and transmitted socially. Thus, in examining fatherhood I consider both patterns of fathering (i.e., behaviors) and conceptualizations of fathers (i.e., beliefs and ideas about fatherhood).

Foraging communities

As previously mentioned, cross-cultural studies of small-scale societies have shown that fathers in hunter-gatherer (a.k.a., forager) communities tend to be more involved with children than in farming or agropastoral (i.e., farming and cattle) or pastoral communities (Hewlett, 1991; Katz & Konner, 1981; Marlowe, 2000). Hewlett and Macfarlan (2010) concluded that there is a general set of integrated cultural characteristics of communities with high father involvement, and that these characteristics are typical among foragers. These cultural characteristics include the following: low population densities, females contributing at least to 50% of the calories of family diets, low or no accumulation of material resources or property, matrilocality (i.e., couples living with or near wife's kin group) or flexible post-marriage residence, low rates of polygyny, infrequent warfare, and husband–wife cooperation in subsistence and social activities. Using data from the Standard Cross-Cultural Sample (SCCS), Marlowe (2000) confirmed that foraging peoples show the highest level of father involvement, followed by horticultural (i.e., simple hoe agriculture) communities, with the lowest rates among pastoral and agricultural (i.e., intensive agriculture, plows and irrigation) communities. Marlowe noted that when fathers have the lowest involvement, they show investment in families through efforts to maintain or increase control over resources and wealth (e.g., land or cattle) that are crucial for survival. Even though these studies focused on global samples, Central and East African populations fall within these described patterns. Table 7.1 highlights differences in father involvement among foragers and farmers in Central and East Africa, and shows that foragers tend to exhibit much higher father involvement than farming communities. Pastoral and agropastoralist communities were not included in the table due to limited data on direct involvement. Despite these differences between foragers and farmers, Table 7.1 also demonstrates that there is considerable variation in father involvement among forager groups.

Hewlett (1991) conducted the first focused study of fatherhood among hunter-gatherers. He looked specifically at Aka fathers' involvement with infants, and questioned Western conceptions of fatherhood by showing that Aka fathers had a much more intimate role in infant care than fathers in the U.S. Fathering among forager groups has also been contrasted with fathering in industrialized Western cultures (Hewlett, 1991; Morelli & Tronick, 1992), showing that while father–child play has been a major

Table 7.1 Cross-Cultural Variation in Father Involvement: Holding and Carrying Infants and Children in Central and East Africa*

Population	Nation, Ecology	Subsistence Type	Age of Children[a]	Father Holding[b]	Source
Aka	Central African Republic, tropical forest	Foraging (nethunting)	1–4 8–12 13–18	22.0 11.2 14.3	Hewlett, 1991
Aka	Republic of Congo, tropical forest	Foraging (nethunting)	18–35 36–47 48–59	5.6 3.1 4.0	Fouts, 2008
Bofi	Central African Republic, tropical forest	Foraging (nethunting)	18–35 36–47 48–59	1.9 5.4 5.4	Fouts, 2008
Efe	Democratic Republic of Congo, tropical forest	Foraging (bow hunting)	1–4	2.6	Winn, Morelli, & Tronick, 1990
Hadza	Tanzania, savanna	Foraging (bow hunting)	0–9	2.5	Marlowe, 1999
Bofi	Central African Republic, tropical forest	Farming	18–35 36–47 48–59	1.16 0.0 0.0	Fouts, 2008
Logoli	Kenya, savanna	Farming	3–18	0.0	Munroe & Munroe, 1992

Notes:

a In months.

b Percentage of total holding by fathers that was observed either in a camp or village setting.

* Partially adapted from Hewlett (1991) and Fouts (2008).

theme in descriptions of Western fathering (Paquette, 2004; Yogman, 1982) forager fathers rarely play with infants or children (Fouts, 2008; Hewlett, 1991; Morelli & Tronick, 1992). Noting that play is rare among Aka forager fathers, Hewlett describes Aka fathering as "characterized by its intimate, affectionate, help-out nature" (1991, p. 168).

Even though cross-cultural analyses indicate that Central and East African forager fathers tend to be more involved in direct social engagement and care of infants and children than farmers and pastoralists (Marlowe, 2000), there are variations between forager groups with respect to the quality and quantity of father involvement. Hewlett's (1991) study of father involvement among Aka foragers in the Central African Republic with infants depicts the highest levels of involvement reported in any society in the world. For example, while observed in camps, Aka fathers were within an arm's reach of their infants for more than 50% of a 24-hour time period and held their infants for 22% of daylight hours. In all contexts in and out of camp, Aka fathers held their infants for 8.7% of daylight hours (Hewlett, 1991). Lower levels of involvement have been reported among other forager groups. From observations of Hadza forager fathers in Tanzania, Marlowe (1999a) found that Hadza fathers held infants (9 months and younger) 2.5% of daylight hours. Furthermore, Morelli and Tronick (1992) noted that Efe forager men and boys jointly spent more time with 1-year-old infants in camp than did fathers. In my own observations of young children (18 months to 4 years of age) in Aka forager communities in the northern Republic of Congo and in Bofi forager communities of Central African Republic, Bofi 3- and 4-year-old children were held by fathers 5.4% of observations while Aka 3- and 4-year-olds were held by fathers between 3% and 4% of observed time between 6 am and 6 pm.

In addition to studies focused on forager populations and intra-cultural variation in fathering, Morelli and Tronick (1992) compared the father involvement with 1-year-olds between the Lese farmers (slash-and-burn horticulturalists) and the Efe foragers (semi-nomadic hunter-gatherers).The Lese and Efe are sympatric communities (i.e., adjoining and somewhat overlapping) in the Ituri Forest of the Congo Basin Rainforest (northeastern Democratic Republic of Congo). As expected, Efe infants were in proximity (within 3 meters) of fathers, other men, and boys far more (i.e., higher proportions of one-hour observations on six different days) than were Lese infants. Specifically, Efe fathers were in proximity to infants in 40% of observations, compared to only 15% for Lese fathers and infants. Of the times in which fathers were in proximity to infants, Lese fathers spent more time playing (18% of time together) than did Efe fathers (7% of time together). Looking broadly at active social engagement with infants (care, holding, playing, and sharing resources), Morelli and Tronick found that Efe fathers were twice as engaged with infants as Lese fathers. However, in both groups mothers and young boys had higher engagement rates than fathers.

Hewlett (1991) has suggested that the high levels of Aka father involvement with infants are supported by the Aka foundational schema of egalitarianism. Particularly, maintenance of gender egalitarianism, through status leveling and extensive sharing in the community, promotes husband–wife daily cooperation in subsistence activities and likewise husband–wife cooperation in childcare. My research, focused on young children rather than infants, in Bofi and Aka forager communities, also supports this point. Specifically, I have observed that Bofi and Aka foragers have relatively high rates of father involvement, value and maintain egalitarianism, and also show similar patterns of husband–wife cooperation in subsistence and childcare (Fouts, 2008). In fact, the Aka and Bofi forager pattern of net-hunting is quite distinct from other Central and East African foragers like the Efe and Hadza who primarily hunt with bows, which seems to facilitate husband–wife cooperation in childcare and subsistence. In each of these foraging groups, husbands and wives both contribute to the family diet, but Aka and Bofi foragers are somewhat unique in that men, women, and children are involved together in net-hunting and gathering. This daily cooperative work also provides a context in which infants are near both parents throughout the day (Hewlett, 1991).

Pastoral, agropastoral, and farming communities

In some of the most extensive observations of children in agropastoral groups, including studies of the Gusii (e.g., LeVine et al., 1996) and the Kipsigis (e.g., Harkness & Super, 1992), father involvement was so rare that scores for holding or carrying were not provided. However, LeVine and colleagues (1996) presented scores for Gusii father–child proximity that were exceedingly low; adult men (including fathers) were the least likely individual to be observed within 5 feet of infants (0–30 months), and presumably holding and carrying was thus similarly rare. Likewise, Harkness and Super (1992) noted that it was rare in the first year of life for Kipsigis fathers to hold infants, and that fathers never carried their infants. For 2- to 3-year-old children, Harkness and Super reported that Kipsigis fathers only occasionally held their infants and rarely carried them.

Most societal characteristics associated with high father involvement, aside from low population densities, are essentially cultural practices i.e., behaviors. These include marriage patterns, husband–wife cooperation, residential patterns, women's work, and lack of material accumulation. Because culture is an integrated set of beliefs and practices, these practices are intertwined with community beliefs and knowledge. LeVine (1980) reported that among the agropastoral Gusii of southwestern Kenya men viewed their role in the family as that of "investors and supervisors of a domestic economy" (p. 102). In these communities, children and wives were the main workers and it was the father's role to protect and expand the family's material resources (e.g., cattle and land) and to reproduce (maximizing the number of offspring). These attributes certainly affect the lives of children but do not support men's active involvement in the direct care of children. Rather, they lead to other forms of investment in children such as resources and wealth. LeVine and his colleagues (1996) discussed how fatherhood is defined socially among the Gusii, who consider biological offspring important but also believe that offspring of any kind represent wealth. For example, "ghost marriages" in which a widow bears children for her deceased husband, or "woman marriages" in which a postmenopausal widow marries a woman to bear sons for the widow's deceased husband, are attempts to increase the father's and his family's wealth. Thus, the cultural meaning of fatherhood with reference to bearing children and thereby promoting wealth and resources for his family, outlives the life cycle of individual fathers. The idea of the father as protector among the Gusii extends beyond wealth. Gusii fathers are also expected to protect children by controlling conflict between their co-wives and the co-wives of their sons. Thus, even though Gusii men were not involved in the direct care of children and were rarely in proximity to their young or infant children, they had a supervisory role in the family system meant to protect children by leveling conflict and maintaining or increasing material resources for the family. LeVine et al. (1996) noted that although containment of conflict between co-wives is meant to protect children, it also fosters resentment toward elder patriarchs and their sons, which in turn results in limited cooperation between co-wives in childcare.

As with the Gusii, Weisner (1997) described how "potency" is a major theme of Abaluyia (i.e., Luyia, Western Kenya) men's life goals. Potency is defined by number of children in combination with the power and longevity of a man's economic and reproductive career. Like the Gusii, Abaluyia fathers emphasize their abilities as protectors and investors, with economic and kin resources intertwined. Furthermore, Weisner observed that the emphasis on accumulation (economic and growth of kin group) led many Abaluyia men to incur substantial risks when they migrated in search of work to support their families and children's education.

Harkness and Super (1992) reported that Kipsigis farmer fathers in Western Kenya were often present with their infants and children, but rarely provided direct care (carrying, holding, dressing, feeding, or bathing). Instead, these fathers' most common form of interaction with their toddlers was verbal discipline. Like the Gusii and Abaluyia, Kipsigis fathers also described their role as fathers in economic terms, and emphasized providing food and clothing, school fees and medical costs for their children.

Also as with the other western Kenyan populations, Kipsigis fathers viewed themselves as family authority figures and valued children's obedience.

Adaptationist perspectives on fathering in Central and East Africa

There is clearly considerable intra- and inter-cultural variation in father-hood roles and fathers' direct involvement with infants and children in Central and East Africa. Most studies that have sought to predict intra- and inter-cultural variation in father investment or involvement with infants or children have adopted an adaptationist perspective. Some have examined how fathering patterns promote reproduction or survival of off-spring, or balance tradeoffs between parenting and reproductive efforts. For example, Katz and Konner (1981) proposed that close husband–wife relations, relatively equal husband–wife contributions to subsistence, and monogamy were all related to high levels of paternal involvement. According to their analysis, when women contribute greatly to subsist-ence they are likely to need help in childcare, and that under these circum-stances fathers as well as grandparents and siblings are likely to provide substantial care to infants and children. They further explained that when wealth accumulation is low and spousal relations are close, cooperation between the husband and wife was facilitated. This is consistent with findings from Marlowe's (2000) cross-cultural survey of father involve-ment, which included Central and East Africa fathers and indicated that the degree of polygyny in populations is associated with lower paternal investment in children.

Likewise, Hewlett (1991) showed that kin resources influenced Aka father involvement, as Aka men with fewer brothers provided less care to infants than did Aka men with more brothers. He explained that the number of brothers was an effective proxy for kin resources because brothers are the core of Aka patriclans and are also the foundation for net-hunting groups. Larger patriclans (i.e., more brothers) typically con-duct larger net-hunts for bigger game, and thus fathers with more broth-ers tend to have more material resources and higher status than fathers with fewer brothers. Hewlett suggested that there was a tradeoff between higher involvement by fathers and lower status, with women choosing mates with few resources if they believe that the males will contribute significantly to childcare. Consistent with Hewlett's findings, my study of father involvement among Bofi and Aka foragers showed that Bofi and Aka fathers with fewer brothers (i.e., kin resources) were more likely to be in close proximity to their children during the day (Fouts, 2008).

Where couples live after marriage also relates to available help from kin, and therefore the necessity of involvement or care of children from moth-ers and fathers may be affected by location. For example, when families live patrilocally (with the husbands' kin group) fathers' kin are more likely to live nearby than when families live matrilocally. Katz and Konner (1981) found that non-patrilocal residence patterns were associated with high levels of father involvement, when fathers have the least amount of kin resources available.

In contrast to Katz and Konner's cross-cultural findings, Meehan's (2005) data indicated that Aka fathers who lived patrilocally were more involved with infants than fathers living matrilocally. Also, in my study of Aka and Bofi foragers (Fouts, 2008), patrilocality was positively associated with three types of father involvement: holding, physical contact, and proximal availability. These results contradict the notion that higher kin resources are associated with lower father involvement, as one would assume that all fathers have access to more resources when they live patrilocally. However, it is important to consider that among Aka and Bofi foragers the number of brothers reflects the status of fathers i.e., having more brothers means higher resources. On the other hand, matrilocal and patrilocal locality represents the current availability of kin helpers and determines the tendency of the helpers to be from the husband's or wife's family. It is well recognized by adaptationist scholars that maternal kin tend to invest more in children than paternal kin, perhaps because paternal kin sometimes are not always certain about the paternity of children (e.g., Trivers, 1972; Xia, 1992).

Also contributing to the lower rates of father involvement in the matrilocal context is the fact that Aka and Bofi forager couples typically live matrilocally during the early years of marriage, when husbands are busy performing bride-service for the wives' families. Hewlett (1991) has described how during bride-service Aka men are often given difficult or dangerous tasks by their in-laws, for example collecting honey from tall trees. Likewise, I observed that Aka and Bofi forager men who were in bride-service were often occupied with such tasks or took long trips to avoid such tasks (Fouts, 2008). Similarly, Marlowe (2005) found that Hadza maternal grandmothers held children more when fathers were not living in the households, and Hawkes and colleagues (Hawkes, O'Connell, & Blurtin Jones, 1997) have shown that Hadza post-menopausal female kin provide crucial provisioning to recently weaned children. Moreover, Hawkes and colleagues explained that Hadza fathers devote considerable effort to big game hunting yielding meat, and share the meat with the wider social group rather than solely with their families. Hadza fathers' big game hunting was further described as an effort to attract mates rather than a parenting effort.

Marriage and reproductive choices are obviously related to fathering. In my work with Aka and Bofi foragers and Bofi farmers, I have found that the foragers and farmers have similarly high fertility rates despite closer birth spacing among the farmers (e.g., Fouts, 2008). Bofi forager mothers often commented to me that the reason that they were able to have many children is because their husbands help with the children, unlike Bofi farmer husbands. Bofi farmer mothers, likewise, often reported difficulties carrying the large burden of farm work along with childcare. Indeed, Bofi farmer women who thought that fathers did not invest in children sufficiently (in terms of money for children's clothing, medicine, and school supplies) often "refused" to have more children and even sought help from traditional health specialists to prevent having more children.

Aside from the preceding studies of father involvement in foraging and farming groups, it makes more sense to focus on investment rather than involvement when studying populations where direct father involvement is rare or nonexistent. Investment may be an indirect form of father involvement or care, by contributing to children's diet, clothing, medical care, education, or wealth inheritance. As mentioned previously, pastoral and agropastoral communities tend to have the lowest levels of father involvement, followed by farming groups; foragers tend to have remarkably high levels of involvement (Marlowe, 2000). Even though their father involvement is quite low, fathers in pastoral and agropastoral communities make some of the largest contributions to subsistence and children's nutrition, followed by farming and forager fathers.

In addition to cross-cultural differences in provisioning, Marlowe's (2003b) study of Hadza men's provisioning of children exemplified intracultural variability in father investment. For example, Marlowe found that when mothers were nursing young babies they were less productive at gathering (i.e., bring fewer calories back to their families) and that during this time fathers provided more than fathers without young nursing babies. Thus, Hadza father provisioning seems strategic in that it occurred at times when families needed it the most. Marlowe (1999b) further questioned the notion that Hadza fathers hunt mainly to show off to their potential mates (referred to by Hawkes, 1991 as the 'show-off hypothesis'), rather than to provide for their children. Instead, Marlowe found that Hadza biological fathers provided more care and resources than did stepfathers. If men's efforts were mostly to show off to potential mates, there would not be a bias toward biological children. Marlowe thus concluded that fathers' direct and indirect provisioning care of children can at least partially be viewed as parenting rather than exclusively as a mating strategy. Even though Hadza father involvement with children did not seem to be driven exclusively by mating effort, however, another study by Marlowe (1999a) found that Hadza fathers spent less time with biological children in camps where there were more fertile women (i.e., potential mating opportunities) than in camps with fewer fertile women.

Related to the tradeoffs between mating and parenting effort, several recent studies have examined testosterone levels of fathers in foraging and pastoral communities of East Africa. Evolutionary theorists (Trivers, 1972;

Marlowe, 2003a) have proposed that human males must make a basic tradeoff between allocation of energy toward parenting (investment and involvement with children) and mating (investment in attracting mates, and competition with other men). Testosterone levels have been positively associated in human and non-human males with mating effort strategies, whereas lower testosterone has been associated with involvement with offspring (see review by Gray & Anderson, 2010). In addition, it is well known that testosterone is related with aggressive behavior in human and non-human animals, and thus would be important for male vs. male competition for mates (for review see Archer, 2006). Lower testosterone levels and resulting reduction of aggressive behavior may support pair-bonding or marriage and father involvement with children; and men who are married and live near children may have decreased levels of testosterone compared to other men (see review by Gray & Anderson, 2010). For example, Gray, Ellison, and Campbell (2007) studied the effects of marriage on men's testosterone levels among Ariaal pastoral communities in northern Kenya, and found that bachelor/warrior men had higher levels of testosterone than monogamously married men. Thus, even in a pastoral society where fathers are rarely involved in direct care of children, there seems to be a hormonal influence that favors marriage and father involvement.

In another relevant study, Muller, Marlowe, Bugumba, and Ellison (2009) compared men's testosterone levels among the Datoga pastoralists and the Hadza foragers in Tanzania. These two populations have distinctly different fathering roles, with Hadza fathers providing direct care of infants and children and Datoga fathers having more distal relationships while being focused on accumulation of wealth (cattle) and subsistence activities. As predicted by the hypothesis that lower testosterone predicts higher levels of father involvement, Datoga fathers' testosterone levels did not differ from those of non-fathers. In contrast, Hadza fathers had significantly lower levels of testosterone than other men, i.e., non-fathers.

In sum, adaptationist studies of fathering in Central and East Africa have promoted a bio-cultural perspective of fathers by highlighting that fathering is strategic and related to kin resources, hormonal levels, marriage, mating and residential patterns, and the constraints of mothers when nursing an infant.

Social Policy Issues Related to Fathering in Central and East Africa

The vast majority of fathering research on Central and East African populations has been conducted in rural communities, mostly on foragers and farmers, and to a lesser degree with pastoral and agropastoralist communities. However, there are also issues relevant here to fathering in urban settings in terms of urban-rural migration, father absence, and paternal or maternal orphans.

For example, Munroe and Munroe (1992) reported that over 30% of the 48 Logoli (Kenya) children (3- to 9-year-olds) they observed were in homes in which fathers were not residents. This was due to a high incidence of men's involvement in migrant wage labor. Weisner (1997) compared Abaluyia (Kenya) men's rural–urban migration and the consequences of migration or multilocal residence (i.e., residence in more than one location, rural/urban) on children's experiences and development, in rural and urban contexts. Weisner noted that Abaluyia men's life goals emphasized the importance of being an economic provider. These men wanted many children, which was associated with wealth and power, but they viewed themselves more as economic providers and supervisors than as caregivers. Thus, for Abaluyia men, wage labor migration fits their schema of fatherhood because rural–urban migration is mainly for the purpose of remittances to one's rural family.

The impact of the HIV/AIDS epidemic on families and children in sub-Saharan Africa has been studied predominantly with a focus on mothers, grandmothers, and other female caregivers; very few studies that specifically address men's role in HIV/AIDS-affected families exist (Hosegood and Madhaven, 2010; United Nations, 2011a). But Hosegood and Madhavan (2010) recently argued that the role of fathers in families affected by HIV/AIDS also must be addressed in order to design more effective policies and interventions. They did not assume that fathers were simply absent or irrelevant. There is some evidence from studies in Southern Africa (e.g., Montgomery, Hosegood, Busza, & Timaeus, 2006; see also Townsend, Ch. 8, this volume) that fathers may play various roles in families affected by HIV/AIDS, for example, care for ailing family members, care for children, or provision of financial support to families. Hosegood and Madhavan's work also underscores the need to think broadly of the father's roles, and to consider the contributions of both the father himself and the father's kin network. Their extensive review clearly shows that biological and social fathers and their extended kin must be included in studies of families with HIV/AIDS. Given the continued prevalence of HIV/AIDS in Central and East Africa and the increasing numbers of orphans in these regions (UNICEF, 2008), it is essential that we understand the father's role in families affected by HIV/AIDS in Central and East Africa.

Consideration of fathers' roles is not common in most epidemiological surveys. Furthermore, given the connections between cultural schema and fathering patterns described throughout this chapter, ethnographic studies of fathers in families affected by HIV/AIDS seem to be especially pertinent. Such studies would help policy makers understand the cultural and community mechanisms that support fathering patterns, and individual variations in how fathers respond to HIV/AIDS in their families.

Contemporary Social/Economic Conditions That Impact Fathering

As is the case throughout the rest of sub-Saharan Africa, urban populations in Central and East Africa are increasing dramatically. In East Africa 23.7% of people lived in urban areas in 2010, up from 14.7% in 1980, and 5.3% in 1950 (United Nations, 2011b; in this report, East Africa included Burundi, Comoros, Djibouti, Eritrea, Ethiopia, Kenya, Madagascar, Malawi, Mauritius, Mozambique, Reunion, Rwanda, Seychelles, Somalia, Uganda, and Tanzania). Meanwhile, in Central Africa, 42.9% of people lived in urban areas in 2010, up from 29% in 1980, and 14% in 1950 (United Nations, 2011b; in this report Central Africa is called "Middle Africa" and included Angola, Cameroon, Central African Republic, Chad, Congo, Democratic Republic of Congo, Equatorial Guinea, Gabon, Sao Tome and Principe). Because substantial populations now live in urban areas, it is problematic that almost all fathering research has taken place in rural communities while very little is known about fathering in urban settings in Central and Eastern Africa. Studies of rural–urban migration suggest that even when contexts change, behavior is still guided by foundational schema or core cultural values (Weisner, 1997). Thus, fathering in urban areas, at least in the early years following such migrations, might be similar to fathering in rural areas. However, given the ample evidence that fathering is facultative (i.e., situation-dependent) and that fathers adapt strategically to the constraints of their current environment, fathering in urban vs. rural settings may also have some distinct characteristics. Most cities of Central and East Africa have experienced a significant population influx, and because of poor economic performance and lack of urban planning this has resulted in vast urban slums, also called informal settlements and shantytowns. UN-HABITAT (2008) estimates that more than 70% of the urban population in sub-Saharan Africa lives in slums. Slum conditions in these cities are marked by overcrowding, make-shift housing, proximity to garbage dumps and industrial areas, poor sanitation, heavy incidence of disease and epidemics, all resulting in higher child mortality rates than in rural areas (APHRC, 2002; Jhpeigo, 2007). For example, a recent comparison of rural and urban mortality in Kenya revealed that under-five mortality rates for Nairobi slums is 151 per 1,000 live-births, compared to the national rate of 112 per 1,000 live-births (Jhpeigo, 2007).

Furthermore, the rate of HIV/AIDS in Nairobi slums is 13%, whereas the national rate for Kenya is 7% (Jhpeigo, 2007).

Thus, many fathers in urban areas are arguably at higher risk than fathers in rural areas in terms of their health and the health of their families, and they often have more limited support or access to kin networks than in rural areas (United Nations, 2011a). These trends have tremendous implications both for social policy and also for our understanding of the nature and diversity of fathering strategies. Studies of fathers in urban areas of Central and East Africa would provide an opportunity to disentangle cultural and ecological influences, because urban slum areas are densely packed with people from many different ethnic groups who live in very similar conditions.

Most studies of Central and East African fathers focus on residential fathers (whether biological, social, or step-fathers). This trend is not surprising given the implications of fathering strategies for children's survival and development. However, migrant fathers who are not predominantly residential are an important subgroup on which research is needed. Understanding the role of migrant fathers and other types of non-residential fathers could broaden our knowledge of father investment in children, and also help us to clarify how fathers strategize and balance their economic and family roles or roles with first and subsequent families in cases of divorce. Issues related to non-residential fathers have been studied in other areas of the world (for reviews see Carlson & McLanahan, 2010; Fabricius, Braver, Diaz, & Velez, 2010; Parkinson, 2010), but little is known about these processes in Central and East African contexts. It is well known that rural areas of sub-Saharan Africa are divided distinctly among various cultural groups, and people from different rural areas and cultural communities migrate to cities. Thus, an examination of fathering in cities would also address inter-cultural interactions, and clarify how fathers from a variety of cultures including small-scale societies adapt to a culturally diverse environment with less extended kin and support from their communities.

Discussion, Speculation, and Conclusions

It is difficult to speculate on how Central and East African fathers compare to fathers in other regions of the world, given that there is tremendous cultural diversity in the Central and East African region. In fact, I am reluctant even to make generalizations about fathers within this region. However, it is clear that given increasingly high rates of urban migration fathering patterns in this region are dynamic. Clearly, many families in this region face changes in their contexts and circumstances. Fathering in general is certainly facultative and changes across the lifespan (Townsend,

Ch. 8, this volume). Most studies in Central and East Africa have been cross-sectional, and it would be valuable to understand how fathering changes from early adulthood through middle and later life. My impression from research among Aka foragers (Congo), Bofi foragers (Central African Republic), and Bofi farmers (Central African Republic) is that in addition to cultural and ecological characteristics (i.e., having few living brothers, living with father's kin, monogamous marriage, and foundational schema related to gender egalitarianism), a father's life stage is an important influence on his involvement. Specifically, fathers' ages but also their experiences with marriage(s) and children are important influences on their fathering behavior. For example, some fathers like Ba'win in the opening Case Story lose more loved ones than others, and I suspect that this would affect the way they approach the care of children. In young adulthood, before fathers have experienced the death or multiple deaths of their children, they may feel less inclined to invest in or care for their children, and indeed may not see the need for involvement or investment. However, fathers who have experienced many losses may change their parenting strategies to prevent further losses. This life course perspective, which focuses more on intra-cultural and individual variation than on larger cross-cultural comparisons, is seldom employed in research in Central and East Africa.

Despite a handful of rich ethnographic studies of fathers in Central and East Africa, there is still much to learn about fathering in this area of the world. It is clear from the research reviewed here that fathers certainly do develop and strategize, and it seems clear that particular cultural, ecological, and biological contexts promote father involvement with children. However, the mechanisms and processes by which fathers develop and strategize is a key area for future inquiry in Central and East Africa.

Even though generalizations about fathers across Central and East Africa are not warranted, there are some lessons to be learned from this region that can broaden our understanding of fathering in others parts of the world. The culture-oriented studies of fathering in Central and East Africa exemplify how core cultural values support and perpetuate dominant patterns of fathering in particular cultures. Furthermore, these studies have shown striking inter- and intra-cultural variation in levels and types of involvement and investment with children. This supports the conclusion that fathering is extremely dependent on context (Hrdy, 2009). Intra-cultural variation of fathering within small-scale cultures that are relatively homogeneous in socioeconomic and cultural terms, for example, Aka and Bofi foragers, underscores the facultative nature of fathering. This volume and other recent books (e.g., Lamb, 2010) demonstrate that fathers in highly stratified industrialized nations and contexts have been studied much more frequently than fathers in less populated small-scale societies. Further, many highly stratified industrialized contexts are quite diverse socioeconomically and culturally. Thus, levels of intra-cultural variation in small-scale fairly homogenous societies, as evidenced in this chapter, suggest the need to carefully disentangle contextual and cultural factors in the study of highly diverse industrialized or urban settings.

Research from an adaptationist perspective of fathering in Central and East Africa has implications for our understanding of fathers around the world. The small-culture studies as a whole exemplify a paradoxical situation – father involvement appears to be both an evolved human feature yet it is facultative, varying tremendously by context (for a review of this paradox see Hrdy, 2009). Indeed fathering, like most aspects of human behavior, involves an inter-play between culture and biology. The evolved biological propensities to support male-care exist for men in any culture or society, but they are activated by cultural systems that support pair-bonding and close proximity or contact with infants. Greater knowledge of the various influences on fathering across cultures would contribute to an understanding of both the biological and social landscapes of men's lives, which policy makers can then apply in support of fathering.

Summary

Most studies of fathers in Central and East Africa have been conducted in rural contexts among small-scale foragers, farmers, and pastoralists. This is in great contrast to the majority of studies of fathering in other parts of the world, which have mostly focused on highly stratified national contexts. Despite the limited contexts in which fathers have been studied in Central and East Africa, it is apparent that there is considerable intra- and inter-cultural variation in both direct and indirect father involvement with children. Studies in this region also underscore how fathering behaviors are related to cultural models of childcare and masculinity. Studies of fathers in Central and East Africa have also contributed to an understanding of the adapted nature of fathering and especially human fatherhood as extremely facultative or dependent on context. There is a need for further studies of fathering in this region to address the role of fathers, particularly in families affected by AIDS/HIV and migration to urban areas and slum communities.

References

APHRC [African Population and Health Research Center]. (2002). *Population and health dynamics in Nairobi's informal settlements.* Nairobi, Kenya: African Population and Health Research Center.

Archer, J. (2006). Testosterone and human aggression: An evaluation of the challenge hypothesis. *Neuroscience and Biobehavioral Reviews, 30,* 319–345.

Carlson, M. J., & McLanahan, S. S. (2010). Fathers in fragile families. In M. E. Lamb (Ed.), *The role of the father in child development* (pp. 241–269). Hoboken, NJ: John Wiley & Sons.

Fabricius, W. V., Braver, S. L., Diaz, P., & Velez, C. E. (2010). Custody and parenting time: Links to family relationships and well-being after divorce. In M. E. Lamb (Ed.), *The role of the father in child development* (pp. 201–240). Hoboken, NJ: John Wiley & Sons.

Fouts, H. N. (2008). Father involvement with young children among the Aka and Bofi foragers. *Cross-Cultural Research, 42,* 290–312.

Gray, P. B., & Anderson, K. G. (2010). *Fatherhood: Evolution and human paternal behavior.* Cambridge, MA: Harvard University Press.

Gray, P. B., Ellison, P. T., & Campbell, B. C. (2007). Testosterone and marriage among Ariaal men of Northern Kenya. *Current Anthropology, 48,* 750–755.

Harkness, S., & Super, C. M. (1992). The cultural foundations of father's roles: Evidence from Kenya and the United States. In B. S. Hewlett (Ed.), *Father-child relations: Cultural and biosocial contexts* (pp. 191–212). New York, NY: Aldine de Gruyter.

Hawkes, K. (1991). Showing off: Tests of a hypothesis about men's foraging goals. *Ethology and Sociobiology, 12,* 29–54.

Hawkes, K., O'Connell, J. F., & Blurton Jones, N. G. (1997). Hadza women's time allocation, offspring provisioning, and the evolution of long postmenopausal life spans. *Current Anthropology, 38,* 551–577.

Hewlett, B. S. (1991). *Intimate fathers: The nature and context of Aka pygmy paternal infant care.* Ann Arbor, MI: University of Michigan Press.

Hewlett, B. S., & Macfarlan, S. J. (2010). Fathers' roles in hunter-gatherer and other small-scale cultures. In M. E. Lamb (Ed.), *The role of the father in child development* (5th ed., pp. 413–434). Hoboken, NJ: Wiley.

Hosegood, V., & Madhavan, S. (2010). Data availability on men's involvement in families in sub-Saharan Africa to inform family-centered programmes for children affected by HIV and AIDS. *Journal of the International AIDS Society, 13,* 55–61.

Hrdy, S. B. (2009). *Mothers and others: The evolutionary origins of mutual understanding.* Cambridge, MA: Harvard University Press.

Jhpiego (2007). *Meeting the health needs of the urban poor in African informal settlements: Best practices and lessons learned.* Baltimore, MD: The Urban Institute.

Katz, M. M., & Konner, M. J. (1981). The role of the father: An anthropological perspective. In M. E. Lamb (Ed.), *The role of the father in child development* (2nd ed., pp. 155–185). Hoboken, NJ: Wiley.

Lamb, M. E. (Ed.). (2010). *The role of father in child development* (5th ed.). New York, NY: Wiley.

LeVine, R. A., Dixon, S., LeVine, S., Richman, A., Leiderman, P. H., Keefer, C. H., & Brazelton, T. B. (1996). *Child care and culture: Lessons from Africa.* New York, NY: Cambridge University Press.

LeVine, R. A. (1980). Adulthood among the Gusii of Kenya. In N. J. Smelser & E. H. Erikson (Eds.), *Themes of work and love in adulthood* (pp. 77–104). Cambridge, MA: Harvard University Press.

Marlowe, F. W. (1999a). Male care and mating effort among the Hadza. *Behavioral Ecology and Sociobiology, 46,* 57–64.

Marlowe, F. (1999b). Showoffs or providers? The parenting effort of Hadza men. *Evolution and Human Behavior, 20,* 391–404.

Marlowe, F. W. (2000). Paternal investment and the human mating system. *Behavioural Processes, 51,* 45–61.

Marlowe, F. W. (2003a). The mating system of foragers in the standard cross-cultural sample. *Cross-Cultural Research, 37,* 282–306.

Marlowe, F. W. (2003b). A critical period for provisioning by Hadza men: Implications for pair bonding. *Evolution and Human Behavior, 24,* 217–229.

Marlowe, F. W. (2005). Who tends Hadza children? In B. S. Hewlett &M. E. Lamb (Eds.), *Hunter-gatherer childhoods: Evolutionary, developmental, and cultural perspectives* (pp. 177–190). New Brunswick, NJ: Aldine.

Meehan, C. L. (2005). The effects of residential locality on parental and alloparental investment among the Aka foragers of the Central African Republic. *Human Nature, 16,* 58–80.

Montgomery C., Hosegood V., Busza J., & Timaeus I. M. (2006). Men's involvement in the South African family: Engendering change in the AIDS era. *Social Scienceand Medicine, 62,* 2411–2419.

Morelli, G. A., & Tronick, E. Z. (1992). Male care among Efe foragers and Lese farmers. In B. S. Hewlett (Ed.), *Father-child relations: Cultural and biosocial contexts* (pp. 231–261). New York, NY: Aldine.

Muller, M. N., Marlowe, F. W., Bugumba, R., & Ellison, P. T. (2009). Testosterone and paternal care in East African foragers and pastoralists. *Proceedings of the Royal Society-B, 276,* 347–354.

Munroe, R. L., & Munroe, R. H. (1992). Fathers in children's environments: A four culture study. In B. S. Hewlett (Ed.), *Father-child relations: Cultural and biosocial contexts* (pp. 213–230). New York, NY: Aldine de Gruyter.

Paquette, D. (2004). Theorizing the father-child relationship: Mechanisms and developmental outcomes. *Human Development, 47,* 193–219.

Parkinson, P. (2010). Changing policies regarding separated fathers in Australia. In M. E. Lamb (Ed.), *The role of the father in child development* (pp. 578–614). Hoboken, NJ: JohnWiley.

Shore, B. (1996). *Culture in mind: Cognition, culture, and the problem of meaning.* New York, NY: Oxford University Press.

Trivers, R. L. (1972). Parental investment and sexual selection. In B. Campbell (Ed.), *Sexual selection and the descent of man 1871–1971* (pp. 136–179). Chicago, IL: Aldine.

UN-HABITAT. (2008). *The state of African cities 2008: A framework for addressing urban challenges in Africa.* Nairobi, Kenya: UN-HABITAT.

UNICEF. (2008). *Africa's orphaned and vulnerable generations: Children affected by AIDS.* New York, NY: The United Nations Children's Fund.

United Nations. (2011a). *Men in families and family policy in a changing world.* Population Division of the Department of Economic and Social Affairs of the

United Nations Secretariat. Retreived August 30, 2011, from http://www. un.org/esa/socdev/family/docs/men-in-families.pdf.

United Nations. (2011b). *World Population Prospect*. Population Division of the Department of Economic and Social Affairs of the United Nations Secretariat. Retrieved April 23, 2011, from http://esa.un.org/unup.

Weisner, T. S. (1997). Support for children and the African family crisis. In T. S. Weisner, C. Bradley, & P. L. Kilbride (Eds.), *African families and the crises of social change* (pp. 20–44). Westport, CT: Bergin & Garvey.

Winn, S., Morelli, G. A., & Tronick, E. Z. (1990). The Infant in the group: A look at Efe caretaking practices, In K. Nugent, B. M. Lester, & T. B. Brazelton (Eds.), *The cultural contexts of infancy* (pp. 87–109). Norwood, NJ: Ablex.

Xia, X. (1992). Uncertainty of paternity can select against paternal care. *The American Naturalist, 139*, 1126–1129.

Yogman, M. (1982). Development of the father–infant relationship, In H. Fitzgerald, B. Lester, & M. Yogman (Eds.), *Theory and research in behavioral pediatrics* (pp. 221–229). New York, NY: Plenum.

Chapter Eight

Complications of Fathering in Southern Africa

Separation, Uncertainty, and Multiple Responsibilities

Nicholas W. Townsend
Brown University, Providence, RI, USA

Case Story: Continuity and Change in One Family

"I am a 'witch doctor'," 70-year-old Khume told me, sitting outside his thatched sleeping-hut in a poor, remote village in South Africa. By using the blunt English term 'witch doctor,' Khume emphasized his commitment to traditional culture, which he also displayed by vehemently opposing trousers for women, having three wives, and sleeping in a thatched hut across his compound from the cattle kraal. But Khume also drove a pick-up truck, owned a bar that he protected with a rifle as well as witchcraft, and had for 27 years worked 400 kilometers (250 miles) away from the village at Johannesburg's International Airport. The fathering of Khume and two of his sons illustrates four crucial features of fathering in Southern Africa: physical separation of employment and family, economic inequality and uncertainty, vulnerability of small families, and the importance of family connections outside the nuclear family.

Khume had lived in several social worlds, and he had faced the challenge of raising children who could do the same. Also, like many men in Southern Africa whose only employment opportunities are distant from their homes, he was physically separated from his children while they were growing up. Khume's experience of fathering had not been one of physical proximity, play, communication, and emotional presence, but he had been a role model of the father as a worker and provider, an authority figure both respected and feared, and a financial support for his wives and children. He had also invested in his children's education and had insisted that they attend school and succeed there.

The lives of two of Khume's sons illustrate the increasing diversity in men's positions in South Africa's extraordinarily unequal economy. Their families of origin have great influence on health and education, and, crucially, determine access to people with the skills and positions to help them find work. Lesedi, Khume's son by his first wife, used money from his father to start his own business and worked with determination to build that business, to crush competition, and to build the network of contacts necessary for business success. At the age of 40 he lived with his wife and three children in the large modern house he had built in a nearby town. Moving away from the village strengthened the autonomy of his nuclear family by distancing it from the culturally supported claims of his numerous kin. It also allowed Lesedi to live in the same house as his wife and children, to send his children to private schools, and to expose them to the activities and experiences that mark members of the middle class in the modern, international sector of South Africa.

Tumelo, Khume's son by his third wife and twelve years younger than Lesedi, is also a competent, intelligent, and articulate man. But because he is not the heir, Khume has not provided him with capital or paid for his higher education. Tumelo does not have the skills or experience he would need for a white-collar position, and there are jobs available for less than half of his generation. Living in his own one-room house within his mother's compound, Tumelo alternates between looking for work in Pretoria and doing occasional small jobs in the village. Without a steady income, he is unable to provide a home or support for his 5-year-old son and the boy's mother, who live with her parents. Tumelo would like to marry his son's mother, but he cannot afford to. Cohabitation is unacceptable to her family and would destroy her chances of finding an alternative husband. Although Tumelo is an affectionate and caring father when his son visits, he is an intermittent presence in his son's life, providing more and seeing him more when he has money, but frequently absent and never essential for the boy's well-being or able to contribute to his opportunities.

Scope and Limits

Across Southern Africa, the meaning of fatherhood, cultural expectations for fathers, men's expectations for themselves as fathers, and the practice of fathering all vary greatly and are changing everywhere. In every place, and for each father, culturally prescribed roles and expectations are the still fluid outcomes of a history in which indigenous cultures have interacted with European invaders, colonial institutions, and the racial policies of the South African state. Any review must necessarily generalize – blurring or

erasing the differences arising from distinct physical environments, economic conditions, and cultural patterns; from men's varied class positions
and social statuses; and from the personal characteristics of individuals.
Recognizing these limitations, the Case Story of Khume and his sons is
not presented as a description of a uniform pattern but as an example
that illustrates general influences, broad problems, and widespread patterns that characterize fathering in Southern Africa: social and physical
separation of men from their children, an uncertain economic situation
that frustrates intentions and constrains possibilities, and complicated
relationships within and between families. One other striking feature of
fathering in Southern Africa, not directly seen in this case but widespread
and important, is "distributed" or "multiple" fathering: a pattern of family life in which male responsibilities to a child are met by several men,
and in which each man's responsibilities towards children are not limited
to his own offspring.

In this chapter "Southern Africa" is restricted to South Africa,
Botswana, Lesotho, and Swaziland, as is shown in the map below. South
Africa has 90% of this region's population; the other three countries
are incorporated into the South African economy by their overwhelm-
ing dependence on bilateral trade and by longstanding patterns of labor
migration. This chapter does not consider fathering among the original
foraging or hunter-gathering population (see Fouts, this volume, for a
discussion of small-scale societies), who were by the time of European
settlement restricted to areas too dry for cattle-herding or cultivation.
Nor is it much concerned with fathering among the white population, for whom aspirations and institutional arrangements concerning
family life are relatively similar to those in Western Europe and North
America (see Khunou, 2006, and Crapanzano, 1985, for descriptions of
this population).

This chapter focuses on the behavioral patterns and problems of
fathering among the 45 million black Africans who make up 81% of the
population of the region. Unless otherwise specified, references to men,
women, families, and population are restricted to black Africans. South
Africa's population is 9% white and 11% "other" (mostly "coloured" or
mixed race, or of South Asian ancestry), and the percentage of the population that is black in Botswana, Lesotho, and Swaziland are 97%, 99%, and
97%, respectively. The national population of South Africa (see Chapter
1, Table 1.1, for demographic statistics) is 49 million; of Botswana and
Lesotho it is 2 million each; and of Swaziland it is 1. 35 million. In the
regional map, the names of ethnic groups are indications of the areas of
their greatest concentration; all the peoples of the region are now widely
distributed.

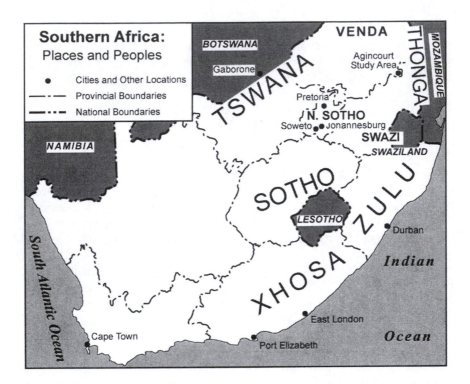

Figure 8.1 Map of Southern Africa, courtesy of Paul R. Larson. White land mass is South Africa.

Cultural and Historical Background as It Influences Fathering

History

The history of Southern Africa has created the circumstances within which men make their lives and become fathers. From the first European settlement at what is now Cape Town in the southwest of the region and throughout its expansion, colonial policy expropriated and exploited the original inhabitants, seizing the desirable land and imposing forced labor. The discovery of diamonds in 1871 and of the gold deposits on the Witwatersrand in 1886 resulted in the rapid growth of cities and urban areas in the region around Johannesburg, where 22% of the population now lives in less than 2% of the country's land. Racial separation and the expropriation of the black population were formalized with particular rigidity and brutality under the apartheid policy of the white-ruled Republic of South Africa (1960–1994), which created a monopoly of mineral wealth and of good arable land for white owners and relegated the African population to small and scattered areas of undesirable land. One consistent consequence of this policy has been that working men, and many women who have been employed in domestic and other service, have been forcibly separated from their families.

The development of mining and industry, in the context of the particular history of racial politics in Southern Africa, was accompanied by a new pattern of population distribution. Specifically, men were concentrated in urban and industrial areas while women and children were restricted to rural areas. This pattern of residence, though radically different from the previous agricultural residence patterns, continued to mean that domestic units and families were (as they have been variously described) divided, broken, separated, stretched, or dispersed (Murray, 1981; Sharp, 1994; Spiegel, 1987; Spiegel, Ross, & Wilkinson, 1996). The profound implications of these arrangements for the expectations and actions of fathers were succinctly stated in *Steering by the Stars: Being Young in South Africa*, a detailed description of the lives of 16 young people growing up in a township in Cape Town, by Mamphela Ramphele, an anti-apartheid activist and social anthropologist. Among Ramphele's (2002) conclusions were:

1. Economic conditions were the root cause of men's abandonment of fatherhood: "Desertion by fathers is often prompted by their inability to bear the burden of being primary providers. The burden of failure becomes intolerable for those who lack the capacity to generate enough income as uneducated and unskilled labourers" (p. 158).
2. Failure at fatherhood is transmitted from one generation to the next: "This decision by many poor men to shed family responsibilities left little room for young men to model themselves on successful males. Conflict between the ideals of a patriarchal system which installs the male as provider, protector and decision-maker on one hand, and the harsh realities of lack of education and skills, compounded by high levels of unemployment and demoralization on the other, leave young men confused" (p. 103).
3. The confusion of young men is only one of the effects on families of men's feeling that they cannot be successful fathers: "Desertion is not always physical, it can also be emotional. Many men 'die' as parents and husbands by indulging in alcohol, drugs or becoming unresponsive to their families" (p. 158).

The men living in the hostels and townships were not only South Africans; workers were recruited from all the countries of the region. South African policy treated Botswana, Lesotho, and Swaziland as labor reserves from which workers could be recruited on contracts, and to which they could be returned when they were no longer needed. Within South Africa, government policy removed the black population of South Africa from their own lands and concentrated them in areas designated successively as "native land areas," "homelands," or *"bantustans."* The object of racial segregation was to preserve desirable areas for white occupation and to guarantee the supply of black labor for commercial farms, mines, domestic work, and industry. Apartheid supplemented land policy with a system of regulations and passbooks designed to ensure that only necessary workers could move to and live in cities. For employers, the enormous advantage of separating races and dividing families was they had to hire and house only currently necessary workers and managed to separate the profit-making processes of production from the biological and social reproduction of the labor force (Burawoy, 1976). Because it crowded the black population into undesirable land, apartheid policy drastically reduced the capacity for subsistence agriculture, making families increasingly dependent on the wages of migrant workers. For the overwhelmingly male African miners and industrial workers employment and access to income were socially and spatially separated and isolated from their homes, domestic lives, families, and children. By the time apartheid was formalized following the election victory of the National Party in 1948, it was almost impossible for African men to both support and to live with their children. Providing support for children, for many the central pillar of modern fatherhood, was made incompatible with living with and caring for them.

Even before the open election of 1994 and the accession to power of the African National Congress, which was the dominant force in the anti-apartheid struggle, under the leadership of Nelson Mandela, the previous stringent forms of population control had been abandoned as unworkable and unenforceable. Since 1994 black South Africans have enjoyed the full rights of citizenship, including the right to move about the country and to live where they choose. But tragically, the practical situation of most Africans has not been equally transformed. South Africa is a relatively prosperous country with a per capita GDP of $10,700 in 2010, developed infrastructure, world-class universities and hospitals, and many people who have a first-world standard of living. However, economic inequality is extreme. For example, 50% of the population lives below the poverty line, 45% of children live in households where there is not enough money for food and clothes (Brookes, Shisana, & Richter, 2004), the official unemployment rate is over 25%, and the top 10% of households accounts for 47% of the total household income while the bottom 10% receives 1.3%. Economic inequality is also marked throughout Southern Africa; very large proportions of the populations of Botswana, Lesotho, South Africa, and Swaziland are desperately poor and a large proportion of men cannot meet the material expectations of fatherhood.

Culture

Cultural patterns help explain several features of fathering in Southern Africa that strike Western observers as markedly different from their own norms, and that they may readily label as pathologies or problems. Among these are: (1) the social and physical separation of the lives of men from those of women and children; (2) a different conception of the ideal male life course; and (3) a pattern of family organization that involves other men than fathers in the lives of children. Showing that certain patterns are consonant with an existing culture should not obscure that fact that they have been imposed by force at the cost of enormous suffering. The fact that in the societies of Southern Africa before the European conquest men and women did different things and frequently lived in different places in no way reduces the inhumanity and human costs of the system of male labor migration. People confronted with forced and rapid changes in their circumstances draw on their existing resources and act in accord with their own cultures, but the consequences of their actions are not necessarily adaptive and may even be catastrophic.

The pre-industrial cultural norms and social structures of the ethnic groups of Southern Africa have been transformed through two centuries of conquest and relocation, industrialization and wage labor, Christianity and literacy, tribalization and nationalism, but they have not been obliterated. Local cultures have been modified, adapted, blended, and differentiated as circumstances have changed, but they remain distinct, recognizable, patterns of belief and behavior and central elements of group and individual identities in multicultural societies. The language spoken at home is an indicator of ethnicity, and in 2001 the population of each ethnic group in the Southern African region, in millions, was Zulu (10.7), Xhosa (7.9), Tswana (5.7), Sotho (5.6), Pedi and other Northern Sotho (4.2), Swazi (2.5), Thonga (2), Venda (1), and Ndebele (0.7). There were also 6 million people who spoke Afrikaans and 3.7 million who spoke English at home (Statistics South Africa, 2004, p. 11).

The following outline is a brief abstract from a remarkable collection of ethnographies from the first half of the twentieth century, most of them written by South Africans. Among the classics are accounts of the Lovedu (Krige & Krige, 1947), Swazi (Kuper, 1947; Kuper, 1986), Thonga (Junod, 1927), Tswana (Schapera, 1966), and Zulu (Krige, 1936; Gluckman, 1950).

The pre-industrial economy was based on cattleherding and cultivation. The balance between herding and cultivation varied, as did the dispersion and concentration of settlements, and the structural importance of patrilineages. But throughout the region, families or extended families were largely self-sufficient and there was a gendered division of labor that made cattle herding a male activity and the focus of men's interest. For

cattle herders and cultivators, the natural environment has favored subsistence strategies in which different productive activities are carried out
in different locations, and men and women have generally worked and
socialized separately. Men spent much of the year at cattle posts or camps
far from the villages and their surrounding farming lands. Even when
men were in the village, their lives revolved around their public meetings,
the cattle kraal, and male socializing. Meanwhile, women's lives centered
on their own single-sex, multi-generational socializing and on organizing
their households, preparing food, and caring for children.

In the 1820s, the establishment of the Zulu empire under Shaka elaborated existing social arrangements to organize the male population into a
succession of "regiments" or cohorts of age-mates who would go through
life together, connected by shared experience and bonds of mutual obligation, and assuming the successive roles of adult manhood together. The
system of age regiments was most elaborated in Zulu society (see Figure
8.1 for main locations of Zulu and other peoples), but the institution was
also widespread in other societies. Even though initiations are no longer
universal, the system had unintended but enduring impacts on cultural
concepts of masculinity and on men's relationships with children: (1) a
man's age grade provides a male setting for social interaction, reinforcing
gendered divisions of labor and social interaction; (2) the age grade system creates social and political connections that cut across family and lineage; and (3) the successive grades express a model of the male life course
and of the responsibilities of each age that is markedly different from the
model introduced from Western Europe.

The gendered division of labor, location, and social life was accompanied by a specific cultural configuration of male responsibility and life
course. Social organization into patrilineages (groups of men descended
from the same male ancestor, with their wives and unmarried sisters and
daughters) combined with patrilineal inheritance (inheritance of wealth
and social position from father to son) meant that a man's chief loyalties
and obligations were to his male kin, who were also his main sources of
social and material support. It also resulted in the fact that marriages were
not simply individual concerns but arrangements between social groups
accompanied by exchanges of goods and services, the most significant of
which was the transfer of "bride wealth" from the family of the groom to
the family of the bride. This transfer ensured that children of the marriage
would be members of their father's patrilineage and signified the importance of the web of relationships created by marriage (Comaroff, 1980).
Since cattle and other wealth were controlled by older men, a young man
had to have the support of his father and other older kinsmen in order to
marry. In a purely agricultural economy, this support was earned through
years of labor herding his father's cattle and cultivating his father's fields.

Initially, labor migration did not disrupt this pattern because young men were recruited from villages on annual contracts with the bulk of their wages remitted to their fathers (Schapera, 1966).

At the time of the transfer of bride wealth, the bride would leave her own father's household and move to that of her husband's father, where she and her children would live under his control. Only when a man had fulfilled his responsibilities to his parents and accumulated the necessary resources could he establish his own household. In a typical village in Botswana near the South African border the cultural consensus was that a woman was not ready to run her own household until she was at least age 30, and no man had established his own household in the village before age 40 (Townsend, 1997). The implications of these patterns for fathering were that (1) a young man's primary responsibility was to his parents, rather than to his young children, (2) fathers of young children often lived apart from their children, and (3) children frequently spent years of their lives under the paternal authority of a grandfather.

There were and continue to be important variations in cultural expectations for fathers in Southern Africa. For example, Zulu culture puts most emphasis on the male institutions of the patrilineage and the group initiation of cohorts of men, making possible both patriarchal oppression and social control of the excesses of individual men. Pedi culture (one of the Northern Sotho groups), on the other hand, establishes strong matrilineal connections and female institutions, with the possibility of more egalitarian marriages and of resilience in the absence of men. Ethnic and linguistic differences are exploited by political figures of all persuasions, and 'ancient tribal animosity' provides an easy but misleading explanation of a variety of social phenomena from violence to differential access to opportunities. Although cultural differences persist, in contemporary Southern Africa the crucial social divisions that affect fathering are actually aspects of social class: income, wealth, and education.

Review of Fathering Research: Patterns and Representations

"Fathers in Africa have remained largely invisible on researchers' agendas; moreover they have not featured on the budgets of research funders … data on fathers is almost non-existent (except for South Africa)" (African Fathers Initiative, n.d., Overview). That is the position of the African Fathers Initiative, an organization that collects and disseminates both research-based knowledge and practical skills about fatherhood throughout Africa. Even in South Africa, a 2006 edited volume summarized what was known and mapped out future research, and claimed accurately to be "the first book to focus specifically on fathers and fatherhood in South Africa" (Richter & Morrell, 2006, p. v). Since 2003, the Fatherhood Project of the South African Human Sciences Research Council (HSRC) has coordinated research and production of resources in support of interventions to encourage responsible fatherhood (Human Sciences Research Council, n.d., Fatherhood Project). Like most research in Southern Africa, research on fatherhood in the region is almost entirely designed to (1) guide and evaluate interventions to deal with problems such as sexual abuse, HIV transmission, substance abuse, violence, teenage parenting, and child support; and (2) document the impact of social conditions such as poverty, public-health, social service provision, unemployment, illiteracy, lack of knowledge, and unemployment on the well-being of families and the behavior of fathers. In this section, I will review four themes that run throughout research, interventions, policy design, and social action about fatherhood: (1) the separation of families and absent fathers, (2) the multiple connections between men and children, (3) public representations of and debates about fatherhood, and (4) the continued impact of poverty and economic uncertainty on men's performance as fathers.

Separation of families and absent fathers

Long-term labor contracts have become much less common in contemporary Southern Africa, but physical separation between work place and family life continues for many fathers. Direct payment of wages to workers and the declining importance of cattle have weakened the control of older men over their sons, and women are now increasingly unwilling to live with their husbands' parents. Instead, many prefer to remain in their own parents' household until they are able to establish their own independent households. These changes have transformed family dynamics but have had less impact on the life-course experience of fathers. In fact, many fathers continue to belong to different households than their children and to be physically distant in order to earn a living, and children continue to live apart from their fathers while sharing households with adult male relatives.

Associated with these different life courses is a pattern of family organization in which several men may have responsibilities for and interests in the same child, and in which a man may have responsibilities for children other than his own. The importance of men other than fathers in the lives of children has been recognized in non-industrialized societies with high fertility rates in general and in Africa in particular (Engle 1997; Greene & Biddlecom, 2000; Lloyd & Blanc, 1996; Fouts, Ch. 7, this volume). However, the design of most surveys and much research unfortunately renders the importance of such men invisible. For example, survey

Figure 8.2 In rural areas, a household of women and children does not necessarily imply father absence. This older woman's husband, father of the child on her lap and of the young woman, supports the family by working in a distant city. The father of the young woman's child is in school and has acknowledged paternity. Photo courtesy of Nicholas Townsend.

research questions that only focus on the absence or presence of fathers and mothers ignore the roles both of fathers who do not live with children and of men who contribute to children's well-being but are not their fathers (Posel, 2006).

Cultural and historic contexts also continue to complicate the questions of the presence or absence of fathers and of their contributions to children's support. Migration data covering the first ten years since the end of apartheid showed neither change in patterns of migration back and forth between rural and urban areas, nor increases in permanent settlement in urban areas (Posel, 2006). While only 38% of the population of South Africa is considered rural, circular migration between urban and rural areas is very common and many long-term residents of urban areas maintain close connections to family in rural areas through visits and remittances. As a result, a considerable majority has strong links to rural areas and retains the possibility of living there. Posel (2006) showed that members of rural households, when given the opportunity, counted labor migrants as temporarily non-resident household members. The most appropriate research in this context allows people to define their own households. These redefinitions of households mean that parents and other family members who do not actually live in a child's rural home but who send money, return periodically, and arrange education are counted as 'non-resident' rather than 'absent,' increasing the observed level of parents' involvement in their children's lives.

The previous section described a pattern of family formation very different from the Western norm by which young people establish new and independent families that are centered on couples, and live in their own homes. In the context of Southern African cultures, marriage is not so much an event as a process that unfolds over years from initial discussion to the final transfer of bride wealth. This transfer was often delayed, sometimes until the time came to arrange the marriages of the children. This situation means that the simple categorization used in many discussions of extramarital births and unmarried fathers underestimates the presence of men in their children's lives. The complexity is compounded by the coexistence of three systems that certify marriages: customary, church, and civil. These three systems have definitions of marriage that are different but compatible, as couples may combine elements of traditional marriage with a marriage certificate obtained in court and an eventual church wedding.

National statistics report low levels of marriage. They also indicate the difficulty of measuring marital status. Botswana, for instance, recognizes both customary and civil marriages, but only civil marriages are registered, while South Africa registers both civil and customary marriages as well as civil unions but coverage is very incomplete. National census and survey records, which depend only on people's responses, show a very low incidence of marriage. In 2006, only 18% of the population of Botswana over the age of 12 was married, with another 11% living together (Botswana Government, 2009, p. 105); for black South Africans in 2001, the equivalent figures for the population over age 14 were 31% and 9%. By comparison, the levels for white South Africans were 61% married and 4% living together (Statistics South Africa, 2004, p. 31).

Consideration of cultural values about marriage helps us to understand that these figures do not reflect moral or social pathology but give a distorted picture of people's actual lives. This is not to say that all legally unmarried women are really in unions when they give birth, or that every union that produces children will eventually be formalized by marriage. But it is important to recognize that a child born to an unmarried mother is not necessarily a child without a father.

Recent research also reveals a complicated view of father presence and absence in Southern Africa. For example, data from a sample of 271 children from the Agincourt Health and Demographic Surveillance System showed that in 2001 only 12% of children were actually living with their fathers and that 24% had no contact at all. Between these two extremes, 41% of fathers were members of their child's household but were not living there; father and child 'shared' a home but did not both live in it. Another 23% were not members of their child's household but had recognized social connections with them. The nuances of these patterns of household membership and residence are relevant to the issue of paternal support. Specifically, co-resident fathers were not the most likely to provide support, most often because they had no income, and 32% of children whose fathers were not even members of the same household received support from them (Madhavan, Townsend, & Garey, 2008). Overall, 13% of the children in this study had never had any contact with their father, half of them received some financial support in a given year, and three-quarters of children over the age of 10 had been supported by their father at some time in their lives. It is difficult to draw firm conclusions from these data, but in a desperately poor population these findings suggest as much involvement as indifference among fathers.

Multiple connections between men and children

Despite the paucity of research directly on fathering, there is an abundant literature on family life in Southern Africa. This literature includes historical descriptions of family life and structure in cultures that had only recently come into direct contact with Europeans, and later ethnographic accounts of family life in cultures that retained considerable autonomy from national governments in their domestic arrangements. For the last 50 years the literature has been dominated by ethnographic and sociological descriptions of the disruption of families by, and their adjustment to, the imposition of a money economy, migrant labor, and racial policies (Burawoy, 1976; Murray, 1981; Niehaus, 1994; Ramphele, 1993; Sharp, 1994; Spiegel, 1987; Spiegel et al., 1996; Townsend, 1997).

The most important use of the literature on African families in discussion of fatherhood is in the analysis of "distributed" (Townsend, 1997), "multiple" (Hewlett & MacFarlan, 2010), or "collective" (Mkhize, 2006) fatherhood. Mkhize, a professor of psychology at the University of KwaZulu-Natal, drew upon his own experience as a Zulu in support of his assertion that "Child-rearing is the collective responsibility of the extended family as a whole." "[W]hen I was growing up ... my father's brothers, my aunts and my grandfather all played an important role in raising us children" (Mkhize, 2006, p. 187). Mkhize cites Townsend's (1997) life history of Mowetsi, a Tswana man from a village near Gaborone, the capital of Botswana, as an example of collective fatherhood. Mowetsi had seven children, born between 1954 and 1975. For 32 years, Mowetsi worked as a miner in South Africa and sent home money to support his wife and children, who lived with his wife's parents. Day-to-day fathering of Mowetsi's children was provided by his father-in-law, whom his children referred to as 'father.' In 1977, Mowetsi retired from the mines and became the head of his own household, where he lived with and raised his younger children and also raised some of his own grandchildren whose parents were away at work.

In societies in which the majority of children are not living in families that include their biological father, we may expect and hope that they will find substitute fathers, or at least men who make positive contributions to their welfare. But the idea of collaborative or distributed fatherhood is so prevalent in the literature on fatherhood and families in Southern Africa, and the practice is so widespread, that distributed fathering is more than a *substitution* for the father. My point here is that these cultures actually *expect* and *require* that men play prescribed roles in the lives of a variety of children besides their own offspring, and that children have legitimate, culturally sanctioned, claims on a variety of men besides their biological father. Fatherhood is *distributed* because the responsibilities, activities, and functions generally attributed to a father are shared among a number of men; it is *multiple* because each child receives paternal care from several men and each man has paternal responsibility to several children; it is *collective* because the child belongs to and is the ultimate responsibility of a social group. In Mowetsi's case the point is not that his father-in-law, his wife's brothers, and his own older sons, had to support, encourage, and protect his children because he was an inadequate father. Rather, these things were expected of them and Mowetsi as a young man was doing what a father was supposed to do. In just the same way, when an older Mowetsi 'fathered' his grandchildren, it was not that he was doing what his own sons should have been doing but rather that, as an older man with an established household, he was again doing what a father was supposed to do. Similarly, in the initial Case Story, Khume was a physically absent but financially supportive father as a young man, and his son Tumelo, who is unable to support his own son, is one of several men involved in his care.

It is understandable that when confronted with the problems of the contemporary situation, authors like Mkhizi and Lesejane report memories of their own childhoods to emphasize the affection and security they experienced rather than the conflicts and unfair distinctions that must also have been part of their family lives. Ethnographic accounts, which have a tendency to depict social institutions as they should operate, also contribute to an image of shared parenthood that worked for all concerned. Given the potential biases in descriptions of distributed fatherhood we should be careful not to regard it as a panacea, but it can certainly provide for the social and physical needs of children and the predictability of interactions necessary to raise culturally competent adults (Super & Harkness, 1986; Weisner, 2002). Although in most chapters in this volume (Chaudhary's Chapter 4 analysis of India being another important exception) grandfathers are seldom mentioned in discussions of fatherhood, grandfathers are often vital people for Southern African children.

References to "the wide range of men who fulfill father roles in children's lives" (Richter & Smith, 2006, p. 158) are pervasive in the literature on families in Southern Africa. Only one of the 16 young people in Ramphele's (2002) study lived with his mother and father, ten were raised mostly by their mothers, though fewer than half had lived continuously with their mother, two by grandmothers, and one by a sister. But many had found support, love, and protection from men other than their fathers (Ramphele & Richter, 2006). In the following discussion of men who act as children's 'other fathers,' I use quotations from essays written by school children excerpted from Richter and Smith (2006) to illustrate the salience of these relationships. For children whose mothers are married, the paternal grandfather may well be the head of the child's household for many years and remain an important authority figure: "Me and my brother call him *Ntata omdala,* which means older father. He is the head of the family therefore he sees to everyone's problems" (p. 159). Many mothers, with or without relationships with fathers, live with their children in their own parents' household, where the maternal grandfather can be a father figure: "My father caused trouble in the family, so now my grandfather is my father" (p. 159). Since brothers are collaborators as well as competitors, a child's paternal uncles may also be important, particularly if the child and its mother are living in the father's natal household. In the patrilineal societies of Southern Africa, the mother's brother (maternal uncle) is another key male figure for children and a link between a child and the mother's natal patrilineage with important social and ritual obligations. The mother's brother (*malome* in Sesotho, literally 'male mother') is generally treated with a respectful familiarity that contrasts with the formality of father–child relationships, and he is expected to serve as a moral guide and material resource: "I live with my uncle. He is like a father to me. When my uncle finds that there is no bread or potatoes, he goes to the shop and buy these things" (p. 159). For mothers living in their natal households, the child's maternal uncle is often a member of the household and may be a crucial support for the child and mother (Niehaus, 1994). As one youth explained, "[T]he best part about being with my mother's mother was that my uncle was there and he looked after me very well. He bought me school uniforms and paid the school fees" (Ramphele & Richter, 2006, p. 77).

Figure 8.3 Men can be fond and attentive fathers, like this man who has taken his son to the market with two of his friends. Unemployed men do not have the material resources to set up their own households, and this man who lives with his mother, herself one of three co-wives, cannot afford to bring his child's mother to live with him. Photo courtesy of Nicholas Townsend.

In high-fertility societies in which women may bear children over a period of twenty years or more, a child's own older brother may also be crucial, especially in Africa where a pattern of 'linking' older and younger siblings is common. For many children, an older sibling pays their school expenses and encourages their schooling, and some do much more than that:

> [My brother] is eighteen years old, he is like a father to me. My father died long time ago. He plays a major role in our lives, though he is a very young boy doing grade 11 at Adams high school. He is responsible … He looks after baby because my mother passed away few months ago. Every afternoon he close the gate so that we are safe inside. He support us in every way. We don't feel that our mother is no longer there for us. He always give us that love we used to get our parents … My brother is like a father to us, we trust him, we love him.
>
> (Fatherhood Project, 2004)

This quote conveys the potential importance of siblings, but it is uncommon for an 18-year-old to be head of household and sole caretaker, as he is here, even in a situation where orphanhood rates are high. For instance, a demographic survey in a Zulu-speaking area of South Africa found that in 2004 of children aged 10 to 14, 12% were maternal, 20% paternal, and 4% double orphans (Hosegood et al., 2007).

Two presidents: Public representations of fathers

One strand of research specifically on fathers is devoted to studying the representation of fathers in the media and public discussion (Clowes, 2006; Prinsloo, 2006). Public portrayals may or may not reflect the actual behavior of fathers, but they do reflect both the aspirations for fathers and the negative image against which they must struggle. Linda Richter's summary of the media picture of fathers in 2009 was in accord with my own observations and with the view of the media communicated to me in research interviews and casual conversations in Botswana and South Africa:

> [T]he public media was, and remains, replete with reports of men's selfishness (spending money on cigarettes and alcohol and, at the high end, on golf and expensive 'toys'), their neglect of their children (failing to pay maintenance or spending long hours at work), their uncontrolled sexuality (multiple, superficial partnerships), their violent behavior, and their abuse, including rape and murder, of women and children.
>
> (Richter, 2009, p. vii)

These public representations are linked to the controversy over whether the failures of contemporary fathers should be blamed on African traditional cultures or on the evil influences of colonialism, Westernization, modernization and globalization (Prinsloo, 2009).

A comparison of the lives and public images of two Presidents of South Africa illuminates the importance both of research on the historical dimensions of fatherhood in the region, and of appeals to African culture as an explanation of men's behavior and a guide to policy. In looking at their public images it is important to remember that the simplified symbolic meanings of their actions become more important in public debate than the complex reality of their personal lives, and that the debate reflects profound differences in attitudes between ethnic groups, generations, and social classes. Nelson Mandela separated from his first wife when their children were still young and did not live with them after that. He was imprisoned for 27 years when his youngest children (with his second wife) were aged three and four, so he was also absent from their childhoods. Mandela's public prominence added to the problems his own children faced, but his commitment to his cause gave him the moral authority to define responsible fathering for the new South Africa.

At a Father's Day lunch hosted by his daughter after the fall of apartheid, Mandela started his speech by condemning the migrant labor system: "One of the most shameful parts of South Africa's apartheid history is in how black family life was ruined by separating fathers from families" (Mandela, 2001, ¶ 2). He endorsed gender equality and recognized that women are "becoming co-providers and breadwinners in families," but he concluded that it "remains the primary task of fathers to provide economic security to families" (¶ 3). Mandela emphasized fathers' roles in "moral regeneration," and their example which "will determine to a large extent how the sons conduct themselves in future, and with how much self-esteem, dignity and self-confidence the daughters go out into life" (¶ 1). Mandela concluded that fathers should "break down" stereotypes of males as "tough and domineering," should make "time for children and for the family," and should become "promoters of love and gentleness in families" (¶ 4).

While Mandela is often referred to with respect and affection as *Tata* (Xhosa for father), descriptions of Jacob Zuma, South Africa's current president and the biological father of 22 children, as "father of the nation" are often satirical (Smith, 2010). Many South Africans have criticized Zuma's actions as undermining the country's anti-AIDS policy which encourages monogamy, as assaults on the equality of women and responsibility of fatherhood, and as inconsistent with moral standards associated with modernity and international respect (*Mail & Guardian*, 2010). On the other hand, Zuma and his defenders appeal to his Zulu culture in defense of his multiple paternity, his polygamy (he has been married five times and currently has three wives and a fiancée), his many sexual relationships (only 13 of his children were born to any of his wives), and his payment of bride wealth in traditional marriage ceremonies. Zuma's case is only one example of the public discussion of fatherhood in South Africa, but his cultural justifications are typical.

Contemporary Social/Economic Conditions That Impact Fathering

Poverty and uncertainty as obstacles to fathering

It is clear that the social organization and cultural context necessary for effective fathering does not exist for many men and children in Southern

Africa. I have already mentioned the problems with conceptual definitions used in, and with the accuracy of the responses to, surveys in Southern Africa. Nevertheless, the finding from a national survey that in 2002 only 37% of African children under 16 in South Africa were living with their fathers and the fathers of 13% had died (in comparison, 87% of White children lived with their fathers) (Posel & Devey, 2006, p. 47) indicates that many fathers play no significant part in their children's lives.

Teenage Tata (Swartz & Bhana, 2009) depicted the experiences and situation of teenage fathers in South African townships and showed clearly that neither these young men nor their fathers from the preceding generation have the cultural or material resources to be adequate fathers, let alone the kind of fathers they would like to be. The authors' analysis of stories told by young fathers about their own experience as children complicates the idea of father absence by distinguishing the impact and meaning of absence caused by death, never knowing anything of one's father, and physical absence with more or less contact. The young men further complicated "father presence" by differentiating between types of fathers, each of which provides examples to emulate or resist. Swartz and Bhana, drawing on the words used by the young fathers themselves, labeled them as "financial," "angry," "faithless," "talking," "caring," "friendly," and "drinking" fathers (p. 42). Like the children and youths quoted earlier from other studies, teenage fathers have also experienced good and bad 'fathering' from men other than their biological fathers, and many of their children are and will be dependent on the fathering of other men. Also similar to the young men who talked to Ramphele (2002), these young fathers are caught in the following cultural bind. On the one hand they see paternity as a proof of manhood, but on the other hand adults, particularly in the mothers' families, see them not as men but as boys and deny them participation in decisions about the custody of their children. The tragedy of the situation and the despair and depression experienced by young fathers are intensified because they have vivid images of what they should do to be good fathers: "To live with my child and the mother of my child [and to] have my own family ... because I think then I'm gonna be a perfect father. Then give my kids love, everything. Everything my kids want. If I can [make] a plan to give her everything ... and love – I think it will make me to be a good father to her" (Swartz & Bhana, 2009, p. 47). Although what they value or miss in their own experience of their fathers is closeness, emotional support, talking and caring, their own expectations of themselves are centered on financial provision: "I don't feel like a real father because I'm not working. I'm not supporting her and that. *A father's job is to be there and support his family* and I'm not doing that and that's what makes me feel a bit down" (Swartz & Bhana, 2009, p. 47, original emphasis).

Social Policy Issues Related to Fathering

The focus of popular and policy interest in Southern African fathering is on the causes of and solutions for what is seen as a crisis in fathering and a related crisis in masculinity. Assertions that these crises are real are usually supported by statements about the situation for which the evidence is sometimes inadequate and always open to interpretation. The most common of these statements are that: (1) marriage rates are very low, (2) a high percentage of births are to unmarried women, (3) for many births, the father is either unknown or never involved, (4) many fathers are absent, (5) many children receive no support from their fathers, (6) children and women are the victims of violence inflicted by men, (7) men are the perpetrators of sexual abuse of children, and (8) adult deaths from AIDS leave many orphans, who are particularly vulnerable in the absence of fathers.

Violence and abuse are notoriously difficult to measure, but there are indications that the people of Southern Africa are correct in seeing their societies as plagued by violence and sexual abuse. For instance, news reports and ordinary conversations describe the common sound of gunshots in the townships, car-jackings and home invasions in the cities, and fights and beatings in the villages. There can be little doubt that most of the violence is perpetrated by men, or that many women and children are subject to routine violence and are safer when they can escape their husbands and fathers. One South African study gave an indication of the scale of the problem when it reported that one-fifth of the 2,000 men surveyed admitted to having had sex with a woman without her consent (Andersson & Mhatre, 2003).

It is almost impossible to determine the incidence of sexual abuse of children in Southern Africa or whether the incidence is increasing, but it is clear that sexual abuse of children has become an issue of public concern in South Africa, as indicated in both press reports and research publications (Posel, 2005). In the great majority of reported cases the perpetrator is a man related to the child. Contributing to the danger of abuse is the fact that 32% of South African children are exposed at least once a month to someone in their household or neighborhood who is drunk (Brookes et al., 2004).

The two common explanations for the fatherhood crisis are not necessarily contradictory but they do emphasize different aspects of the situation. The first suggests a moral failure and a crisis of masculinity in which men pursue their own immediate ends without concern for the interests of others or the welfare of the community. The second explanation emphasizes the history of assaults on African masculinity, the physical subjugation of African men, the brutal removal from men of control over their land and lives, generations of being treated at best as 'boys' and at worst as sub-human, and a contemporary economy that allows barely half of them the ability to support a family.

One public 'policy' response corresponding to explanations in terms of moral failure or psychological damage takes the form of moral exhortation, such as Mandela's Father's Day speech and Anglican Archbishop Desmond Tutu's statements, and public education campaigns for personal responsibility in sexual relationships and parenthood such as those sponsored by the Fatherhood Project, the African Fathers Initiative, and Love Life (www. lovelife. org. za/index. php). These campaigns usually emphasize 'responsible' fatherhood in the context of nuclear or marital families, but they also recognize the desirability of wider definitions of paternity, and become oriented towards broader reformulations of masculinity:

> Many men can play the role of father to a child, including grandfathers, uncles, stepfathers, foster-fathers, older brothers, cousins or family friends. Outside the family boyfriends, male carers, teachers, pastors, policemen and others can all fill the need expressed by children themselves for male nurturing in their lives.
>
> (Davies, 2011, ¶ 3)

This wider definition, though it is applicable worldwide, is generally presented as a distinctively African phenomenon, and the research on Southern African families cited above is often deployed to defend policies that are considered specific to culture, nation, or region. For example, Lesejane (2006), a leader in faith-based social policy formation, used Tswana culture as emblematic of African culture more broadly, and urged a revival of what he depicted as the 'responsible patriarchy' of traditional culture. Specifically, he argued for the continued relevance of boys' initiation, the initiation regiment, the men's council, and the clan as models for the reformation of fatherhood in contemporary society. News reports and personal communications indicate that initiation ceremonies have been reintroduced in Botswana and in northern areas of South Africa where they had been previously outlawed or abandoned; in Swaziland, Lesotho, and for many Zulus, the practice had never ceased. The meaning of the ceremonies has shifted from reinforcement of kinship-based social structure to emphases on cultural identity, individual rites of passage, and the values of education, self-discipline, and individual responsibility.

There have been three types of explicit policy interventions potentially relevant to fathering: (1) policies directly targeted at men to compel or coerce them into being responsible fathers; (2) policies directed towards the well-being of children and their mothers designed to help them resist abuse and to survive in the absence of financial support from men; and (3) general social and economic policies aimed at creating employment and education opportunities for men so that they can earn the income needed to support their families.

Botswana, with a 50-year experience of democratic elections and functioning governments, and South Africa, with a constitution that codifies gender equality among a large number of individual rights, have made formal commitments to gender-neutral policies and policies directed specifically at men. A common complaint is that these formal declarations have not been translated into concrete actions. One policy that is targeted at families is the attempt to determine the amount of child support and to enforce its payment. In both Botswana (Garey & Townsend, 1996; Mokomane, 2005) and South Africa actual payment of child support is limited by women's doubts that going to court will have any result, widely held ideas that payment of support for children implies an ongoing relationship between the child's father and mother, weak enforcement and the ease of evading payments, and the poverty of many fathers.

Government policy and many development programs operating in Southern Africa emphasize opportunities and services for women, and gender equity in employment and income (Beardshaw, 2006). This is a necessary policy priority in societies in which women are heavily responsible for their own maintenance and for the support of children. These policies and programs, however, reduce Southern African women's need for the economic support of men and weaken the cultural supports for men's presence as providers. The system of child support grants (and grants to the elderly, which allow many grandparents to contribute to the support of children) has clearly improved the well-being of children but is overwhelmingly directed at women. Similarly, campaigns against gender-based violence are appropriately aimed at women by providing the moral and physical resources to avoid abuse; programs directed at men are much less common.

Reducing poverty, creating jobs, encouraging small-scale farming, building adequate homes, providing basic services, and improving schools are all expensive and would require a redistribution of wealth and access to resources that is impossible politically. The governments of Botswana and South Africa do implement programs designed to mitigate the effects of economic inequality, but the scope of the problems remains enormous. In contrast, the monarchy of Swaziland has shown very little interest in either social reform or the redistribution of resources.

Speculation, Predictions for the Future, and Cultural Comparisons

Recent transformations in Southern African societies are not only increasing sub-cultural and individual variation in fathering, but also widening a divide among men, families, and children. On one side are men who have stable work and incomes. They face the same problems that fathers face anywhere, and show the same range of responsibility and attention to their children. On the other side are men who do not have much prospect of finding steady employment. For them, successful fathering is a severe challenge and a rare accomplishment.

The research on rural children in the Agincourt survey area described above (Madhavan et al., 2008) revealed a marked division in the stability of paternal support. Among children in the 10 to 20 age group in 2001, 41% had been supported by their fathers throughout their lives, 24% had never received any support, and 36% had received intermittent support. Nearly all those who had been supported consistently were the children of men who had work in distant urban areas; these children are adequately provided for and have relatively stable living situations, although their future prospects as rural children with rural educations are generally limited. Khume, in the opening Case Story, was this kind of father, as was Mowetsi, the father from Botswana (see pp. 185–186). Children who never received paternal support were not all destitute, and many of them lived in households that included grandfathers, uncles, or stepfathers who contributed to their well-being. But they certainly exemplified father absence and their chances in life were surely diminished. The 36% of fathers who provided intermittent support were a mixed group; some of them had died or abandoned their children, but most were like Tumelo in the Case Story, unable to find stable work and unable to provide consistently and adequately.

Although the Agincourt study population includes long-term migrant workers, it does not describe the lives of children whose entire families are permanently urban. More children in urban areas live with their fathers than do children in the rural areas, but even if those fathers are employed their children are not necessarily better fed or housed because of the higher costs of living in urban areas. The extreme poverty of shanty towns and informal settlements, where poverty is compounded by crowding, violence, and pollution, is one face of urban life in Southern Africa, and provides an environment even less supportive of successful fathering than the rural areas. But urban areas are also home to people who have moved away from rural life or circular migration socially and economically as well as physically, and have the skills and resources to take advantage of urban services and opportunities. Although they are often referred to as 'middle class,' these people cover a wide range of incomes and aspirations and are 'middle' only in the sense that they live somewhere between destitution and affluence. What members of the urban middle class have in common is the aspiration and opportunity to provide their children with education, mastery of English, and connections to people with modern-sector jobs that can secure their children's position in the modern economy.

One way that fathers conserve resources and advance their own children is to selectively 'prune' kinship relationships with poorer or demanding kin. At the same time they cultivate connections with kin who can be useful by providing contacts, a place to live while looking for work in a new town, a cheap rural base in hard times, lodging for children near a good school, or any of the many services that are still provided primarily by kin rather than formal institutions. Lesedi, in the Case Story, is separating his life from his rural kin, including his half-brother Tumelo, in just this way. One consequence of this pattern of behavior is a sharp divergence of life courses within extended families, and the emergence of restricted sub-sets of kin who combine culturally sanctioned mutual aid with the resources to make that aid effective. In the struggle to reach or retain middle-class status, the employment and income of individuals is crucial because children depend more on a single earner rather than on a group of kin. As a result, the various facets of fatherhood become concentrated rather than distributed, and children's improved prospects are coupled with vulnerable dependence on an individual adult.

Men in Southern Africa – economic successes and failures alike – are vulnerable to economic circumstances beyond their control and cannot base successful fatherhood on income alone. There is an urgent need for a massive transformation in men's aspirations and for cultural definitions of masculinity that do not entirely depend on being hard workers and material providers. If children do not and cannot depend on men for financial support, or can only do so if their fathers are providers at the expense of all other contributions to their children's well-being, Southern African cultures must emphasize and reinforce other good reasons for the stable presence of men in the lives of children. Men and women both understand those reasons, and children clearly value them, but the following aspects of the father's role need to be taken more seriously looking ahead, in the Southern African context: (1) living with children and participating in their daily lives; (2) establishing children's social identities and positions and their relationships with kin; (3) enabling children's positive social relationships outside the family with employers, patrons, and peers; (4) connecting children to institutions and services such as schools, medical care, churches, and voluntary associations; (5) encouraging children to develop their individual skills and resources for future success; (6) being close, trusted, affectionate, and emotionally supportive figures for their children; and (7) providing children with appropriate role models for adulthood.

Conclusion

It is certainly possible to look at fathering in Southern Africa and see a bleak picture and dire prospects. Closer examination of family life in

Southern Africa in its historic and cultural contexts, without denying the many social problems facing the region, provides a more complex, nuanced, and hopeful prognosis. After all, Southern African states are not ineffective, many institutions of civil society operate vigorously, their national economies are productive, and the people of the region continue to hope, dream, and work. Indeed, many Southern Africans live in strong and supportive families and raise children with all the energy, optimism, and abilities of children anywhere.

Summary

Southern African cultures include important roles for men in the lives of children even though the care of young children is seen as women's responsibility within a gendered division of labor and social activity. In a system of distributed or collective fatherhood, the father is one of several men expected to contribute to a child's well-being and fathers are expected to play a role in the lives of children other than their own offspring. More than a century of white domination, labor migration, and racial segregation have separated families. Social policy and cultural attitudes increasingly emphasize financial support as the central aspect of adequate fathering, but massive unemployment and economic inequality make it impossible for many fathers to provide financial support to their children. Families and governments must acknowledge and encourage the many non-financial ways that men can contribute to the lives of children.

References

African Fathers Initiative. (n.d.). *Research overview*. Retrieved September 25, 2011 from http://www.africanfathers. org/page. php?p_id=99

Andersson, N., & Mhatre, S. (2003). Do unto others – and pay the price: Combating sexual violence in the south of Johannesburg. *SA Crime Quarterly, 3*, 5–9.

Beardshaw, T. 2006. Taking forward work with men in families. In L. Richter & R. Morrell (Eds.), *Baba: Men and fatherhood in South Africa* (pp. 306–316). Cape Town, South Africa: HSRC Press.

Botswana Government. (2009). *Botswana demographic survey, 2006.* Gaborone, Botswana: Central Statistics Office.

Brookes, H., Shisana, O., & Richter, L. (2004). *National household HIV prevalence and risk survey of South African children.* Cape Town, South Africa: HSRC Press.

Burawoy, M. (1976). The functions and reproduction of migrant labor: Comparative material from Southern Africa and the United States. *American Journal of Sociology, 81*, 1050–1087.

Clowes, L. (2006). Men and children: Changing constructions of fatherhood in *Drum* magazine, 1951–1965. In L. Richter & R. Morrell (Eds.), *Baba: Men and fatherhood in South Africa* (pp. 108–117). Cape Town, South Africa: HSRC Press.

Comaroff, J. L. (Ed.). (1980). *The meaning of marriage payments*. New York, NY: Academic Press.

Crapanzano, V. (1985). *Waiting: The whites of South Africa*. New York, NY: Random House.

Davies, T. (2011). The fatherhood revolution is long overdue. *African Fathers Initiative*. Retrieved September 25, 2011, from http://africanfathers. org/article. php?a_id=69

Engle, P. (1997). The role of men in families: Achieving gender equity. *Gender and Development, 5* (2), 31–40.

Fatherhood Project. (2004). *Briefing on the fatherhood project 2004*. Cape Town, South Africa: HSRC. Retrieved September 25, 2011, from http://www. hsrc. ac. za/ Page-70.phtml

Garey, A. I., & Townsend N. W. (1996). Kinship, courtship, and child maintenance law in Botswana. *Journal of Family and Economic Issues, 17,* 189–203.

Gluckman, M. (1950). Kinship and marriage among the Lozi of Northern Rhodesia and the Zulu of Natal. In A. R. Radcliffe-Brown & D. Forde (Eds.), *African systems of kinship and marriage* (pp. 166–206). London, UK: Oxford University Press.

Greene, M. E., & Biddlecom A. E. (2000). Absent and problematic men: Demographic accounts of male reproductive roles. *Population and Development Review, 26,* 81–115.

Hewlett, B., & Macfarlan S. J. (2010). Fathers' roles in hunter-gatherer and other small-scale societies. In M. E. Lamb (Ed.), *The role of the father in child development* (5th ed.). Hoboken, NJ: Wiley.

Hosegood, V., Floyd, S., Marston, M., Hill, C., McGrath, N., Isingo, R., ... Zaba, B. (2007). The effects of high HIV prevalence on orphanhood and living arrangements of children in Malawi, Tanzania, and South Africa. *Population Studies, 61,* 327–336.

Human Sciences Research Council. (n.d.). *The Fatherhood Project*. Retrieved September 25, 2011, from http://www. hsrc. ac. za/Page-67. phtml

Junod, H. A. (1927). *The life of a South African tribe* (2nd ed.). London, UK: Macmillan.

Khunou, G. (2006). Fathers don't stand a chance: Experiences of custody, access, and maintenance. In L. Richter & R. Morrell (Eds.), *Baba: Men and Fatherhood in South Africa* (pp. 265–277). Cape Town, South Africa: HSRC Press.

Krige, E. J. (1936). *The social system of the Zulus*. London, UK: Longmans, Green.

Krige, E. J., & Krige J. D. (1947). *The realm of a rain-queen: A study of the pattern of Lovedu society*. New York, NY: Oxford University Press.

Kuper, H. (1947). *An African aristocracy: Rank among the Swazi*. New York, NY: Oxford University Press for the International African Institute.

Kuper, H. (1986). *The Swazi: A South African kingdom* (2nd ed.). New York, NY: Holt, Rinehart, and Winston.

Lesejane, D. (2006). Fatherhood from an African cultural perspective. In L. Richter & R. Morrell (Eds.), *Baba: Men and fatherhood in South Africa* (pp. 173–182). Cape Town, South Africa: HSRC Press.

Lloyd, C. B., & Blanc, A. K. (1996). Children's schooling in sub-Saharan Africa: The role of fathers, mothers, and others. *Population and Development Review, 22,* 265–298.

Madhavan, S., Townsend, N. W., & Garey, A. I. (2008). 'Absent breadwinners': Father–child connections and paternal support in rural South Africa. *Journal of Southern African Studies, 34*, 647–663.

Mail & Guardian. (2010). Zuma's conduct undermines his own govt's message. *Mail and Guardian online.* February 1, 2010. Retrieved September 25, 2011, from http://mg. co. za/article/2010–02–01–zumas-conduct-undermines-his-own-govts-message

Mandela, N. (2001). Address at father's day lunch hosted by Zindzi Mandela: Madiba pays warm tribute to Nkosi. *Nelson Mandela Foundation.* Retrieved September 25, 2011, from http://db.nelsonmandela.org/speeches/pub_view. asp?pg=search&opt=basic

Mkhize, N. (2006). African traditions and the social, economic and moral dimensions of fatherhood. In L. Richter & R. Morrell (Eds.), *Baba: Men and fatherhood in South Africa* (pp. 183–198). Cape Town, South Africa: HSRC Press.

Mokomane, Z. (2005). Cohabitation in Botswana: An alternative or a prelude to marriage? *African Population Studies, 20*, 19–37.

Murray, C. (1981). *Families divided: The impact of migrant labour in Lesotho.* Cambridge, UK: Cambridge University Press.

Niehaus, I. (1994). Disharmonious spouses and harmonious siblings: Conceptualizing household formation among urban residents of Qwaqwa. *African Studies, 53*, 115–136.

Posel, D. (2005). Sex, death and the fate of the nation: Reflections on the politicization of sexuality in post-Apartheid South Africa. *Africa, 75*, 125–153.

Posel, D. (2006) Moving on: Patterns of labour migration in post-apartheid South Africa. In M. Tienda, S. Tollman, & E. Preston-Whyte (Eds.), *African migration and urbanisation in comparative perspective* (pp. 217–231). Johannesburg, South Africa: University of the Witwatersrand Press.

Posel, D., & Devey R. (2006). The demographics of fatherhood in South Africa: An analysis of survey data, 1993–2002. In L. Richter & R. Morrell (Eds.), *Baba: Men and fatherhood in South Africa* (pp. 38–52). Cape Town, South Africa: HSRC Press.

Prinsloo, J. (2006). Where have all the fathers gone? Media(ted) representations of fatherhood. In L. Richter & R. Morrell (Eds.), *Baba: Men and fatherhood in South Africa* (pp. 132–146). Cape Town, South Africa: HSRC Press.

Prinsloo, J. (2009). Theorising news mediations of the Zuma rape trial: Citizens and subjects in collision. *Critical Discourse Studies, 6*(2), 81–96.

Ramphele, M. (1993). *A bed called home: Life in the migrant labor hostels of Cape Town.* Columbus, OH: Ohio University Press.

Ramphele, M. (2002). *Steering by the stars: Being young in South Africa.* Cape Town, South Africa: Tafelberg.

Ramphele, M., & Richter L. (2006). Migrancy, family dissolution and fatherhood. In L. Richter & R. Morrell (Eds.), *Baba: Men and Fatherhood in South Africa* (pp. 73–81). Cape Town, South Africa: HSRC Press.

Richter, L. (2009). Foreword. In S. Swartz and A. Bhana (Eds.), *Teenage Tata: Voices of young fathers in South Africa* (pp. vii–viii). Cape Town, South Africa: HSRC Press.

Richter, L., & Morrell R. (Eds.). (2006). *Baba: men and fatherhood in South Africa*. Cape Town, South Africa: HSRC Press.

Richter, L., & Smith, W. (2006). Children's views of fathers. In L. Richter & R. Morrell (Eds.), *Baba: Men and fatherhood in South Africa* (pp. 155–172). Cape Town, South Africa: HSRC Press.

Schapera, I. (1966). *Married life in an African tribe*. Evanston, IL: Northwestern University Press.

Sharp, J. (1994). A world turned upside down: Households and differentiation in a South African bantustan in the 1980s. *African Studies, 53*, 71–88.

Smith, D. (2010). 'Father of the Nation' Jacob Zuma leaves South Africa feeling deflated. *The Guardian*, 26 February, 2010. Retrieved September 25, 2011, from http://www. guardian.co.uk/world/2010/feb/26/david-smith-letter-from-south-africa

Spiegel, A. (1987). Dispersing dependants: A response to the exigencies of labour migration in rural Transkei. In J. Eades (Ed.), *Migrants, workers and the social order* (pp. 113–129). London, UK: Tavistock.

Spiegel, A., Ross F., & Wilkinson D. (1996). Domestic fluidity in Die Bos. *Social Dynamics, 22*, 55–71.

Statistics South Africa (2004). *Census 2001: primary tables South Africa: census '96 and 2001 compared* (Report No. 03/02/04 (2001)). Pretoria: Statistics South Africa. Retrieved September 25, 2011, from http://www. statssa. gov. za/census01/html/C2001PrimTables. asp

Super, C. M., & Harkness S. (1986). The developmental niche: A conceptualization at the interface of child and culture. *International Journal of Behavioral Development, 9*, 545–569.

Swartz, S., & Bhana A. (2009). *Teenage tata: Voices of young fathers in South Africa*. Cape Town, South Africa: HSRC Press.

Townsend, N. W. (1997). Men, migration, and households in Botswana: An exploration of connections over time and space. *Journal of Southern African Studies, 23*, 405–420.

Weisner, T. S. (2002). Ecocultural understanding of children's developmental pathways. *Human Development, 45*, 275–281.

Part Four

Americas

Chapter Nine

Fathers in Caribbean Cultural Communities

Jaipaul L. Roopnarine
Syracuse University, Syracuse, NY, USA

Case Story: Fathering in an Extended Family

Rakesh and Chitra (both 30 years of age and of East Indian origin) live with their 2- and 5-year-old sons in the municipality of Penal/Debe in southern Trinidad. They met while they were working at a bookstore, and in consultation with their parents they arranged their own marriage. Because Chitra grew up in a Hindu household and Rakesh in a Christian household, two separate wedding ceremonies were performed. This couple represents a growing trend among young Indo Caribbeans to choose their own marital partners and embrace different religious beliefs, yet remain traditional in other aspects of their lives. After marriage, they moved into a flat above Rakesh's family residence that is located about a half-mile from Chitra's ancestral home. This living arrangement is viewed as temporary; they hope to save enough money for a down payment on a piece of land to build their own house.

Rakesh is very reserved and maintains a good deal of distance from his father and brothers due to family disputes. Work is unpredictable and wages are generally low in his town. On most days, he appears worried and the demands of work keep him away from the children. Chitra normally cleans the flat, prepares breakfast, and gets the older child ready for school. The maternal grandmother has been caring for the 2-year-old while Chitra and Rakesh are at work. When the children are at the maternal grandparents' residence, Chitra's younger brother and sister assist in caring for them.

On weekday mornings, Rakesh drops the older child off at his full-day early childhood program and the younger one off at the maternal grandparents' home before going to work. He fusses about the older child's behavior and often threatens to discipline him when he misbehaves.

When he disciplines the older child, the treatment can be harsh involving physical punishment and a series of stern verbal reprimands. By all
accounts, Rakesh is more involved in the care of his children than men of
the previous generation. But his involvement is mostly confined to taking
the children to places and events (e.g., church social gatherings), physical
discipline, and watching television with them (e.g., wrestling and sporting events). Rakesh sometimes looks puzzled and uncertain about how he
should approach his responsibilities as a father. He remains quiet for long
stretches of time when he is with the children.

Life in this extended family in southern Trinidad provides a glimpse into
the internal dynamics of paternal responsibilities in one Caribbean cultural
community. Yet it by no means captures the diverse family structural and
social arrangements within which fatherhood and fathering are situated
across the Caribbean. Over the last two decades, my colleagues (Anderson,
2007; Brown, Anderson, & Chevannes, 1993; Samms-Vaughan, 2005) and
I have documented different aspects of father involvement with young
children (0–8 years) in different ethnic groups and in non-marital and
marital family systems in English-speaking Caribbean countries. Several
other researchers (e.g., Flinn, 1992; Munroe & Munroe, 1992; Wilson &
Kposowa, 1994) contributed to these efforts in seminal ways by examining father availability and caregiving interactions with biological and non-
biological offspring. More recent studies (Anderson, 2007; Roopnarine &
Krishnakumar, 2010) have moved beyond demonstrating that Caribbean
fathers are involved in the care and socialization of young children, to test
paradigms about male parenting practices in different family constella-
tions and ethnic groups. In this chapter, I situate the findings of these later
studies and those of Caribbean immigrant men in North America within
a socio-historical and cultural context and elucidate their implications for
childhood development and for social policies on fathering. My primary
focus is on fathers and young children in Indo Caribbean and African
Caribbean families in English-speaking Caribbean countries. With their
respective histories of social and political oppression, these two major ethnic groups have established contrasting family structural and residential
patterns for entrance into parenthood and for fathering.

Cultural and Historical Background as It Influences Fathering

Cultural and cross-cultural researchers (e.g., Greenfield, Keller, Fuligni, &
Maynard, 2003) have emphasized the importance of socio-historical influences on developmental pathways, and the cultural adaptations families

make to accomplish childrearing and socialization goals in the face of social and economic hardships (Ogbu, 1981). In different Caribbean countries, couple/partner and father–child relationships have evolved out of the inter-related histories of conquest, slavery, and indentured servitude. The arrival of the Spanish, English, French, and Dutch in the New World marked the beginning of long periods of enslavement, indentured servitude, and socio-political domination that would last for centuries. Through the periods of slavery, post-emancipation, indentureship, and post-independence, Caribbean families experienced cycles of social, political, economic, and population transformations that were attributed to social and economic exploitation by the European colonial powers (Barrow, 1998). Of interest here are the social changes that affected the structural arrangements of families, the role of men in families, and the childrearing patterns of native peoples, slaves from Africa, and indentured servants brought from India between 1838 and 1917 after slavery was abolished (Barrow, 1998; Brereton, 1974). On the topic of fathering, European colonization, slavery, and indentured servitude have been discussed in terms of the emergence of women-headed families, "male marginality" in family life, and the retention and/or modification of ancestral religious and cultural practices (Deen, 1995; Leo-Rhynie, 1997). In African Caribbean families today, mate-shifting wherein men and women move on to other relationships through the life cycle, low marriage rates, and child-shifting (a form of fosterage whereby children are cared for by relatives and non-relatives) are all vestiges of the dehumanizing effects of slavery and persistent poverty. For instance, the offspring born to slaves belonged to the master of the woman slave, and the relationship between parent and child was determined through the mother, ignoring paternal rights (Patterson, 1967). According to some scholars, this set in motion matrifocal family structures and affiliations, often at the expense of separating men from families (Frazier, 1951; Patterson, 1967; Smith, 1996).

The matrifocal family, with extended female networks, was predominant among poor women and persisted over time. Affected by poor economic conditions, this family structure, in which marriage became less central to male–female relationships, has been credited with shaping family-based attitudes about mating, marital relationships, and childcare roles in Caribbean societies (Brunod & Cook-Darzens, 2002). Other scholars (e.g., Higman, 1973) have disagreed with this perspective and proposed instead that slave families were more diverse in structural arrangements under the plantation system (e.g., Craton, 1979; Higman, 1973), mirroring African ancestral patterns of family organization. In my opinion, although these historical accounts provide insights into the structural organization of slave families in the Caribbean plantation system and into the impact of slavery on families (e.g., Beckles, 1989; Frazier, 1951), current patterns

of male roles in Caribbean societies are probably more influenced by difficult economic conditions and men's views about manhood than historical
experiences *per se*. Economic conditions have often forced men to migrate
to find work and leave family members behind. At the same time, values
of male dominance and traditional conceptions of women's roles as caregivers have contributed to low levels of paternal involvement.

As in slavery, indentureship was not meant to preserve Indian family
structure or traditions (Barrow, 1998). Because its aim was to procure cheap
labor, disproportionate numbers of East Indian males (68%) were brought
to the Caribbean. Most of the females who came were widows, women
abandoned by their husbands, unmarried pregnant women, or prostitutes
(Reddock, 1994). The gender imbalance, poor living conditions in the bar-
racks, and lack of legal recognition of Hindu and Muslim marriages in
Guyana and Trinidad and Tobago all conspired against the continuance of
the traditional Indian family (Barrow, 1998). In addition, unstable family
patterns stemming from infidelity and polyandry led to increased violence
toward women (Sharma, 1986) and undermined the establishment of conjugal unions. Nevertheless, during the immediate post-indenture period
(after 1917) a system of arranged marriages (including pre-pubescent and
pubescent boys and girls) was put in place whereby men and women
were considered married if they lived together (Mohammed, 1997). It
was not until a hundred years after the indenture system was instituted
that marriages became more recognized for Indo Caribbeans. Over time,
the gender imbalance disappeared and more traditional forms of family
organization resurfaced. Descriptions of family life during the post-indentureship period through the latter part of the 20th century suggest that
Indo Caribbean men were more concerned about their role as economic
providers than with childrearing (Jayawardena, 1963; Rauf, 1973).

There are still debates about the impact of degrading socio-historical
experiences on family structure and relationships and the extent to which
ancestral beliefs and practices were integrated into modern day childrearing. Cultural and social elements of African and Indian traditions have
been incorporated into family life in the Caribbean. For example, multiple caregiving, extended living arrangements, and some religious beliefs
and practices (e.g., Orisha, Hindu) have their roots in ancestral traditions
(see Chaudhary, Ch. 4, this volume). Moreover, in indigenous African cultures, marriage was central to male–female intimacy, childbearing, and
childrearing within an extended family network (Nsamenang, 2010). Due
to the disintegrative effects of slavery, it is difficult to draw conclusions
about connections between ancestral traditions and male parenting among
African Caribbean men. Arguably, a better case can be made for such historical continuities for Indo Caribbean men because of the symbolic rituals
and practices expressed during marriage ceremonies (e.g., knotting of the

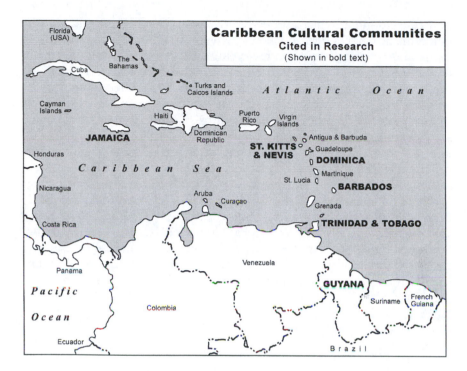

Figure 9.1 Map of the Caribbean, courtesy of Paul R. Larson.

wedding garb of the bride and groom), after the birth of children (e.g., naming and head-shaving ceremonies that call upon the father to participate), and during childhood transitions (e.g., *janew*, in which the Indian father ushers his son into manhood), all of which may be traced back to India. Yet tremendous caution should be exercised in generalizations about cultural continuity and the carryover of male attitudes and childrearing practices from India to the Caribbean. In short, even though Caribbean researchers (Samuel & Wilson, 2009) have emphasized the continuity of childrearing practices from ancestral cultures, men's roles in childhood socialization in both Indo Caribbean and African Caribbean family systems have not been adequately considered in the context of periods of slavery, indentured servitude, and pre-independence.

Contemporary Social Conditions That Affect Fathering: Family Configurations and Manhood

Fatherhood and fathering in Caribbean cultural communities occur in diverse and complex family systems. In some family systems marriage and co-residential living lay the foundation for having children and for emerging father–child relationships, whereas in other family systems sexual relationships and pair-bonds develop and dissolve around the birth of children outside of marriage (Brown et al., 1993; Samuel & Wilson, 2009). The prevalence of non-marital mating systems in Caribbean communities over the last two centuries runs counter to the two-parent nuclear family in European and European-heritage cultures that has been the benchmark for assessing paternal involvement with young children worldwide. On several fronts, Caribbean family living arrangements challenge theoretical frameworks that have emphasized the importance of the biological father and strong male–female emotional bonds as prerequisites for high levels of paternal investment in offspring (Hofferth & Anderson, 2003). They also raise questions about clinical treatment programs for children that are premised on the prototypical two-parent, married family model. Anthropologists sensitive to the role of social and biological factors have discussed the importance of non-biological fathers in children's lives and men's investment in caregiving when other adults contribute to childrearing (e.g., Fouts, Ch. 7, this volume; Hewlett & McFarlan, 2010; Townsend, Ch. 8, this volume).

Indo Caribbean fathers

For Indo Caribbeans, marriage (71%, 74% and 67% in three different samples in Guyana and Trinidad were married) remains a basis for family formation, definition of manhood, and subsequently fatherhood (Rauf, 1973). Heavily influenced by the patriarchal conceptions (e.g., *pativrata* – the subservient wife) and marriage systems of northern India, the Indo Caribbean family subscribes to marriage rituals, roles and responsibilities articulated in ancient Hindu and religious texts (e.g., *Ramayana, Mahabharata*) – monogamy and devoted son/husband to family of origin (Chaudhary, Ch. 4, this volume). The religious beliefs and rituals described in these texts are conservative, assigning responsibility for nurturance and childcare to women, and for providing and protection to men (Hossain, Ch. 5, this volume; Kakar & Kakar, 2007). Dominance, virility, and sexual control of women are still valued and exercised by Indo Caribbean males in Trinidad and Tobago and Guyana (Roopnarine et al., 1997).

Insofar as traditional masculine values are present across ethnic groups in Caribbean societies, economic ascendancy and better educational attainment among Indo Caribbeans have led to some modifications of ancient marriage rituals and patriarchal traditions. The much maligned dowry system that contributed to asymmetric husband–wife roles has largely been discarded, as couples choose their own marital partners, and Hindu marriage ceremonies performed in Indo Caribbean communities

Figure 9.2 A 62-year-old Indo Caribbean immigrant male extended kin engaging in pretend play with 6- and 3-year-old girls in Hamilton, Ontario. Photo courtesy of Jaipaul Roopnarine.

increasingly emphasize the joint efforts of men and women to raise sons and daughters (Barrow, 1998; Nevadomsky, 1980). Further, the nuclear family has replaced the paternal extended family as the norm (e.g., 64.6% of Indo-Guyanese designated their families as nuclear; only 24% described them as extended). All of these trends may weaken the grip of patriarchal traditions on childhood care and socialization (Samuel & Wilson, 2009). This is in sharp contrast to what is witnessed in some parts of India, where traditional practices regarding marriage and husband–wife roles still prevail (Chaudhary, this volume), and 67% of the elderly live with an adult child amid dramatic economic and technological changes (Desai et al.,

2010). As in the ancestral culture, most Indo Caribbean children live with biological fathers in married nuclear units, or extended and transitional extended households. Increasing divorce rates (although low, e.g., 2% in Guyana) have led to the rise of single mother/extended living arrangements (Roopnarine & Krishnakumar, 2010; Samuel & Wilson, 2009).

African Caribbean fathers

By comparison, becoming a father in African Caribbean communities is more likely to begin in non-married mating unions than in married relationships (marriage rates of 29.2%, 23.7%, and 37.3% in three different Jamaican samples; Anderson, 2007; Brown, Newland, Anderson, & Chevannes, 1997; Samms-Vaughan, 2005). In this context, men and women enter visiting unions, in which they have sexual relationships while living apart, before moving on to common-law unions. After achieving relative economic security, men/fathers may eventually marry (Brown et al., 1997). Of course, marriage remains an entry point into male–female relationships for some men, and across age groups marriage becomes more likely with higher educational training, material resources, and church membership (Anderson, 2007). With the birth of children in visiting and common-law relationships where a couple shares a residence and resources but are not married, men and women acquire the status of "baby father" and "baby mother," even when biological paternity may be dubious. Having a child confers manhood and brings social status to men in the community (Anderson, 2007; Brown et al., 1997). Surveys conducted on fathers in Jamaica show that about 26% of men report having two "baby mothers" and 11% had three "baby mothers" (Anderson, 2007; Brown et al., 1997). Thus, men become biological fathers in different mating unions with concurrent opportunities for "social fatherhood" (fathering of other men's biological offspring), as female partners may also have offspring from previous mating relationships. Interestingly, African Caribbean women do not see marriage as necessary for motherhood (Powell, 1986). Their marriage rates and mating patterns contradict some of the basic tenets of family formation and intimacy espoused by Christianity, which is practiced in most African Caribbean communities. A distressing fact is that a significant number of children in these multiple mating situations grow up without their biological fathers (as many as 61.1%), having little or no contact with them (Anderson, 2007).

Visiting relationships are evident in other cultural groups in North America (e.g., low-income African American men; Carlson & McLanahan, 2010; Tamis-LeMonda & McFadden, 2010) and short-term cohabitation in European societies may result in the birth of children (e.g., Norwegian men and women; Seltzer, 2005; Haas & Hwang, Ch. 13, this volume). However,

African Caribbean men/fathers distinguish themselves from men in other cultural groups in that mate-shifting has a long, adaptive history and follows a life-course developmental process in which a stable relationship is the ultimate goal (Brown et al., 1997). There is also the possibility of conceptual separation between fathering and the spousal/partner relationship due to men's adherence to traditional definitions of masculinity, as discussed later (Anderson, 2007). Marriage rates increase appreciably as men age (44.3% for men over 35), but conjugal or relationship stability is often threatened by poor economic resources that lead fathers to migrate away from family members in search of better employment opportunities. This may force women to terminate current relationships and mating unions – the latter is characterized as "no romance without finance" (Brown et al., 1997).

Sub-Cultural and Cultural Variations in Fathering in Different Caribbean Cultural Communities

About 15 years ago, Brown and her colleagues (Brown et al., 1997) asserted that Caribbean fathers were generally neglected in international attempts to understand parenting practices and childhood outcomes. Unfortunately, this is still true today. As stated above, data on Caribbean fathers are rather deficient and confined mostly to low-income African Caribbean families in Jamaica (e.g., Brown et al., 1997). I have provided detailed overviews of research on father involvement conducted between 1950 and 2000 in prior papers (Roopnarine, 2002, 2004). Below I offer only a summary of a few major findings on father involvement with young children from that time period and then concentrate more on recent efforts to understand qualitative aspects of parenting among Caribbean fathers.

Because of the practice of mate-shifting, it was popularly assumed that African Caribbean men were irresponsible and therefore uninvolved in children's lives (see Clarke, 1957, for the concept of "my mother who fathered me"). Likewise, based on the precepts of ancient Hindu traditions, Indo Caribbean fathers were characterized as strict and distant from young children. Thus, many earlier studies sought to find out what men actually did when they were around children and whether they were involved in "minding" children (see Brown et al., 1993, for a discussion of "minding").

Two sets of findings on fathers' involvement in feeding and cleaning infants and in care interactions with young children have since dispelled claims about male marginality in Caribbean families. First, a study on African Caribbean men in common-law relationships in Kingston, Jamaica (Roopnarine et al., 1995) showed that fathers spent as much time in primary care activities such as feeding and cleaning 1-year old infants as fathers in African American (Hossain & Roopnarine, 1994), rural Malay (Hossain et al., 2005), and Kadazan Malaysian families (Hossain et al., 2008). A second study on Indo Caribbean and African Caribbean men in the Georgetown area of Guyana (Wilson, Wilson, & Berkeley-Caines, 2003) indicated that the percentage of fathers involved in feeding and attending to infants' needs at night were similar to percentages for fathers in technologically developed societies. Further, observations of families in northern Trinidad revealed that father care interactions occurred in conjunction with multiple caregivers: fathers engaged in about 10.3% of all caregiving interactions, compared to 44.2% by mothers, 17.6% by grandparents, 16.3% by siblings, 4.5% by aunts/uncles, and 7.2% by distant kin and non-relatives (Flinn, 1992). Father care is embedded in multiple caregiving (alloparenting) in several other cultural communities. For example, in India grandmother care increased between 7 and 11 months and care by aunts increased between 24 and 36 months during infancy (Sharma, 2000). But most studies have continued to use a dyadic, mother-centric model in assessing paternal care across the world (Brunod & Cook-Darzen, 2002; Fouts, Roopnarine, Lamb, & Evans, 2012).

Taken together, these and other findings from studies conducted in earlier decades (e.g., Brown et al., 1993, 1997) suggest that, as in other technologically developing societies, Caribbean fathers care for children in the context of alloparenting. Male caregiving and the socialization and upbringing of children are often situated in a network of female caregivers (termed "emotional expansiveness" by Brodber, 1975) with strong intergenerational bonds (Brunod & Cook-Darzen, 2002). Recent research investigations have shown that Caribbean men are involved in minding and caring for children, and can be good fathers independent of being family men. There have also been attempts to document the qualitative dimensions of parenting practices, that is, the warmth and sensitivity Caribbean fathers display during parenting and their links to cognitive and social functioning in young children. I turn to these newer findings next.

Indo Caribbean fathers

As described above, during the late- and post-indentureship periods, gender ratios improved considerably among Indo Caribbeans, and they were able to gradually restore different aspects of the traditional, patriarchal family that still exists in India (Barrow, 1998). Accordingly, it has been proposed that there is good intergenerational stability – the retentionist thesis – in present family organization patterns. This is seen in high rates of marriage and commitment to marriage in Indo Caribbean families, regardless of the quality of husband–wife relations. The patriarchal extended family has been evident in East Indian diasporas in Fiji, Mauritius, South Africa, Sri Lanka, Malaysia, and the Caribbean (Jayawardena, 1963; Mansinghe, 2001). Within this family system, men/fathers assume a dominant role, are peripheral to caregiving, and are emotionally distant from children (Jayawardena, 1963; Rauf, 1973; Roopnarine et al., 1997; Roopnarine, Evans, & Pant, 2011). Additionally, because of a preference for sons among East Indians, fathers routinely avoid engaging in close interactions with teenage daughters (Jayawardena, 1963). Is the Indo Caribbean family of the twenty-first century still steeped in these traditional parenting practices?

It is repeatedly proposed but seldom tested that Caribbean parents use a combination of warmth and control and harsh disciplinary practices during socialization (Leo-Rhynie, 1997). For example, harsh discipline (hitting with an object, slapping, pulling, etc.) and verbal insults and threats (e.g., "hardened" or stubborn in Trinidad; *A-betant* or troublesome in Dominica) are strongly endorsed by parents and children alike across Caribbean countries (Durbrow, 1999). In other cultures, physical discipline has consistently been shown to be associated with behavioral and emotional problems, regardless of society-wide acceptance of physical punishment as an approved way of addressing inappropriate childhood behaviors (McLoyd, Kaplan, Hardaway, & Wood, 2007).

In two recent studies, we determined the prevalence of parenting practices in Indo Caribbean fathers that reflect culturally-based childrearing tendencies and their associations with child development outcomes. A series of cluster analyses performed on responses provided on the Parental Acceptance-Rejection Questionnaire (PARQ) by Indo Caribbeans in Guyana ($N =139$ mothers) and a multi-ethnic sample ($N = 180$ mother–father pairs; 72% Indo Caribbean, 32% African Caribbean, and mixed-ethnic parentage) in Trinidad revealed that both mothers and fathers were high in warmth and affection and behavioral control, while displaying moderate levels of hostility and indifference toward preschool-aged children (Roopnarine & Krishnakumar, 2010). For low- to middle-income families in Trinidad, paternal and maternal warmth were significantly related. Mothers displayed slightly more warmth and punished children more frequently and more severely than fathers did, but mothers and fathers did not differ on behavioral control, hostility and aggression, indifference and neglect, or undifferentiated rejection. Fathers delayed punishing children far longer than did mothers. Among low-income Indo-Guyanese families fathers used physical punishment more often with their preschool-aged sons (70%) than with their daughters (52%) (Pant, Roopnarine, & Krishnakumar, 2008). The severity of Trinidadian fathers' physical punishment was significantly associated with teachers' assessments of physical aggression in preschoolers – a trend that emerged for other cultural groups (see Gershoff, 2002).

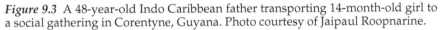

Figure 9.3 A 48-year-old Indo Caribbean father transporting 14-month-old girl to a social gathering in Corentyne, Guyana. Photo courtesy of Jaipaul Roopnarine.

These data are suggestive of the ethos and quality of parenting practices among Indo Caribbean fathers. Perhaps, as with the ancestral culture, it appears that the patriarchal context for childrearing in Indo Caribbean families may be changing, as the Case Story of Rakesh suggests. For example, fathers in India have been observed to engage in affectionate displays with infants as much as mothers did and to engage in a range of sensitively-attuned interactions like hugging and soothing infants (Roopnarine, Talukder, Jain, Joshi, & Sristastav, 1990). Comparable observational work has not been conducted on Indo Caribbean families, but the high levels of warmth toward preschoolers reported by fathers and greater involvement of mothers in disciplining children may signal a shift away from paternal emotional distance from preschool-aged children, and to a diminished role of Indo Caribbean fathers as disciplinarians. There are two possible reasons for these trends, in my view: (1) assimilation into multi-ethnic Caribbean cultural communities with an increase in nuclear families whereby women are employed and fathers are pressed to become more involved in childrearing out of necessity, and (2) movement away from more orthodox Hindu traditions that still govern much of family life in contemporary India. In other words, while there remain semblances of East Indian family life in the Caribbean, a creolization process began some time ago whereby Indo Caribbean fathers have incorporated elements of childrearing practices through extensive exposure to other cultural groups.

African Caribbean fathers

There is general agreement that African Caribbean men in different mating/marital unions are also increasing their involvement in parenting young children, in very positive ways (Anderson, 2007; Roopnarine & Krishnakumar, 2010). Yet fathering in African Caribbean families has largely been conceptualized with respect to men's conjugal or union status with their mating partners. This approach has ignored the possibility that African Caribbean fathers could be, as Anderson (2007, p. iii) put it, "good fathers but bad husbands." In other words, there may be conceptual separation between what it means to be a good father and to be committed to a relationship with a woman. In this regard, it may be incorrect to situate African Caribbean fatherhood and fathering in the context of a model of two-parent, marital stability. In view of the life course progressive relationship pattern of African Caribbean families, three issues are relevant here: (a) how men see themselves as fathers in terms of childrearing and culture-based socialization beliefs and practices, (b) family processes and developmental outcomes in children, and (c) fathering and partner relationships.

Using two newly developed scales (the Mandad Fatherhood Scale and Macho Scale) that measure fathering commitment and attitudes toward male dominance, virility, and domestic freedom, Anderson (2007) provided insight into Jamaican men's ($N = 1142$) beliefs about good fathering and its achievement. Similar to the findings of prior studies in Jamaica (Brown et al., 1993), men across socioeconomic groups identified economic support to children as a key characteristic of being a good father. However, they also emphasized emotional support, showing love, and responsibility as expectations of fathering. In line with regional cultural values about socialization (see Durbrow, 1999; Wilson et al., 2003), fathers thought that it was important to transmit manners, respect for others, honesty and integrity, to be loving and kind to others, and to exhibit 'the fear of God' and self-discipline to children during parenting. Men saw the need to encourage daughters to be independent and self-reliant and to "toughen" boys through harsh discipline for the economic and social realities of life. To implement these childrearing desires and goals, most fathers indicated that it was necessary to provide good role models, provide guidance, and spend time with children and reason with them. The main ways in which fathers showed approval of children's behaviors were through hugging, telling children that they were pleased with what they had done, offering encouragement and praise, giving rewards, and by kissing them (Anderson, 2007). These findings contrast with findings from earlier decades (Leo-Rhynie, 1997) that had suggested low levels of emotional expression and an inclination toward authoritarian socialization practices with young children by Caribbean parents.

In one of the few studies to assess developmental outcomes of family processes, Samms-Vaughan (2005) followed a group of 241 preschool-aged Jamaican children from diverse socioeconomic backgrounds through their transition to first grade. This research mapped families' socioeconomic resources and living arrangements very carefully and measured children's cognitive skills and achievement (Peabody Picture Vocabulary Test–PPVT, Raven's Progressive Matrices, McCarthy Scales of Children's Abilities, Wide Range Achievement Test, MICO Diagnostic Reading Test) and behavioral skills (Jamaican Child Behavior Checklist). It also assessed adult mental health (Brief Symptom Inventory–BSI), parenting stress (Parenting Stress Index), and family functioning (Family Adaptability and Cohesion Environment Scale–FACES-II). Approximately 80% of the children in Samms-Vaughan's sample lived with biological mothers and 50% were with biological fathers; for 65% of children both biological parents assumed the parenting role regardless of residential living status, and 14.8% only had female relatives acting as parents. Children whose parents had professional jobs were more likely to have biological parenting figures than children in households where parents had unskilled jobs. Despite the absence of active biological fathers in one-third of the households, most families reported good cohesion: 44.5% were connected or very connected (17.8%), with 24.6% separated and 13.1% disengaged. Moreover, a majority of families were assessed as flexible or very flexible (63.5%) showing good latitude in adapting to family social circumstances.

Not surprisingly, preschool-aged children who lived in homes that were crowded, lacked modern facilities, had fewer material possessions, or who lived in homes in which parents had unskilled jobs, had lower cognitive scores than their more privileged preschool-aged peers. There were significant positive associations between family functioning (cohesion and adaptability) and children's receptive vocabulary scores, and between paternal and maternal education and achievement and cognitive scores. Children from married households performed better academically and had better cognitive scores than children in other family arrangements. Child-shifting by father figures was associated with internalizing problem behavior in children, and children who had multiple father figures exhibited more withdrawn behavior. Similarly, children who lived with biological fathers and surrogate mothers fared poorly, both academically and behaviorally, perhaps because children had difficulty forming close relationships and maintaining ties to paternal and maternal figures who moved in and out of family systems.

These findings underline the importance of family stability and family cohesion and adaptability for children's social and cognitive development. However, achieving family stability is not easy for Caribbean men because of perennial economic hardship, physical separation from children, the desire to be independent, and conflicts with partners. For example, Jamaican men who had experienced little or no contact with their own fathers stressed the need to be different, but those from the lowest income levels stated that labor market constraints prevented them from being fully responsible fathers (Anderson, 2007). The inability to provide economic support was the major source of dissatisfaction in men's role as fathers (56.1%). Lower-income Jamaican men were more likely than their more affluent counterparts to have more baby mothers and more children, and to use violence during partner conflicts. Religiosity, as measured by church membership and attendance, was associated with greater commitment to fathering and with less stereotyped views about masculinity (Anderson, 2007).

Recent scholarship about fathering in African Caribbean families has suggested that the fathering role and partner/spousal relationships can be distinguished (Anderson, 2007). Put differently, men may understand the requirements of being a good father and feel a sense of fulfillment in their role as fathers but may be reluctant to become solely committed to partners as "family men." Anderson wrote that "Jamaican men move within a world where there is a strong attachment to child-bearing and children, but a world which is colored by their expectations of domestic freedom and dominance. These two sets of ideals and expectations are potentially in conflict" (Anderson, 2007, p. 113). From this perspective, fathering in African Caribbean men cannot be viewed entirely within the parameters of a household, or a well-defined marriage (Anderson, 2007; Smith, 1996). I propose that currently fatherhood and fathering (for Indo Caribbean men, too) are more likely to be located in male identity via dominant male values and practices rather than in deeply-committed, mutually beneficial emotional relationships with a partner, or for that matter in egalitarian roles. Most low-income African Caribbean men are reluctant to express emotional feelings toward their partners/spouses and to respond to queries regarding their whereabouts in the community and activities with friends (Anderson, 2007). At the same time, they need baby mothers to cooperate and collaborate with them in meeting paternal responsibilities. The scant available evidence demonstrates that children from homes with the least economic resources and with child-shifting fathers perform progressively worse as they move from preschool to elementary school (Samms-Vaughan, 2005). Yet it is in these very low-income families that more traditional views about masculinity prevail, compounding the difficulties of those who want to have access to and to meet the emotional and intellectual needs of young children. New research is needed to clarify how African Caribbean fathers' investment in and care of children is affected by the resources of mating partners, number and presence of female and male caregivers available to children, and the age and gender of children.

Social Policy Issues Related to Fathering: Caribbean Immigrant Fathers

With the exception of Barbados and Trinidad and Tobago, economic development has remained anemic for decades throughout most of the Caribbean. This has spawned widespread internal, region-wide, and external migration to North America and Europe, contributing to the separation of fathers from children and the development of new family forms (Foner, 2001; Roopnarine & Shin, 2003). Migratory patterns vary, as some parents and children migrate together as family units, while others migrate serially and leave children behind. There are transnational living arrangements where parents move between cultural communities. The available data about Caribbean transnational families suggest that, as in other cultural groups, they establish social and economic ties in the sending country and their new cultural communities for various reasons which include business ventures, schooling, childrearing support and disciplinary practices, and seasonal work (Roopnarine & Shin, 2003). Studies on Caribbean immigrant families cover wide-ranging issues such as mental health and adjustment difficulties in the new cultural community (Broman, Neighbors, Delva, Torres, & Jackson, 2008; Seeman, 2011), cultural capital and ethnic identity (Reynolds, 2006), the impact of parental separation (Pottinger, 2005), and schooling and educational outcomes (Roopnarine, Krishnakumar, Metindogan, & Evans, 2006). I focus here on two topics of relevance to father–child relationships: (1) the impact of paternal separation due to migration, and (2) paternal involvement with children, specifically in North America.

In a common scenario among low-income Caribbean families, fathers and mothers migrate together or serially to North America, Europe, or another country of the Caribbean Community and Common Market ("CARICOM") to live or work for short periods, leaving children behind to be cared for by relatives and non-relatives. These parents literally ship material goods in barrel-like containers from North America and Europe to their children back in the Caribbean and are known pejoratively as "barrel children" families. Although children's material circumstances may be enhanced and parents maintain social contacts with their children via cell phones and the internet, children's emotional needs may languish. In these circumstances, the children left behind are forced to form new social ties with non-parental caregivers while simultaneously coping with separation from primary attachment figures. In a small-scale study conducted in Jamaica (Pottinger, 2005), 74% of the children were separated from fathers, with about half separated from a parent for an average of four years; 59% of the children were cared for by mothers, 22% by grandparents and 19% by other relatives. Contrary to claims about the disadvantages experienced by children who are separated from fathers, children in this study whose parents had migrated to England, Canada, and the U.S. did not show poorer psychological condition, lower academic performance, or any more behavioral difficulties in school, compared with peers whose parents had not migrated. Nevertheless, feelings of anger, loneliness, and isolation were evident in separated children, and these were negatively associated with their academic performance. Further, children who had someone to talk to and who viewed their parents' migration in positive terms tended to perform better in school (Pottinger, 2005). Apparently immigration itself did not lead to negative childhood outcomes in Pottinger's sample, because support mechanisms and children's self-regulation also contributed to their adjustment to changing life circumstances (see Aptaker, 2004; Masten & Osofsky, 2010).

Caribbean immigrant fathers in North America and Europe may face several challenges as they meet the demands of responsible fathering. Some fathers experience generational or cultural dissonance between family structural arrangements and parental practices (e.g., excessive use of physical punishment) that are commonly accepted in the Caribbean as opposed to what is expected in their host country (Hassan, Rousseau, Measham, & Lashley, 2008). In other words, difficulties may arise from acculturation demands to conform to the two-parent, residential family structural arrangement, more egalitarian roles, and child support standards in the new cultural community, all of which are in direct contrast with the more loosely organized Caribbean systems of mating and parenting. Research has shown that there is cultural continuity in parenting beliefs and practices among Caribbean immigrants in Canada (Hassan et al., 2008), New York (Roopnarine, Krishnakumar, & Xu, 2009), and other immigrant groups (Updegraff, Delgado, & Wheeler, 2009). Qualitative accounts of men of Caribbean ancestry living in England indicate that cultural capital in the form of ethnic solidarity and extended social support can facilitate their social adjustment and attempts to be effective fathers (Reynolds, 2006).

Data on Caribbean immigrant fathers are sparse. In one mixed-ethnic sample of Caribbean immigrant two-parent families who lived in the New York City area (Roopnarine et al., 2006), we found that fathers and mothers did not differ significantly in assessments of authoritarian, authoritative, and permissive parenting styles as measured by the Parental Authority Questionnaire (PAQ). Mothers exceeded fathers in academic socialization of preschoolers at home (engagement in homework, reviewing school work, reading, etc.) and on a measure of parent–school contact (attempts to contact children's school about academic progress, behavioral/disciplinary issues, and involvement in school functions). Again, drawing on cultural and social capital, paternal involvement with children occurred in collaboration with diverse caregivers. Compared to mothers (45.5% of the time), fathers accounted for 24.4%, grandparents 10.2%, other relatives (uncles, aunts, cousins) 12.1%, and non-relatives (neighbors and sitters) for 7.8% of the time spent engaged in academic activities at home with children.

Our subsequent study focused on ethno-theories about the distribution of childcare responsibilities in 60 Indo Caribbean immigrant families living in the New York City area (Roopnarine et al., 2009). Analysis of responses to questions about gender roles indicated that men and women held conservative beliefs about financial, emotional, and physical caregiving responsibilities even after living for an average of 12 years in a more egalitarian society. Their beliefs paralleled the traditional role dichotomy found in the Caribbean communities from which they migrated and those found in their ancestral culture. Fathers spent less time than mothers in basic childcare activities and in getting children ready for school, but there were no significant differences between maternal and paternal involvement in educational activities with children at home or in taking children to school. It was noteworthy that in 33% of the families, fathers provided more childcare during weekdays than did mothers, and that the gap between maternal and parental childcare narrowed on weekends. It may be that, irrespective of beliefs about gender roles, men are forced by necessity to perform childcare duties in households when women contribute appreciably to the economic support of their families.

Conclusions about Caribbean immigrant fathers would be premature at this point in time. Most of these fathers are twice removed from their ancestral cultures and have been influenced by diverse social and economic factors in the Caribbean. Their destinations are usually industrialized nations, but they may also live temporarily in developing CARICOM nations on their way to the developed world. It can at least be said that as in other immigrant groups that originated in patriarchal cultures, Caribbean immigrant men seem to hold on to traditional belief systems about role distribution and parenting practices. They also spend less time than women in childcare activities and use support from relatives and non-relatives in everyday childrearing situations. Further, when the immigration experience is viewed by children in a positive light, parental separation due to migration has less severe consequences for childhood social adjustment.

Research and Social Policy Implications

More research is needed to better understand fathering in native Caribbean and Caribbean immigrant communities. Our knowledge would be greatly enhanced by increased focus on processes that influence father involvement and childhood outcomes. For instance, across cultures, family stability influences parenting skills and childhood outcomes. Therefore, researchers need to examine links between relationship stability, family cohesion and adaptability, developmental and relationship history, emotional support, gendered ideologies and parenting practices and childhood social and cognitive functioning in diverse Caribbean ethnic groups. Factors such as material resources, family size, extended support from male and female adult caregivers, sibling care, and child–adult relationships must be considered as potential mediators or moderators. The conceptual separation between fathering and partner/spousal roles in African Caribbean families is intriguing and needs to be examined more systematically. Such work would contribute to the development of fathering theories that are not wedded to the two-parent, married family model that has governed most previous fathering research.

Fathering in the Caribbean must be understood as fully entrenched in patriarchal traditions and in the context of scarce economic resources. For Indo Caribbean and African Caribbean men, fatherhood and fathering are defined through conceptions of manhood whereby men understand what it takes to be a good father, although the quality of pair-bonds may not be very strong or mutually fulfilling. Fathers of Caribbean ancestry in North America seem to maintain these ideologies but may be compelled to care for young children because their spouses or partners work. The two-parent, heterosexual family is held as the prototypical norm in technologically developed societies. In these societies, men have greater opportunities to develop improved father–child relationships by participating in social programs and by accessing information in parenting books, magazines, and websites (see O'Brien & Moss, 2010) than do men in the Caribbean. Most fathers in Caribbean cultural communities do not subscribe to the two-parent, married model, and some choose to forego their economic responsibilities to biological children.

A prudent approach to the development of policies for Caribbean fathers would be to consider the impact of economic conditions, belief systems, and family living arrangements. With meager resources and underdeveloped social service agencies, it makes little sense to suggest social policies based on the same ideals of parenting as in the technologically developed world. Caribbean governments may have to rely on home health personnel, workers in home visiting programs sponsored by NGOs and donor agencies (e.g., the Bernard van Leer Foundation), early childhood teachers, and religious leaders to educate men about the importance of their support for partners during pregnancy and birth and about the beneficial effects of father–child interactions during infancy and early childhood. Television and radio programs and announcements about appropriate parenting techniques, domestic violence, and dominant male values have been used with some success in Trinidad and Tobago and Jamaica. At the community level, older men, particularly those in religious organizations, can encourage fathers to register the births of children, have their children immunized, and become involved in providing safe homes and social and intellectual stimulation to children.

Like Rakesh in the opening Case Story, most Caribbean men struggle to meet the economic needs of their families and the contemporary demands of responsible fatherhood. Although they would be a step in the right direction, economic policies alone will not increase the level of paternal responsibility to children in Caribbean communities. At the base of Indo Caribbean and African Caribbean cultural communities are issues of gender mistrust and male dominance that privilege men to act in a patriarchal manner toward family members. For example, Caribbean men rarely realize the implications of harmonious interpersonal relationships with partners/spouses for successful parenting. It is crucial, as we apply our growing understanding of Caribbean fathers, that policy initiatives incorporate an awareness of men's beliefs about what it means to be a man and a father in different Caribbean communities.

Summary

After providing a socio-historical background of African Caribbean and Indo Caribbean families, this chapter discussed the quality of paternal parenting practices and childhood outcomes. The disintegrating impact of slavery and indentured servitude on male investment with children was acknowledged. Marriage is a basis for entry into fatherhood and for childrearing in Indo Caribbean families, but among a majority of African Caribbean families fatherhood is realized and takes shape in non-marital unions where mate-shifting is a common practice. Unlike previous assertions about the lack of involvement with children among Caribbean fathers, contemporary studies of parenting practices indicated that (a) paternal involvement occurs within the context of multiple male and female caregivers, (b) both groups of fathers displayed moderate levels of warmth and sensitivity toward young children, (c) family stability and cohesion and economic conditions influenced the quality of paternal involvement and childhood outcomes among African Caribbean fathers, and (d) Caribbean immigrant fathers in North America drew on cultural and social capital to enhance childrearing that is embedded in multiple caregiving and follow a gender-differentiated pattern. Policies that focus on men's conceptions of fatherhood and manhood, economic factors, and religiosity may be more meaningful for Caribbean cultural communities.

Acknowledgments

The author was supported by the Jack Reilly Institute for Early Childhood and Provider Education during the preparation of this manuscript.

References

Anderson, P. (2007). *The changing roles of fathers in the context of Jamaican family life*. Kingston, Jamaica: Planning Institute of Jamaica and the University of the West Indies.

Aptaker, L. (2004). The changing developmental dynamics of children in particularly difficult circumstances: Examples of street and war-traumatized children. In U. Gielen & J. Roopnarine (Eds.), *Childhood and adolescence: Cross-cultural perspectives and applications* (pp. 377–410). New York, NY: Praeger.

Barrow, C. (1998). *Family in the Caribbean: Themes and perspectives*. Kingston, Jamaica: Ian Randle.

Beckles, H. (1989). *Natural rebels: A social history of enslaved Black women in Barbados*. London, UK: Zed Books.

Brereton, B. (1974). The experience of indentureship: 1845–1917. In J. La Guerre (Ed.), *Calcutta to Caroni: The East Indians of Trinidad* (pp. 25–38). London, UK: Longman Caribbean.

Brodber, E. (1975). *A study of yards in the city of Kingston*. Mona, Jamaica: Institute for Social and Economic Research: Mona, Jamaica: University of the West Indies.

Broman, C. L., Neighbors, H. W., Delva, J., Torres, M., & Jackson, J. S. (2008). Prevalence of substance use disorders among African Americans and Caribbean Blacks in the National Survey of American Life. *American Journal of Public Health, 98*, 1107–1114.

Brown, J., Anderson, P., & Chevannes, B. (1993). *The contribution of Caribbean men to the family*. Report for the International Development Centre, Canada, Caribbean Child Development Centre, Mona, Jamaica: University of the West Indies.

Brown, J., Newland, A., Anderson, P., & Chevannes, B. (1997). In J. L. Roopnarine & J. Brown (Eds.), *Caribbean families: Diversity among ethnic groups* (pp. 85–113). Norwood, NJ: Ablex.

Brunod, R., & Cook-Darzens, S. (2002). Men's role and fatherhood in French Caribbean families: A multi-systemic resource approach. *Clinical Child Psychology & Psychiatry, 7*, 559–569.

Carlson, M., & McLanahan, S. S. (2010). Fathers in fragile families. In M. E. Lamb (Ed.), *The role of the father in child development* (pp. 241–269). Hoboken, NJ: Wiley.

Clarke, E. (1957). *My mother who fathered me: A study of family in three selected communities in Jamaica.* London, UK: George Allen & Unwin.

Craton, M. (1979). Changing patterns of Slave families in the British West Indies. *Journal of Interdisciplinary History, X*, 1–35.

Deen, S. (1995). *Research into Indian family history in Trinidad.* Paper presented at ISER-NCIC Conference on challenge and change, University of the West Indies, St. Augustine, Trinidad.

Desai, S., Dubey, A., Joshi, B., Sen, M., Sharrif, A., & Vannenman, R. (2010). *Human development in India challenges for a society in transition.* New York, NY: Oxford University Press.

Durbrow, E. H. (1999). Cultural processes in child competence: How rural Caribbean parents evaluate their children. In A. S. Masten (Ed.), *Cultural processes in child development: The Minnesota symposia on child psychology* (Vol. 29, pp. 97–121). Mahwah, NJ: Lawrence Erlbaum Associates.

Flinn, M. (1992). Paternal care in a Caribbean village. In B. Hewlett (Ed.), *Father–child relations: Cultural and biosocial contexts* (pp. 57–84). New York, NY: Aldine de Gruyter.

Foner, N. (2001). *Islands in the city: West Indian migration to New York.* Berkeley, CA: University of California Press.

Frazier, E. F. (1951). *The Negro family in the United States.* New York, NY: Dryden Press.

Fouts, H., Roopnarine, J. L., Lamb, M. E., & Evans, M. (2012). Infant social interactions with multiple caregivers: The importance of ethnicity and socio-economic status. *Journal of Cross-Cultural Psychology, 43* (2), 328–348.

Gershoff, E. T. (2002). Corporal punishment by parents and associated child behaviors and experiences: A meta-analytic and theoretical review. *Psychological Bulletin, 128*, 539–579.

Greenfield, P. M., Keller, H., Fuligni, A., & Maynard, A. (2003). Cultural pathways through universal development. *Annual Review of Psychology, 54*, 461–490.

Hassan, G., Rousseau, C., Measham, T., & Lashley, M. (2008). Caribbean and Filipino adolescents' and parents' perspectives of parental authority, physical punishment, and cultural values and their relation to migratory status. *Canadian Ethnic Studies, 40* (2), 171–186.

Hewlett, B. S., & Mcfarlan, S. J. (2010). Fathers' roles in hunter-gatherer and other small-scale societies. In M. E. Lamb (Ed.), *The role of the father in child development* (pp. 413–434). Hoboken, NJ: Wiley.

Higman, B. (1973). Household structure and fertility on Jamaican Slave plantation: A nineteenth century example. *Population Studies, 27*, 527–550.

Hofferth, S. L., & Anderson, K. (2003). Are all dads equal? Biology versus marriage as a basis for paternal involvement, *Journal of Marriage and the Family, 65,* 213–232.

Hossain, Z., & Roopnarine, J. L. (1994). African-American fathers' involvement with infants: Relationship to their functioning style, support, education, and income. *Infant Behavior and Development, 17,* 175–184.

Hossain, Z., Roopnarine, J. L., Isamel, R., Menon, S., & Sombuling, A. (2008). Fathers' and mothers' reports of involvement in caring for infants in Kadazan families in Sabah, Malaysia. *Fathering, 5,* 58–78.

Hossain, Z., Roopnarine, J. L., Masud, J., Muhamed, A. A., Baharudin, R., Abdullah, R., & Jahur, R. (2005). Mothers' and fathers' childcare involvement with young children in rural families in Malaysia. *International Journal of Psychology, 40,* 385–394.

Jayawardena, C. (1963). *Conflict and solidarity in a Guyanese plantation.* London, UK: (University of London) Athlone.

Kakar, S., & Kakar, K. (2007). *The Indians: Portrait of a people.* New Delhi, India: Penguin/Viking.

Leo-Rhynie, E. (1997). Class, race, and gender issues in child rearing in the Caribbean. In J. L. Roopnarine & J. Brown (Eds.), *Caribbean families: Diversity among ethnic groups* (pp. 25–55). Norwood, NJ: Ablex.

Mansinghe, V. (2001). *Callaloo or tossed salad? East Indian and the cultural politics of identity in Trinidad.* Ithaca, NY: Cornell University Press.

Masten, A., & Osofsky, J. (2010). Disasters and their impact on child development: Introduction to the special issue. *Child Development, 81,* 1029–1039.

McLoyd, V. C., Kaplan, R., Hardaway, C., & Wood, D. (2007). Does endorsement of physical discipline matter? Assessing moderating influences on the maternal and child psychological correlates of physical discipline in African American Families. *Journal of Family Psychology, 21,* 165–175.

Mohammed, P. (1997). The idea of childhood and age of sexual maturity among Indians in Trinidad: A sociohistorical scrutiny. In J. L. Roopnarine & J. Brown (Eds.), *Caribbean families: Diversity among ethnic groups* (pp. 115–146). Norwood, NJ: Ablex.

Munroe, R., & Munroe, R. (1992). Fathers in children's environments: A four culture study. In B. Hewlett (Ed.), *Father–child relations: Cultural and biosocial contexts* (pp. 213–229). New York, NY: Aldine de Gruyter.

Nsamenang, B. A. (2010). Fathers, families, and children's well-becoming in Africa. In M. E. Lamb (Ed.), *The role of the father in child development* (pp. 388–412). Hoboken, NJ: Wiley.

Nevadomsky, J. (1980). Abandoning the retentionist model: Family and marriage change among the East Indians in rural Trinidad. *International Journal of Sociology of the Family, 10,* 181–197.

O'Brien, M., & Moss, P. (2010). Fathers, work, and family policies in Europe. In M. E. Lamb (Ed.), *The role of the father in child development* (pp. 551–557). Hoboken, NJ: Wiley.

Ogbu, J. (1981). Origins of human competence: A cultural ecological perspective. *Child Development, 52,* 413–429.

Pant, P., Roopnarine, J. L., & Krishnakumar, A. (2008). *Parenting styles among*

Indo-Guyanese Fathers: Links to early cognitive and social development. Paper presented at the Society for Cross-Cultural Research, New Orleans, LA.

Patterson, O. (1967). *The sociology of slavery: An analysis of the origins, development and structure of Negro slave society in Jamaica.* London, UK: McGibbon & Kee.

Pottinger, A. M. (2005). Children's experience of loss by parental migration in inner-city Jamaica. *American Journal of Orthopsychiatry, 75,* 485–496.

Powell, D. (1986). Caribbean women and their responses to familial experience. *Social and Economic Studies, 35,* 83–130.

Rauf, M. A. (1973). *Indian village in Guyana: A study of cultural change and ethnic identity.* Leiden, the Netherlands: E. J. Brill.

Reddock, R. (1994). *Women, labor, and politics in Trinidad and Tobago: A history.* London, UK: Zed Books.

Reynolds, T. (2006). Caribbean young people, family relationships and social capital. [Special Issue: Social capital, migration and transnational families]. *Journal of Ethnic and Racial Studies, 29,* 1087–1103.

Roopnarine, J. L. (2002). Father involvement in English-speaking Caribbean families. In C. S. Tamis-LeMonda & N. Cabrera (Ed.), *Handbook on father involvement: Multidisciplinary perspectives* (pp. 279–302). Mahwah, NJ: Lawrence Erlbaum Associates.

Roopnarine, J. L. (2004). African American and African Caribbean fathers: Levels, quality, and meaning of involvement. In M. E. Lamb (Ed.), *The role of the father in child development.* New York, NY: Wiley & Sons.

Roopnarine, J. L., Evans, M., & Pant, P. (2011). Parenting and socialization practices among Caribbean families: A focus on fathers. In D. Chadee & J. Young (Eds.), *Current themes in social psychology.* Mona, Jamaica: University of the West Indies Press.

Roopnarine, J. L., & Krishnakumar, A. (2010). *Parenting styles and childhood outcomes in Trinidadian and Guyanese families.* Unpublished manuscript, Syracuse University, NY.

Roopnarine, J. L., Krishnakumar, A., & Xu, Y. (2009). Beliefs about mothers' and fathers' roles and the division of childcare and household labor in Indo-Caribbean immigrant families. *Cultural Diversity and Ethnic Minority Psychology, 15,* 173–182.

Roopnarine, J. L., Krishnakumar, A., Metindogan, A., & Evans, M. (2006). Links among parenting styles, academic socialization, and the early academic and social skills of pre-Kindergarten and Kindergarten-age children of English-speaking Caribbean immigrants. *Early Childhood Research Quarterly, 21,* 238–252.

Roopnarine, J. L., & Shin, M. (2003). Caribbean immigrants from English-speaking countries: Sociohistorical forces, migratory patterns, and psychological issues in family functioning. In L.L. Adler & U. P. Gielen (Eds.), *Migration, immigration, and emigration in international perspectives* (pp. 123–142). Westport, CT: Praeger.

Roopnarine, J., Snell-White, P., Riegraf, N., Wolfsenberger, J., Hossain, Z., & Mathur, S. (1997). Family socialization in an East Indian village in Guyana: A focus on fathers. In J. L. Roopnarine & J. Brown (Eds.), *Caribbean families: Diversity among ethnic groups* (pp. 57–83). Norwood, NJ: Ablex.

Roopnarine, J., L., Brown, J., Snell-White, P., Riegraf, N. B., Crossley, D., Hossain, Z., & Webb, W. (1995). Father involvement in child care and household work in common-law dual-earner and single-earner families. *Journal of Applied Developmental Psychology, 16,* 35–52.

Roopnarine, J. L., Talukder, E., Jain, D., Joshi, P., & Srivastav, P. (1990). Characteristics of holding, patterns of play and social behaviors between parents and infants in New Delhi, India. *Developmental Psychology, 26,* 667–673.

Samms-Vaughan, M. (2005). *The Jamaican pre-school child: The status of early childhood development in Jamaica.* Kingston, Jamaica: Planning Institute of Jamaica.

Samuel, P. S., & Wilson, L. C. (2009). Structural arrangements of Indo-Guyanese family: An assessment of the assimilation hypothesis. *Journal of Comparative Family Studies, 40,* 439–454.

Seeman, M. V. (2011). Canada: Psychosis in the immigrant Caribbean population. *International Journal of Social Psychiatry, 57*(5), 462–470.

Seltzer, W. (2005). Norwegian families from a psychocultural perspective. In J. L. Roopnarine & U. Gielen (Eds.), *Families in global perspective* (pp. 259–276). Boston, MA: Allyn & Bacon.

Sharma, D. (2000). Infancy and childhood in India: A critical review. *International Journal of Group Tensions, 29,* 219–251.

Sharma, K. N. (1986). Changing forms of East Indian marriage and family form in the Caribbean. *The Journal of Sociological Studies, 5,* 20–58.

Smith, R. T. (1996). *The matrifocal family: Power, pluralism, and politics.* London, UK: Routledge.

Tamis-LeMonda, C., & McFadden, K. (2010). Fathers from low-income backgrounds: Myths and evidence. In M. E. Lamb (Ed.), *The role of the father in child development* (pp. 296–318). Hoboken, NJ: Wiley.

Updegraff, K. A., Delgado, M. Y., & Wheeler, L. A. (2009). Gender and culture in Mexican immigrant families: Comparing mothers versus fathers and sons versus daughters. *Sex Roles, 60,* 559–574.

Wilson, L. C., & Kposowa, A. J. (1994). Paternal involvement with children: Evidence from Guyana. *International Journal of Sociology of the Family, 24,* 23–42.

Wilson, L. C., Wilson, C. M., & Berkeley-Caines, L. (2003). Age, gender and socioeconomic differences in parental socialization preferences in Guyana. *Journal of Comparative Family Studies, 34,* 213–227.

Chapter Ten

Fathering in Brazil
A Diverse and Unknown Reality

Ana Cecília de Sousa Bastos, Vívian Volkmer-Pontes,
Pedro Gomes Brasileiro, and Helena Martinelli Serra
Catholic University of Salvador/Federal University of Bahia, Salvador, Brazil

Case Story: Three Generations of Fathers

Lauro is silent at his 89th birthday party. He watches his children and grandchildren laughing and moving around the room. He has been a loving father, concerned with all his nine children, but even so he is a little emotionally distant from them. He had rarely beaten them, unlike other men of his generation, yet he was still the moral authority in the family and had the last word when it came to discipline. Perhaps that role kept him from becoming closer to his children. Lauro's closeness to his little ones had changed into distance as they grew into teenagers with whom he just couldn't talk, ever.

A long road brought him to this day. Lauro came from a black family in northeastern Brazil. His family was poor and all his life, even after moving to the big city, he struggled with money problems. He and his young wife had left their hometown just a year before their first child was born. He now remembers how happy he was then, so proud of accomplishing what he considered an important step in affirming his masculinity. The moment he became a father, he felt stronger as a man.

The image of his own father comes to mind now ... how hard his father had worked as a carpenter so that his children could go to school ... childhood days in his father's workshop. Besides working together, he can't remember any conversations or physical interactions with his father. His father was a great storyteller, and Lauro often relates to his children and grandchildren the same stories he heard as a child.

"Times have really changed," he thinks. Lauro realizes how proud he feels of one of his sons' caring parenting style. Unlike Lauro, Daniel makes a point of participating in his baby's daily care – bathing her and changing her diapers. The other day, Daniel was saying how anxious he was the day his daughter was born. He was not embarrassed by the topic of childbirth, and had no problem telling people how hard he cried or confessing his fear of holding a newborn in his arms – a fear that he had soon overcome. Daniel is deeply proud of having witnessed his children's developmental milestones, the first smiles, the first words, the first steps.

Now Lauro realizes that something is missing for him: there is too much silence surrounding his own feelings about fatherhood. He recalls the day he intended to write down the first words of his first child, but never did. How much do his children know about his feelings and worries as a father? Is it possible that he is somehow a stranger to his children? Lauro looks at his family and realizes how many different ways there are to be a father. He gazes at his children and grandchildren, some of them adolescents and young adults. He is certainly the only one in the small crowd who is fully aware of what it means to have raised nine children, providing them an education and caring for their well-being, values and morality.

Fathering in the Brazilian Context

Fathering in Brazil is complex and diverse, varying widely with the father's socioeconomic condition and educational level. It is therefore not possible to speak simply about one pattern of Brazilian fathering. A Brazilian father can be caring and close to his children, but he also can be absent or violent, and these features cannot be exclusively associated with social class. Our Case Story took place at a middle-class birthday party. Lauro, whose birthday was being celebrated, reflects on changes and contrasts he has observed in his own fathering experiences across three generations. Although his story exemplifies important generational themes in fathering, we cannot say that Lauro represents all fathers in Brazil, even in the middle class. Yet his story documents an array of changes that have attracted the interest of most Brazilian psychologists who have studied fathering.

Brazil has seen the same demographic changes noted in the other industrialized countries discussed in this volume: a decline in fertility and family size, changes in the timing of onset of parenthood, increased participation of women in the workforce, a rising divorce rate, and growing numbers of single-parent families (Parke, 2002; see also Table 1.1, this volume). In Brazil, declining family sizes and slight increases in the numbers of families without children have also been prominent demographic trends. Specifically, between 1999 and 2009 the average family size dropped from 3.4 to 3.1. During this time women retained primary responsibility for household chores and for child and family care – what we call in Brazil the "invisible work." In 2009, while employed women spent an average of 22.0 hours per week on household chores, the average for men was only 9.5 hours. Between 1999 and 2009, increased numbers of men and women had formal jobs in the expanding economy, and there are more employed men than women. Specifically, in 2009 the proportion of men with registered jobs reached 53.2%, while for women this proportion reached 48.8%. Despite averaging more years of formal education than men, however, Brazilian women earned only 70.7% of the average income of employed men (IBGE, 2009, 2010, 2011).

Although such demographic data are plentiful, historical information about Brazilian fathers is scarce and the history of Brazilian fatherhood has yet to be written. Laqueur (1992) viewed this "silence" on the subject of fathering as a kind of pathology and Brazil still lacks a movement analogous to feminism to foster the study of men. This chapter breaks through the silence about Brazilian fathering.

In Brazil, a new movement is under way whereby men are just beginning to talk about their right to fathering as a life experience. Who are these men? What are their stories, backgrounds and motivations? Psychological research has focused mainly on the absence of the father and its consequences for family and child development. But that does not tell us who Brazilian fathers *are*; in this chapter we emphasize research about father *presence*. After a brief analysis of the connections of Brazilian culture and history to fathering, we review the Brazilian literature on fathering. Finally, we analyze three portrayals of the extent and diversity of fathers' experiences in Brazil.

Cultural and Historical Background as It Influences Fathering: The Legacy of Patriarchy

The transformation of the wild and unexplored Southern lands into a prolific colony was directed by the strong hands of Brazil's very first patriarchs (Freyre, 1933/2005). In this context, fathers were the heads and masters of their families, and related to everything and everyone through possession, control and domination (Almeida, 1986). Hollanda (1936/2006) remarked that the Portuguese transplanted in Brazil a patriarchal model of the family, with the *pater famílias* as the only citizen; his slaves, wife, children and aggregates (mostly relatives) were part of his wealth. The patriarchal father held distinct powers (legal, political, and religious), and occupied the vacuum left by the distant Portuguese rulers as the central socializing agent in the newly colonized lands. He was the sole arbiter of daily rural life, and his rule and domination often made the family a place of violence (Filgueiras & Petrini, 2010).

Although this portrayal of the patriarchal father cannot be generalized to the role of the father in other contexts during either the colonial period or today (natives, slaves, or the semi-urban and urban middle class), it has become a significant symbol of fatherhood in traditional Brazilian society (Samara, 2002; Filgueiras & Petrini, 2010). The decline of patriarchy came in the 19th century with urbanization and the rise of institutions such as the Catholic Church, schools, and government, which took on some of the authority once held by patriarchal fathers. The rural patriarch thus changed from a symbol of power to a symbol of an outdated society, so strongly rejected that it ultimately has harmed the image of fatherhood throughout Brazil to this day. However, with the decline of family patri-archy, Brazilian fathers could also reach out in expressive ways (e.g., with affection and care) which were less associated with patriarchy yet indis-pensable to the family (Filgueiras & Petrini, 2010).

However, it is interesting to note that laws continued to reflect fam-ily patriarchy well beyond the colonial era. The Brazilian Constitution of 1916, for example, presumed that the father of a child was the husband of the mother, even in cases where the mother had confessed to adultery and claimed that another man was the biological father. Until 1988, the Constitution contained the term "paternal power" implying paternal rights and duties and stressing the father's role as protector; under this law, only the children of married parents were legally recognized by the father (Thurler, 2006). Today all children have the same rights, whether they are born from married or unmarried parents.

In Brazil, the custom is for fathers to claim paternity soon after child-birth, but only the mother is identified on the birth certificate. Nationwide data are unavailable, but for Brasília (the federal district and Brazil's polit-ical and administrative center) Thurler (2006) reported that from the 1960s through the present 12% of birth records did not establish paternity, and she estimated that this was true for 25% of the births nationwide. Thurler attributed this failure to establish paternity to traditional patriarchal prac-tices and particularly to the notion that manhood entitled men to behave freely as they wished, without legal consequences. If a patriarch is defined by his arbitrary, unrestricted power, she claimed, the mass abdication of fatherhood re-actualizes old patriarchal practices. Further, the high pro-portion of one-parent families headed by women calls our attention to Brazilian father absence. The challenge for researchers is to understand multiple levels of father absence and to identify their social and psycho-logical antecedents and effects.

Multiple traditional and modern views and values coexist in Brazilian fathering. The prevailing social representation of the ideal father combines characteristics of classical masculinity (responsibility, authority, resource control, social recognition) with a new vision that is more democratic and participatory. One could say that men today are reevaluating their social identity. This movement has been called "the new forms of fathering" (Levandowski, Antoni, Koller, & Piccinini, 2002; Orlandi & Toneli, 2005, 2008; Levandowski & Piccinini, 2006) and "New Fatherhood" (Trindade & Menandro, 2002; Dias & Aquino, 2006; Freitas, Coelho, & da Silva, 2007), and the emergence of the father-as-caregiver is one of the primary dimensions of the redefined father's role.

Yet the new Brazilian ideal of fatherhood may not be as different from the traditional image as it appears. The new father is, in Fuller's words (2000), "one who protects, provides, shapes, educates and represents authority" (p. 387). Thus, the idea of fatherhood remains associated with masculinity and is consequently connoted by power and control over one's wife and children. It is possible, Fuller says, that in the past there were also men who were highly involved in child rearing. What is changing is that young men now position themselves in clear opposition to the old model, and seek increased closeness and commitment to their children. Such men face not only new demands to maintain marital relationships, but are also committed to a personal quest to find a place in domains once monopolized by women, including care of the children, home and family. The father with this new identity is no longer just a provider, in that he also takes responsibility for the physical, emotional and educational condition of his children.

Review of Fathering Research

The father's role

Traditionally, the Brazilian father was the unquestioned moral authority in the family. He was the owner of his family in the same way that he owned material goods. But new roles have brought new opportunities for men to fully experience the rich emotional aspects of fathering and to participate in their children's lives in ways they find personally relevant and gratifying. It is easy to observe the process by which men experience the transition to parenthood, as Lauro and Daniel's Case Story illustrated. Life transitions reinforce and often promote a new and more complex family dynamics and composition. In the transition to parenthood, both men and women may find themselves beset by a mixture of new feelings, doubts and insecurities. Their personal ability to cope with new situations is challenged, for example, by the idiosyncrasies of the pregnancy and disagreements between cultural and scientific knowledge about the care of the pregnant woman and the baby. As pointed out by Bustamante and Trad (2005), fragility in the notion of a new father imposes multiple expectations on men. On the one hand, it demands that as breadwinners they participate actively in the economic sphere, serve as providers for their families, and build family identity. On the other hand, they are expected to be present at home, share childcare duties with their partners, and to be emotionally close to their children.

For some authors, contemporary fatherhood in Brazil is a phenomenon of the middle class (La Rossa, according to Bustamente, 2005). Indeed, one major limitation of psychological studies conducted in Brazil on fatherhood is the tendency to ignore socioeconomic, educational, ethnic and cultural variations. For example, Bustamante and Trad (2005) remarked that in low-income families, roles are defined in advance because of the sexual division of labor, and also by the hierarchical relationships between men and women and between parents and children. Thus, while men are moral authorities and are responsible for familial respectability, women assume another type of authority, to maintain the unity of the family through caretaking. Women's authority rests on the performance of their role as mothers and on their ability to manage resources. Costa (2001/2002) found a similar representation of men's and women's roles after interviewing men at a family planning and treatment center in São Paulo. These participants expressed the view that working men should support their families, while women should be responsible for children and decisions about whether or not to get pregnant. Still, fathers appear in women's narratives as a relevant support and participant in childbirth, second to only the grandmother (Borges & Bastos, 2011). However, in cases of recurrent miscarriages, the husband's support is reported as the most important (Pontes, 2011).

At first glance, Brazilian studies of fatherhood do not place much emphasis on the emergent reality of the "new father." Actually, the literature focuses on a broad array of themes concerning fatherhood. But most studies are limited to relatively small numbers of research participants and do not consider diversity related to locality, social class, ethnicity, or educational background.

Muzio (1998) identified three main ways in which Brazilian fatherhood had been approached by researchers. The first was based on a psychoanalytical framework and almost exclusively emphasized the mother and her relationship to the child as a basis for development. This approach was the most influential from the 1940s until the 1960s. From the 1960s through the 1980s, the father came into focus in terms of the absence of the father from family life, the absence of his authority and material support, and the association between father absence with negative outcomes such as poor adjustment, suicide, delinquency, and gender identity problems. This emphasis on father absence was precisely what Pleck (Foreword, this volume) described as the focus of U.S. fathering research through the early 1970s. The third and newest approach, which emerged in Brazil more than a decade after it appeared in the U.S., focuses on the personal attributes of multiple individuals responsible for childcare, including fathers. These latter studies take into account the contemporary restructuring of paternal and maternal roles.

Many fathering researchers have concentrated on adolescent fatherhood, as identified by Souza and Benetti (2009) in a recent review. For example, adolescent pregnancy has been a major problem with significant social consequences, and the impact of adolescent fatherhood on the personal development, fathering skills and commitment of the large numbers of mostly young Brazilian men is a significant challenge. This social problem has accordingly begun to draw the attention of fathering researchers.

Caregiving is another focus of research, and appears as a major and visible dimension of contemporary Brazilian father behavior (Sutter & Bucher-Maluschke, 2008). As Lyra et al. (2008) stressed, childcare has so often been associated with motherhood that it is taken for granted, supporting the notion of a maternal instinct. As a result, when a man becomes a father he may internalize the notion that his caregiving cannot be as good as the mother's, and that he is by definition an inadequate parent. In the same vein, Nolasco (1993) suggested the existence of socially constructed mechanisms that deprives Brazilian fatherhood of its meanings, goals and functionality. One consequence of this mentality is that fathers feel incapable of meeting their children's physical and emotional needs. As noted by Levandowski and Piccinini (2006), many new Brazilian fathers feel increasingly lost and confused as expectations rise for their involvement.

Changes in family organization, especially the increasing participation of women in the work force, have substantial impact on relationships between men and women, and on marital and paternal roles (Gomes & Resende, 2004). As this process destabilizes the Brazilian father's authority, new patterns, roles and images will be required, and men will need to master a multiplicity of ways to pursue fatherhood (Bustamante & Trad, 2005). Considering the coexistence between traditional and contemporary fatherhood, Cerveny and Chaves (2010) contrasted the traditional role of the man as financial provider and family decision-maker on moral and economic issues, with the demands of a more collaborative role within the family and society. Greater participation in childcare, again, may conflict with the hallmark of traditional fatherhood (Souza & Benetti, 2009; Levandowski & Piccinini, 2006).

In practical terms, these tensions reveal that Brazilian fathers are in transition, searching for ways to re-create their role by synthesizing these complex and sometimes contradictory social demands. Gomes and Resende (2004) claimed that contemporary fathers are increasingly willing to "recognize their feelings and to confront the constraints of the male role" (p. 123). Some studies show that the new father is an emotionally involved and engaged participant as capable as the mother of bringing up his children (Souza & Benetti, 2009; Bustamante, 2005; Gomes & Resende, 2004). However, Souza and Benetti also concluded that there are many "barriers in men's everyday practice, revealing that the transformation of values does not follow the pace of social change" (p. 98).

Some signs of change are beginning to appear in Brazilian research data, in younger fathers' perceptions of their own parents. Men are often referred to as role models, but by tradition this did not include teaching their sons how to be fathers. For example, Gomes and Resende (2004) conducted a study which had as its central focus the man's/father's perspective on the process of being and becoming a father in contemporary Brazil. The participants reflected on their experiences as children and realized the difficulty their own fathers had expressing their feelings, which was exactly the case for Lauro in our opening Case Story. Like Lauro's son Daniel, Gomes and Resende's participants also reported a willingness to walk away from the model of fathering they had witnessed in childhood, recreating fatherhood on a more affective and participative basis. Similar findings were reported by Silva and Piccinini (2007) in a study of younger fathers in Porto Alegre, the main city in the state of Rio Grande do Sul. These fathers considered themselves to be quite different from their own fathers, although they often viewed them as role models. Likewise, adult and teenage fathers-to-be in a study by Levandowski and Piccinini (2006) reportedly hoped to have good relations with their children and to successfully fulfill 'new' paternal roles. In doing so they attempted to be more involved than their own fathers and to avoid their fathers' mistakes, while incorporating the positive aspects of their fathers' behavior. In the same locale, Krob, Piccinini, and Silva (2009) interviewed young fathers about the negative aspects of their experiences with their own fathers. These participants reported that their fathers were distant, absent physically and psychologically, spent little time with them as children, were rigid and closed, formed only superficial bonds with them, and focused mainly on material support.

Other Brazilian studies have cast an eye on fathers as caregivers from the moment that pregnancy is confirmed. Piccinini, Silva, Gonçalves, Lopes, and Tudge (2004) investigated the involvement of fathers, aged 21 to 40, during the third trimester of gestation of their first children. They found that the majority of participants felt emotionally attached and were very involved in some aspects of the pregnancy. Many reportedly attended ultrasound exams and medical appointments, sought contact and responded to movement and heartbeat of the baby in the womb, and expressed concerns about the baby. Nevertheless, childbirth and pregnancy remained of interest primarily to women. Only a few fathers in their sample reported seeking information about the baby, and still fewer wished to attend the birth. In other words, fathers were not very involved with pregnancy and childbirth, although they felt attached to the babies. These results seem to support Trindade's (1993) conclusion that, despite rejecting the traditionally distant model of fatherhood, some fathers still fit the distancing model.

Brasileiro, Pontes, Bichara, and Bastos (2010) investigated the transition to fatherhood among young middle-class men in the city of Salvador, the capital of the state of Bahia. The participants presented themselves as effectively involved in the private sphere of family life. Examples of this involvement including the following: active support for their partners during pregnancy, equitable sharing of baby care tasks, joint organization of work and entertainment schedules, and shared responsibility for living both in public (financial support) and private (running the household). Silva and Piccinini (2007) reported similar results concerning fathers' involvement with preschool-age children. Their participants noted that husbands and wives shared the responsibilities for children even though men's participation was inconsistent. They also generally believed that

Figure 10.1 A 26-year-old father plays peek-a-boo with his 11-month-old daughter in their bedroom, in Salvador, Bahia. Brazilian fathers of preschool-age children generally believe that involvement in children's lives is very important, and report a high degree of satisfaction with fatherhood (Silva & Piccinini, 2007). Photo courtesy of Helena Martinelli Serra.

involvement in the lives of children was very important, and reported a high degree of satisfaction with fatherhood. It was noteworthy, however, that in both studies the fathers interviewed had relatively high levels of schooling. Another important issue to be considered, according to Silva and Piccinini (2007), was the quality of the marital relationships, which may have facilitated paternal involvement of fathers with their children.

Piccinini and his collaborators are exceptional among Brazilian developmental psychologists, in that they consistently focus on fathering and explore different dimensions of father–mother–child interactions with children of various ages. They also observed an increase in sharing of childcare by fathers and mothers in other studies in the state of Rio Grande do Sul. For instance, Piccinini's group compared the educational practices of fathers and mothers with 18-month-old children, in 34 families from different socioeconomic levels (Piccinini, Marin, Alvarenga, Lopes, & Tudge, 2007). This study identified similarities between fathers' and mothers' educational choices, which could be explained in terms of beliefs and values about education, experiences with their own care givers, marital conflict, and the characteristics of their children. In another study by the same team, Levandowiski and Piccinini (2006) also found a growing commitment to equality in contemporary couples. Even so, fathers sampled during their wives' pregnancy reported that they lacked confidence about their future performance in baby care, despite their willingness to participate.

Moreira, Carvalho, and Almeida (in press) studied 150 families living in Salvador, Bahia, to further explore fathers' attitudes and behavior. They interviewed mothers and fathers about the distribution of childcare tasks among various caregivers. Their results showed that mothers performed almost all caregiver chores (physical care, leisure/conviviality, education, discipline, and outdoor activities), while the fathers' involvement was either complementary or peripheral. In fact, Moreira and her colleagues observed not only maternal but also female predominance in the care of young children, especially in daily physical care such as changing diapers, bathing, and feeding. Both mothers and fathers engaged in outside tasks like taking the child to the doctor, shopping for clothing or food, as well as in the education and discipline of the children, and playing with them. Fathers were involved in some physical care activities when their work schedules permitted (for example, putting the child to sleep at night), and this tendency was more common for younger children and in the middle to high SES families.

Bustamante and Trad (2005) also investigated the fathers' participation in the care of children under six years of age, in low-income families in a regional capital city of northeastern Brazil. They found that fathers were involved in three domains: (a) education, where they contributed to the establishment of moral values and discipline; (b) personal hygiene, once regarded as the mothers' domain but increasingly performed by men even when they do not report it; and (c) preservation of physical safety, providing the structure and construction of homes.

Tudge's (2008) cross-cultural study of child rearing across social classes, in seven countries (Brazil, Estonia, Finland, Kenya, Russia, Korea, and the U.S.), yielded interesting observational data about father–children interactions in diverse everyday situations. His Brazilian participants were from Porto Alegre, Rio Grande do Sul. In all seven countries, the mothers were the adults most likely to be involved with children in the various activities. Tudge also focused on the nature of activities in which fathers and children were involved. Unlike the other countries studied, when both parents were present Brazilian fathers were as likely to be involved with the children as mothers, whether in lessons ("deliberate attempts to impart or elicit information," p. 93) or work (household activities or shopping). The Brazilian fathers also distinguished themselves on another dimension as well. According to Tudge:

> Middle-class fathers in Porto Alegre typically spent a greater proportion of the time with their children engaging in lessons (4.4% vs. 4.2%), and play (30.6% vs. 24,1%) than did mothers, while working-class fathers there spent a greater proportion of time conversing with their children than did mothers (10.7% to 7.7%).
>
> (Tudge, 2008, p. 216)

Tudge's cross-cultural, longitudinal and observational data are not only methodologically impressive but also important, because they suggest that in Brazil and elsewhere fathers can be meaningfully involved with children in diverse everyday activities. However, Tudge concluded that "it is generally the case that the adult world with which these young children engaged was a female world" (p. 220). According to Silva and Piccinini (2009), Brazilian and international studies have also shown that fathers can act as a protective factor for the mental health of the mother and the child when the men are actively involved and mentally healthy. The small literature on the perceptions, attitudes, and behavior of Brazilian fathers makes it clear that men and women assume and carry out domestic tasks in distinctive ways. It is undeniable that transformations are taking place in the father's role in the family with increased involvement and responsibility towards their children. However, according to Silva and Piccinini (2004), this new conception of Brazilian fatherhood is more clearly evident in the discourse of scholars and society in general than in fathers' actual behavior.

Sub-Cultural Variations in Fathering: Social Class

In Brazil, sub-cultural variations in fathering are mainly related to social class. Tudge's cross-cultural study (2008) was conclusive in this regard: there were more similarities between families from the same social class across different countries, than between families from different social classes in the same country, including Brazil.

Different models of parenting are apparent in Brazilian families from every social class. The Case Story of Lauro illustrated this coexistence of models of fathering over the course of three generations. For example, Lauro reflected on the differences between his fathering behavior and that of his son. In the background was Lauro's memory of his own father, who had represented the model of a father who transmitted skills and attitudes related to work. An intergenerational gap was evident in this case, yet some continuity can also be identified, for instance in the centrality of the authority of the father, and the transmission of values through storytelling. Other aspects of fathering saw a break in continuity across the generations of Lauro's family. Specifically, the tradition of fathers teaching sons through father–son involvement in work was replaced by teaching skills through games and sports, which is more common today among middle-class fathers.

Most of the research reviewed in this chapter was conducted in the more developed regions of Brazil, where changes may take place more rapidly and may be more intense. To discuss sub-cultural variations in fathering, three views of fathering are articulated here, based on qualitative studies conducted by Bastos and her collaborators in a different context. This research considered fathers in three everyday family contexts: (1) work as a father–son socialization strategy, (2) the father's image as described in mothers' conversations, (3) fathers as family guardians.

Bastos (2001, 2009) has studied the daily lives of families living in poverty in two neighborhoods in Salvador, Bahia. In the first neighborhood, she and her collaborators carried out a 10-year longitudinal investigation from 1991 to 2000. In the second neighborhood, a sequence of studies took place between 1999 and the present. As in most Brazilian studies of family life, a mother or grandmother was selected by both the researcher and family to be the "natural" source regarding routines and experiences in the family context, especially when the focus was on relationships and interactions with children. Only after successive visits to the family, and after a trusting relationship was established, did a man become involved on his own initiative in conversations about child rearing and domestic routines. In contrast with women's unquestioning willingness to participate in the study, men often posed questions about the goals and potential uses of the data. Men's attitudes toward the researchers clearly defined the limits of domestic territory.

In both communities, only two of the single-parent families that participated in this research were composed of a father and children. In one of these families, an unemployed carpenter named Lourenço and his two boys (7 and 9 years old) were part of the longitudinal study. It was possible to visit the family at least once a week during the first year. Lourenço had custody of the children because he did not want to pay alimony to their mother, who was living with another man. He reported that he did not want to see his children mistreated by another man. Lourenço's case illustrates the model of socialization through father–son work, which is common among poor families in Brazil who believe that this is the only way to prevent delinquency and to prepare children to later enter the adult work force. The older boy went with his father to work occasionally on those intermittent occasions when Lourenço was employed, and the two boys were expected to do all the household chores. Lourenço believed that the only way to train children was harshly, and he spanked the boys when they did not do the tasks he assigned them to do. He said this was the way his own father had brought him up, through beatings, and he believed that this is why he had not become a delinquent. His neighbors once reported him to the police after he had severely beaten his older son, and he also left the boys dirty and abandoned "in the street." But Lourenço did not understand why the neighbors should interfere in his business, stating that "a father can't teach his sons any more because the police would arrest him for it. I beat my children today so that the police won't kill them tomorrow."

The example of Lourenço cannot be taken as typical of most poor fathers in Brazil, except regarding his work. In the socialization-through-work model where fathers teach boys and mothers teach girls, both parents promote the early engagement of children in various tasks inside or outside the household. Fathers, in particular, are supposed to teach values and skills related to work. To meet the goal of socialization-through-work, the first strategy is to engage in joint father–son involvement in tasks of varied complexity. In our study, skills with multiple tasks and hard work were often emphasized in fathers' discourse with children. The fact that these fathers were often unemployed or under-employed made this scenario more complex.

The father-as-worker model is not too different from the father-as-provider model, which seems to constitute the core of the ideal image of the father in women's conversations in poor communities. Bastos, Gomes, Gomes, and Rego (2007) analyzed narratives provided by parents in their conversations at weekly group meetings, over the course of a year. There was a dramatic contrast between fathers' and mothers' narratives. Specifically, women's narratives primarily conveyed an image of family life in which maternal care was prevalent and fathers were absent or harmful. According to mothers, when present, fathers were the authorities who children respect and obey, and they "kept quiet" when mothers went out and left the children with them. Mothers also portrayed fathers as men who offered negative models of behavior and tended to be ignorant, aggressive, and rough. More positive evaluations, although not frequent, referred to fathers as providers who helped with childcare.

Negative experiences with men seemed to influence mothers' orientation toward their daughters, for example, "She has to learn to control herself. Now she is a child, but when she grows up and marries you do not know what kind of man will try to treat her like a doormat." Another woman said that it was humiliating to ask men for money, as was the case between her and her ex-husband. She had to fight hard to be free of him and now tries to teach her daughters to be independent of men. Many women complained about men acting as if they were the "owner" of the family: "He doesn't give anything to me and the children … he beats us and thinks he owns me."

On the other hand, women tended to make alliances (mother–daughter–grandmother) which excluded fathers from the family when they did not conform to the provider role. On the few occasions when men participated in the conversation group, one father talked about his struggles to see his children; he was unemployed and for a while was not able to pay alimony to his ex-wife. But he expressed how much he missed his children and remarked that his daughter "had a psychological fever" because she also missed her father. Another interesting contrast between mothers' and fathers' narratives was that fathers were more likely to adhere to traditional values and seemed to be more convinced of their point of view. Women more often expressed their doubts and uncertainties, and seemed to be more aware of a transition concerning Brazilian child rearing, fathering, and family life.

Finally, a third model of the father-as-guardian was evident in many observations in our sequence of studies (Bastos, 2001; Bastos et al., 2007). When present, fathers spoke on behalf of the family to outsiders. This was observed not only in communications with the researchers, but also in fathers' interactions with schools and other institutions that impinge on the family. For example, even when men were not available to talk to teachers (work schedules are usually stricter for men than women), they decided what to do and gave directions. Such fathers got personally involved in more serious situations. Paulo, one of the fathers interviewed in Bastos et al.'s longitudinal study, spoke about the case in which he personally went to the school to complain about his son's grades, which he considered unfair. He commented to the researcher, "Someone needed to show them that my son has a father who fights for him!" In this example it was interesting to observe the construction of meaning; despite his ineffectiveness it was the father's desire to protect the family that was important. In this sense, he believed that he fulfilled his role as a guardian.

Figure 10.2 A 40-year-old father teaches his 5-year-old daughter the rules of chess in their living room, in Cachoeira, Bahia. Unlike in other countries, Tudge (2008) found that Brazilian fathers were as likely to be involved with the children as mothers, in lessons or work. Photo courtesy of Janailda Santos Vatin.

This same model was also illustrated in negative examples. For example, the father-as-guardian referred usually to protecting the family, but it also applied to a sense of ownership of the family or being abusive. In both situations, the father seemed to believe that he was acting in accordance with social expectations.

Many different dimensions are required to describe fathering in Brazil. The examples presented in this section do not exhaust the subject, but when contrasted with the studies reviewed in the previous section, they illustrate the coexistence of sub-cultural variations. Social class contextualizes these variations, although it is important to recognize that a variety of fathering styles are found in every social class.

Social Policy Related to Fathering

In terms of social policies, fathers have recently been pressured to assume new postures and attitudes toward mothers, children and 'caring activities,' and fathers' failure to behave accordingly have been severely criticized (Lyra et al., 2008). In opposition to this emerging movement, however, public policies may actually serve as an obstacle to active involvement by fathers (Mioto, 2010). Medrado et al. (2010) pointed out that paternity leave as currently proposed is one of these policies. Specifically, maternity leave in Brazil lasts four months (or in some cases six months, depending on labor negotiations), while paternity leave is currently limited to five days. Paternity leave was instituted in Brazil in 1943 and originally lasted for only a single day. In 1988 leave was expanded to five days, but it was still a temporary rule and was subject to the discretion of the employer (Marcon, 2010).

There is currently a proposal to expand paternal leave to 15 days. However, most men do not use the leave even for five days, for fear of losing their jobs. Paternity leave is a major topic of discussion because it exposes the limited, neglectful way that fatherhood is viewed by Brazilian policy makers. However, the increasing participation of fathers in the care and support of their partners and children has prompted a movement toward changes with regard to leave policies. We expect that in this context new role models and new values will emerge.

In a large-scale effort, the Health Ministry of Brazil formulated a specific policy concerned with the health of the male population called the "National Policy of Integral Attention to Men's Health" (BRASIL, 2008). The initiative has yet to be approved and implemented. Some authors are convinced that it is possible to construct more solid initiatives recognizing fathers as central agents in family health, and to address their needs effectively (Bustamante, 2005; Bustamante & Trad, 2005; Corrêa & Ferriani, 2007, and Mioto, 2010).

Finally, we note the potential benefits of the work by the Family Health Program's professionals with the father/male population. We recommend as an example of a possible activity the implementation of men's groups (see Nakazawa & Shwalb's discussion of Japanese fathering advocacy groups, Ch. 3, this volume). Non-profit organizations could provide a critical space and opportunity for men of different ages and trajectories to exchange experiences about manhood and fatherhood. In this setting it would be possible for participants and professionals to reflect on the modification of these relationships over time and to observe fathers' needs. Therefore, new proposals about the concerns of men and fathers should be formulated and implemented as both government programs and by non-governmental organizations.

Conclusions, Speculation, and Predictions for the Future

In a country as diverse as Brazil, it is not a simple task to give a precise account of how fatherhood is changing. We are still a long way from being able to approach in any comprehensive way the complexities involved in fathering as practice or personal experience. The best we could do in this chapter was to identify in a broad sense the directions in which these changes are heading, to contextualize general patterns of fathering, and to discuss some sub-cultural variations related to social class.

Lamb and Lewis (2011) drew our attention to the biases that result from the fact that parenting has heretofore been equated with mothering. This bias applies perfectly to research on fathers in Brazil. We noted the absence of systematic Brazilian research on the main dimensions which define fatherhood: responsibility (material and psychological support), involvement, authority, affect, transmitting cultural values, knowledge, specifics of father–son and father–daughter relationships, and the impact of fathering on children's development. Despite the growing body of literature on family issues in Brazil, at present there is only a preliminary approach to fatherhood, in contrast with the rich and quite elaborated research developed in other countries and reported in several chapters of this volume.

Brazilian psychological research on fathering focuses precisely on how well fathers are prepared to perform tasks and functions traditionally carried out by mothers. Certainly, to address this point, inequalities related to gender and the ideological preeminence of mothering must be taken into account. Even more importantly, researchers must develop a comprehensive approach to fatherhood by emphasizing the father's perspective. The past approach of studying fathers from the perspective of mothers still limits our knowledge of fathering, and this problem is not limited to Brazil.

The absent father has been a recurrent concern of researchers and practitioners in Brazil as in other countries. The consequences of absence are said to be persistent and pervasive, and are related in Brazil to the high number of children who are not even recognized by their fathers. This absence can be literal or symbolic; the reality of a father who is physically present but psychologically absent as the family's provider and moral authority is unfortunately very common. Actually, a father who is emotionally distant may still fulfill his roles, as was suggested in Lauro's Case Story.

Brazilian fathers are changing in a social and historical context, where the coexistence of many diverse forms of families and a blend of tradition and modernity are the rule rather than the exception. Traditional gender roles are also changing in Brazil. For example, the mother in some families now acts as the provider in addition to her responsibility for domestic tasks and childcare, while the father is unemployed or under-employed. The new fathers who are emerging in the Brazilian middle class are not typical of the majority of Brazilian fathers, and are not even typical of fathers within the middle class. In addition, the inversion of traditional roles establishes an experience which according to Zaluar (1983) is symbolically characterized as familial privation and suffering. That is, a family is considered to be deficient when the father is not the main breadwinner, even if the mother is able to assume the role of provider.

In low-income families, fathers' and mothers' roles are predefined because of a strict sexual division of labor. As a result, there are more rigid hierarchical relationships between men and women in these families, and between parents and children. The father in this context is the moral authority and is responsible for familial respectability, discipline, and transmission of moral values and rules. Meanwhile, the mother assumes another dimension of authority as the one who maintains family unity through care giving. As a result, fathers seldom share childcare responsibility and only do so under very special conditions, for example when the mother has a full-time job and the father is unemployed. Petrini (2010) reminds us that the father is not easily replaceable in his function of introducing children to the world outside the family. To be able to live outside the family requires knowledge of the harsh rules and codes of the world of adulthood, and is not common for mothers to fulfill the bridge role of imparting such knowledge to children.

A final issue of concern for the future of Brazilian fathering concerns how a man becomes a father. Brazil is still a country where the work of men and women is not equally remunerated, and which tolerates sexism and violence against women. Although there has been much progress in recent years, especially in the formal education of females, Brazil still cannot be considered a country that treats men and women equally. It has one of the lowest rates of female membership in parliament in Latin America and in 2010 was ranked in the second to last position on ISOQuito, an index of gender equality by the NGO Feminist Articulation Mercosur (Articulación Feminista Marcosur, 2010) which examined official data from 16 South American countries between 1997 and 2007.

Given these economic and social tendencies, it would be naïve in the short run to expect a 'new Brazilian father' to prevail and become a personal and social reality. In fact, the socialization of boys does not support the emergence of a new father, and instills a restricted view of how men are cast into public. Young men learn while playing to struggle for power, and to develop abilities to compete (Lyra et al., 2008) rather than to become fathers. It is no wonder in light of their role models and childhood socialization that it is difficult for Brazilian fathers to cooperate with, empathize with, care for, and depend on others.

Despite a growing body of literature on the Brazilian family, at present there is only a tentative literature on fatherhood, in contrast with the rich and elaborated research developed in many other countries.

Indeed, only recently has fathering become a legitimate subject of psychological research. The complexities of Brazilian society, as it goes through an intense process of economic and social growth and struggles with chronic poverty and social inequality, make the absence of systematic research on fathering all the more regrettable. However, a new movement has been observed, and men are beginning to talk about their right to fathering as a life experience.

Summary

After an initial discussion of Brazilian fatherhood in historical and cultural contexts, this chapter reviewed the current conditions of fathering in Brazil. Our review indicated that the father's involvement in childcare has been the main focus of Brazilian fathering research. We also discussed the emergent tendency in recent studies to consider fathers' perspectives, expectations and representations regarding parenthood, especially in the transition to fatherhood. Brazilian sub-cultural variations in fathering appeared to be mainly related to social class, as documented in qualitative, ethnographic, and longitudinal studies of families' lives. Finally, we demonstrated that consideration of fathers has been absent from Brazilian public policies. There are new possibilities for policies, but also obstacles to efforts to promote pro-fathering measures, particularly in the field of health.

References

Almeida, A. M. (1986). Sexuality and marriage in the Portuguese settling of Brazil. *Análise Social, XXI*, 697–705.

Articulación Feminista Marcosur. (2010). *ISOQuito: A tool for monitoring the Agreement*. Retrieved June, 18, 2011, from: www.mujeresdelsurafm.org.uy/isoquito.pdf

Bastos, A. C. S. (2001). *Ways of sharing: The child and family's daily life*. Taubaté, São Paulo, Brazil: Cabral Editora Universitária.

Bastos, A. C. S. (2009). Studying poor families in Salvador, Brazil: Reflections after two decades. In A. C. S. Bastos & E. P. Rabinovich (Eds.), *Living in poverty: Developmental poetics of cultural realities* (pp. 69–97). Charlotte, NC: Information Age Publishing.

Bastos, A. C. S., Gomes, M. M., Gomes, M. C. C., & Rego, N. N. (2007). Talking with families: Crisis, coping, and novelty. In L. Moreira & A. M. A. Carvalho (Eds.) *Família, subjetividade, vínculos* (pp. 157–193). São Paulo, Brazil: Paulinas.

Borges, A. P., & Bastos, A. C. S. (2011). Meanings through the transition to motherhood: Women before and after childbirth. In A. C. S. Bastos, K. Uriko, & J. Valsiner (Eds.), *Cultural dynamics of women's lives*. Charlotte, NC: Information Age Publishing.

Brasil (2008). *National policy of comprehensive health care for men: Principles and guidelines*. Brasília: Mimeo.

Brasileiro, P. G. L., Pontes, V. V., Bichara, I. D., & Bastos, A. C. S. (2010). The transition to fatherhood and fatherhood in transition. In L. V. C. Moreira, G. Petrini, & F. B. Barbosa (Eds.), *The father in contemporary society* (pp. 145–166). Bauru, Brazil: EDUSC.

Bustamante, V. (2005). Being a father in the Rail Suburbs of Salvador: A case study with working class men. *Psicologia em Estudo, 10*, 393–402.

Bustamante, V., & Trad, L. A. B. (2005). Paternal participation in the care of young children: An ethnographic study with families of working classes. *Cadernos de Saúde Pública, 21*, 1865–1874.

Cerveny, C. M. O., & Chaves, U. H. (2010). Father? Who is this? The experience-fatherhood in the new millennium. In. L. V. C. Moreira, G. Petrini, & F. B. Barbosa (Eds.), *The father in contemporary society* (pp. 41–52). Bauru, Brazil: EDUSC.

Corrêa, A. C. P., & Ferriani, M. G. C. (2007). Teenage fatherhood: A challenge faced by health services. *Cienc Cuid Saúde, 6*, 157–163.

Costa, R. G. (2001/2002). Dream of the past versus plan for the future: Gender and representations of infertility and the desire to have children. *Cadernos Pagu, 17–18*, 105–130.

Dias, A. B., & Aquino, E. M. L. (2006). Motherhood and fatherhood in adolescence: Some observations in three cities in Brazil. *Caderno de Saúde Pública, 22*, 1447–1458.

Filgueiras, M. R., & Petrini, G. (2010). The patriarchal father according to Gilberto Freyre. In L. V. Moreira, G. Petrini, & F. B. Barbosa (Eds.), *The father in contemporary society* (pp. 23–40). Bauru, Brazil: EDUSC.

Freitas, W. M. F., Coelho, E. A. C., & da Silva, A. T. M. C. (2007). To feel a father: The male experience from the gender perspective. *Caderno de Saúde Pública, 23*, 137–145.

Freyre, G. (2005). *The masters and the slaves*. Recife, Brazil: Global Editora. (Original work published 1933).

Fuller, N. (2000). *Fatherhoods in Latin America*. Lima, Peru: Fondo de Cultura.

Gomes, A. J. S., & Resende, V. R. (2004). The present father: The unveil of fatherhood on a contemporary family. *Psicologia: Teoria e Pesquisa, 20*, 119–125.

Hollanda, S. B. de (2006). *Roots of Brazil*. São Paulo, Brazil: Companhia das Letras. (Original work published 1936).

IBGE [Instituto Brasileiro de Geografia e Estatística]. (2009). *National Household Sample Survey-PNAD*. Rio de Janeiro, Brazil: IBGE.

IBGE [Instituto Brasileiro de Geografia e Estatística]. (2010). *Synthesis of social indicators: An analysis of the population's living conditions*. Rio de Janeiro, Brazil: IBGE.

IBGE [Instituto Brasileiro de Geografia e Estatística]. (2011). *Synopsis of the 2010 census*. Rio de Janeiro, Brazil: IBGE.

Krob, A. D., Piccinini, C. A., & M. R. Silva (2009). The transition to fatherhood: From pregnancy to the second month of the baby's life. *Psicologia USP, 20*, 269–291.

Lamb, M., & C. Lewis (2011). The role of parent–child relationships in child development. In M. E. Lamb & M. E. Bornstein (Eds.), *Social and personality development: An advanced textbook* (pp. 259–307). New York, NY: Psychology Press.

Laqueur, W. (1992). *Europe in our time: A history, 1945–1992.* New York, NY: Penguin.

Levandowski, D. C., Antoni, C., Koller, S. H., & Piccinini, C. A. (2002). Teenager fatherhood and the risk and protection factors for violence in the father–child interaction. *Interações VII,* 77–100.

Levandowski, D. C., &Piccinini, C. A. (2006). Expectations and feelings about fatherhood among teenagers and adults. *Psicologia: Teoria & Pesquisa, 22,* 17–28.

Lyra, J., Leão, L. S., Lima, D. C., Targino, P., Crisóstomo, A., & Santos, B. (2008). Men and care: Another family? In A. R. Acosta & M. A. F. Vitale (Eds.), *Vitale family: Networks, bonds and public policies* (pp. 79–92). São Paulo, Brazil: Cortez/Instituto de Estudos Especiais/PUC-SP.

Marcon, G. B. (2010). *Expansion of paternity leave.* Retrieved June, 18, 2011, from http://www.administradores.com.br/informe-se/artigos/ampliacao-da-licenca-paternidade/47173/

Medrado, B., Lyra, J., Oliveira, A. R., Azevedo, M., Nanes, G., & Felipe, D. A. (2010). Public policies as paternities-producing devices. In L. V. C. Moreira, G. Petrini, & F. B. Barbosa (Eds.), *The father in contemporary society* (pp. 53–80). Bauru, Brazil: EDUSC.

Mioto, R. C. T. (2010). The family as a reference in public policy: Trends and dilemmas. In L. A. B. Trad (Ed.), *Contemporary family and health: Meanings, practices and public policies* (pp. 51–66). Rio de Janeiro, Brazil: Editora FIOCRUZ.

Moreira, L., Carvalho, A. M. A., & Almeida, O. (in press). The maternal and feminine prevalence in the daily care of young children. In M. G. Castro, A. M. A. Carvalho, & L. V. C. Moreira (Eds.), *Family dynamics on care: Affect, imaginary and fathers' involvement in the care of children.*

Muzio, P. A. (1998). *Fatherhood (being a father) ... What's the use? The exercise of fatherhood.* São Paulo, Brazil: Artes Médicas.

Nolasco, S. (1993). *The myth of masculinity.* Rio de Janeiro, Brazil: Plural.

Orlandi, R., & Toneli, M.J.F. (2005). Sobre o processo de constituição do sujeito face paternidade na adolescência [An approach to the process of subject constitution in face of paternity in adolescence]. *Psicologia em Revista, 11* (18), 257–267.

Orlandi, R., & Toneli, M. J. F. (2008). Adolescence and paternity: On the rights to create projects and procreate. *Psicologia em Estudo, 13,* 317–326.

Parke, R. R. (2002). Fathers and families. In M. H. Bornstein (Ed.), *Handbook of parenting: Being and becoming a parent* (Vol. 3, pp. 27–74), Mahwah, NJ: Lawrence Erlbaum Associates.

Petrini, G. (2010). Introduction. In L. V. C. Moreira, G. Petrini, & F. B. Barbosa (Eds.), *The father in contemporary society* (pp. 15–20). Bauru, Brazil: EDUSC.

Piccinini, C. A., Silva, M. R., Gonçalves, T. R., Lopes, R. S., & Tudge, J. (2004). The father involvement during pregnancy. *Psicologia: Reflexão e Crítica, 17,* 303–314.

Piccinini, C. A., Marin, A. H., Alvarenga, P., Lopes, R. C. S., & Tudge, J. (2007). Maternal responsiveness in single-parent families and nuclear families in the third month of the child's life. *Estudos de Psicologia (Natal), 12,* 109–117.

Pontes, V.V. (2011). Having recurrent gestational losses: Persistence in living. In A.

C. S. Bastos, K. Uriko, & J. Valsiner (Eds.), *Cultural dynamics of women's lives*, Charlotte, NC: Information Age Publishing.

Samara, E. M. (2002). What changed in the Brazilian family? From the colony to the present. *Psicologia USP* [Online], *13*, 27–48. Retrieved June, 18, 2011, from: www.scielo.br/scielo.php?pid=S0103656420020002000004&script=sci_abstract &tlng=pt.

Silva, M. R., & Piccinini, C. A. (2004). The fatherly involvement in non-resident fathers: Some theoretical questions. *Psico (PUCRS), 35*, 185–194.

Silva, M. R., & Piccinini, C. A. (2007). Feelings about fatherhood and fatherly involvement: A qualitative study. *Estudos de Psicologia (Campinas), 24*, 561–573.

Silva, M. R., & Piccinini, C. A. (2009). Fatherhood in the context of maternal post-partum depression: A literature review. *Estudos de Psicologia, 14*, 5–12.

Souza, C. L. C., & Benetti, S. P. C. (2009). Contemporary fatherhood: A survey of the academic production from 2000 to 2007. *Paidéia, 19*, 97–106.

Sutter, C., & Bucher-Maluschke, J. S. N. F. (2008). Fathers who take care of their children: The male experience in participative fatherhood. *PSICO, 39*, 74–82.

Thurler, A. L. (2006). Other horizons for fatherhood Brazil in the XXI century. *Sociedade e Estado, 21*, 681–707.

Trindade, Z. A. (1993). Social representations and everyday life: The issue of maternity and paternity. *Psicologia: Teoria e Pesquisa, 9*, 535–546.

Trindade, Z. A., & Menandro, M. C. S. (2002). Teenage parents: Experiences and meaning. *Estudos de Psicologia, 7*, 15–23.

Tudge, J. (2008). *The everyday lives of young children: Culture, class and child rearing in diverse societies*. New York, NY: Cambridge University Press.

Zaluar, A. (1983). Women and the management of the household consumption (study of family roles on urban working classes). In M. S. Almeida, C. A. Brandão, M. Corrêa, B. Feldmann-Bianco, V. Stolcke, & A. Zaluar (Eds.), *Patchwork: Studies on the family in Brazil* (pp. 161–184). São Paulo, Brazil: Brasiliense.

Chapter Eleven

Fathers in the U.S.

Karen E. McFadden and Catherine S. Tamis-LeMonda
New York University, New York, NY, USA

Case Story: Bicultural American Fathering

Salvino is a U.S. father of a 6-year-old son, Filippo. He lives with his wife, Anne Marie (an American-born Ph.D. in Italian who is a college teacher) in New York City. Salvino was born in Switzerland but raised in Sicily by his Italian parents, and immigrated to the U.S. in 1991. He first worked at a restaurant in San Diego and finally settled in New York City where he met Anne Marie, whom he married in 1995. Over the years, he continued his work at various restaurants, and through perseverance, dedication, and a belief in the American Dream, he eventually achieved a prestigious position with an Italian company that imports wines. His work takes him back to Italy on a regular basis. Salvino studied for many years in preparation for U.S. citizenship, which he received in July, 2000. He and his wife share household responsibilities, childcare, and living expenses, with Salvino doing most of the cooking and Anne Marie being in charge of childcare arrangements.

Their son is bilingual and attends Italian programs in the city so as to remain connected to his Italian heritage. Salvino mostly speaks Italian with Filippo, to ensure that his son's Italian skills remain strong, and the two enjoy watching Italian soccer on television. Salvino is a very involved father; he attends school PTA meetings, looks after Filippo whenever there are conflicts with Anne Marie's teaching schedule, attends his son's sporting events, and regularly takes Filippo to special outings, for example, to see the *Thomas the Tank Engine* live-on-stage show, and to family community events such as Easter egg hunts and Halloween parades. At least one night a week, when Anne Marie teaches, Salvino and Filippo have "pal night" during which they play and have a special dinner that they prepare together. At the end of the evening, Salvino reads Filippo Italian books as a part of the bedtime routine. Salvino's fathering differs from that of his own father, who constantly worked and was less involved in the raising of his children and household responsibilities.

Salvino's story typifies the ideals of freedom and opportunity, equality and negotiations between fathers and mothers, highly involved fathering (in this case with his one child), and the cultural diversity of U.S. fathers and families, which we will emphasize in this chapter.

Cultural and Historical Background as It Influences Fathering

Our discussion of fathers in the U.S. begins with consideration of the socio-cultural forces that have shaped the current opportunities and constraints of American men and families. Three converging and overlapping forces are central to this discussion: shared ideals, economic opportunities, and cultural diversity. First, the core ideals of equality and freedom – the founding principles on which America was established – are expressed in both shared and unique roles of U.S. fathers. The American ideal of equality influences how citizens view the fathering role. Many U.S. fathers today are partners in the parenting process, and thus expect to negotiate their partnership with the mothers of their children. However, the American ideal of freedom also means that fathers and families have choices about the roles and responsibilities men have in family life. Many American fathers devote substantial time to childcare, and a growing number of men (albeit a small minority) are taking on the role of primary caregiver or "stay-at-home dad." Other men assume other combinations of parenting roles, engaging directly with their children as playmates or disciplinarians. Overall, the majority of men also continue to endorse the importance of financial provisioning, but with the high rates of divorce and out-of-wedlock births in the U.S., many fathers provide for their children from outside the household.

Second, the United States has a free market economy, and the majority of men and families in the U.S. reap the financial benefits of a capitalist society with educational, employment, and lifestyle opportunities. These opportunities have meant that the majority of work-eligible men in the U.S. participate in the labor market and contribute economically to the needs of their children and families. Family visits to restaurants, attendance at cultural and sporting events or religious services, family vacations, birthday parties for children, access to new technologies (computers, cell phones, notebooks), and residence ownership are normative for many families in the U.S.

However, other families confront financial hardship, and some rely on various forms of public assistance. Economic expansion in the context of economic stratification has always been a part of U.S. history, as for example when the surge of industrial growth in the late 1800s, concentrated along the East and West coasts, led to resource disparities across regions depending on access to commerce and trade (e.g., North vs. South, and urban vs. rural areas in America). Moreover, unemployment continues to be a problem for many men in the U.S., with rates at 8.7% for White men over age 20 years (March 2011) and reaching a staggering 15.5% for Black men (Bureau of Labor Statistics, 2011).

Finally, the U.S. has always been a land of immigration and cultural diversity. The opportunities of the free market have attracted new immigrants to this country throughout its history. Consequently, fathers in the U.S. come from a range of backgrounds and communities that vary widely in traditions of dress, food, music, religion, holidays, languages, and child-rearing views and practices. Moreover, men and fathers in the U.S. have the freedom to act in accordance with their religious beliefs, and religious beliefs continue to play a key role in the lives of many American fathers and families today. Diversity is part of the fabric of U.S. society, and economic and cultural variations have powerful implications for the faces of

Figure 11.1 The Case Story father proudly watches his son blow out the candles at his 6th birthday party in New York City, as friends sing "Happy Birthday." Attending such an important event is typical for an American father. Photo courtesy of Catherine S. Tamis-LeMonda.

fatherhood in America. There is no single American definition of a good or bad father, because U.S. ideals around freedom result in diverse definitions of fathering, including those that emphasize fathers as breadwinners, as nurturers and equal care providers (to mothers), and as disciplinarians, etc.

In this chapter we show how cultural ideals, economic opportunities, and cultural diversity influence the research and theoretical questions that are asked and answered about fathers in the U.S. We begin with a review of the socio-cultural forces that have shaped father involvement in the U.S., and then consider a set of questions and findings on: (1) father presence–absence; (2) the father's role in the broader family context; (3) father–child relationships; and (4) fathers from diverse backgrounds. We conclude with a discussion of policy directions and reflections about how fathering in the U.S. differs from fathering in other societies.

Socio-cultural forces in the United States

As in many nations, the U.S. has experienced substantial changes in perceptions about and enactments of fathers' role in family life over its relatively short history (Rotundo, 1985). These shifts resulted from changing economic and social contexts at different periods in United States history, from the Colonial era to the present.

Stories surrounding colonial history in the U.S. are rife with imagery emphasizing liberty, freedom, and the entrepreneurial experiences of men and fathers who made the most of opportunities afforded by a new land. One of the earliest U.S. narratives (aside from the narratives of Native Americans) describes the voyage of Pilgrims on the Mayflower, who came to the New World in search of freedom to practice the religion of their choice. Historical accounts of freedom and equality continue to dominate the popular view of colonial history in America, most notably in descriptions of the Revolutionary War and patriots' sacrifices to preserve the personal and political liberties they sought in America. When liberty was threatened, colonists rose to protect and maintain their freedom to make and pursue their choices. The term "patriarchal" father has been used to refer to men's roles during the period of approximately 1600–1800 (Rotundo, 1985), during which men controlled material resources (e.g., property ownership) and wielded enormous control over the moral and spiritual development of their children. In accordance with colonists' focus on religious values, fathers in this era took on the role of teacher of morals, communicating ethical standards primarily based in Biblical teachings (Pleck & Pleck, 1997).

Following the colonial era in America, the rise of industry became the dominant influence on U.S. fathers and families. The industrial revolution established the basis for further division of labor in American households and solidified fathers' role as breadwinners, which also reinforced men's role as head of household (Rotundo, 1985). Mothers were responsible for the care of children at home while fathers labored in industrial work and factories. This pattern persisted into the next century and reinforced cultural expectations with respect to male and female parental roles, and in turn the typical tasks performed by mothers and fathers. Divisions of household labor common in 19th and early 20th century America established the notion of traditional parental roles, whereby fathers were responsible for financial provisioning, and childcare and homemaking were the purview of mothers (Amato, 1998).

However, during the mid-20th century, major new work opportunities for women coupled with emergence of the women's movement led to a redefinition and expansion of fathers' and mothers' roles. Not only did their roles begin to change, but the U.S. also experienced a cultural shift in expectations and values surrounding both fatherhood and motherhood (Thornton, 1989). A marked rise in rates of paid female employment led to rapid change in the typical division of labor of the American family. Consistent growth in the American economy was accompanied by a steady stream of mothers leaving unpaid work at home for paid employment in the outside world. Specifically, in 1950 approximately 12% of married women with young children held jobs outside of the home, but by 2000 this percentage had risen to two-thirds of this group of women (Baxter, Hewitt, & Western, 2000). Accordingly, a new style of fatherhood emerged – "Androgynous Fatherhood"– in which sex roles were reshaped to minimize differences between the sexes (Rotundo, 1985).

Statistics on women's work outside the home are often linked to higher rates of children spending significant time in non-maternal care (Bureau of Labor Statistics, 1997; Tamis-Le Monda & Cabrera, 2002). Such trends in women's work-force participation are also connected to the shift towards later timing of first marriage and family formation by American women and men in the latter half of the 20th century (Goldstein & Kenney, 2001; Thornton & Young-DeMarco, 2001). Additionally, during this time period, out-of-wedlock births jumped from 4% in 1950 to 33% by the end of the 20th century, suggesting that marriage was no longer a prerequisite for family formation (Heuveline & Timberlake, 2004; Ventura & Bachrach, 2000). Such demographic trends have altered the landscape of U.S. family life and forced American families to renegotiate divisions of labor.

These historical and cultural shifts have had substantial implications for expectations regarding fathers' roles in family life and child development. Household financial provisioning was formerly expected mainly of fathers, but now is substantially shared by mothers; perhaps in response, expectations for fathers' participation in childcare has increased (Thornton, 1989). Currently, many fathers in the U.S. are expected to feed and dress children and change their diapers, tasks that would never have been normative for men hitherto. Additionally, because of the rise in divorce rates and out-of-wedlock births, fathers do not necessarily live with their children. Never-married and divorced parents have had to redefine norms for paternal care, and the focus of these fathers' roles outside the household has mainly been on child support and financial responsibilities (Nepomnyaschy, 2007; Seltzer & Bianchi, 1988; Waller, 2002).

In response to the preceding socio-cultural changes, research on the father's role in child development burgeoned from the latter part of the 20th century through the present (Lamb, 2000, 2010). We next discuss how socio-cultural shifts have affected questions about and research findings on father involvement in the U.S.

Review of Fathering Research: Key Questions

Studies on fathering in the U.S. are motivated by a core set of questions that are firmly rooted in the U.S. cultural experience: (1) Does father *presence or absence* matter for children's development, and how? (2) What are the pathways through which fathers' *financial provisioning* influences children? (3) What are the *roles of fathers in families*, and how do family members negotiate these roles? (4) Which aspects of the *father–child relationship* lead to positive or negative development in children, and how? And (5) How does fathering (including presence–absence, financial provisioning, role in family life, and quality of the father–child relationship) compare across *culturally diverse U.S. populations*?

Each of these questions is subordinate to our fundamental, overarching question: *Why study fathering in the U.S.?* The simple answer is that we study fathers because of a firm conviction in American culture that who parents are, how they think, and what they do powerfully affects children's development. Just as the U.S. economy was built on the idea that all individuals have the potential to succeed in the marketplace through hard work (Weber, 1958), the literature on child development was founded in the U.S. and internationally on the assumption that children are in part the products of socialization by parents. This guiding principle has been the impetus for thousands of studies on parenting, most of which provide solid evidence for the impact of parents on children's development (e.g., Bornstein, 2002; Collins, Maccoby, Steinberg, Hetherington, & Bornstein 2000; Maccoby & Martin, 1983). Moreover, parents' influence on children is evident across domains of social, language, cognitive, and emotional development, and these influences may start even before birth. Furthermore, differences in children's experiences with parents largely explain disparities in developmental trajectories among subgroups in the U.S.

Father presence and absence

Socio-cultural shifts in the U.S. during the 20th century spurred a focus on the role of father presence/absence in children's development. Rising divorce rates in the mid-20th century heightened concerns about the benefits of fathers' continued presence in children's lives, and whether and how divorce and separation from fathers influenced children's development (e.g., Furstenberg & Nord, 1985; Seltzer & Bianchi, 1988). This research continues into the 21st century due to the continued high rates of divorce and family reformation. Fathers' presence and absence has also been investigated in the context of out-of-wedlock births. The proportion of children born to unmarried parents rose dramatically in the last four decades, and has remained somewhat stable since the 1990s, with rates being highest among poor minority parents (Gibson-Davis, Edin, & McLanahan, 2005; Ventura & Bachrach, 2000). Additionally, while many of these births are to cohabitating couples, the likelihood that low-income parents will establish a household together or marry varies by race, ethnicity, and economic factors; for example, low-income Black mothers are less likely to marry at all than low-income White mothers (Gibson-Davis et al., 2005; Manning & Smock, 1995). As a result of these trends, father presence/absence has continued to be a focus of research on children and fathers.

For the most part, American studies of divorce and out-of-wedlock childbearing reveal negative effects of father absence on children. These adverse effects can be attributed to several mechanisms (Silverstein & Auerbach, 1999), including the absence of co-parents (Kelly, 2000), economic stress related to single motherhood (Pearson & Thoennes, 1990), emotional stress as a result of social isolation and disapproval (Hetherington, Cox, & Cox, 1985), a sense of abandonment experienced by children (Lamb, 1999; Thompson & Laible, 1999), and marital conflict regarding divorce (Cummings, Goeke-Morey, & Raymond, 2004; Kelly, 2000).

But while many fathers do not reside with their children, non-resident fathers are not necessarily absent from their children's lives. National, large-scale studies indicate that, of the 21% of American children who live in mother-headed households, about 87% have regular contact with their fathers (Federal Interagency Forum on Child and Family Statistics, 2010; Flanagan & West, 2004; McLanahan, Garfinkel, Reichman, & Teitler, 2001). Moreover, reports about father involvement based on several large-scale national studies of minority and low income families (e.g., National Survey of Black Americans; Early Head Start Fatherhood Study–EHS; the Early Childhood Longitudinal Study-Birth Cohort–ECLSB; and Fragile Families–FF) indicate that the majority of non-resident fathers are actively engaged in their children's lives, and that their involvement has a positive impact on children's learning and social development (Black, Dubowitz, &

Starr, 1999; Bowman & Forman, 1997; Cabrera et al., 2004). Across studies, approximately 80% of fathers are involved through pregnancy, birth, and early childhood, express commitment to raising their children, and continue to see their children regularly during the preschool years (e.g., Cabrera et al., 2004; Johnson, 2001). In-depth interviews with such men revealed their strong desire to "be there" for their children and acknowledge the importance of remaining part of their children's lives (Summers, Boller, Schiffman, & Raikes, 2006).

Fathers' financial provisioning

The division of household responsibilities that accompanied the industrial revolution solidified the ideology of the American father's role as family breadwinner, and the opportunities afforded by a free, capitalist society led to expectations that men should provide economically for their children. Moreover, economic theory posits that households tend to be organized in the manner most efficient to family needs (Becker, 1991). Men's generally higher income potential has largely reinforced traditional division of labor patterns, in which women perform most household work. This fact has typically played out in a model where men focus on paid work outside of the home to provide for the financial needs of the household, while women provide the labor necessary for the adequate functioning of the household.

Widespread expectations for fathers' financial provisioning have continued through the present, leading to extensive research on the effects of family resources on children's development (Duncan & Brooks-Gunn, 1997). Indeed, scholars assert men's financial provisioning to be the most important form of father involvement (Working Group on Conceptualizing Male Parenting, 1997). Mothers also consider men's financial provisioning to be of prime importance, especially in the case of non-resident fathers (Argys, Peters, Brooks-Gunn, & Smith, 1998; Gassman-Pines, Yoshikawa, & Nay, 2006).

Furthermore, the rising rate of out-of-wedlock births, coupled with the fact that unmarried mothers and fathers are unlikely to establish households together, are related to the economic challenges faced by growing numbers of single mothers in the U.S. in a number of ways. For example, in one qualitative study, the majority of low-income mothers from three different Eastern metropolitan areas in the U.S. stated that they were not inclined to marry their children's fathers unless marriage provided economic benefits (Edin, 2000). Low marriage rates among non-married parents have been explained partially as a shortage of 'marriageable men' accounting for increases in single motherhood in low-income minority populations, and have intensified focus on the financial provisioning role fathers may or may not play in families (Lichter, McLaughlin, Kephart, & Landry, 1992). Declines in educational attainment and consistently high rates of incarceration for low-income fathers in the U.S. (and low-income Black fathers in particular) have created a landscape that continues to be bleak in terms of fathers' potential to provide economically for children (Mincy, 2006; Western & McLanahan, 2000). These trends have highlighted the fact that economic patterns and racial/ethnic trends in family formation should be examined jointly (Wilson, 1987), due to the broad income inequalities that exist in the U.S. by race and ethnicity.

Furthermore, fathers' financial provisioning has been of interest to researchers as a result of studies showing that child support payments seem to influence children's academic achievement and predict positive child outcomes more strongly than other sources of income (Graham & Beller, 2002). Research shows that fathers who pay child support are more likely to be committed to their children, to have better relationships with the mothers of their children, to visit their children more often, or to have the financial ability – and tendency – to support them. Research data thus show that fathers' economic provisioning has wide-ranging benefits for children, although other aspects of father involvement that accompany financial provisioning may be just as important for children's development as the dollars *per se*.

Fathers' role in the family

Although equality and even freedom were not legalized for non-Whites over centuries in America, the incorporation of these ideals into the Declaration of Independence, the U.S. Constitution, and the Bill of Rights gave women and people of color the grounds to challenge inequality and injustices during the women's suffrage movement in the early 20th century and the civil rights movement in the 1950s and 1960s. As a result, women worked toward and achieved increased participation in the labor force over the latter part of the 20th century, applying the American ideal of equal rights for women and men to educational and employment opportunities. As such, current American ideology suggests that the time devoted to outside employment, household chores, and the care of children should be shared by men and women. When couples do not share these roles, the cultural expectation is that men and women have negotiated and settled upon a system that best suits the common needs of household members; this in part explains the data on fathers' financial provisioning, and is also linked to interest in the other roles that fathers might play in the family. Consequently, many researchers have analyzed the time fathers spend with children in childcare and in household work, and documented changes in these activities between the 1950s and the end of the 20th century (Blair & Lichter, 1991; Kamo & Cohen, 1998; Pleck, 1997; Pleck & Masciadrelli, 2004).

Of course, ideologies around shared division of labor by men and women vary by region, family socioeconomic status, religion, and ethnicity. Moreover, despite the U.S. ideology of equality, on average modern fathers continue to spend substantially less time with their children than mothers (Pleck, 1997; Pleck & Masciadrelli, 2004). In two-parent families in which mothers are unemployed, fathers spend about a quarter as much time as mothers directly engaged with their children, and about a third as much time accessible to their children.

However, the rising level of employment among American women has led to growing expectations that men should share responsibilities of childcare, and this expectation has engendered increases in paternal involvement (Lamb, Pleck, Charnov, & Levine, 1987; Pleck, 1985). For example, in one 1966 survey that was replicated in 1986, U.S. fathers' total time spent with children over these two decades increased by 33% (Robinson, Andreyenkov, & Patrushev, 1988). In addition, federal childcare data indicated that 21% of married employed mothers reported fathers to be the primary childcare providers for their children in 2005 compared to 17% in 1977 (O'Connell, 1993; U.S. Census Bureau, 2008).

Moreover, in two-parent families where both parents are employed, the average levels of father engagement and accessibility are substantially higher than in families with stay-at-home mothers. However, fathers do not necessarily spend more time interacting with their children when mothers work; rather, the proportions increase because employed mothers contribute less time to household and childcare responsibilities. Fathers are thus proportionately more involved when mothers are employed, even though the absolute extent of their involvement may not change to a meaningful extent. Over time, levels of paternal involvement in dual-earner families have increased, but these changes are smaller than popular accounts suggest (Pleck & Masciadrelli, 2004).

Current research on fathers' role in the family system has also focused on tradeoffs men and women make regarding work within and outside the household. Economic theory suggests that household labor is rationally divided on the basis of family composition and outside work schedules (Pinto & Coltrane, 2009). According to this theory, the amount of work required to support a household rises with the number of people in the home, but as individuals work more hours outside the home, their participation in household labor decreases. Theories of household labor and resources have also focused on the relative economic power men and women wield in the market place, such as earned income, education, and occupational status or prestige (Becker 1991; Blood & Wolfe, 1960; Gupta, 2006). Couples who are more balanced on these indicators of occupational power tend to

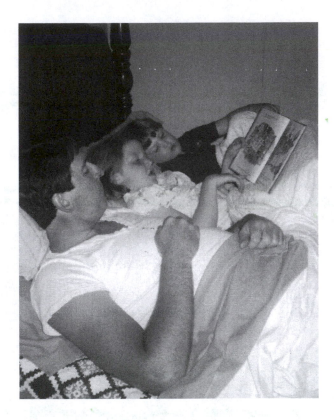

Figure 11.2 A 36-year-old father with his 3-year-old son and 6-year-old daughter, reading a bedtime story while on summer vacation at Seaside Park, New Jersey. Fathers like him are highly involved in activities beyond those of financial provider or physical playmate. Photo courtesy of Karen E. McFadden.

have more egalitarian divisions of labor in their households (Blair & Lichter, 1991; Kamo & Cohen, 1998). As parents' education, salary, or occupational prestige increases, there is less incentive to spend commensurate time in household work. In modern families where both parents have prestigious occupations, both parents often engage in this tradeoff and leave childcare to paid caregivers, because the cost of these services is less than what parents can earn as a result of the time saved by employing caregivers.

The father–child relationship

Questions about the consequences of father presence/absence, financial contributions, and fathers' role in the family generally neglect to highlight the importance of the *quality* of fathering in supporting positive development in children. U.S. ideology regarding equality and opportunity, together with the principle that parents matter for children's development, asserts that the quality of the father–child relationship should be equally (1) supportive or positive (based on mean level comparisons) and (2) influential (based on the magnitude of associations), compared to the mother–child relationship. Empirical studies present solid support for these assumptions. The quality of fathers' relationships with their children does not differ dramatically from that of mothers, even though fathers spend less time overall with their children. In addition, variations in the quality of father–child relations predict a range of developmental outcomes in children, including language development, cognitive development, emotional and behavioral regulation, and social competence. The importance of father–child relationship quality also generalizes to families from different SES and ethnic/racial backgrounds and remains after controlling for fathers' education and employment, and for the quality of the mother–child relationship (e.g., Tamis Le-Monda, Shannon, Cabrera, & Lamb, 2004).

Comparing father–child and mother–child relations, studies of infant attachment indicate that infants are equally likely to become attached to their fathers and mothers (Lamb, 2002). Moreover, observational studies comparing mother–child and father–child interactions on a number of dimensions indicate that, on average, fathers do not differ from mothers, when rated for supportiveness (sensitivity, cognitive stimulation, positive regard or warmth), negativity, and intrusiveness during naturalistic play with toddlers (Ryan, Martin, & Brooks-Gunn, 2006; Tamis-LeMonda et al., 2004). Studies of parents' communication with infants and young children also suggest more similarities than differences in the language used by fathers and mothers. Specifically, the literature on U.S. parent–child communication has shown the following: (a) fathers and mothers do not differ in the frequencies with which they refer to objects and events in the environment during parent–child free play (Bornstein, Vibbert, Tal, & O'Donnell, 1992); (b) both fathers and mothers produce more explicit than implicit directives when talking to their infants (Golinkoff & Ames, 1979); (c) they do not differ in the number of utterances, words used, communicative functions, or diversity of word types expressed towards 2-year-olds (Tamis-LeMonda, Baumwell, & Cristofaro, in press); and (d) when responding to infants' language, fathers and mothers use repetition and expansion similarly (Gleason, 1975). In addition, measures of parents' syntactic complexity reveal no differences in mean lengths of fathers' and mothers' utterances (i.e., MLU; Gleason, 1975; Pancsofar & Vernon-Feagans, 2006; Tamis-LeMonda, Baumwell, & Cristofaro, in press), and both mothers and fathers use shorter utterances and adjust their speech to children aged 9 months to 3 years (e.g., Golinkoff & Ames, 1979).

Yet there is also evidence that fathers and mothers offer their children different experiences. For example, fathers challenge children's conversational skills more frequently than mothers. In particular, when talking to children who are at the early stages of language development, fathers produce more directives, requests for clarification, wh- questions, references to past events, and imperatives than mothers (e.g., Leaper, Anderson, & Sanders, 1998; Malone & Guy, 1982; McLaughlin, White, McDevitt, & Raskin, 1983). These differences may occur because fathers spend less time with their children than mothers, and are therefore less able to understand what their young children attempt to say. Fathers also spend proportionately more time than mothers engaging their young children in physical play (e.g., throwing infants in the air; mock fighting, Lamb, 2004; Lamb et al., 1987), which may reflect their unique role in activating children's emotions (Paquette, 2004).

In support of the widespread American belief that parent involvement is vital for children's development, there is ample evidence of the benefits of positive father–child relationship quality for a range of children's skills. Fathers' direct engagements with their children matter even from infancy, and disparities in children's development are often explained by differences in paternal involvement (Furstenburg, Brooks-Gunn, & Morgan, 1987; McLanahan & Sandefur, 1994). In particular, numerous investigators have documented the importance of fathers' supportive engagements for children's development in infancy and the preschool years, including studies in our laboratory (e.g., Shannon, Tamis-LeMonda, London, & Cabrera, 2002; Tamis-LeMonda et al., 2004). Fathers' supportiveness also continues to predict children's language and cognitive development over time, after controlling for demographic characteristics, maternal engagement and children's characteristics (Tamis-LeMonda et al., 2004). Other investigators have shown that children of positively involved fathers are more socially competent and demonstrate better emotional regulation than children with less involved fathers (Fitzgerald, McKelvey, Schiffman, & Montanez, 2006; Parke et al., 2002). In the area of language development, fathers' word types, grammatical complexity, and breadth of word usage predict the same measures of language development in children (Tamis-LeMonda et al., in press), and children's communicative skills increase when they spend time talking with both fathers and mothers (Rowe, Coker, & Pan, 2004; Tomasello, Conti-Ramsden, & Ewert, 1990). Indeed, some researchers have documented *stronger* associations between father and child language than between mother and child language (Pancsofar & Vernon-Feagans, 2006; Pancsofar, Vernon-Feagans, & The Family Life Project Investigators, 2010). Finally, positive interactions between fathers and children present children with opportunities to learn social skills that enhance children's engagements with others (Parke & O'Neil, 1997), and father–child attachment and relationship quality predicts the quality of children's peer relationships concurrently and over the childhood years (see Parke et al., 2002 for review).

Sub-Cultural Variations in Fathering: Immigrants from Diverse Cultures

Because the U.S. is a land of cultural diversity, fathers from different ethnic and cultural communities view and enact the fathering role differently, in line with community norms and expectations. In the U.S., the values placed on freedom and diversity imply that men and families can decide on the roles fathers will play in the family, and these choices vary in the extent to which they reflect or do not reflect U.S. mainstream cultural orientations. Researchers in turn have asked what significance these choices have for children's development.

Accurate knowledge about the characteristics of immigrant fathers in the United States is limited, especially since the ethnic/racial composition of the U.S. is constantly shifting. In addition, some immigrant children in the U.S. are separated from one or both parents and their fathers have little opportunity to regularly interact with them. For example, in a sample of Dominican youth living in the U.S., 25% were separated from their fathers only, while 61% were separated from both parents for periods ranging from 6 months to over 5 years (Suarez-Orozco, Todorova, & Louie, 2002). In other instances, men from other countries come to the U.S. to pursue economic prospects while leaving their wives and children behind (see Roopnarine, Ch. 9, this volume, for discussion of serial immigration from Caribbean communities). This pattern has been documented in a qualitative study of Mexican fathers (Dreby, 2006) and in Chinese immigrants from Fujian Province (Gaytan, Xue, Yoshikawa, & Tamis-LeMonda, 2006). In the latter study, over 70% of undocumented Fujanese families sent their 3- to 6-month-old infants back to China to live with grandparents for several years, with the intention to bring their children back to the U.S. in time for school entry. Even among families whose infants were not sent back to China, fathers sometimes worked in towns or cities removed from their children, and only returned home on weekends. Thus, family separation may be a common experience for immigrant men who either have families in the U.S. or leave their families to seek U.S. employment. Separated fathers cannot experience the same levels of childcare, play, and daily activities with their children as in the majority of U.S. families, which may diminish their influence on children's cognitive, language, social and emotional development. Nonetheless, questions that are asked about foreign as well as immigrant fathers largely mirror the questions asked about fathers in general. Familial separations raise questions about father absence, the benefits of fathers' financial provisioning for children, and how mothers and fathers negotiate and accommodate varying levels of father involvement.

Research indicates that economic provisioning is a major role played by fathers in immigrant communities. For example, Dreby (2006) found that Mexican fathers in the U.S. maintained contact with their children through phone calls and sending money despite being separated from them. It was only when fathers were unable to fulfill their role as family breadwinners that they became distant from their children. Research on Mexican familial values corroborates this finding, because fatherhood is associated with providing economic resources for the family (Gutmann, 1996) and is closely bound with the notion of honor (Melhuus, 1996). Similarly, our research has shown a high commitment to the breadwinner role among immigrant fathers from Mexican and other backgrounds. For example, 78% of low-income Dominican fathers worked at the time of their infants' births; over half worked more than 40 hours per week, and 20% worked over 50 hours per week. The comparable percentages for Mexican fathers in our study were 94% working, 65% working over 40 hours, and 40% working over 50 hours/week. Chinese fathers, of whom 76% were working, put in the longest hours of the three immigrant groups: over 84% worked over 50 hours per week (Tamis-LeMonda, Niwa, Kahana-Kalman, & Yoshikawa, 2008). Long work hours may come at a cost, because they limit men's availability for everyday activities with their children. However, tradeoffs between fathers' work hours and time spent engaged with children are not always straightforward. For example, the above percentages might imply that Mexican fathers have less time available to spend with their children. Yet this is not the case. The vast majority reside with their infants, share meals with their families on a daily basis, and are more likely than low-income men from other backgrounds to engage in play and other activities with their toddlers (Tamis-LeMonda, Kahana-Kalman, & Yoshikawa, 2009).

Researchers often focus on the first-generation experiences of immigrant families from less materially affluent backgrounds. However, many U.S. fathers are second-, third- (or above) generation citizens with roots in other lands (e.g., Africa, South America, Eastern and Western Europe, the Middle East, and Asia), and immigrants include skilled workers and families with financial resources, although these groups are less often studied. Men from various backgrounds are all integral to the socio-cultural fabric of the U.S. and reflect stories of high aspirations and success in their U.S. experiences, as exemplified by our Case Study of Salvino.

In short, research on the role of fathers in immigrant families is limited (not only in the U.S., but also as described in nearly every chapter of this volume), and researchers are only beginning to learn about the nature of father–child activities and relationships across societies and immigrant communities. Although little is known about the ways in which U.S. immigrant fathers engage with children, expectations about the fathering role may vary according to cultural values and economic circumstances. At the same time, most fathers are free to accept new roles or modify traditional ones when they come to the U.S., and more research is needed on how immigration affects men's involvement with their children and families.

Social Policy Issues Related to Fathering

U.S. policies on fathering have been shaped by socio-cultural context. For example, many social policies have been implemented in response to rising rates of divorce and out-of-wedlock childbearing (Cabrera, 2010), and policies also shifted in response to political changes. For example, during the Clinton administration the federal response to social changes was mainly organized around promoting father involvement through the Fatherhood Research Initiative (Cabrera, Brooks-Gunn, Moore, West, & Boller, 2002; Cabrera & Peters, 1999). Subsequently, George W. Bush supported policies to enhance father involvement through the promotion of marriage (Administration for Children and Families, Healthy Marriage Initiative, 2006). Despite these different emphases, both administrations shared the goal of supporting father involvement in the form of time, financial provisioning and positive relationship quality. We next review several public policies that arose from U.S. socio-cultural trends in family life in the late 20th century (declines in marriage, increases in out-of-wedlock births) and in reaction to research evidence on the importance of fathers for children's development.

Healthy marriages initiative

During the 1990s, studies on the Early Head Start and Fragile Families projects highlighted the need to understand fathering in populations of "missing men," i.e., fathers who were not married to the mothers of their children and/or men from understudied groups (e.g., non-resident fathers, minority fathers including Blacks and Latinos; Cabrera, 2010). At the same time, several policies were implemented to support current marriages and encourage marriage between parents who had given birth to children out-of-wedlock. The Healthy Marriages Initiative coalesced in 2002 and provided funding for research on marriage, marriage education, and marriage programs in faith-based and community-based organizations (Pear & Kirkpatrick, 2004). Funds were reallocated in 2005, and this collection of marriage promotion policies comprised the main thrust of the federal response to single parenthood and welfare dependency (Struening, 2007). Related research indicated that marriage promotion could be beneficial in certain contexts but not others. For instance, the value of such policies are questionable in families characterized by substance abuse or domestic violence (Edin & Kefalas, 2005; Waller, 2002) and when couples are no longer romantically involved (Cabrera et al., 2004; Carlson & Furstenberg, 2006). The current Obama administration has signaled an interest in returning to policies that encourage father involvement and responsibility rather than marriage *per se*, although it has not yet implemented any such programs.

In-hospital paternity establishment

Concerns about the legal responsibility of men who were not married to the mothers of their children also fueled U.S. policies regarding paternity. In 1984, Congress introduced guidelines for paternity establishment, providing the legal grounds for actions to establish paternity of a child in court (Roberts, 2006). Paternity action suits were often conducted under hostile circumstances and brought by welfare officials outside of the family, to offset state monies allocated to men's children. In response, researchers encouraged the creation of more voluntary measures to ensure the establishment of legal paternity (Cabrera & Peters, 1999; Sonenstein, Holcomb, & Seefeldt, 1994). As a result, federal welfare reform legislation in 1996 required hospitals to provide programs for voluntary paternity acknowledgement at the time of a child's birth (Roberts, 2006). At present, the paternity of the vast majority of children is established when children are born in American hospitals (Mincy, Garfinkel, & Nepomnyaschy, 2005).

Child support

Grounded in research on the importance of fathers' financial provisioning for children, child support is strongly valued in the U.S. as essential for children's well-being (Curran, 2003). Child support policy is also a key element of welfare reform, in that fathers' financial provisioning reduces costs to the state, and an unmarried woman who applies for welfare is required to supply the name of her child's father (Laakso, 2000). Although child support policy was enacted through federal legislation, enforcement of the policy is determined by individual states which have adopted numerous strategies, including paycheck garnishing, license suspensions, and even arrests (Cabrera, 2010). Other research has shown that fathers who pay child support are more likely to visit children, and that when fathers do not make sufficient payments mothers are less likely to encourage father visitation (King, Harris, & Heard, 2004; Seltzer, 1991). Causal inferences about the direction of these associations are not warranted, however, and one qualitative study has suggested that child support payment is preferable when it is voluntary (Edin & Kefalas, 2005). This latter finding suggested that because of the American ideals of autonomy and self-reliance, men may have more positive attitudes toward their roles as fathers when they are able to provide for their children voluntarily.

Parental custody

U.S. policies regarding parental custody following divorce were traditionally biased in favor of mothers. However, evidence on the importance of father involvement for children's development has led some to challenge the assumption that "mother knows best." For example, the Marriage and Divorce Act of 1970 called for custody decisions to be made in the "best interests" of the child rather than on the basis of gender (Fineman & Opie, 1987; Hall, Pulver, & Cooley, 1996). However, for the most part, the assumption persisted that a child's best interests were equated with maternal custody, and many fathers cited discrimination in custody decisions (Braver & O'Connell, 1998). More recently, in the context of growing gender equality in labor market and households, custody decisions increasingly favor neither parent, and shared custody has become increasingly common.

Parental leave

U.S. values also promote equality in childcare and household management. For instance, the Family and Medical Leave Act of 1993 enabled both mothers and fathers to take up to six weeks of unpaid leave from work after the birth of a child, although fathers have tended not to opt for unpaid leave, particularly when mothers have paid leave options (Hyde, Essex, & Horton, 1993; Jutta, 1997). The gap between opportunity and practice again reflects the importance placed on men's role as breadwinners and documented disparities in women vs. men's involvement with childcare and household work. Although there are no current federal provisions for paid parental leave, public interest in alternative childcare options makes it part of current social policy discussions.

Interventions with families

The American ideals of personal achievement and fulfillment of one's potential has been an impetus for many family- and parenting-oriented policies, which aim to improve the lives of children and ensure equal opportunities for children from disadvantaged backgrounds. For example, parenting classes and education are cornerstones of Early Head Start intervention programs, which were implemented to support young children in low-income U.S. families. Interventions to strengthen families and promote positive parenting were also part of programs under the Healthy Marriages Initiative. Fathers are encouraged to participate in most parenting programs, but data suggest that they participate more in programs that target fathers specifically rather than parents generally.

Conclusions: American Fathers in a Global Context

Fathers in the U.S. are similar to fathers all over the world in many ways. Most of them are strongly invested in raising healthy, well adjusted children who will grow up to become valuable contributors to society, and they influence their children in various ways through social and economic provisioning. Like fathers everywhere, American fathers are the products of many converging forces, including broader cultural ideology, the socio-political histories of their communities, and the needs, constraints and opportunities of their families. To some extent, fathers in the U.S. represent a kaleidoscope of cultures and therefore vary in their childrearing views and practices.

However, the melting pot metaphor of the U.S. also implies that U.S. fathers collectively differ from fathers in the vast majority of countries around the world. In contrast to more homogenous societies such as Japan and Sweden (Chs. 3 and 13, this volume), U.S. fathers may be highly diverse in terms of both their socioeconomic and cultural backgrounds, and their fathering roles. Also by comparison, in Arab societies where the majority follows a religious faith that opposes divorce, we may expect fewer single-parent households, out-of-wedlock births, and non-resident fathers, than in the U.S. (see Ahmed, Ch. 6, this volume). American fathers consequently are observed across a wider range of family contexts than elsewhere, and research questions and policies (about father presence-absence, responsibility, and custody payments) reflect this diversity.

Finally, American values and constitutional rights centered on equality and freedom uniquely distinguish the U.S. ideology of fathering from that seen in other countries. As discussed earlier, traditional gender roles characterize many U.S. families, where mothers take on responsibilities at home and fathers spend the majority of their time at work. However, in a substantial proportion of U.S. families, men and women strive for the equitable division of labor within and outside the household. Fathers' and mothers' roles are negotiated, and many women are not expected to stay at home if they want to return to work. Thus, in the U.S. context, it is not surprising to see men share household tasks, childcare, and household expenses with women, or even take on the role of stay-at-home dads. When they do not share household duties, it is acceptable for women to complain about workload inequities and push men to pull their weight at home. This may contrast with more homogeneous cultures where expectations and roles for mothers and fathers are prescribed as mutually exclusive.

Finally, while there appears to be a contradiction between the two main tenets of the chapter – the *shared* ideals that formed the basis of the U.S. and the notion of *diversity* – the two are not inconsistent. The shared ideal of freedom recognizes personal choice. That is, the expression of diversity, as discussed here through a lens on fatherhood, can only be sanctioned in a society that respects a person's freedom of choice. Similarly, although social and economic disparities among fathers and families in the U.S. lead some to question the shared ideal of equality, this ideal has underpinned many social movements, policy decisions and programs in the U.S. Indeed, the ideal of equality has been a key catalyst for historical changes in American fathers' impact on child development, as reflected in shifts from men's patriarchal role in colonial times to the present-day father–mother negotiations illustrated in our opening Case Story.

Summary

Shared ideals regarding equality and freedom, economic opportunity, and cultural diversity frame both the face of fatherhood in America and the questions asked in research on fathering. The effect of these shared ideals is that contemporary U.S. fathers and mothers are increasingly expected to share in the task of parenting, although they have the freedom to define and negotiate their roles within the family system. Research on fathers' roles in the family and child development, including emphases on "division of household labor" and "father engagement in childcare," also reflects these shared ideals. In terms of economic opportunity, American fathers have access to education and employment not universally available in many countries of the world. Nonetheless, large disparities in income and work are seen among men from different ethnic/cultural backgrounds and regions of the U.S. As a result, much research has been dedicated to comparing the role of fathers' financial provisioning for children's development between population groups. Finally, the cultural diversity of men and fathers in the U.S. has the effect that customs, values, roles, and traditions in families vary across religious backgrounds, race/ethnicity, and immigration histories. Consequently, recent research has focused on identifying similarities and differences in fathering across groups of fathers, and on examining links between such variability and children's developmental trajectories. In sum, the chapter demonstrates that diversity is a defining characteristic of fathers in America – as seen in their roles, economic circumstances, and backgrounds – and current fathering research reflects this variation.

Acknowledgments

We acknowledge funding by NSF BCS grant #021859 and NSF IRADS grant #0721383, and thank our colleagues from the National Early Head Start Fatherhood Consortium, including Natasha Cabrera and Jacqueline Shannon. We are grateful to the hundreds of mothers, fathers, and children who have participated in our research over the years.

References

Administration for Children and Families, Healthy Marriage Initiative. (2006). *Healthy marriage initiative achievements and accomplishments, 2002–2005.* Retrieved from www.acf.hhs.gov/healthymarriage/about/mission.html.

Amato, P. R. (1998). More than money? Men's contributions to their children's lives. In A. Booth & A. C. Crouter (Eds.), *Men in families: When do they get involved? What difference does it make?* (pp. 241–278). Mahwah, NJ: Lawrence Erlbaum Associates.

Argys, L. M., Peters, E., Brooks-Gunn, J., & Smith, J. R. (1998). The impact of child support dollars on cognitive outcomes. *Demography, 35* (2), 159–173.

Baxter, J., Hewitt, B., & Western, M. (2000). Post-familial families and the domestic division of labor. *Journal of Comparative Family Studies, 36* (4), 583–600.

Becker, G. S. (1991). *A treatise on the family.* Cambridge, MA: Harvard University Press.

Black, M. M., Dubowitz, H., & Starr, R. H., Jr. (1999). African American fathers in low income, urban families: Development, behavior, and home environment of their three-year-old children. *Child Development, 70,* 967–978.

Blair, S. L., & Lichter, D. T. (1991). Measuring the division of household labor: Gender segregation of housework among American couples. *Journal of Family Issues, 12*(1), 91–113.

Blood, R. O., & Wolfe, D. M. (1960). *Husbands and wives: The dynamics of family living.* Oxford, UK: Free Press Glencoe.

Bornstein, M. H. (2002). Parenting infants. In M. H. Bornstein (Ed.), *Handbook of parenting: Vol. 1. Children and parenting* (2nd ed., pp. 3–43). Mahwah, NJ: Lawrence Erlbaum Associates.

Bornstein, M. H., Vibbert, M., Tal, J., & O'Donnell, K. (1992). Toddler language and play in the second year: Stability, covariation and influences of parenting. *First Language, 12* (36, Pt. 3), 323–338.

Bowman, P. J., & Forman, T. A. (1997). Instrumental and expressive family roles among African American fathers. In R. J. Taylor, J. S. Jackson, & L. M. Chatters (Eds.), *Family life in Black America* (pp. 216–247). Thousand Oaks, CA: Sage Publications.

Braver, S. L., & O'Connell, D. (1998). *Divorced dads.* New York, NY: Putnam.

Bureau of Labor Statistics. (1997). Marital and family characteristics of the labor force. *Current Population Survey.* Washington, DC: U.S. Department of Labor.

Bureau of Labor Statistics (2011). *Employment status of the civilian population by race, sex, and age.* Retrieved from http://www.bls.gov/news.release/empsit.t02. htm

Cabrera, N. J. (2010). Father involvement and public policies. In In M. E. Lamb (Ed.), *The role of the father in child development* (5th ed., pp. 517–550). Hoboken, NJ: John Wiley.

Cabrera, N., Brooks-Gunn, J., Moore, K., West, J., & Boller, K. (2002). Bridging research and policy: Including fathers of young children in national studies. In C. Tamis-LeMonda and N. Cabrera (Eds.), *Handbook of father involvement: Multidisciplinary perspectives* (pp. 489–523). Mahwah, NJ: Lawrence Erlbaum Associates.

Cabrera, N., & Peters, E. (1999). Public policies and father involvement. *Marriage and Family Review, 29,* 295–331.

Cabrera, N., Ryan, R., Shannon, J. D., Brooks-Gunn, J., Vogel, C., Raikes, H., et al. (2004). Fathers in the Early Head Start National Research and Evaluation Study: How are they involved with their children? *Fathering: A Journal of Theory, Research, and Practice About Men as Fathers, 2,* 5–30.

Carlson, M. J., & Furstenberg, F. F., Jr. (2006). The prevalence and correlates of multipartnered fertility among urban U.S. parents. *Journal of Marriage and Family, 68* (3), 718–732.

Collins, W. A., Maccoby, E. E., Steinberg, L., Hetherington, E. M., & Bornstein, M. H. (2000). Contemporary research on parenting: The case for nature and nurture. *American Psychologist, 55,* 218–232.

Cummings, M. E., Goeke-Morey, M. C., & Raymond, J. (2004). Fathers in family context: Effects of marital quality and marital conflict. In M. E. Lamb (Ed.), *The role of the father in child development* (4th ed., pp. 196–221). Hoboken, NJ: John Wiley.

Curran, L. (2003). Social work and fathers: Child support and fathering programs. *Social Work, 48* (2), 219–227.

Dreby, J. (2006). Honor and virtue: Mexican parenting in the transnational context. *Gender & Society, 20*(1), 32–59.

Duncan, G., & Brooks-Gunn, J. (1997). *Consequences of growing up poor.* New York, NY: Russell Sage.

Edin, K. (2000). What do low-income single mothers say about marriage? *Social Problems, 47,* 112–133.

Edin, K., & Kefalas, M. (2005). *Promises I can keep: Why poor women put motherhood before marriage.* Berkeley, CA: University of California Press.

Federal Interagency Forum on Child and Family Statistics. (2010). *America's children: Key national indicators of well-being 2010.* Washington, DC: U.S. Government Printing Office.

Fineman, M. L., & Opie, A. (1987). The uses of social science data in legal policy-making: Custody determinations at divorce. *Wisconsin Law Review,* 107–157.

Fitzgerald, H. E., McKelvey, L. M., Schiffman, R. F., & Montanez, M. (2006). Exposure of low-income families and their children to neighborhood violence and paternal antisocial behavior. *Parenting: Science and Practice, 6* (2–3), 243–258.

Flanagan, K., & West, J. (2004). *Children born in 2001: First results from the base year of the Early Childhood Longitudinal Study, Birth Cohort (ECLS-B)* (NCES 2005–036). [U.S. Department of Education]. Washington, DC: National Center for Education Statistics.

Furstenberg, F.F., Brooks-Gunn, J., & Morgan, S. P. (1987). *Adolescent mothers in later life.* New York, NY: Cambridge University Press.

Furstenberg, F. F., Jr., & Nord, C. W. (1985). Parenting apart: Patterns of child rearing after marital disruption. *Journal of Marriage and the Family, 50,* 893–904.

Gassman-Pines, A., Yoshikawa, H., & Nay, S. (2006). Can money buy you love? Dynamic employment characteristics, the New Hope program and entry into marriage. In H. Yoshikawa, T.S. Weisner, & E. Lowe (Eds.), *Making it work: Low-wage employment, family life, and children's development* (pp. 206–232). New York, NY: Russell Sage Foundation.

Gaytan, F. X., Xue, Q., Yoshikawa, H., & Tamis-LeMonda, C.S. (2006). *Transnational babies: Patterns and predictors of early childhood travel to immigrant mothers' native countries.* Paper presented at Head Start's Ninth National Research Conference, Washington, DC.

Gibson-Davis, C. M., Edin, K., & McLanahan, S. (2005). High hopes and even higher expectations: The retreat from marriage among low-income couples. *Journal of Marriage and Family, 67,* 1301–1312.

Gleason, J. B. (1975). Fathers and other strangers: Men's speech to young children. In D. P. Data (Ed.), *Developmental psycholinguistics: Theory and application* (pp. 289–297). Washington, DC: Georgetown University Press.

Goldstein, J. R., & Kenney, C. T. (2001). Marriage delayed or marriage forgone? New cohort forecasts of first marriage for U.S. women. *American Sociological Review, 66*(4), 506–519.

Golinkoff, R. M., & Ames, G. J. (1979). A comparison of fathers' and mothers' speech with their young children. *Child Development, 50,* 28–32.

Graham, J. W., & Beller, A. H. (2002). Nonresident fathers and their children: Child support and visitation from an economic perspective. In C. Tamis-LeMonda & N. Cabrera (Eds.), *Handbook of father involvement: Multidisciplinary perspectives* (pp. 431–454). Mahwah, NJ: Lawrence Erlbaum Associates.

Gupta, S. (2006). Her money, her time: Women's earnings and their housework hours. *Social Science Research, 35* (4), 975–999.

Gutmann, M.C. (1996). Imaginary fathers, genuine fathers. In M. C. Guttman (Ed.), *The meaning of being macho: Being a man in Mexico City* (pp. 50–88). Thousand Oaks, CA: Sage.

Hall, A. S., Pulver, C. A., & Cooley, M. J. (1996). Psychology of best interest standard: Fifty state statues and their theoretical antecedents. *American Journal of Family Therapy, 24* (2), 171–180.

Heuveline, P., & Timberlake, J. M. (2004). The role of cohabitation in family formation: The United States in comparative perspective. *Journal of Marriage and Family, 66* (5), 1214–1230.

Hetherington, E. M., Cox, M., & Cox, R. (1985). Long-term effects of divorce and remarriage on the adjustment of children. *Journal of the American Academy of Child Psychiatry, 24* (5), 518–530.

Hyde, J. S., Essex, M. J., & Horton, F. (1993). Fathers and paternal leave: Attitudes and experiences. *Journal of Family Issues, 14*(4), 616–641.

Johnson, W. E. (2001). Paternal involvement among unwed fathers. [Special Issue: Fragile families and welfare reform (Part II)]. *Children and Youth Services Review, 23* (6–7), 513–536.

Jutta, J. M. (1997). Paid leave and the time of women's employment before and after birth. *Journal of Marriage and Family, 59,* 1008–1021.

Kamo, Y., & Cohen, E. L. (1998). Division of household work between partners: A comparison of Black and White couples. [Special Issue: Comparative perspectives on Black family life]. *Journal of Comparative Family Studies, 29*(1), 131–145.

Kelly, J. B. (2000). Children's adjustment in conflicted marriage and divorce: A decade review of research. *Journal of the American Academy of Child & Adolescent Psychiatry, 39* (8), 963–973.

King, V., Harris, K. M., & Heard, H. E. (2004). Racial and ethnic diversity in nonresident father involvement. *Journal of Marriage and Family, 66,* 1–21.

Laakso, J. H. (2000). Child support policy: Some critical issues and the implications for social work. *Social Work, 45,* 367–370.

Lamb, M. E. (1999). Noncustodial fathers and their impact on the children of divorce. In R. A. Thompson & P. R. Amato (Eds.), *The postdivorce family: Children, parenting, and society,* (pp. 105–125). Thousand Oaks, CA: Sage Publications.

Lamb, M. E. (2000). The history of research on father involvement: An overview. [Special Issue: Fatherhood: Research, interventions and policies, Part I]. *Marriage and Family Review, 29*(2–3), 23–42.

Lamb, M. E. (2002). Infant-father attachments and their impact on child development. In C. S. Tamis-LeMonda & N. Cabrera (Eds.), *Handbook of father involvement: Multidisciplinary perspectives* (pp. 93–117). Mahwah, NJ: Lawrence Erlbaum Associates.

Lamb, M. E. (2004). *The role of the father in child development* (4th ed.). Hoboken, NJ: John Wiley & Sons.

Lamb, M. E. (Ed.). (2010). *The role of father in child development* (5th ed.). New York, NY: Wiley.

Lamb, M. E., Pleck, J. H., Charnov, E. L., & Levine, J. A. (1987). A biosocial perspective on paternal behavior and involvement. In J. B. Lancaster, J. Altmann, A. S. Rossi, & L. R. Sherrod (Eds.), *Parenting across the life span: Biosocial dimensions* (pp. 111–142). Hawthorne, NY: Aldine Publishing Co.

Leaper, C., Anderson, K. J., & Sanders, P. (1998). Moderators of gender effects on parents' talk to their children: A meta-analysis. *Developmental Psychology, 34,* 3–27.

Lichter, D. T., McLaughlin, D. K., Kephart, G., & Landry, D. J. (1992). Race and the retreat from marriage: A shortage of marriageable men? *American Sociological Review, 57,* 781–799.

Manning, W. D., & Smock, P. J. (1995). Why marry? Race and the transition to marriage among cohabitators. *Demography, 32* (4), 509–520.

Maccoby, E., & Martin, J. (1983). Socialization in the context of the family: Parent-child interaction. In E. Hetherington (Ed.), *Handbook of child psychology* (Vol. 4, pp. 1–101). New York, NY: Wiley.

Malone, M. J., & Guy, R. F. (1982). A comparison of mothers' and fathers' speech to their 3-year-old sons. *Journal of Psycholinguistic Research, 11*(6), 599–608.

McLanahan, S., Garfinkel, I., Reichman, N. E., & Teitler, J. O. (2001). Unwed parents or fragile families? Implications for welfare and child support policy. In L. L. Wu & B. Wolfe (Eds.), *Out of wedlock: Causes and consequences of nonmarital fertility* (pp. 202–228). New York, NY: Russell Sage Foundation.

McLanahan, S., & Sandefur, G. (1994). *Growing up with a single parent: What hurts, what helps.* Cambridge, MA: Harvard University Press.

McLaughlin, B., White, D., McDevitt, T., & Raskin, R. (1983). Mothers' and fathers' speech to their young children: Similar or different? *Journal of Child Language, 10,* 245–252.

Melhuus, M. (1996). Power, value and the ambiguous meanings of gender. In M. Melhuus & K. A. Stolen (Eds.), *Machos, mistresses, madonnas: Contesting the power of Latin American gender imagery.* London, UK: Verso.

Mincy, R. B. (2006). *Black males left behind.* Washington, DC: Urban Institute Press.

Mincy, R., Garfinkel, I., & Nepomnyaschy, L. (2005). In-hospital paternity establishment and father involvement in fragile families. *Journal of Marriage and Family, 67,* 611–626.

Nepomnyaschy, L. (2007). Child support and father-child contact: Testing reciprocal pathways. *Demography, 44* (1), 93–112.

O'Connell, M. (1993). *Where's papa? Fathers' role in child care.* Washington, DC: Population Reference Bureau.

Pancsofar, N., & Vernon-Feagans, L. (2006). Mother and father language input to young children: Contributions to later language development. *Journal of Applied Developmental Psychology, 27,* 571–587.

Panscofar, N., Vernon-Feagans, L., & The Family Life Project Investigators. (2010). Fathers' early contributions to children's language development in families from low-income rural communities. *Early Childhood Research Quarterly, 25* (4), 450–463.

Paquette, D. (2004). Dichotomizing paternal and maternal functions as a means to better understand their primary contributions. *Human Development, 47* (4), 237–238.

Parke, R., McDowell, D.J., Kim, M., Killian C., Dennis, J., Flyr, M.L., & Wild, M.N. (2002). Fathers' contributions to children's peer relationships. In C. S. Tamis-LeMonda & N. Cabrera (Eds.), *Handbook of father involvement: Multidisciplinary perspectives* (pp. 141–168). Mahwah, NJ: Lawrence Erlbaum Associates.

Parke, R. D., & O'Neil, R. (1997). The influence of significant others on learning about relationships. In S. Duck (Ed.), *The handbook of personal relationships* (2nd ed., pp. 29–60). New York, NY: Wiley.

Pear, R., & Kirkpatrick, D. (2004). Bush plans $1.5 billion drive for promotion of marriage. *New York Times.* January 14, p. A1.

Pearson, J., & Thoennes, N. (1990). Custody after divorce: Demographic and attitudinal patterns. *American Journal of Orthopsychiatry, 60* (2), 233–249.

Pinto, K. M., & Coltrane, S. (2009). Divisions of labor in Mexican origin and Anglo families: Structure and culture. *Sex Roles, 60* (7–8), 482–495.

Pleck, J. H. (1985). *Working wives, working husbands.* Beverly Hills, CA: Sage.

Pleck, J. H. (1997). Paternal involvement: Levels, sources, and consequences. In M.

E. Lamb (Ed.), *The role of the father in child development* (3rd ed., pp. 66–103). Hoboken, NJ: John Wiley & Sons.

Pleck, E. H., & Masciadrelli, B. P. (2004). Paternal involvement by residential fathers: Levels, sources, and consequences. In M. E. Lamb (Ed.), *The role of the father in child development* (4th ed.). Hoboken, NJ: John Wiley & Sons.

Pleck, E. H., & Pleck, J. H. (1997). Fatherhood ideals in the United States: Historical dimensions. In M. E. Lamb (Ed.), *The role of the father in child development* (3rd ed., pp. 33–48). Hoboken, NJ: John Wiley & Sons.

Roberts, P. (2006). *Update on the marriage and fatherhood provisions of the 2006 federal budget and the 2007 budget proposal.* Washington, DC: Center for Law and Social Policy.

Robinson, J. P., Andreyenkov, V. G., & Patrushev, V. D. (1988). *The rhythm of everyday life: How Soviet and American citizens use time.* Boulder, CO: Westview Press.

Rotundo, E. A. (1985). American fatherhood: A historical perspective. [Special Issue: Perspectives on fatherhood]. *American Behavioral Scientist, 29*(1), 7–23.

Rowe, M. L., Coker, D., & Pan, B. A. (2004). A comparison of fathers' and mothers' talk to toddlers in low income families. *Social Development, 13* (2), 278–291.

Ryan, R. M., Martin, A., & Brooks-Gunn, J. (2006). Is one good parent good enough? Patterns of mother and father parenting and child cognitive outcomes at 24 and 36 months. *Parenting: Science and Practice, 6* (2–3), 211–228.

Seltzer, J. (1991). Legal custody arrangements and children's economic welfare. *American Journal of Sociology, 96* (4), 895–929.

Seltzer, J. A., & Bianchi, S. M. (1988). Children's contact with absent parents. *Journal of Marriage and the Family, 50,* 663–677.

Shannon, J. D., Tamis-LeMonda, C. S., London, K., & Cabrera, N. (2002). Beyond rough and tumble: Low-income fathers' interactions and children's cognitive development at 24 months. *Parenting: Science and Practice, 2,* 77–104.

Silverstein, L. B., & Auerbach, C. F. (1999). Deconstructing the essential father. *American Psychologist, 54,* 397–407.

Sonenstein, F. L., Holcomb, P. A., & Seefeldt, K. S. (1994). Promising approaches to improving paternity establishment rates at the local level. In I. Garfinkel, S. S. McLanahan, & P. K. Robins (Eds.), *Child support and child well-being* (pp. 31–59). Washington, DC: Urban Institute.

Struening, K. (2007). Do government sponsored marriage promotion policies place undue pressure on individual rights? *Policy Sciences, 40,* 241–259.

Suarez-Orozco, C., Todorova, I. L. G., & Louie, J. (2002) Making up for lost time: The experience of separation and reunification among immigrant families. *Family Process, 41* (4), 625–643.

Summers, J. A., Boller, K., Schiffman, R. F., & Raikes, H. H. (2006). The meaning of "good fatherhood": Low-income fathers' social constructions of their roles. *Parenting: Science and Practice, 6* (2–3), 145–165.

Tamis-LeMonda, C. S., Baumwell, L. B., & Cristofaro, T. (in press). Parent–child conversations during play. *First Language.*

Tamis-LeMonda, C. S., & Cabrera, N. (Eds.). (2002). *Handbook of father involvement: Multidisciplinary perspectives.* Mahwah, NJ: Lawrence Erlbaum Associates.

Tamis-LeMonda, C. S., Kahana-Kalman, R., & Yoshikawa, H. (2009). Father involvement in immigrant and ethnically diverse families from the prenatal period to the second year: Prediction and mediating mechanisms. *Sex Roles, 60* (7–8), 496–509.

Tamis-LeMonda, C. S., Niwa, E., Kahana-Kalman, R., & Yoshikawa, H. (2008). Immigrant fathers and families at the transition to parenthood. In S. Chuang & R. Moreno (Eds.), *On new shores: Understanding fathers in North America* (pp. 229–253). Lanham, MD: Lexington Books.

Tamis-LeMonda, C. S., Shannon, J. D., Cabrera, N. J., & Lamb, M. E. (2004). Fathers and mothers at play with their 2- and 3-year olds: Contributions to language and cognitive development. *Child Development, 75* (6), 1806–1820.

Thompson, R. A., & Laible, D. J. (1999). Noncustodial parents. In M. E. Lamb (Ed.), *Parenting and child development in "nontraditional" families* (pp. 103–123). Mahwah, NJ: Lawrence Erlbaum Associates.

Tomasello, M. Conti-Ramsden, G., & Ewert, B. (1990). Young children's conversations with their mothers and fathers: Differences in breakdown and repair. *Journal of Child Language, 17*, 115–130.

Thornton, A. (1989). Changing attitudes toward family issues in the United States. *Journal of Marriage and the Family, 51* (4), 873–893.

Thornton, A., & Young-DeMarco, L. (2001). Four decades of trends in attitudes toward family issues in the United States. *Journal of Marriage and the Family, 63*, 1009–1037.

U. S. Census Bureau. (2008). *Who's minding the kids? Child care arrangements: Spring 2005.* Retrieved from www.census.gov/population/www/socdemo/childcare.html.

Ventura, S. J., & Bachrach, C. A. (2000). *Non-marital childbearing in the United States, 1940–99* (National Vital Statistics Reports, No. 16). Hyattsville, MD: National Center for Health Statistics.

Waller, M. R. (2002). *My baby's father: Unmarried parents and paternal responsibility.* Ithaca, NY: Cornell University Press.

Weber, M. (1958). *The Protestant ethic and the spirit of capitalism* (Trans, Talcott Parsons). New York, NY: Charles Scribner's Sons. (Original work published as two separate essays, 1904–05)

Western, B., & McLanahan, S. (2000). Fathers behind bars: The impact of incarceration on family formation. In G. R. Fox & M. L. Benson (Eds.), *Families, crime and criminal justice: Contemporary perspectives in family research* (Vol. 2). New York, NY: Elsevier.

Wilson, W. J. (1987). *The truly disadvantaged: The inner city, the underclass, and public policy.* Chicago, IL: University of Chicago Press.

Working Group on Conceptualizing Male Parenting. (1997). *Social fatherhood and paternal involvement: Conceptual, data, and policymaking issues.* Paper presented at the NICHD Conference on Fathering and Male Fertility: Improving Data and Research, Bethesda, MD.

Part Five

Europe

Chapter Twelve

Men on the Margins of Family Life
Fathers in Russia

Jennifer Utrata
University of Puget Sound, Tacoma, WA, USA

Jean M. Ispa
University of Missouri, Columbia, MO, USA

Simone Ispa-Landa
Northwestern University, Evanston, IL, USA

Case Story: Dmitri's Family Values and Commitment to Provide

Dmitri Mikhailovich sees himself as exceptional among Russian men. Others agree. Olga, a single mother and former classmate of Dmitri's, proclaimed, "If more men were like Dmitri, Russia would have far fewer problems!" Dmitri married for love when he was 19, and his first daughter was born shortly thereafter. His wife, Katya, quit work to care for a second daughter with health problems. Dmitri worked constantly, coming home only to sleep. They had problems living with their parents, first hers and then his. Although they managed to rent their own apartment for a short while, he and Katya never got used to living together and eventually divorced. He did not marry again, but when his girlfriend Lena got pregnant and had a baby a few years ago, he decided to help provide for his third child. Since he left Lena five months ago, Dmitri has lived with his parents. He does not pay formal child support but pays "more than half" of his salary for his three children. His ex-wives will not sue him for support because they would get much less if they did. Dmitri earns at least four times what the average man earns in the provincial Russian city of Kaluga (100 miles southwest of Moscow), but most of his income is "unofficial."

Dmitri compares himself favorably to other Russian men, whom he describes as a weak, irresponsible, untrustworthy, hard-drinking lot who "let" their wives work while a grandmother helps to raise the children. After a divorce, most men abandon their children, but Dmitri considers himself a family man. He wants to live in a family – he'd like three more kids – but worries about unduly burdening a future wife. Any "normal woman" would resent the time and money he would have to spend on his other children. Dmitri is stretched to his limits.

For Dmitri, being a father means loving his children by providing for them. Despite living apart from his kids, Dmitri feels proud that his children know their father will always protect them, dress them, feed them, and provide for them. Yet it was difficult to find out if Dmitri actually enjoyed being a father.

Dmitri may be exceptional in some ways, but his story provides clues for understanding contemporary Russian fatherhood. Fatherhood in Russia has long been marginalized relative to motherhood, and the effects of this isolation on fathers and children are palpable today. Even though women have worked for wages outside the home for several generations, in Russia it is men who are expected to be successful primary breadwinners. Good fathers are sober and competent providers, and according to this limited definition Dmitri feels he is doing alright. Yet even Dmitri, a well-to-do divorced father who abstains from drinking and supports his three children financially, has a hard time juggling fatherhood with the new demands and uncertainties of market capitalism in post-Soviet Russia. He clearly is not alone.

There is much less research about fatherhood than motherhood in Russia. In this chapter, we pull together the limited research that has been conducted on expectations for Russian fathers and the cultural and socio-economic contexts that affect fathering. We begin by tracing themes relevant to fatherhood from the Kievan period to the period just before the Soviet Union collapsed in 1991. Some of the themes that remain prominent today are not new, for example, a patriarchal society with marginally engaged fathers.

Cultural and Historical Background as It Influences Fathering

The historical literature suggests five interrelated themes that appear to form the backdrop for fatherhood even today. The first concerns the importance of extended family ties. While it is less common today for fathers and their families to live with in-laws, grandmothers (and much less frequently grandfathers) have been and remain closely involved in raising their grandchildren. A second theme concerns fathers' low levels of responsibility for childcare; typically mothers and grandmothers have been expected to care for children. Third, authoritarian child-rearing beliefs predominate alongside a fourth pattern: fathers have been psychologically if not physically distant from their children. Fifth, marital relationships in Russia are often fragile (Rotkirch, 2000), with tension, detachment, and separation frequently characteristic of relations between fathers and mothers. We note that all of these themes were apparent in the experiences of Dmitri. In what follows, we sketch the contours of this historical legacy, to situate our discussion of contemporary fatherhood.

Before the Soviet period (10th through to the late 19th centuries)

Family forms in Kievan Rus (Russia's predecessor state, which lasted from the 9th through to the 13th centuries) are noteworthy in part because many centuries later Russian revolutionaries would depict their ancestors as embodying equality and cooperation between the sexes (Terras, 1985). This depiction was used to support claims of a "true" egalitarian heritage to which Russia should return. However, folklore and historical documents refute this claim. Instead, they depict women as cunning in relation to men even as they are devoted and selfless in relation to their children. There seem to have been no comparable images of paternal love or dedication. Men were instead portrayed as mischievous or despotic in relation to both their wives and their children (Atkinson, 1977; Hubbs, 1988).

Russian Orthodoxy, introduced to Kievan Rus in the 10th century and accelerating in influence throughout the Medieval Period (13th through to the end of the 17th century), built on traditional ideas about gender to create contradictory views of women and men in their marital and parental roles. On the one hand, women in the maternal role were hailed as virtuous and all-giving, emulating the Virgin Mary. On the other hand, based on teachings that sexuality had Satanic origins, women were portrayed as devious and fickle temptresses in their roles as wives or potential wives, posing a risk to men's salvation. Given this paradoxical set of assumptions, the Church taught that children's moral upbringing was the responsibility of fathers and not mothers (Hubbs, 1988; Levin, 1989). Historians suggest that traces of the dualistic view of women still survive today, contributing to problems in contemporary Russian spousal relationships (Atkinson, 1977; Gray, 1990).

What little we know about peasant fathers' interactions with their children during the centuries before the Soviet Era indicates that they strongly preferred sons over daughters but spent minimal time with either sex when their children were less than 7 years old (Dunn, 1974; Rappoport, 1913). According to Matossian (1968), in rural areas when boys reached the age of 7, fathers began to teach them farming, crafts, and trade skills. Peasant proverbs stressed the need for fathers to provide their sons with early moral and vocational training, for example: "If you don't teach him when he lies across the width of the sleeping bench, then you will not be able to teach him when he stretches out along its whole length" (Matossian, 1968, p. 23). In addition to modeling and direct instruction, teaching by fathers involved corporal punishment. Proverbs and court records indicate that fathers had the right and duty to flog even adult children (Morley, 1866).

It was also important, however, that in many peasant families the preceding pattern of father dominance was tempered by men's long absences from home. Typical reasons for separation included military conscription, landowner orders that men leave their families to work on distant parts of their estates, or as became more common in the 19th century, migration to work in factories. Many migrant workers lived apart from their families for years (Engel, 1996; Mitterauer & Kagan, 1982).

Among the upper classes, the fathering themes of strictness and detachment also dominate the biographical and family history literature (e.g., Tolstoy, 1964). Through the 19th century, before the age of 7 children of the noble and gentry classes typically spent their days in the company of nursemaids and governesses. At the age of 7, many boys were sent away to boarding schools and thus saw little of either parent, especially their fathers. Based on her review of 19th century memoirs written by men of the nobility, Dunn (1974) concluded that fathers tended to be alternately restrictive and aloof from their children, and made no efforts to understand their children's feelings and thoughts. This stance was in accord with the *Domostroi*, an influential 16th century treatise on home management prepared by Tsar Ivan III in collaboration with the Church. The *Domostroi* held fathers responsible for the welfare and moral standing of everyone in the household, and maintained that fathers must wield authority from children's earliest years, using fear to save them from sin and divine condemnation to hell.

Exceptions to the ideology of authoritarian fathering seem to have emerged in the 18th and 19th centuries as Western democratic ideas gained in popularity as an alternative (Engel, 1996). Dunn (1974), for example, cited 19th century revolutionaries who described their fathers as affectionate, wise, warm, and encouraging. Such fathers, however, appear to have been in the minority.

The Soviet period (1917–1991)

The meager literature on fatherhood during the Soviet period falls largely into two categories: histories of laws concerning paternal rights and obligations, and time-use studies on gender-typed domestic activities. As in the pre-Soviet period, themes of paternal absence, detachment, and low responsibility predominate. We believe that contemporary fathering was partially shaped by intergenerational transmission of this long legacy of minimal father involvement.

The Marxist and feminist ideologies that eventually contributed to the downfall of Tsarist Russia called for an end to patriarchal oppression. As one means to that end, new legislation allowed either spouse to obtain a no-fault, uncontested divorce by simply sending a postcard to the local registrar. An unintended consequence of this policy ensued: an epidemic of child abandonment by fathers. To address this problem, the 1926 Family Code recognized common-law marriages and required a father to pay child support whether or not he continued to be involved with his children's mother (Bazyler, 1990). Nonetheless, the pattern of broken families and illegitimate children continued, leading to a tightening of divorce laws in the 1930s. However, as it became a national priority to boost the birth rate, a contradictory policy was next instituted. The Family Code of 1944 recognized only registered marriages and abolished the mother's right to file a paternity suit. In fact, there was no way for a father to take legal responsibility for his child born out of wedlock even if he wished to (Bazyler, 1990). The law effectively sanctioned male adultery for the sake of replenishing the population lost because of collectivization, famines, and especially the Second World War. These policies promoted male irresponsibility in family life and allowed "huge numbers of children" to grow up without fathers (Kelly, 2007, p. 386).

The right to file paternity suits against absent fathers was reinstituted and divorce procedures were simplified, after Stalin's death in 1953. Historians note that divorce rates throughout the late Soviet era were comparable to rates in urban centers of Western Europe and the U.S. (Kelly, 2007). Laws required all biological fathers to pay child support, with the rate set by the court as a percentage of income dependent on the number of children. But cultural attitudes tying women but not men to children surfaced in the details. A mother who filed a paternity suit was required to submit evidence that the father had in the past lived with her, acknowledged paternity, or helped in the rearing or support of their children (Bazyler, 1990). In effect, these requirements continued to allow fathers to avoid responsibility for their offspring.

Social science writings on Russian parenthood during and after the Soviet years have almost uniformly indicated that mothers spent a far greater amount of time and had a wider breadth of responsibilities than fathers, even in married households (Boss & Gurko, 1994; Ispa, 1984, 1988). Most men were fathers and were expected to fulfill their duty to the state as workers or soldiers, and to their families as primary bread-winners. Women, in contrast, were expected to be "worker-mothers," who worked for pay outside the home while bearing primary if not sole responsibility for child rearing and home management in the difficult con-text of a shortage economy (Ashwin, 2000; Kay, 2007; Kukhterin, 2000). Grandmothers were often the mothers' main support (Zdravomyslova, 2010). In one study of Moscow families, mothers were found to inter-act with adolescents more than fathers in every way except in help with homework. Accordingly, children and adolescents reported feeling closer to their mothers than to their fathers. In another study of young Moscow families, grandparents were found to spend more time caring for children than fathers (Boss & Gurko, 1994).

Scholars have attributed the persistence of these patterns to tradi-tional beliefs that males and females differ in their family roles because of unalterable biological differences in their abilities and predilections, high rates of male alcoholism, and unbalanced sex ratios. We will return to the first two of these likely causal factors (roles and alcoholism) in the follow-ing section on contemporary issues. Unbalanced sex ratios and attendant shortages of men were especially salient during the Soviet years, and have been blamed for the willingness of women to accept low standards for male participation in family life. Scholars have further suggested that low sala-ries, required subservience and conformity in the work place, and fathers' lack of influence in the political life of the country were also determinants of their lack of involvement with their children. Perhaps men's feelings of powerlessness outside the home spilled over into depression and inaction at home or, conversely, into compensatory authoritarian behaviors vis-à-vis wives and children (Maddock & Kon, 1994; Neimark, Nikolskaya, & Sadomskaya, 1981; Zdravomyslova, 2000). Additionally, Boss and Gurko (1994) asserted that because many young Soviet fathers grew up without the involvement of their own fathers as role models, they did not know how to behave as fathers and did not believe that their participation in their children's daily lives was needed.

Other scholars have argued that frequent father absence over many generations, whether due to death, divorce, or desertion, has led to self-perpetuating patterns of maternal over-protectiveness and unilateral con-trol over household decision-making, even when husbands are physically present. Bronfenbrenner (1970) wrote that this pattern of father absence was especially unhealthy for their sons, contributing to passivity and irresponsibility. Of course, there were exceptions to these patterns. Hart, Nelson, Robinson, Olsen, and McNeilly-Choque (1998) remarked on the diversity of fathering styles across families in the years just after the collapse of Soviet rule; some of this variation certainly applied to the Soviet period as well. Other observers have commented that Soviet Jewish fathers tended to be more involved in daily childcare than ethnic Russian fathers, and that fathers living in the western parts of the country were less authoritarian than fathers in the Central Asian republics (Boss & Gurko, 1994; U. Bronfenbrenner, personal communication, 1974). Nevertheless, on a broad societal level the historical legacy of father absence and detachment was clearly evident and continued into the present era.

Fatherhood in post-Soviet Russia (1991 to the present)

Despite the increased interest in fatherhood and gender relations since the 1990s, there remains a dearth of social science research on post-Soviet men in general and fatherhood in particular (Janey, Janey, Goncherova, & Savchenko, 2006; Kukhterin, 2000). The small empirical literature on men, of which an even smaller subset is on men as fathers, emphasizes how dramatic changes accompanying the transition to capitalism since 1991 have affected fathers' engagement in family life. Most research underscores both the effects of the Soviet state's marginalization of fathers and the ways in which the new post-Soviet environment shapes fatherhood. Three patterns are discernible in the literature on post-1991 fatherhood. First, there is a focus on how Russian men are "in crisis" due to premature mortality rates, high stress and accident rates, and poor health (Ashwin & Lytkina, 2004; Kay & Kostenko, 2006). If Russian men are in crisis, then fatherhood by extension is also on shaky ground.

Second, post-Soviet empirical research on fatherhood draws attention to how and why the Soviet state glorified and protected motherhood but neglected fatherhood. Most researchers emphasize how this legacy of marginalized fatherhood continues to shape contemporary fathering, e.g., "the tendency to equate the family with women goes on to this day" (Kay, 2006, p. 139). Some have argued that because the Soviet state itself existed as a "universal and exclusive 'father'" (Kukhterin, 2000, p. 71), it minimized the role of men in families by enforcing gender relations whereby fathers and mothers were more dependent on the state than they were on each other (Ashwin, 2000).

Third, a few researchers offer an alternative, more favorable interpretation of Russian men as fathers. For example, Kay (2006, 2007) argued that we need to emphasize men's resiliency in spite of their lack of support systems. Rather than being unable to cope with various crises related to post-Soviet transition, men from this viewpoint are seen as adapting as best they can in the face of a lack of societal and state supports. Attention to gender relations and analysis of the contemporary post-Soviet environment unites these three streams of research on Russian fatherhood and manhood.

The following section explores these three approaches and highlights the importance for fathers of the transition from the Soviet system to post-Soviet market capitalism.

Contemporary Social/Economic Conditions That Impact Fathering

Culture, historical legacies, and contemporary conditions always shape parenting beliefs and practices. This seems especially true for fatherhood, in that "fathering is influenced, even more than mothering, by contextual forces in the family and the community" (Doherty, Kouneski, & Erickson, 1996, p. i; see also Fouts, Ch. 7, this volume, for a discussion of the situation-dependent nature of fathering in small-scale societies). Because the context of fatherhood is so critical for an understanding of attitudes and behavior, most recent fathering research in Russia has focused on the massive societal upheaval associated with the transition from state socialism to capitalism. These changes have had profound effects on fathers because men are expected to prioritize material support for their families.

Employment issues and breadwinner expectations

On the surface, it appears that current fathering practices are continuous with the Soviet past, when men were chiefly encouraged to be primary breadwinners and ceded most family concerns to women. Today men are still expected to be the primary breadwinners for their families. In fact, research has found that men's connection to the family is maintained mainly through their monetary contributions. Without money, men are seen as almost superfluous (Ashwin & Lytkina, 2004; see also Roopnarine's reference to the African Caribbean notion of "no romance without finance," Ch. 9, this volume).

However, in the transition to market capitalism, new challenges have arisen for men in providing for their families. In the late-Soviet era, citizens were guaranteed employment, and salary differentials across workers were modest. Today there is no employment guarantee, and because the labor market is increasingly competitive, jobs have become more demanding and income inequality has increased dramatically. Difficulty in adaptation to capitalism has led to much economic uncertainty for ordinary Russian families (Burawoy, Krotov, & Lytkina, 2000; Rotkirch, 2000). For example, Alexei, a 34-year-old unemployed man in Kaluga interviewed by our first author (unless stated otherwise, all interview excerpts in this chapter are from the fieldwork of the first author in Kaluga, Russia in 2003–2004) reflected as follows on how his life changed since 1991: "Of course, my outlook changed. Before one didn't have to think about anything, where you were going to work or whatever. You'd work your shift, and go home, work a shift, and go home. Now you need to really think. First you need to find a good job, meaning a well paid one, but you're also supposed to like it."

Utrata (2008a) found that in addition to these pressures Russian fathers increasingly confront rather unrealistic societal expectations of what men should be able to provide for their families in a market economy. For example, Dmitri, our Case Story manager, argued that fathers should ensure that their children have everything that other children have. But post-Soviet Russia is a society with vast inequalities, where most jobs barely pay enough to buy basic foodstuffs and rent. Alex, a 36-year-old doctor of alternative medicine argued that "A father must be more than a wallet. He should provide for the spiritual development of his children," but he admitted that he failed to see his child in another city in part because he did not have enough money for nice gifts. Another father, a 37-year-old successful security services businessman, observed that "People used to have real values, goals, and there used to be real love. Now money has changed everything, and has made people anxious and insecure." In uncertain economic times when good jobs are hard to come by, it is especially dangerous to limit fatherhood to the narrow role of "adequate" financial provider.

Not only are men facing higher expectations in terms of how much financial provision is sufficient, but some research suggests that women's expectations of men have also increased because of the decline in state support for families. State guarantees and benefits have eroded steadily since the collapse of the Soviet Union, with childcare centers, child support payments and other Soviet-era benefits either disappearing or diminishing in value (Teplova, 2007). Indeed, perhaps too much is expected of men in these difficult times, as even fathers who can provide for their families materially face stress from multiple jobs with longer hours. Longer hours at work give men less time to develop close relationships with children. Stephan, a 35-year-old government employee, described feeling tired when he got home from work: "Perhaps I could have spent more time with my daughter. But my wife was home all day, and she was doing a good job … . Yeah, she wanted me to do more, but it seemed to me like she [his wife] had it covered. Maybe if she was working at that time I would have felt compelled to do more at home." Stephan, like many Russian fathers, is not really convinced of the importance of fathering in children's lives. Unemployed and low-wage earning fathers face even greater struggles in that their masculine identity and sense of self-worth are seriously challenged (Kiblitskaya, 2000; Kukhterin, 2000; Townsend, 2002).

Increased geographic and occupational mobility has also compounded fathers' struggles. In the post-Soviet period, the societal belief that men should do whatever it takes to provide for their families often puts men under pressure to travel great distances to higher-paying regions and cities to earn money. Indeed, migration to larger cities for better job opportunities is mostly a male phenomenon. In White's (2009) study of internal Russian labor migration, fathers were especially likely to temporarily migrate to other cities in search of better paying work, since it is easier for men to find work as manual laborers. Jobs as manual workers such as drivers, builders, welders, and metal workers, are male-dominated. Even if fathers are able to send money home, migration pulls them away from their families. Women are unlikely to leave their children for employment elsewhere unless a grandmother is available to provide constant childcare (Utrata, 2011). Thus, financial constraints and pressure to migrate exert more strain on the Russian father–child emotional bond than on the mother–child emotional bond.

Detached fatherhood and engaged motherhood as cultural norms

We know little about the actual behavior of Russian fathers in their families, although involvement appears to be minimal relative to what mothers and grandmothers do, and fathers are focused primarily on provisioning. In a cross-national study of Russian preschoolers and their parents' engagement in conversation, work, lessons, and play with their children, Tudge et al. (2000, p. 7) noted that in the city of Obninsk "Mothers … were more likely than fathers not only to be around their children, and to engage actively with them, but even when fathers were in the same setting as their children they were less likely to be involved. …" This finding of much greater maternal engagement with children was replicated in the U.S., Kenya, Korea, Estonia, and Russia, but the authors emphasized that this tendency was "dramatically so" in Russia and Korea (Tudge et al., 2000, p. 8).

Some researchers attribute such patterns to a resurgence of neo-traditional ideas about gender in the post-Soviet era. Most Russians agree that each child should have a man in his/her life to provide for material needs (Utrata, 2011). However, the relational bond between fathers and children is seldom acknowledged, and few household tasks except home repairs are seen as masculine. Fathers may agree with the ideal of broader paternal involvement, but they lack the cultural and social support necessary to help put this ideal into practice. Some view this gender 'essentialism' as a backlash against the Soviet-era gender system which imposed ideals of equality without an effort to reduce women's dual burdens of work and family.

Russian women may inadvertently contribute to fathers' disengagement from the household (Ashwin & Lytkina, 2004). Some studies on this issue emphasize the frailty of marriages in Russia. Scholars have shown that working mothers almost invariably turn to their mothers for support with housework and childcare, rather than to their children's fathers (Utrata, 2011; Zdravomyslova, 2010). Grandmothers' provision of extensive support to adult daughters may in effect discourage fathers from a greater involvement in family life (Rotkirch, 2000, 2004; Utrata, 2011). In illustration of this point, Mikhail, a 35-year-old successful married businessman with a 4-year-old son by his girlfriend in another city, acknowledged that he would like to be a 'real father' someday and provide more than money. However, in his interview he also observed that "… [his child's] mother is of course completely crazy about him. She loves that kid so much … And his grandma and grandpa, well they simply idolize him. He's like a little czar in the family!" Mikhail believed that his girlfriend solicited her parents' help because of his failure to propose marriage. As it turns out, however, this extended family involvement makes Mikhail feel rather superfluous during his monthly visits to see his girlfriend and son.

Other scholars posit that a widespread negative cultural discourse about men justifies and perpetuates fathers' peripheral roles in family life (Kay, 2006; Utrata, 2008a; Vannoy et al., 1999). According to this discourse, men are infantile, weak, irresponsible, and even somewhat non-essential in families, apart from their role in financial provision (Ispa-Landa, 2009). This view has a long historical legacy, and may contribute to a self-fulfilling prophecy whereby fathers "are kept at one remove from the responsibilities of childcare" (Kay, 2007, p. 132) and women continue to feel primarily responsible for home and family.

State policies generally reinforce and reflect cultural norms that make fathers unviable and invisible. Even though there have been a few policy changes to shift from a primary focus on Soviet motherhood to parenting in general, they have been minimal and reveal at best ambivalence toward fatherhood. For example, unlike Soviet policies that protected and valorized motherhood, the Russian Family Law passed in 1995 used gender-neutral language to delineate parental rights and responsibilities (Kay, 2007). Yet the key government agency dealing with family issues at the federal level still tends to define parenthood almost exclusively as motherhood (Kay, 2004; Rotkirch, Temkina, & Zdravomyslova, 2007). Gender-neutral language might initially seem to be an improvement, especially since some of the language references "paternal rights." But there is little acknowledgement by policy makers that fathers should share in a family's domestic and childcare work, or that something should be done about women's frequent experiences of discrimination as mothers in the workplace (Rivkin-Fish, 2010). In a commentary about a 2006 speech by

President Putin, Rivkin-Fish (p. 714) noted that "… the language of parenthood was replaced with explicit statements that women needed assistance combining work and family responsibilities. Men's responsibilities to the family were again invisible."

The "maternity capital" program that began in 2007 is also illustrative of the invisibility of fathers. Valued at around $10,000 and indexed to inflation, "capitals" are paid to women who give birth to a second or third child. The money is paid out after a child turns 3 years old (Rivkin-Fish, 2010). In 2009, it amounted to the largest bonus payments for childbearing in the world relative to income (Zavisca, 2012). Zavisca's research shows how maternity capital reinforces women's primary responsibility for the home and family, *with almost no mention of fatherhood.* Although the certificates are officially called "maternity (family) capital" *(materinskii (semeinnyi) kapital)*, the term "family" is dropped in ordinary use. Mothers alone are entrusted to use the funds to benefit the entire family. While maternity capital is designed to increase the birth rate, it thus does so in a way that continues to marginalize fathers.

Here it is important to note Tartakovskaya's (2000) alternative argument that, in the post-Soviet period, gender relations are in flux, allowing for many ideas about gender, including about the notion of proper fathering behaviors and attitudes (Johnson & Robinson, 2007). The younger generation, for instance, is more supportive of egalitarian relationships (Tikhomirova, 2011) and expresses less willingness than its forebears to conform to traditional expectations of parenthood (Gurko, 2000). Nonetheless, it is clear that ideas about fatherhood remain contested and vague in Russia, in stark contrast to ideas about motherhood.

Life expectancy and alcohol consumption

The Russian gender gap in mortality is among the highest in the world. In the mid-1960s, Russian life expectancy approximated rates in the U.S. but then began to slowly decline. By the mid-1990s, the gender gap in life expectancy was more than 13 years, twice the gap of other industrialized countries, with men having a life expectancy of just over 59 years (Shkolnikov, Field, & Andreev, 2001). Today the gender gap remains high at 12 years, with men's life expectancy now 62 years and women's 74 (Bobrova, West, Malyutina, Malyutina, & Bobak, 2010). Heavy drinking among men as well as a high incidence of accidents, violent deaths, and stress-related illnesses are some of the problems contributing to men's lower life expectancy.

Much of the focus of the "men in crisis" research stream concerns drinking. Russia is one of the hardest-drinking nations in the world, with a primarily male drinking culture (White, 1996) and high rates of binge

Figure 12.1 A group of men and women in their late 30s gather at a park out-side Kaluga for a school reunion. Drinking is a major part of Russian culture and is prominent in social events, especially among men. Drinking also shapes both fatherhood and family life. Here a father of two leads the group in the first of several rounds of vodka toasts. Most participants left their children with friends or grandparents for the afternoon, to fully relax with old friends. Photo courtesy of Jennifer Utrata.

drinking and other risky drinking practices. A World Health Organization (WHO) report stated that, "By far the highest proportion of alcohol-attributable mortality is in the Russian Federation and neighbouring countries, where every fifth death among men and 6% of deaths among women are attributable to the harmful use of alcohol" (World Health Organization, 2011, p. 27). Russians consume approximately 4.75 gallons of pure alcohol per person annually, more than double the amount considered a health threat by the WHO (Levy, 2009).

Russian culture condones heavy drinking as an essential part of Russian masculinity (Zdravomyslova & Chikadze, 2000). Drinking in groups is a firmly rooted and socially expected aspect of male friendships and work. It may also be viewed as a normal masculine response to life's stresses and failures (Ashwin & Lytkina, 2004). Sergei, a man working in a factory in "appalling conditions" as described in Ashwin & Lytkina's study (2004, p. 202), admittedly turned to alcohol to ease his pain: 'Work's getting to me. Things are getting worse and worse. I've started to drink. The strong stuff. ... I have to ease the stress somehow.' Men's limited domestic responsibilities create more opportunities for leisure drinking (Bobrova et al., 2010). Drinking creates a vicious circle since it appears to then reduce fathers' emotional and financial contributions to their families.

The consequences of drinking practices for fathering and family life are vast and require the attention of scholars and policy makers. Utrata (2008b) found that some men define themselves as good fathers simply because they have a job and keep their drinking within 'reasonable' limits. They set these personal limits in comparison to their own fathers and other Russian men (Utrata, 2008b). In addition, men frequently do not count drinking small quantities of beer after work as "a real drink" (Bobrova et al., 2010). Slava, a 47-year-old director of a children's club and a body-guard, mentioned drinking in reference to his own absent father when he was growing up. His comments supported our point about how expected and ordinary male drinking is in Russia:

> I assume my father drank as all men do ... . All men drink in Russia! ... What's the difference between "getting drunk regularly" or just "drinking"? There's no real difference. I can drink two liters of vodka without collapsing. But I don't do this. Or if I do, then it's only once a month or so. I don't have time for more than that. But someone can drink every day yet only have half a glass. That person also drinks.

Russia has one of the largest gender differences in drinking patterns in the world. For example, a study in Novosibirsk found that 30% of Russian men compared to 1% of women reported binge drinking at least once a month, such as the kind referenced by Slava in the preceding interview excerpt (Bobak et al., 2004). Another interviewee, Alexei, an unemployed stepfather who feels he is now a decent father in his new marriage, judged himself harshly in terms of how drinking had affected him as a father during his first marriage. He explained that "... in terms of alcohol, well, he [a good father] shouldn't even glance at a shot glass ... I mean in terms of raising the kid, I didn't spend enough time, nothing was enough ... Sometimes I'd drink and then not go to see my son because I didn't want him to see me in an unattractive light" (Utrata, 2008a, p. 1306). Government efforts to curtail alcohol consumption, including recent initiatives to raise taxes on alcohol, have met with resistance. But given the strong association between drinking, poor health and family breakdown, we believe that reduction of alcoholism in Russia would almost certainly facilitate fathers' contributions to family life.

Single and nonresident fatherhood

Formal divorce rates are high in Russia, and there is reason to believe that there are many additional unregistered separations. As in many countries, failure to pay child support and loss of emotional ties with children too often follows divorce or separation. Unfortunately, today there is weaker legal enforcement of child support payment than during the Soviet era, when most citizens worked for state-owned enterprises and fewer worked in the informal sector, and the state had more control in garnishing wages. The current trends toward couples living together without marrying and informal separations also hamper such enforcement (Klugman & Motivans, 2001; Zakharov, Vishnevskii, & Sakevich, 2005; Utrata, 2008a). In 2000,

Figure 12.2 A Russian father in his mid-30s named Andrei poses with his 2-year-old daughter in a Moscow public park. Unlike many fathers who feel somewhat superfluous compared to mothers, Andrei is committed to being a more active and engaged father than his own father was with him. But his new job demands long hours that limit his time with his young daughter. Photo courtesy of Jennifer Utrata.

adequate child support was received by only 12% of divorced women in Moscow, according to the Committee for Child Support (Gurko, 2008), in contrast to countries like the United States where 77% of custodial parents receive at least some form of payments owed them (U.S. Census Bureau, 2007). Here we recall that even Dmitri, our "exemplary" Case Story father, maintained control over how much and when he paid child support to his children's mothers.

In addition, as in the Soviet period there is little or no expectation that fathers will maintain ties to their children after divorce, apart from their legal obligation to pay child support. It is almost routine for fathers to become absent after divorce (Gurko, 2003). Thus, the general Soviet pattern of men's loss of emotional contact with their children after divorce continues today (Kay, 2006), along with a newer pattern of non-payment of child support. In an ethnographic study of Russian homelessness, Höjdestrand (2009) observed a paradox: homeless Russian men and women expressed the belief that parents should sacrifice themselves for the sake of their children. But at the same time, only mothers were actually expected to make those sacrifices. She explained this situation as follows:

> "Parents" can be substituted by "mother" because most parents *are* mothers – fathers die earlier, or they disappear in divorces – and because unlimited self-sacrifice primarily is conceived of as a female and motherly quality.
>
> (p. 125)

In Höjdestrand's study, homeless fathers felt that their inability to provide for family members justified a total abandonment of family life. They seemed to define fatherhood solely in terms of material support (Höjdestrand, 2009).

Thus, a critical challenge for Russian policy makers is to increase divorced fathers' involvement through enforcement of child support obligations and encouragement of fathers to spend time with their children. Evidence that fathers want to maintain ties with their children comes from Gurko's (2008) survey data. This study indicated that while child support payments have declined since the late-Soviet period, in the post-Soviet period increasing numbers of fathers turn to the courts to gain custody of their children. These fathers may have sufficient income to support their children, but they nevertheless evade child support payments, in some cases because they do not trust their ex-wives to use the payments for their children's care (Gurko, 2008).

Despite the increase of custody disputes in courts, it must be kept in mind that ordinary Russians rarely turn to the legal system to help resolve problems (Hendley, 2010). In fact, Russians generally are suspicious about the courts and the law. It is unlikely in most cases, therefore, that fathers would use the courts to seek more contact with their children. Instead, development of informal mechanisms would probably encourage fathers' contact with their nonresident children more effectively. At the same time, we believe that policies regarding custody need to be written with sensitivity toward cases involving fathers who are prone to violence or heavy drinking (Utrata, 2008b). Social service workers and psychologists should help determine the amount of support and attention required by children in various family situations.

Comparisons with Fathers in Other Societies

The father's role is in flux around the world, and Russian fathers are hardly unique as they face a variety of competing fathering ideals and practices. Such diversity appears on cross-cultural, intra-cultural and individual levels. Writing about fatherhood in the U.S., Roy and Cabrera (2010, p. 306) noted that "While there are large numbers of men who are increasingly disengaged from their children, there are also increasing numbers of men who are more involved than ever before." Western scholars tend to agree that fathering patterns are becoming more diverse, as different subpopulations exhibit simultaneous intra-cultural trends toward involvement or detachment. On the individual level, men who were disengaged from their children from a first marriage may later become engaged fathers with the children from a second marriage. In countries such as the U.S., involved fathers coexist alongside disengaged fathers (Gerson, 1993; Waller, 2002, 2009). Indeed, ideals and practices related to fatherhood are more contested and in greater transition than those pertaining to motherhood.

Based on what we have learned from studies of Russian single and nonresident fathers (Kay, 2004, 2007; Utrata, 2008a, 2008b), we can speculate that wider variations in fatherhood ideals and practices are also emerging in Russia. Russians now have more exposure to images of involved fathers in other countries than they did during the Soviet period, through the media and travel, and change seems likely to come to Russian fathering, albeit slowly. As we predict that a trend toward involved fathering will be gradual, we are mindful of Russia's historical and cultural legacy of marginalized fatherhood, the entrenched negative discourse on men, and the still new economic pressures men face as they try to be successful primary breadwinners in a market economy.

In addition, the demands of global capitalism are at odds with the kind of involved and intensive fathering that many societies value. The pressure to work long hours to be able to afford an array of consumer goods and experiences is still relatively new, as most Russians grew up in a more stable society where employment was guaranteed and consumers had few choices. It may still be too early to expect a movement towards involved fatherhood while most Russians are focused on adapting to the new economic system.

Fathers in many developed countries also face the challenge of providing for their families, especially given the effects of globalization and the spread of competitive capitalist markets worldwide. Many of these countries have limited paternity leave and other supports for involved fatherhood. Long work hours, for example, deprive fathers of time that might be spent building relationships with their children (Townsend, 2002, and Ch. 8, this volume). We also believe that Russian fathers face some unique pressures. Russian men are discovering their identities as fathers in the context of a strong historical legacy and cultural assumptions that diminish or even dismiss their role as fathers. Moreover, the new post-Soviet environment thwarts many fathers' desire for greater family involvement, by demanding longer work hours and harder work.

Conclusions, Speculation, and Predictions for the Future

We can highlight the fact that the conversation about what defines a "good father" has begun in Russia. This conversation has begun to widen, at least relative to the Soviet period, in spite of the pressures of the new capitalist system and the state's weakening of the legal ties that once bound men to their families. Perhaps when socioeconomic conditions improve, ideals of involved fatherhood will gain a stronger foothold. As Igor, a 22-year-old computer programmer said in reference to his daughter's stepfather: "It's painful to admit it, but that man is a better father than I am. He truly cares about my daughter, provides for the family well, and seems to spend a lot of time with her." His statement exemplifies some Russian fathers' growing awareness that fatherhood can be about affection and time spent with children, and not just about economic provision.

Although most of the diverse Russian fathers who participated in Utrata's (2008a) study ended up accepting the limited role of economic provider, several fathers showed a clear awareness of and sympathy for ideals of fatherhood whereby fathers spend time with children, offer moral guidance, and pay careful attention to children's needs. Many want to be better fathers and some imagined that they would be better fathers in the future, as in the words of 35-year-old Mikhail: "I would like to be a normal father. To live with my child, to participate in raising him. To teach him what I was never taught as a child … ." However, many fathers who expressed support for the ideals of involved fatherhood also argued that they might become involved fathers only at some vague point in the future. Some asserted that fathers are only really necessary after children are about 10 years old or that only sons really need fathers.

There have been some efforts in recent years to reform current attitudes and practices relevant to fathering, on the regional and institutional levels. For example, the Altai Regional Crisis Centre for Men studied by Kay (2004, 2006, 2007) seeks to counter cultural stereotypes by promoting responsible fatherhood. The staff at this institution recognizes the importance of fathering and promotes increased awareness of the importance of fatherhood. Kay noted that as men told their stories at the center, they spoke about their children passionately, even as they mentioned that such expressions of fatherly love were unusual and unexpected in Russia. Although behavioral changes in the overall population may occur only gradually, a significant number of Russian fathers clearly already think differently about fatherhood, and recognize that low levels of paternal involvement can cause problems for their children, as happened in their own childhoods (Utrata, 2008a).

While we are optimistic that a movement toward a more involved, multi-dimensional father's role will grow in Russia, we also realize that ideals of fatherhood tend to change faster than actual practices in many countries. Policy makers could contribute to this movement by exploring ways in which fathers, along with the state and women, can create a culture that promotes men's involvement in families and positive impact on child development. An expansion of rigid Russian conceptions of masculinity to include engaged and active fathering will help ensure that most men, but especially those facing trouble in the labor market, can find fulfillment as fathers.

In conclusion, we expect that despite a historical legacy of negative discourse on men and the marginalization of fatherhood, a wider range of ideas about fathering and gender will increasingly flourish in Russia. Fathers are already becoming freer to draw on varied ideas and practices concerning fathering. On the other hand, the ties that bind men to their families have been weakened in some respects in the post-Soviet period. Despite the fact that more people now expect fathers to be involved in their children's lives, "fathers in post-Soviet Russia are objectively freer to opt out of this involvement" (Utrata, 2008a, p. 1308). New freedoms permeate many aspects of Russian life, and as is the case in other developed countries, freedom will probably pull Russian fathers in many directions.

Summary

A long history of absence and marginal involvement in family life shapes contemporary Russian fatherhood. Relative to mothers, fathers are still often considered superfluous in families apart from their contributions of income. Grandmothers are frequently involved in raising grandchildren, which may exacerbate the problem of paternal distancing. Some fathers have begun to embrace a more engaged ideal of fatherhood, yet at the same time, fathers have struggled in the face of increased economic pressures during post-Soviet Russia's transition to a market economy. Economic stresses and long hours typical of men's work in this transition to capitalism are often at odds with the ideal of involved fathering that many societies value. This puts Russian fathers in a double bind. However, gender and family relations are in flux in Russia, and newer discourses about involved fatherhood are beginning to compete for space alongside older discourses that marginalized fathers. Indeed, awareness about the importance of fathers is now increasing, although evidence suggests that fathers' behavior lags behind their ideals. State policies and cultural attitudes could do much more to support father involvement, for example by enforcing child support laws, discouraging heavy drinking, increasing the availability of well-paying jobs, and encouraging paternal involvement and closeness in family life, especially after divorce.

References

Ashwin, S. (Ed.). (2000). *Gender, state and society in Soviet and post-Soviet Russia.* London, UK: Routledge.

Ashwin, S., & Lytkina, T. (2004). Men in crisis in Russia: The role of domestic marginalization. *Gender & Society, 18* (2), 189–206.

Atkinson, D. (1977). Society and sexes in the Russian past. In D. Atkinson, A. Dallin, & G. W. Lapidus (Eds.), *Women in Russia* (pp. 3–38). Stanford, CA: Stanford University Press.

Bazyler, M. J. (1990). Soviet family law. *Kansas Law Review, 39,* 125–176.

Bobak, M., Room R., Pikhart H., Kubinova, R., Malyutina, S., Pajak, A., ... Marmot, M. (2004). Contributions of drinking patterns to differences in rates of alcohol related problems between three urban populations. *Journal of Epidemiology and Community Health, 58,* 238–242.

Bobrova, N., West, R., Malyutina, D., Malyutina, S., & Bobak, M. (2010). Gender differences in drinking practices in middle aged and older Russians. *Alcohol and Alcoholism, 45* (6), 573–580.

Boss, P. G., & Gurko, T. A. (1994). The relationships of men and women in marriage. In J. W. Maddock, M. J. Hogan, A. I. Antonov, & M. S. Matskovsky (Eds.), *Families before and after Perestroika: Russian and U.S. perspectives* (pp. 9–35). New York, NY: The Guilford Press.

Bronfenbrenner, U. (1970). *Two worlds of childhood: US and USSR.* New York, NY: Sage.

Burawoy, M., Krotov, P., & Lytkina, T. (2000). Involution and destitution in capitalist Russia: Russia's gendered transition to capitalism. *Ethnography, 1,* 43–65.

Doherty, W. J., Kouneski, E. F., & Erickson, M. F. (1996). *Responsible fathering: An overview and conceptual framework*. [Final Report prepared for the Administration for Children and Families in the Office of the Assistant Secretary for Planning and Evaluation of the United States Department of Health and Human Services].

Dunn, P. (1974). 'That enemy is the baby': Childhood in Imperial Russia. In L. deMause (Ed.), *History of childhood* (pp. 383–405). New York, NY: The Psychohistory Press.

Engel, B. A. (1996). *Between the fields and the city: Women, work, and family in Russia, 1861–1914*. New York, NY: Cambridge University Press.

Gerson, K. (1993). *No man's land: Men's changing commitments to family and work*. New York, NY: Basic Books.

Gray, F. (1990). Reflections: Soviet women. *New Yorker*, February 19, 1990, pp. 48–81.

Gurko, T. A. (2000). Variativnost' predstavleniy v sfere roditel'stva. ["Variations in the sphere of parenthood]. *Sotsiologicheskie Issledovaniya, 26*, 90–97.

Gurko, T. A. (2003). *Roditel'stvo: Sotsiologicheskie aspekty*. [Parenthood: Sociological aspects]. Moscow, Russia: Tsentr obshchechelovecheskikh tsennostei.

Gurko, T. A. (2008). Faktor kachestvennogo i kolichestvennogo vosproizvodstva naseleniia. [Alimonies: A factor for qualitative and quantitative population reproduction]. *Sotsiologicheskie Issledovaniya, 34*, 110–120.

Hart, C. H., Nelson, D. A., Robinson, C. C., Olsen, F., & McNeilly-Choque, M. K. (1998). Overt and relational aggression in Russian nursery-school-age children: Parenting style and marital linkages. *Developmental Psychology, 34* (4), 687–697.

Hendley, K. (2010). Varieties of legal dualism: Making sense of the role of law in contemporary Russia. *Wisconsin International Law Journal*. [University of Wisconsin Legal Studies Research Paper No. 1119]. Available at SSRN: http://ssrn.com/abstract=1619478

Höjdestrand, T. (2009). *Needed by nobody: Homelessness and humanness in post-socialist Russia*. Ithaca, NY: Cornell University Press.

Hubbs, J. (1988). *Mother Russia: The feminine myth in Russian culture*. Bloomington, IN: Indiana University Press.

Ispa, J. (1984). A comparison of Soviet and American women's perceptions of the postpartum period. *Journal of Comparative Family Studies, 15*, 95–108.

Ispa, J. M. (1988). Soviet immigrant mothers' perceptions regarding the first childbearing year: The 1950s and the 1970s. *Slavic Review, 47*, 291–306.

Ispa-Landa, S. (2009). *The persistence of the 'strong woman/infantile man' discourse in Post-Soviet Russia*. Unpublished manuscript.

Janey, B. A., Janey, N.V., Goncherova, N., Savchenko, V. (2006). Masculinity ideology in Russian society: Factor structure and validity of the multicultural masculinity ideology scale. *The Journal of Men's Studies, 14*, 93–108.

Johnson, J. E., & Robinson, J. C. (2007). Living gender. In J. E. Johnson & J. C. Robinson (Eds.), *Living gender after Communism* (pp. 1–21). Bloomington, IN: Indiana University Press.

Kay, R. (2004). Working with single fathers in western Siberia: A new departure in Russian social provision. *Europe-Asia Studies, 56* (7), 941–961.

Kay, R. (2006). *Men in contemporary Russia: The fallen heroes of Post-Soviet change?* Burlington, VT: Ashgate.

Kay, R. (2007). 'In our society it's as if the man is just some kind of stud': Men's experiences of fatherhood and fathers' rights in contemporary Russia. In R. Kay (Ed.), *Gender, equality and difference during and after state socialism* (pp. 125–145). New York, NY: Palgrave Macmillan.

Kay, R., & Kostenko, M. (2006). Men in crisis or in critical need of support? In sights from Russia and the UK. *Journal of Communist Studies & Transition Politics, 22*(1) (March), 90–114.

Kelly, C. (2007). *Children's world: Growing up in Russia, 1890–1991*. New Haven, CT: Yale University Press.

Kiblitskaya, M. (2000). Once we were kings: Male experiences of loss of status at work in post-Communist Russia. In S. Ashwin (Ed.), *Gender, state and society in Soviet and post-Soviet Russia* (pp. 90–104). London, UK: Routledge.

Klugman, J., & Motivans, A. (Eds.) (2001). *Single parents and child welfare in the New Russia*. UNICEF. New York, NY: Palgrave.

Kukhterin, S. (2000). Fathers and patriarchs in Communist and post-Communist Russia. In S. Ashwin (Ed.), *Gender, state and society in Soviet and post-Soviet Russia* (pp. 71–89). London, UK: Routledge.

Levin, E. (1989). *Sex and society in the world of the Orthodox Slavs, 900–1700*. Ithaca, NY: Cornell University Press.

Levy, C.J. (2009). Russia tries, once again, to rein in vodka habit. *The New York Times*. November 3, 2009. Retrieved from http://www.nytimes.com

Maddock, J. W., & Kon, I. S. (1994). Sexuality and family life. In J. W. Maddock, M. J. Hogan, A. I. Antonov, & M. S. Matskovsky (Eds.), *Families before and after Perestroika: Russian and U.S. perspectives* (pp. 96–134). New York, NY: The Guilford Press.

Matossian, M. (1968). The peasant way of life. In W. Vucinich (Ed.), *The peasant in nineteenth century Russia* (pp. 1–40). Stanford, CA: Stanford University Press.

Mitterauer, M., & Kagan, A. (1982). Russian and Central European family structures: A comparative view. *Journal of Family History, 7,* 103–131.

Morley, H. (1866). *Sketches of Russian life before and during the emancipation of the serfs*. London, UK: Chapman and Hall.

Neimark, M., Nikolskaya, A., & Sadomskaya, N. (1981). *Soviet families of two post-war generations*. Report prepared for the National Council for Soviet and East European Research, Inc., Washington, DC.

Rappoport, A. S. (1913). *Home life in Russia*. New York, NY: The Macmillan Co.

Rivkin-Fish, M. (2010). Pronatalism, gender politics, and the renewal of family support in Russia: Towards a feminist anthropology of 'maternity capital'. *Slavic Review, 69* (3), 701–724.

Rotkirch, A. (2000). *The man question: Loves and lives in late 20th century Russia*. Helsinki, Finland: University of Helsinki.

Rotkirch, A. (2004). 'Coming to stand on firm ground': The making of a Soviet working mother. In D. Bertaux, P. Thompson, & A. Rotkirch (Eds.), *On living through Soviet Russia* (pp. 146–175). London, UK: Routledge.

Rotkirch, A., Temkina, A., & Zdravomyslova, E. (2007). Who helps the degraded housewife? Comments on Vladimir Putin's demographic speech. *European Journal of Women's Studies, 14,* 349–357.

Roy, K., & Cabrera, N. (2010). Not just provide and reside: Engaged fathers in low-income families. In B. J. Risman (Ed.), *Families as they really are* (pp. 301–306). New York, NY: W. W. Norton.

Shkolnikov, V. M., Field, M. G., & Andreev, E. M. (2001). Russia: Socioeconomic dimensions of the gender gap in mortality. In T. Evans, M. Whitehead, F. Diderichsen, A. Bhuiya, & M. Wirth (Eds.), *Challenging inequalities in health: From ethics to action* (pp. 139–155). New York, NY: Oxford.

Tartakovskaya, I. (2000). The changing representation of gender roles in the Soviet and Post-Soviet press. In S. Ashwin (Ed.), *Gender, state and society in Soviet and post-Soviet Russia* (pp. 118–136). London, UK: Routledge.

Teplova, T. (2007). Welfare state transformation, childcare, and women's work in Russia. *Social Politics, 14*, 284–322.

Terras, V. (1985). *Handbook of Russian literature.* New Haven, CT: Yale University Press.

Tikhomirova, V. V. (2011). The value orientations and sense of social well-being of the young family. *Russian Education and Society, 53, 3*, 74–86.

Tolstoy, L. (1964). *Childhood, boyhood, youth* (Trans. R. Edmonds). London, UK: Penguin Books.

Townsend, N. (2002). *The package deal: Marriage, work and fatherhood in men's lives.* Philadelphia, PA: Temple University Press.

Tudge, J., Hayes, S., Doucet, F., Odero, D., Kulakova, N., Tammeveski, P., ... Lee, S. (2000). Parents' participation in cultural practices with their preschoolers. *Psicologia: Teoria e Pesquisa, 16* (1), 1–11.

U.S. Census Bureau. (2007). *Custodial mothers and fathers and their child support: 2007.* [Issued November 2009]. Retrieved June 10, 2011, from http://www.census.gov/hhes/www/childsupport/reports.html

Utrata, J. (2008a). Keeping the bar low: Why Russia's nonresident fathers accept narrow fatherhood ideals. *Journal of Marriage and Family, 70* (December), 1297–1310.

Utrata, J. (2008b). *Counting on motherhood, not men: Single mothers and social change in the New Russia.* Ph.D. dissertation, University of California, Berkeley, CA.

Utrata, J. (2011). Youth privilege: Doing age and gender in Russia's single-mother families. *Gender & Society, 25* (October), 616–641.

Vannoy, D., Rimashevskaya, N., Cubbins, L., Malysheva, M., Meshterkina, E., & Pisklakova, M. (1999). *Marriages in Russia: Couples during the economic transition.* Westport, CT: Praeger.

Waller, M. R. (2002). *My baby's father: Unmarried parents and paternal responsibility.* Ithaca, NY: Cornell University Press.

Waller, M. R. (2009). Family man in the other America: New opportunities, motivations, and supports for paternal care giving. *The Annals of the American Academy of Political and Social Science, 624*, 156–176.

White, A. (2009). Internal migration, identity and livelihood strategies in contemporary Russia. *Journal of Ethnic and Migration Studies, 35*, 555–573.

White, S. (1996). *Russia goes dry: Alcohol, state and society.* Cambridge, UK: Cambridge University Press.

World Health Organization. (2011). *Global status report on alcohol and health.* Geneva, Switzerland: WHO.

Zakharov, S. V., Vishnevskii, A. G., & Sakevich, V. I. (2005). Brachnost i rozhdae-most [Marriage and fertility]. *Naselenie Rossii* [Population of Russia]. Edited by A.G. Vishnevskii.

Zavisca, J. (2012). *Housing the new Russia*. Ithaca, NY: Cornell University Press.

Zdravomyslova, O. M. (2000). O vozmozhnosti izmenenia statusa zhenshchini v sem'e [About the possibility of changing the status of women in the family]. *Narodo Nacelenie, 2*, 56–61.

Zdravomyslova, E., & Chikadze, E. (2000). Scripts of men's heavy drinking. *Idatutkimus, 2*, 35–52.

Zdravoymyslova, E. (2010). Working mothers and nannies: Commercialization of childcare and modifications in the gender contract (a sociological essay). *Anthropology of East Europe Review, 28* (2), 186–199.

Chapter Thirteen

Fatherhood and Social Policy in Scandinavia

Linda L. Haas
Indiana University-Purdue University, Indianapolis, IN, USA

C. Philip Hwang
University of Gothenburg, Gothenburg, Sweden

Case Story: The Opportunity of Paternal Leave

Patrik is a 36-year-old father of two boys, Filip (4 years old) and Jesper (1 year old) and has a problem with his work supervisor. He has used parental leave to work part-time for a total of 15 months since his eldest son was born. He has worked for several years at a small high-tech company with international business dealings. Patrik's supervisor, who has two teenage children but did not take parental leave, is getting tired of this arrangement, and at the latest company progress meeting he commented about the leave and asked when exactly Patrik planned to come back to work full-time. At the same time, the supervisor emphasized that he knows that all employees, male and female alike, have the right to take parental leave. But the company is small and competitive and so certain key people need to work full-time …

For about five years Patrik has lived with Anna, who is 34 years old. Patrik and Anna plan to marry but haven't got around to it yet. Anna also works full-time at the small company, but in a completely different branch than Patrik. Both are interested in and committed to their jobs and decided early in their relationship that when they had children they would take turns staying at home. When Filip was born, Anna was home full-time for six months and after Filip began pre-school they both took leave part-time and worked part-time. But when their second son Jesper was born, both parents wanted Patrik to get involved earlier, so they chose to begin sharing parental leave when Jesper was just 3 months old.

Patrik is really satisfied with this arrangement. Compared to Anna who meets other mothers, he has no social network of fathers whom he can meet with during the days. But he is happy being at home and taking care of the children – dropping off and picking Filip up at daycare, being outside taking a walk with Jesper in the baby carriage. Anna, on the other hand, is busy with different activities during the day and meets many other mothers. Soon Jesper will be enrolled in preschool and then both parents will work full-time. Patrik says, "It is a very short time in one's life when a person can be home to take care of his children, so it is more important for me to be home than to satisfy my boss."

> When a child is born, there are a thousand opportunities these days, when there is a shortage of housekeepers, for an enterprising father to show his interest and love for the baby …

The preceding was a line from a popular 1945 Swedish handbook titled *Parents and Children*. The father's main task in those days was to be a breadwinner and from time to time to help out with the baby, and by so doing relieve pressure on the mother. He was not perceived as having an independent role in relation to his child.

A dramatic change in Scandinavian fathers' relationships with children began three decades later, in the mid-1970s. At that time, Denmark, Norway and Sweden became pioneers with regard to gender equality, setting the stage for fathers to become equal and independent parents. These three nations have developed social policies designed to promote a family pattern often called the dual-earner/dual-caregiver model, where both fathers and mothers are responsible for breadwinning and childcare. Comparisons of the three Scandinavian nations reveal, however, that there are significant differences between them in terms of policy and popular support for fathers' active participation in childcare; support for active fatherhood is strongest in Sweden and weakest in Denmark, with Norway in-between. According to Leira (2006, p. 44), "Among the Nordic countries, Sweden's policies come closest to facilitating the dual-earner, care-sharing family, in which both mothers and fathers are economic providers and carers for children." As demonstrated below, Norway's family policies follow a dual track, one encouraging equality in childrearing and another reinforcing women's traditional responsibility for children. Denmark's policies, on the other hand, support mothers' full-time employment, facilitated more by subsidized childcare than by fathers' taking on a more equal responsibility for childcare. Borchorst (2006, p. 102) maintains "the role of Danish men as carers and fathers within marriage has not been politicized to the same extent as in Sweden and Norway."

The purposes of this chapter are to: (1) describe the development of social policies affecting fathers in Scandinavia; (2) assess the impact of policy on fathers' participation in childcare and the realization of the dual-earner/dual-caregiver model; and (3) analyze workplace barriers still preventing Scandinavian fathers' from becoming equal parents. The Scandinavian nations are ahead of most others in terms of policies to expand the role of father to include close relationships with children and active participation in childcare. European policies that promote dual-earner families and fathers' participation in childcare have been found to contribute positively to a nation's economic development and fertility level and to lower child poverty rates (Duvander, Lappegård, & Andersson, 2010; Ferrarini & Duvander, 2010. Therefore many nations seeking to improve these important indicators of societal well-being look to the Scandinavian countries as models for policymaking.

Socio-Cultural, Historical and Economic Background

The population of Denmark is 5.5 million, Norway 4.7 million and Sweden 9.1 million (Nordic Council of Ministers, 2011). Of the three nations, Sweden appears to be the most culturally heterogeneous. Immigration, especially by asylum seekers, has led to a situation where 13% of Swedish residents are foreign-born compared to 8% in Norway and Denmark (Nordic Council of Ministers, 2011). In Denmark, the largest groups of immigrants are from Turkey, the former Yugoslavia, and Poland (Danish Immigration Service, 2010). In Norway, the largest immigrant groups are from Poland, Sweden, and Iraq (Statistics Norway, 2008), and in Sweden, the three largest groups are from Denmark, Poland, and Iraq (SCB, 2005). The three countries share a common history as they were all once united in one kingdom; Norway became completely independent of Sweden as late as 1905. The three national languages are closely related. All three nations are characterized by the "Scandinavian welfare state model," where all citizens have equal rights to social security services and benefits are financed by relatively high taxes on individuals and corporations. A relatively high proportion (3%) of the gross domestic product in each nation is spent on family benefits (OECD, 2010b). Relatively low proportions of the populations (5% in Denmark and Sweden, 7% in Norway) live in poverty, which is defined as living in a household with half or less of national median income. In comparison, the U.S. poverty rate is 17%, while the U.K.'s rate is 8% (OECD, 2010a). All three nations have advanced industrialized economies based on the capitalist model. Rapid industrialization and welfare state expansion in the mid- to late 20th century created a demand for workers that could not met by men. This prompted their national governments to enact equal employment legislation protecting the rights of mothers to work. To promote women's continued participation in the labor market, women gained the right to paid maternity leave (now ranging between 9 and 18 weeks in the three nations) as well as a family entitlement for paid parental leave which now ranges between 32 and 38 weeks (Brandth & Kvande, 2010; Duvander, Haas, & Chronholm, 2010; Rostgaard, 2010).

Each government substantially subsidizes early childhood education and care to facilitate mothers' employment and to support children's development. For example, Swedish parents pay on average only 4% of their after-tax income for childcare (Lundin, Mörk, & Öckert, 2008). Denmark has been the leader in terms of providing early childhood education and care; Sweden has in turn been ahead of Norway, which has only recently managed to provide coverage sufficient to meet the demand. In 2008, 90% of 1- to 2-year-olds in Denmark were in public care, compared to 70% in Sweden and 75% in Norway. The vast majority of 3- to 5-year-olds benefit from public subsidies of their care, including 97% in Denmark and Sweden and 96% in Norway (Eydal & Rostgaard, 2011).

With institutional and cultural support for mothers' working, having children does not force Scandinavian women to leave the labor market. Their labor force participation rate is therefore close to men's; in 2009, 84–87% of Scandinavian women aged 25–54 were employed compared to 90–93% of men (ILO, 2010). The gender wage gap is also relatively small; in 2006, full-time employed Danish women earned 92% as much as men, while Norwegian and Swedish women made 91% (OECD, 2010b).

Partly because of these political and economic factors, family patterns in Scandinavia are distinctive. As a result of the emphasis on women's labor force participation, women wait relatively long to marry, complete their education, and become established in occupations. In 2008, the average age of first marriage was 31–32 for Scandinavian women and 32–34 for men (United Nations, 2010). In contrast, the average age of first marriage for American and British women is 25 and 26, respectively (Cherlin, 2009). The average age for American men to first marry is 28 (U.S. Census, 2011b) and for U.K. men it is 29 (Office for National Statistics, 2011). Over time, the majority marry, but not the vast majority. For example, 37% of Swedish men and 28% of women have never been married by age 45. Marriage is more common in Norway where only 27% of 45-year-old men and 19% of women have never been married (Wiik, Bernhardt, & Noack, 2009). In comparison, by age 40, 27% of U.K. women and only 16% of U.S. women remain unmarried (Cherlin, 2009). In the U.S. among men 45 and older, only 14% have never been married (U.S. Census, 2011a). The Scandinavian nations are similar to other post-industrialized countries in having relatively high separation and divorce rates (2.2–2.3 per 1,000 population in 2006; United Nations, 2010). Moreover, divorce rates continue to increase as elsewhere in the West (OECD, 2010c).

Perhaps because of the tendency to promote women's economic independence and low religiosity, cohabitation is widespread. About half of all Scandinavian couples living together are unmarried (OECD, 2010b). In all three nations, both heterosexual and gay couples can register domestic partnerships, so marriage (available to all couples regardless of sexual orientation) yields little or no legal advantage. Another important characteristic of Scandinavian family life is that delayed parenthood is commonplace, likely because of the emphasis on women's labor force participation. Swedish and Danish women become mothers on average at 29, while Norwegian women become mothers at 28; Swedish men become fathers for the first time on average at age 31 (Nilsson & Strandh, 2009; Statistics Denmark, 2010; Statistics Norway, 2010). In contrast, the average age of first motherhood in the U.S. is 25 (Livingston & Cohn, 2010).

Despite this relatively late start for parenthood, Scandinavian nations have higher fertility levels than almost all other nations in Europe. The total fertility rate in 2010 was 1.9 live births per woman in Norway and Sweden, and 1.8 in Denmark (Hausmann, Tyson, & Zahidi, 2010). In Sweden, there is a strong positive relationship between women's labor force participation and their fertility (Nilsson & Strandh, 2009). Demographers have concluded that steady employment for both parents provides the most secure economic foundation for family formation, if family policies contain strong supports for working parents and incentives for gender equality (Rønsen & Skrede, 2006).

In Scandinavia, a high proportion of births are to unmarried mothers because of the prevalence of cohabitation, and not due to teenage fertility, which is very low. In 2008, the proportion of children born to unmarried mothers was 55% in Sweden, 54% in Norway and 46% in Denmark. In comparison, the U.S. rate is 41% (National Center for Health Statistics, 2009). The majority of young Scandinavian children, however, live with both biological parents. This includes 85% of Swedish children aged 0–5 and 89% of Danish children under one year of age (Nilsson & Strandh, 2009; Statistics Denmark, 2010).

Social Policy Issues Related to Fathering

Parental leave

Since the 1970s, Scandinavian social policies have aimed to support a new family model, the dual-earner/dual-carer family, which calls for men and women to share breadwinning and childcare (Leira, 2006). Described above were policies that support the dual-earner family – equal employment legislation, paid employment leaves, and subsidized early childhood education and care. Government policies have also developed in Scandinavia to support the dual-caregiver family, specifically emphasizing fathers as caregivers. To understand fatherhood and how it has developed in Scandinavia, it is important to examine how national social policies encourage or constrain men's and women's sharing of breadwinning and childcare roles.

Sweden was the first nation in the world to set a political course that called for fathers to be more involved in caring for children. Analysis of the history of Swedish family policy suggests that interest in expanding men's role beyond being breadwinners to become active caregivers of children occurred first in the 1960s and 1970s, during the time of a major labor shortage. At that time, feminist journalists and social scientists questioned how women could achieve equality in the labor market if they were expected to take on a "double role" as worker and homemaker-mother. They advocated an abolition of "sex roles," in favor of transforming men's and women's roles so that men could become more involved in family life. To this end, a government commission was established to reform family law, so that both partners should support themselves and share domestic duties (Roman, 2009). Maintenance obligations to spouses after divorce and widow's pensions were phased out; individual taxation on earned income became mandatory to symbolize women's economic independence.

The commission recommended that parents of both sexes be supported in staying at home with small children, calling for changes in the social insurance system that replaced maternity leave with gender-neutral parental leave in 1974 (Roman, 2009). Sweden was also the first country in the world to allow fathers to share what was mothers' right to take leave after childbirth, granting fathers the right to take three of the six paid months of leave formerly available only to mothers. Fathers could, however, still transfer their rights to mothers.

Norway was the next nation in the world to make paid parental leave available to fathers, four years after Sweden in 1978. Fathers were granted the right to share up to 12 of the 18 weeks of parental leave formerly available to mothers. In 1984, Danish men were granted the right to share up to 10 weeks with mothers, but gender equality was less clearly articulated as a policy goal, and no strong efforts were made to encourage fathers to use their parental leave. In all Scandinavian nations, extending parental leave to fathers is widely regarded as an important way to develop strong father–child bonds and relationships that will continue and develop through the years (Valdimarsdottir, 2006).

While the inclusion of fathers as potential users of parental leave was ground-breaking, Roman (2009) claims these changes to family law did not really alter Scandinavian men's roles as fathers, because few fathers took advantage of their new rights. In 1992, Swedish fathers took only

10% of all parental leave days taken by parents, Danish fathers took 5%, and Norwegian fathers took 1% (Haataja, 2009). This lack of progress toward fathers sharing care for young children prompted Norwegian policymakers in 1993 to make a revolutionary change in leave legislation, setting aside four weeks of parental leave for fathers as an individualized nontransferable entitlement, in order to increase children's contact with fathers (Brandth & Kvande, 2009). This "father's quota" could not be transferred to mothers. By 2011, this quota was extended to 12 weeks (Eydal & Rostgaard, 2011). While Norway has taken the lead in offering a father's quota, conservative parties oppose this policy because it takes away family choice by forcing fathers to take leave, and the conservatives would likely abolish it if they took power (Brandth & Kvande, 2010).

Sweden followed Norway's lead by offering fathers one non-transferable month of parental leave in 1995 and a second month in 2002. Policymakers hoped that fathers' use of more leave would help maintain women's position in the labor force and facilitate father–child relationships, which would in turn lead to more equal sharing of childcare (Klinth, 2002). The proposal for the first "daddy's month" was controversial, because mothers' "lost" a month of leave. The second daddy's month was accompanied by an expansion of parental leave by one month, which reduced opposition. There has been more political consensus in Sweden than in Norway concerning the desirability of keeping the father's quota.

Inspired by Norway and Sweden, Denmark decided to offer fathers a two-week, non-transferable leave entitlement in 1997. However, with the election of a center-right government which indicated it did not want to interfere with private life, the father's quota was abolished in 2002 (Borchorst, 2006). A recent national survey indicated that only a minority of parents – 37% of men and 23% of women – wanted the quota reintroduced (Rostgaard, 2010). This development shows that in Scandinavia there is a range of opinions about the father's role in early childcare.

All Scandinavian nations' parental leave programs provide parents with a similar earnings-based wage replacement: 80–100% of wages, up to a high income ceiling (Haas & Rostgaard, 2011). Such compensation sends a strong message that parental care is socially valued, an important prerequisite for the development of a dual-earner/dual-caregiver society. Providing high compensation for parental leave also makes taking leave more attractive to fathers, who still tend to be their families' higher earners. Another important feature of parental leave that is important to fathers is scheduling flexibility. All three nations allow parents to take leave until children are at least 8 years old (Norway extends this to age 10). Sweden offers the most flexibility in taking leave part-time, since parents can take it in increments of as little as one hour. If Norwegian men want to take the family entitlement part-time, they need their employers' permission.

Denmark makes no provision for part-time leave (Fine-Davis, Fagnani, Giovannini, Hijgaard, & Clarke, 2004; Haas & Rostgaard, 2011).

Fathers' use of their non-transferable right to wage-based parental leave is very high in Norway and Sweden. The vast majority (90%) of Swedish fathers took advantage of their leave for children born in 1998; 89% of Norwegian fathers took it in 2003 (Brandth & Kvande, 2010; Duvander et al., 2010a). Brandth and Kvande (2009, p. 182) explain this high usage rate: "Having a right that applies to male employees as a group … makes it easier to avoid the stress and strain of being in the minority, or being the only one to take leave to provide care for children."

While Scandinavian fathers clearly take advantage of parental leave when it is their non-transferable right, they are much less likely to share the wage-based leave that is a family entitlement (which ranges between 32 and 37 weeks). Danish fathers take the most (one-fourth), probably because they have no individualized entitlement (Rostgaard, 2010). In the two nations with a fathers' quota, the percentage is lower: 16% for Norway and 12% for Sweden (Brandth & Kvande, 2010; Försäkringskassan, 2009). This low percentage of fathers' use of the family entitlement led the Swedish government to institute a "gender-equality bonus" in 2008, worth about $1,300 annually, for couples where the father takes some shared family entitlement (Duvander et al., 2010a). This has not yet significantly increased the proportion of leave that fathers take (Ferrarini & Duvander, 2010).

Research suggests that native-born Scandinavian fathers are more likely to take parental leave than immigrant men from non-Western nations (Bernhardt & Goldscheider, 2007; Naz, 2010). Scandinavian fathers are more likely to take leave when they are highly educated and hold prestigious jobs with high incomes (Duvander & Lammi-Taskula, 2010; Eydal & Rostgaard, 2011; Lammi-Taskula, 2006). Naz (2010) argues that Norwegian men are more likely to take leave when their partners are better educated – the type of employee who finds it difficult to take leave. Lappegård (2008b, p. 139) found that Norwegian fathers take more leave when partners earn income close to theirs, suggesting that the "gender balance in breadwinning has a strong effect on fathers' use of parental leave."

Government-mandated parental leave policies designed to increase Scandinavian fathers' involvement in early childcare have so far had only modest effects, yet the existence of such policies and the publicity that surrounds them may still send out an important political message to citizens that fathers should be active participants in the care of young children. This appears to be particularly true in Sweden, where the government has been much more involved than in Denmark and Norway in advertising the desirability of fathers taking parental leave. This publicity, which has extended over three decades, has helped to develop a norm of involved fatherhood (Johansson and Klinth, 2007).

BARNLEDIG PAPPA!

Figure 13.1 1978 poster promoting parental leave in Sweden. Pictured is famous weight-lifter Hoa-Hoa Dahlgren. The baby is now 33 years old and recently became a father himself. He and his wife strongly favor sharing parental leave, and he wants to stay at home and take care of his daughter. Photo courtesy of C. Philip Hwang.

While there is popular support for Swedish fathers to take parental leave, a different picture emerges when parents are asked about sharing parental leave in their families. One survey found that only 19% of fathers and 14% of mothers wanted a more even division of parental leave than they had (Josefsson, 2007). Research suggests that fathers have more options than mothers regarding leave; they can choose whether or not to take any of the shared family entitlement while mothers are expected to take most of it (Bekkengen, 2002).

Additional types of parental insurance

In addition to parental leave, there are three "parental insurance" benefits offered to Scandinavian fathers to encourage them to take care of young children. The first is "paternity leave," 10 days off work to be taken soon after childbirth (in Sweden within the first month, in Denmark within the first 14 weeks). In Denmark and Sweden, this leave is paid by the government; in Norway it is paid through employers. The vast majority (89%) of fathers use this in Denmark and Norway, while 80% of Swedish fathers use it (Brandth & Kvande, 2010; Duvander et al., 2010a; Rostgaard, 2010).

The second type of parental insurance is "temporary parental leave," whereby fathers as well as mothers have the right to stay home from work with pay to care for sick children. This leave is most generous in Sweden, where either parent can stay home with pay when children are sick, or stay home to care for children when their regular caregiver is sick, up to 120 days per year for each child under the age of 12. In 2009, mothers took a majority (65%) of the days taken (Duvander et al., 2010a). Norway also allows parents to stay home to care for sick children with wage compensation that is similar to Sweden's, but only up to 10 days per year for one child. Danish law allows parents to miss work for this reason, but compensation is not government-mandated in the private sector as it is in Sweden and Norway (Brandth & Kvande, 2010; Duvander et al., 2010a; Moss & Deven, 2010).

A third type of parental leave benefit in Norway and Sweden is the right to reduce work hours by three-fourths without pay (Brandth & Kvande, 2010; Duvander et al., 2010a). In Norway, employers can deny this if it would cause a "significant inconvenience" (Dommermuth & Kitterød, 2009). Statistics concerning fathers' use of this benefit do not appear to be kept. Lack of compensation for reduced hours probably discourages fathers from using this benefit, reinforcing mothers' traditional responsibility for childcare.

Cash for care policies

While the introduction of the father's quota for parental leave in Scandinavian countries in the 1990s was designed as a policy to encourage fathers to participate more in early childcare, another family policy emerged during the same decade that has the potential to have the opposite effect. Often labeled "cash for care," this policy establishes a caregiver's allowance for the one parent who stays home to care for children, typically between the ages of 1 and 3; the family thereby gives up the opportunity for the child to be placed in publicly subsidized childcare. The Norwegian caregiver's leave is the best established, originating in 1998, offering $557 per child per month for up to 24 months in 2010 (Andenaes, 2005; Brandth & Kvande, 2010); this seems to be the direct opposite approach to that in states which force single mothers to look for work. This is about the same amount as the state subsidy for public early childhood education and care.

According to Brandth and Kvande (2009, p. 194), this policy "supports a traditional division of work in the family, the male breadwinner family model, facilitating one of the parents (in practice, the mother) staying home." About three-quarters of eligible families in Norway have taken advantage of "cash for care" since 2000 (Statistics Norway, 2010). Both Andenaes (2005) and Leira (2006) claim that this high utilization has been due to the inadequate supply of daycare facilities in Norway.

Sweden also offers a caregiver's allowance at $428 per child per month. The policy has been intermittently in effect when the more conservative coalition is in power, and has now been in force in about half of municipalities since 2009. Less than 2% of families use this allowance, perhaps because daycare supply is readily available and social norms do not strongly support mothers staying at home (Ferrarini & Duvander, 2010). This policy tends to be used most often by ethnic minorities who have more traditional views about childrearing. Since 2002 Danish parents have been able to apply for this stipend in some municipalities, but very few appear to have done so (Eydal & Rostgaard, 2011).

Fathers' rights to custody and visitation

Scandinavian prioritization of the caregiving role of both parents is reflected not just in policies like parental leave but also in the laws that govern visitation rights and custody decisions following the breakup of the relationships between mothers and fathers (Eydal & Gislason, 2008). Given the high rate of nonmarital childbearing, the prevalence of cohabitation and the high divorce rate, fathers' relations with children following union breakup could potentially be difficult to sustain in Scandinavia. However, the Scandinavian nations have put into place legal rights for fathers to custody and visitation designed to help the majority of nonresident fathers and children remain in close contact.

Fathers gained the right to petition the court for sole or joint custody in the late 1960s in Denmark, in the 1970s in Sweden and in the early 1980s in Norway. The right to "joint custody" does not guarantee shared physical custody (i.e., children alternating residence at both parents), but is meant to encourage both parents to take responsibility for a child's welfare and upbringing. These rights have been strengthened over time, so that married and single fathers enjoy the same rights as mothers when it comes to custody. The law was originally changed from giving preference to mothers to realize "the best interests of the child," which includes close contact with both parents (Annfelt, 2009). All three nations have also seen a strengthening of fathers' visitation rights (Andersen & Ravn, 2009). As the political goal of gender equality became institutionalized in the 1990s, the gender equality principle was increasingly mentioned as an additional reason to ensure fathers' custodial and visitation rights (Annfelt, 2009; Roman, 2009).

Today, courts enforce the norm of joint custody (unless one parent is unable to function as a legal guardian), which guarantees fathers an equal share in decision-making about matters affecting children's welfare, regardless of whether or not children reside with them (Melby, Ravn, & Westerberg, 2009). In Sweden, the court can award joint custody over the objection of one parent (Ferrarini & Duvander, 2010).

Fathers' equal rights with mothers for custody and visitation have been somewhat controversial in Scandinavia. Research suggests that some separated and divorced fathers in Sweden enjoy "conditional parenting." Although they share custody with mothers, fathers still choose how actively they participate in childcare, while normative expectations give single mothers no choice (Ahlberg, Roman, & Duncan, 2008).

Impact of Policies on Fathers' Participation in Childcare and Breadwinning

Scandinavian policies support the establishment of families where both parents are active in paid employment and caring for children. This shared responsibility for children is expected to continue even if parents stop living together. While there has been a dramatic increase in the proportion of children with two employed parents, and attitudes about fathers' involvement have undergone a revolutionary transformation, there is still a gap between Scandinavian social policy and parental practices. Scandinavian policymakers' focus on the importance of fathers' development of ties with children encourages men to develop a more child-oriented type of masculinity, but this does not necessarily lead fathers to share childcare equally with mothers (Brandth & Kvande, 2009; Duvander & Jans, 2009).

Fathers' participation in childcare

Time use data show that Scandinavian mothers perform more childcare than fathers in two-parent families. In 2000, fathers' share of all time parents spent in childcare for children aged 0–6 was 36% in Norway and Sweden (Finch, 2006). For Danish fathers of children aged 0–4, the percentage was slightly lower at 33% (Craig & Mullan, 2010). There is variation between the three nations in terms of fathers' percentage of total non-leisure time spent on childcare. Looking only at those with young children, this percentage ranges from 5% in Denmark to 13% in Norway, and 12% in Sweden. These proportions are lower than for mothers, demonstrating again the unequal division of childcare. Mothers' percentage of non-leisure time spent in childcare ranged from 10% in Denmark to 22% in Norway and 20% in Sweden (Finch, 2006). According to Boje (2006), Danish families tend to rely less on fathers for childcare and more on paid private caregivers, compared with Swedish families.

Since fathers' rights to non-transferable parental leave were instituted, Scandinavian fathers in two-parent families have only slightly increased

Figure 13.2 A 33-year-old father, dressed in his usual work clothes, with his 7-month-old and 3-year-old children outside Stockholm in a public park in the suburb of Hägersten. The picture was intended to show that even men in traditional male jobs want and are capable of having close relationships with their children. Photo courtesy of Ulla Lemberg.

the time they spend in childcare. For example, using time-use data, Sullivan, Coltrane, Mcannally, and Altintas (2009) compared the minutes of childcare per day that Norwegian fathers and Swedish fathers spent in 1990 and 2000, in two-parent families, with at least one child under the age of 5. Both Norwegian and Swedish fathers' average time spent in childcare increased only 10 minutes per day for Norwegians and 6 minutes for Swedes. Norwegian fathers spent slightly more time in childcare than Swedish fathers in both years (10 minutes per day in 2000).

Fathers' participation in childcare appears greater when "indirect" forms of childcare are included. For example, a 2000 survey of Swedish parents of children aged 0–2 years using time diaries found that fathers' share increased to 37% from 31%, when time spent in the presence of children while doing something else was added to direct childcare time. Fathers' share of childcare was higher for preschool-age children (3–6); with fathers spending 39% of all direct childcare time spent by the couple, but 42% of all time spent if time spent in the company of children was also counted (Berggren & Duvander, 2003).

While time-use studies are instructive about men's participation in childcare, it is difficult to capture responsibility for childcare with this method. Bø's (2008, p. 444) study of Norwegian families noted greater maternal responsibility in that "the mother was the one who 'does the thinking to see to it that things work out or fit in.'" Only about half of Danish and Swedish parents with children under age 15 shared responsibility for childcare equally in 2001, with men slightly more likely than women to make this claim (Boje, 2006).

Fathers' likelihood of sharing childcare is strongly related to mothers' employment status in Sweden. Results from Thomas and Hildingsson's (2009) survey one year after childbirth showed that fathers' share of childcare was associated with mothers' return to full-time employment. For example, full-time employed mothers reported that their male partners were responsible for 43% of the time spent bathing the baby; in comparison, the percentages were 31% in families where mothers worked part-time and 27% where only fathers were employed. Patterns for playing with children were similar. Chuang, Lamb, and Hwang's (2004) longitudinal study of Swedish families and Haas and Hwang's (2008) investigation of fathers employed in private Swedish companies also found that fathers participate in childcare more when mothers worked longer paid hours. Mothers' full-time employment was not associated with fathers' increased contributions to childcare in Norway however (Kitterød & Pettersen, 2006).

A few Scandinavian studies have compared parent–child relations between non-married vs. married fathers living with mothers. A Norwegian study found no difference between married and cohabiting fathers in willingness to allocate time to family over work or interest in being a good parent (Reneflot, 2009). Meanwhile, a Swedish study found no differences in psychological well-being between children raised in families with both biological parents and children raised in single-parent families. The same study also observed no differences in well-being between children whose parents worked full-time, part-time, or not at all (Låftman & Ostberg, 2004).

While it is difficult to locate specific studies about childcare sharing among separated parents, the majority of Scandinavian children appear to have meaningful contact with their fathers after their parents separate. In 2003, for example, about two-thirds of Danish parents shared custody of children after their relationships ended (Andersen & Ravn, 2009). It is still most common for the majority of Scandinavian children to live with mothers after the parents' relationship has ended. For example, in 2004, 82% of Norwegian and 86% of Danish children lived with their mothers after their parents' relationships ended (Fine-Davis et al., 2004; Statistics Norway, 2010). Shared residential custody appears to be highest in Sweden, where in 2006, 28% of children of separated parents split their time living with mothers and fathers (Ferrarini & Duvander, 2010).

Scandinavian children frequently visit their nonresidential fathers. Over three-quarters of Danish children visit the parent they did not live with at least every two weeks, which is typically the father; only 13% never visit them (Andersen & Ravn, 2009). In Norway, nonresidential fathers reported seeing children 8.0 days per month on average, with the vast majority (79%) having seen their children within the last month (Statistics Norway, 2010). In Sweden, separated fathers spend 5.4 days a month with their children; only 20% of children do not see fathers regularly (Duvander & Jans, 2009).

In summary, it appears that Scandinavian men have more autonomy and more choice than women when it comes to sharing childcare, concerning the types of childcare they provide (Ahlberg et al., 2008). Men can be considered to be good fathers even if their share of childcare is under 40% and mothers remain more responsible for meeting children's needs.

The impact of parental leave on fathers' participation in childcare

Most research on the impact of parental leave on fathers' participation in childcare has been conducted in Sweden. Early studies found modest effects of fathers' taking paternal leave on father–child relations. For example, a longitudinal study in the 1970s and 1980s found that effects varied depending on the outcome measured. At ages 8–16 months, infants and toddlers showed a greater preference for and attachment to mothers over fathers. Further, they displayed the same level of preference and attachment to fathers who had taken care of them on parental leave (on average for three months) as those who had taken no leave (Frodi, Lamb, Hwang, & Frodi, 1982; Lamb, Frodi, Frodi, & Hwang, 1982; Lamb, Frodi, Hwang, Frodi, & Steinberg, 1982). Fathers who had or had not taken leave were just as likely to play and show affection toward infants when mothers were in the room. But when mothers left the room, fathers who took leave did play more and showed more affection toward their infants than fathers who had not taken leave (Hwang, 1986). When these children were somewhat older (16–28 months of age), Lamb et al. (1988) found that fathers' involvement in childcare activities and overall responsibility for childcare were positively related to whether or not they had taken parental leave earlier. This impact, however, was only temporary. While past experience with childcare acquired during one's parental leave was positively associated with men's later time spent caring and being responsible for toddlers, it had little impact on childcare sharing by the time children reached the age of 7 (Chuang et al., 2004).

Two Swedish studies with larger samples of parents, during this same time period, found that fathers who took leave were more likely than fathers who did not to be equally responsible for childcare, regardless of the children's ages (Haas, 1992; SOU, 1978). In addition, a large-scale longitudinal time-use study of Norwegian fathers found that fathers spent more time with children after the father's quota was introduced in 1994 than they did before the advent of the quota (Rege & Solli, 2010).

By the 21st century, taking leave *per se* did not seem to affect Swedish men's participation in childcare or their relationships with children, according to Haas and Hwang (2008), who studied fathers working in large private companies whose children were 12 years old or younger. If fathers in their sample had taken more days of leave when their children were younger, they were more likely to have sole responsibility for childcare while their partners worked, spend more time doing things for or with their children on work days, engage in more physical caregiving, and report more satisfaction with contact with their children.

Qualitative studies offer insights into what fathers learn by taking parental leave. Chronholm's (2004) research on Swedish fathers who took 120 or more days found that leave enabled them to develop close emotional relationships with their children and made them feel responsible for childrearing. Based on another study of Swedish fathers, Premburg, Hellström, and Berg (2008, p. 61) revealed "when the fathers were alone with their children that they had a deeper contact … men postpone their emotional attachment to the child when the woman is there to comfort and take care of the child." Further, a qualitative study in Norway noted "a development of competence as the fathers get to know their children by having the main responsibility and spending a great deal of time with them" (Brandth & Kvande, 2003, p. 66). After taking six months of parental leave, one Swedish physical education teacher said: "I know her, what she wants, I am not a foreigner to her. She knows us both equally well. I'm not just a baby sitter filling in for Mom." His wife agreed, saying, "She is secure with both of us. ... I am not raising a child alone. He can do things as well, knows her as well" (Haas, 1992, p. 154). Research by Bekkengen (2006, p. 155) suggested that Swedish men who take long parental leaves also contribute to a change in societal norms concerning masculinity towards a "child-oriented masculinity," which "implies having space for close relationships with children."

Taking parental leave has also been found to have a significant impact on single fathers' time spent with children. For instance, Swedish fathers who took more than 60 days of parental leave saw their children more days a month (6.5) after they separated from mothers than fathers who had not taken leave (4.6) (Duvander & Jans, 2009). Other Swedish studies show that fathers' leave use reduces couple break-ups. Two explanations have been offered for this finding. Nilsson and Strandth (2009) suggested that women are more likely to leave partners who fail to live up to the strong social norm of equal parenthood. Alternatively, Oláh (2001) posited that conflict is reduced among couples that have common experiences of employment and family work, and there by understand each other's problems.

The impact of fatherhood on men's participation in the labor force

Fathers' opportunities to develop close relationships with children and participate actively in childcare can be negatively affected by men's preoccupation with paid employment and families' reliance on men as the main breadwinners. The "dual-earner/dual-caregiver model" of family life calls on fathers to share wage-earning with mothers, thereby freeing men up for childcare. But to what extent is there evidence that this in fact has taken place in Scandinavia? In this regard, it is useful to examine Scandinavian men's paid work hours after the transition to parenthood, likelihood of working long hours, chances of adopting part-time employment to allow for increased participation in childcare (relative to that by mothers), and the extent to which they remain more responsible than mothers for income-earning.

Scandinavian research has found that fathers on average work more hours than other men if they embrace the traditional breadwinner role (Dommermuth & Kitterød, 2009; Dribe & Stanfors, 2009). In examining Scandinavian fathers' work hours over the transition to parenthood, it is clear that they do not *increase* their work hours, as fathers are likely to do elsewhere. One Danish study showed there was no difference in paid hours between fathers and childless men (Craig & Mullan, 2010); another found that about one-fifth of fathers of pre-school-aged children decreased their working time after having children (Fine-Davis et al., 2004). Norwegian fathers shorten their work week by one hour when they have preschool-aged children (Dommermuth & Kitterød, 2009). Swedish men's hours also declined somewhat when they became parents, although not as much as women's (Dribe & Stanfors, 2009). When fathers have taken considerable parental leave (60 days or more), their work hours are less than men who do not take long leave (41 hours vs. 45) (Duvander & Jans, 2009).

Scandinavian fathers are relatively unlikely to work long hours (46+ hours per week) that would undoubtedly cut into childcare time. The average proportion of fathers of children aged 0–15 years in two-partner households working such long hours was 25% in Denmark and 24% in Sweden in 2004–05. While this was considerably higher than the percentage of mothers who worked long hours in both nations (11% and 8% respectively), it was substantially lower than the average (38%) for 11 other European nations (Lewis, 2009). In Norway, 15% of fathers worked 50 or more hours in 2000, compared to 3% of mothers (Kitterød & Kjelstad, 2003). Sayer and Gornick's (2011) study which looked only at fathers with young children aged 4 and under found that only 7% of Swedish fathers and 10% of Norwegian fathers worked 51 hours or more per week, compared to 22% of American and 26% of U.K. fathers.

Although legislation permits fathers in all three Scandinavian nations the right to request a reduction of their work hours to part-time status, Scandinavian fathers are much less likely than mothers to work part-time. In 2009, only 9% of Swedish working fathers with one child aged 1 to 2 worked part-time (30 hours or less a week), compared to 40% of Swedish working mothers (SCB, 2010). Swedish research also shows that there is a gap in work time between women and men even if they both take parental leave. For example, among white-collar workers, 88% of women and 95% of men worked full-time before taking parental leave. After taking leave, the proportion of women working full-time dropped to 50%, while men's proportion remained at 95% (Westerlund, Lindblad, & Larsson, 2005). Apparently, the types of jobs women tend to hold in more traditional women's fields have been flexible in terms of work hours, while traditional men's jobs so far have not. Fathers are also unlikely to work part-time in Norway. In 2000, only 4% of Norwegian fathers of children aged 0–15 worked part-time, compared to 50% of mothers (Kitterød & Kjelstad, 2003). Statistics about Danish fathers are not available, but only 5% of Danish men aged 15–66 worked part-time in 2010 compared to 30% of Danish women (Statistics Denmark, 2010).

Because men work more hours and their jobs pay more than women's, men's contributions to family income are much larger than women's. For example, Swedish fathers in 2002 provided 75% of the income in households where the youngest child was under 2, the same proportion they contributed in 1987. When the youngest child was older (aged 3 to 6), the fathers' share was 63%, down slightly from 67% (Haataja & Nyberg, 2006).

Swedish research suggests that fathers' use of parental leave can potentially increase women's share of family income (Johansson, 2010). Each month that their partners took leave increased mothers' later earnings by 7%. Johansson hypothesized that fathers on leave acquire "child care human capital" which makes them more likely to do childcare in the future and frees women up to engage in the labor market.

Ellingsaeter (1998) analyzed Scandinavian parents' preferences for which parent should provide financial support. Danish parents were more likely than Norwegian and Swedish parents to say that the ideal model of family support was the equal-sharing model (63% vs. 56% and 55%). Relatively few parents (8% in Denmark, 16% in Norway and 11% in Sweden) preferred the male-breadwinner model, while a substantial minority preferred a mix somewhere in between equal sharing and the father's assuming responsibility.

Workplace Barriers to Scandinavian Fathers' Becoming Equal Parents

Given men's strong attachment to the labor market and role as family breadwinners, it is essential for the workplace to be supportive if men are to be encouraged to play an active role in childcare. Yet research suggests that perhaps the most formidable barrier to fathers becoming equal and independent parents in Scandinavia is the structure and culture of the workplace (see Li & Lamb, Ch 2, this volume, for a discussion of how workplace barriers have stymied Chinese paternal leave policies). While social policies such as parental leave for fathers set up possibilities for involvement in childcare, whether fathers can take advantage of them depends on how these policies are implemented at the workplace. Workplace policies and practices tend to be organized along the model of the ideal worker (male) who is unencumbered with family responsibilities, and thus full-time and uninterrupted work has historically been a sign of a man's organizational commitment (Haas & Hwang, 2007).

Research on fathers' use of parental leave in Scandinavia indicates that workplace issues are often cited as a reason why fathers do not take more leave (Brandth & Kvande, 2003; Lammi-Taskula, 2006). Danish fathers, who take leave less often than Swedes and Norwegians, are more likely than Swedes to name the workplace as a barrier (EC, 2004). Swedish fathers have been found to take less parental leave when they lack support for active fatherhood from top managers and work groups (Haas, Allard, & Hwang, 2002). It is more difficult for men to take leave if their work is based on individual specialization, than if it is easily shared with co-workers (Bekkengen, 2002).

The most consistent difference in fathers' leave-taking in Scandinavian countries is between work organizations in the public vs. private sectors. Fathers working in the public sector are much more likely than fathers in the private sector to take parental leave in all three Scandinavian nations (Lammi-Taskula, 2006; Lappegård, 2008b). For example, two-thirds (67%) of Danish men who take parental leave are in the public sector where men make up only 48% of the workers (Rostgaard, 2010).

There are three possible reasons for the "implementation gap" for fathers working in the private sector. First, fathers in the private sector are less likely to receive information about fathers' rights to leave, and lack of knowledge about fathers' rights is often mentioned as one of the obstacles to fathers' taking parental leave (Försäkringskassan, 2010; Rostgaard, 2010). Second, fathers may be less likely to take parental leave in the private sector because they are less likely to be eligible for enhanced compensation, which typically takes the form of raising the wage-replacement percentage to 90% or 100% or by eliminating the income ceiling for benefits – all benefits that have been won by unions in the public sector (Lammi-Taskula, 2006). Third, fathers in the private sector may be less likely to take parental leave than others because these workplaces tend to be male-dominated, so that employee concerns about harmony between work and family life have historically been less likely to come up (Lappegård, 2008a). In the public sector, because more employees are women, employers have more experience accommodating leave requests (Bygren & Duvander, 2006).

Since fathers are less likely to take leave in the private sector, it is interesting to learn about what might bring companies in this sector to become father-friendly. In contrast to traditional workplaces, a father-friendly workplace would take for granted that fathers as well as mothers are capable of and interested in providing early childcare, and would adopt policies and practices that facilitate fathers' participation in childcare.

In the 1990s, Haas and Hwang (2000) found that the vast majority of Swedish companies were not father-friendly, lagging dramatically behind men's growing interest in active fatherhood. Comparing representative samples of profitable companies in 1993 and 2006, Haas and Hwang (2009) discovered there has been a dramatic increase in Swedish companies' support for fathers' taking parental leave, as measured by the presence of formal policies and practices, informal support by co-workers and managers, and the establishment of a norm for fathers' leave-taking. Companies were more likely to support fathers' taking leave when they espoused caring values, women made up a larger share of the workforce, women made up a larger proportion of top managers, and company policy prioritized women's advancement. Prospects for companies providing more support for fathers' participation in early childcare likely depend on company commitment to improvement in women's position in the labor market.

Conclusions

Before the 1960s, Scandinavian fathers were unlikely to be involved in childcare activities, because of norms that emphasized their breadwinning role. Since the 1960s, this has changed dramatically in that normative fatherhood has expanded to include men's involvement in everyday childcare activities. From an international perspective, Scandinavian nations are unique in that their governments have pioneered the idea that active fatherhood can and should be shaped by social policy. Policy has been driven by a desire to realize the dual-earner/dual-caregiver family model, which is seen as helping to establish a firm economic foundation for families, women's economic independence, and better relations between fathers and children. Most policies have targeted fathers to provide them the opportunity to be released from work to stay home to care for young children, with wage compensation. Policies also address the need for fathers and children to maintain relations following parental separation.

Why have the Scandinavian nations been so progressive in this regard? First, each nation is a social welfare state where the well-being of children has high political priority (Eydal & Rostgaard, 2011). Second, grass-roots activists and social scientists have been particularly influential in convincing policymakers and the public that children's well-being is enhanced by policies that promote children having a secure economic base with two working parents and a secure emotional base with two parents who are actively involved in and responsible for their care (Lundqvist, 2011). Third, policies that support the dual-earner/dual-caregiver model have been enacted by Parliaments that involve more representation of women than in most of the rest of the world. In 2010, women made up 38% the Parliamentary membership in Denmark, 40% in Norway, and 46% in Sweden, compared to women holding 17% of U.S. Congress seats and U.K. women holding 22% in Parliament (Hausmann et al., 2010).

The dual-earner/dual-caregiver model, however, has only been partially realized in Scandinavia despite the prevalence of social policy. A gendered division of labor persists, with fathers more responsible for paid work and breadwinning and mothers more responsible for childcare. Women's roles have changed more than men's roles; paid work is no longer optional for women, but shared involvement in childcare is still optional for men (Ahlberg et al., 2008). While mothers as well as fathers are active in the paid labor force, aided by a strong government-subsidized high-quality system of early childcare education, there is a tendency for mothers to work fewer work hours than fathers and to contribute substantially less to family income. Fathers as well as mothers are active in childcare (including physical caregiving not just social interaction), but there is a tendency for mothers to still do the majority of childcare and retain responsibility over this important area of social life. At least one social policy, the "cash for care" caregiver's allowance, has the potential to reinforce this gender-based division of labor, by offering a non-taxed wage to parents (typically women) who stay home to care for children once paid parental leave is over.

Each of the three Scandinavian nations has its own distinctive patterns of parenting. In Denmark, mothers typically work full-time and rely heavily on daycare; fathers do not receive the same encouragement or pressure to take on more active roles. In Norway, there exists what has been called a "dualistic policy regime" (Ellingsaeter, 2006), with one policy strand encouraging fathers to participate equally in childcare (e.g., offering non-transferable rights to three months of paid parental leave), while another offers families choice concerning childcare arrangements that typically lead mothers to stay home collecting caregivers' allowances.

Of the three, Sweden has set the boldest course toward a society where fathers participate in childcare at the same level as mothers, with progressive social policies such as the gender equality bonus and aggressive attempts through the social insurance office to change the cultural discourse about men's role in society. Expectations for Swedish fathers to share childcare are higher than in Denmark, Norway, or most other countries. However, in some respects Swedish fathers' actual participation in childcare is similar to men's elsewhere. They are not likely to share responsibility for childcare equally with mothers, they are less likely to engage in physical caregiving than play, and they are unlikely to reduce work hours significantly to promote work-family integration.

What does the future hold for fatherhood in Sweden, the nation that has made so much progress? Without increasing equal labor market opportunities for women, including access to full-time jobs, men remain more responsible for income; therefore, there is less pressure on men to expand their role as fathers to accept shared responsibility for children. While Swedes generally support the goal of equal parenthood, individual parents – responding to the reality of men's and women's unequal labor force participation – seem ambivalent about equality, and seldom aspire toward this ideal in their own families, where decisions are made often on rational economic grounds. Consequently, the division of domestic labor tends to fall somewhere in between policymakers' goals of a dual-earner/dual-caregiver society and the traditional gender-based division of labor for breadwinning and childcare.

In speaking about fatherhood policies in Nordic countries, Lammi-Taskula (2006, p. 95) concluded that "Policies promoting father's care of young children appear to be more significant on the symbolic level of gender relations than on the level of actual division of labor between mothers and fathers." Policies to promote active fatherhood would seem likely to be more effective when they are structured in ways that make it difficult for couples to fall back into the traditional division of labor. One example of a policy already in place is the "father's quota" that offers families additional paid parental leave only if the father takes it, which is now up to two to three months in Sweden and Norway and is taken by the vast majority of fathers. Additional parental leave that could not be transferred to mothers could be offered. Another policy that could be enacted that might encourage fathers to be more active in childcare would be wage compensation for reduced work hours, that would enable fathers to continue to contribute to family income while becoming more available to be with children.

Summary

A dramatic change in Scandinavian fathers' relationships with children began in the mid-1970s. At that time, Denmark, Norway and Sweden became innovators with regard to gender equality, setting the stage for fathers to become equal and independent parents. From an international perspective, Scandinavian nations are unique in that governments have pioneered the idea that active fatherhood can and should be shaped by social policy. Social policies are designed to promote a family pattern often called the dual-earner/dual-caregiver model, where both mothers and fathers are responsible for breadwinning and childcare. This model is seen as helping to establish a firm economic foundation for families, women's economic independence, and better father–child relations. Most policies provide fathers the opportunity to be released from work with pay to stay home to care for young children; others address the need for fathers and children to maintain relations following parental separation. We concluded that the dual-earner/dual-caregiver model has only been partially realized in Scandinavia, despite the prevalence of social policy. A gendered division of labor persists, whereby fathers remain more responsible for paid work and breadwinning and mothers are still more responsible for childcare.

References

Ahlberg, J., Roman, C., & Duncan, S. (2008). Actualizing the 'democratic family'? Swedish policy rhetoric versus family practices. *Social Politics, 15* (1), 79–100

Andenaes, A. (2005). Neutral claims. *Feminism & Psychology, 15* (2), 209–226.

Anderson, C., & Ravn, A.-B. (2009). From powerful to powerless fathers. In K. Melby, A.-B. Ravn, & C. Wetterberg (Eds.), *Gender equality and welfare politics in Scandinavia* (pp. 135–148). Bristol, UK: Policy Press.

Annfelt, T. (2009). The 'new father.' In K. Melby, A.-B. Ravn, & C. Wetterberg (Eds.), *Gender equality and welfare politics in Scandinavia* (pp. 119–134). Bristol, UK: Policy Press.

Bekkengen, L. (2002). *Man får vilja* [One can choose] Malmö, Sweden: Liber.

Bekkengen, L. (2006). Men's parental leave. In L. Gonäs & J. Karlsson (Eds.), *Gender segregation* (pp. 249–262). Aldershot, UK: Ashgate.

Berggren, S., & Duvander, A.-Z. (2003). Family assets: Time and money. In *Social Insurance in Sweden 2003*. Stockholm, Sweden: National Social Insurance Board.

Bernhardt, E., & Goldscheider, F. (2007). Gender and work-family balance. In E. Bernhardt, C. Goldscheider, F. Godscheider, & G. Bjerén (Eds.), *Immigration, gender, and family transitions in adulthood in Sweden* (pp. 96–112). Lanham, MD: University Press of America.

Boje, T. (2006). Working time and caring strategies: Parenthood in different welfare states. In A. Ellingsaeter & A. Leira (Eds.), *Politicising parenthood in Scandinavia* (pp. 195–216). Bristol, UK: Policy Press.

Bø, I. (2008). Equal gender opportunity: Couples in the gap between principles and practices. *Community, Work & Family, 11* (4), 439–455.

Borchorst, A. (2006). The public–private split rearticulated. In A. Ellingsaeter & A. Leira (Eds.), *Politicising parenthood in Scandinavia* (pp. 101–120). Bristol, UK: Policy Press.

Brandth, B., & Kvande, E. (2003). Father presence in childcare. In A.-M. Jensen & L. McKee (Eds.), *Children and the changing family* (pp. 61–75). London, UK: RoutledgeFalmer.

Brandth, B., & Kvande, E. (2009). Gendered or gender-neutral care politics for fathers? *The Annals of the American Academy of Political and Social Sciences, 624,* 177–189.

Brandth, B., & Kvande, E. (2010). Country note: Norway. In P. Moss (Ed.), *International review of leave policies and related research 2010* (pp. 174–180). [Employment Relations Research Series No. 115]. London, UK: Department for Business, Innovation and Skills.

Bygren, M., & Duvander, A.-Z. (2006). Parents' workplace situation and fathers' parental leave use. *Journal of Marriage and Family, 68,* 363–372.

Cherlin, A. (2009). *The marriage go-around.* New York, NY: Alfred Knopf.

Chronholm, A. (2004). *Föräldralediga pappa* [Father on parental leave]. Doctoral dissertation, Göteborg University, Department of Sociology, Göteborg, Sweden.

Chuang, S., Lamb, M., & Hwang, C. (2004). Internal reliability, temporal stability, and correlates of individual differences in paternal involvement. In R. Day & M. Lamb (Eds.), *Conceptualizing and measuring father involvement* (pp. 129–148). Mahwah, NJ: Lawrence Erlbaum Associates.

Craig, L., & Mullan, K. (2010). Parenthood, gender and work-family time in the United States, Australia, Italy, France, and Denmark. *Journal of Marriage & Family, 72,* 1344–1361.

Danish Immigration Service. (2010). *Statistical overview: Migration and asylum 2009*. Copenhagen, Denmark: Ministry of Refugee, Immigration and Integration Affairs.

Dommermuth, L., & Kitterød, R. (2009). Fathers' employment in a father-friendly welfare state. *Community, Work & Family, 12* (4), 417–436.

Dribe, M., & Stanfors, M. (2009). Does parenthood strengthen a traditional household division of labor? Evidence from Sweden. *Journal of Marriage and Family, 71*, 33–45.

Duvander, A.-Z., & Jans, A.-C. (2009). Consequences of fathers' parental leave use: Evidence from Sweden. *Finnish Yearbook of Population Research 2009* (pp. 49–62). Helsinki, Finland: Population Research Institute.

Duvander, A.-Z., Haas, L., & Chronholm, A. (2010a). Country note: Sweden. In P. Moss (Ed.), *International review of leave policies and related research 2010* (pp. 223–229). [Employment Relations Research Series No. 115]. London, UK: Department for Business, Innovation and Skills.

Duvander, A.-Z., & Lammi-Taskula, J. (2010). Föräldraledighet [Parental leave]. In I. Gislason & G. Eydal (Eds.), *Föräldraledighet, omsorgpolitik och jämställdhet i Norden* [Parental leave, care politics and gender equality in the Nordic countries]. *Tema Nord* 2010: 595. Copenhagen, Denmark: Nordiska ministerråd [Norwegian Council of Ministers].

Duvander, A.-Z., Lappegård, T., & Andersson, G. (2010b). Family policy and fertility. *Journal of European Social Policy, 20*, 45–57.

Ellingsaeter, A. (2006). The Norwegian regime and its paradoxes. In A. Ellingsaeter & A. Leira (Eds.), *Politicising parenthood in Scandinavia* (pp. 121–144) Bristol, UK: Policy Press.

Ellingsaeter, A. (1998). Dual-breadwinner societies. *Acta Sociologica, 41* (1), 59–73.

Eydal, G., & Gislason, I. (2008). Paid parental leave in Iceland. In G. Eydal & I. Gislason (Eds.), *Equal rights to earn and care* (pp. 15–44). Reykjavik, Iceland: Felagsvisindastofnun Haskola Islands.

Eydal, G., & Rostgaard, T. (2011). Gender equality revisited. *Social Policy & Administration, 43* (2), 161–179.

Ferrarini, T., & Duvander, A.-Z. (2010). Earner-carer model at the crossroads. *International Journal of Health Services, 40* (3), 378–393.

Finch, N. (2006). Gender equity and time use. In J. Bradshaw & A. Hatland (Eds.), *Social policy, employment and family change in comparative perspective* (pp. 255–281). Cheltenham, UK: Edward Elgar.

Fine-Davis, M., Fagnani, J., Giovannini, D., Hojgaard, L., & Clarke, H. (2004). *Fathers and mothers*. Dordrecht, the Netherlands: Kluwer.

Frodi, A., Lamb, M., Hwang, C., & Frodi, M. (1982). Father–mother–infant interaction in traditional and non-traditional Swedish families. *Alternative Lifestyles, 1*, 3–22.

Försäkringskassan. (2009). *Rapport av uttaget av föräldrapenning* [Report on parental leave use]. Stockholm, Sweden: National Social Insurance Office.

Försäkringskassan. (2010). Föräldrars syn på Försäkringskassans information på föräldraförsäkringen [Parents' views on Social Insurance Office information about parental insurance]. *Socialförsäkringsrapport* 2010: 3.

Haas, L. (1992). *Equal parenthood and social*. Albany, NY: SUNY Press.

Haas, L., Allard, K., & Hwang, C. P. (2002). The impact of organizational culture on men's use of parental leave in Sweden. *Community, Work & Family, 5* (3), 319–342.

Haas, L., & Hwang, C. P. (2000). Programs and policies promoting women's economic equality and men's sharing of childcare in Sweden. In L. Haas, C.P. Hwang, & G. Russell (Eds.), *Organizational change and gender equity* (pp. 133–161). Thousand Oaks, CA: Sage.

Haas, L., & Hwang, C. P. (2007). Gender and organizational culture. *Gender & Society, 21* (1), 52–79.

Haas, L., & Hwang, C. P. (2008). The impact of taking parental leave on fathers' participation in childcare and relationships with children. *Community, Work & Family, 11*(1), 85–104.

Haas, L., & Hwang. C. P. (2009). Is fatherhood becoming more visible at work? Trends incorporate support for fathers taking parental leave in Sweden. *Fathering, 7*(3), 303–321.

Haas, L., & Rostgaard, T. (2011). Fathers' rights to paid parental leave in the Nordic countries. *Community, Work & Family 14* (20), 179–197.

Haataja, A. (2009). *Fathers' use of paternity and parental leave in the Nordic countries.* [Online working papers 2/2009]. Helsinki, Finland: The Social Insurance Institution of Finland.

Haataja, A., & Nyberg, A. (2006). Diverging paths? In A. Ellingsaeter & A. Leira (Eds.), *Politicising parenthood in Scandinavia* (pp. 217–240). Bristol, UK: Policy Press.

Hausmann, R., Tyson, L., & Zahidi, S. (2010). *The global gender gap report.* Geneva, Switzerland: World Economic Forum. Retrieved from www3.weforum.org.

Hwang, C. P. (1986). Behavior of primary and secondary caretaking fathers in relation to mothers' presence. *Developmental Psychology, 22* (6), 749–751.

ILO [International Labour Organisation]. (2010). *Key indicators of the labour market.* Retrieved from www.kilm.ilo.org.

Johansson, E.-A. (2010). *The effect of own and spousal parental leave on earnings.* [IFAU Working Paper 2010: 4]. Uppsala, Sweden: Institute for Labor Market Policy Evaluation (IFAU).

Johansson, T., & Klinth, R. (2007). Caring fathers. *Men and Masculinities, 11* (1), 42–62.

Josefsson, J.(2007). Uppdelning av föräldraledighet [Division of parental leave]. *Working Papers in Social Insurance* 2007: 2.

Kitterød, R., & Kjeldstad, R. (2003). A new father's role? *Economic Survey* 1/ 2003. Retrieved from www.ssb.no/english/subjects/08/05/10/es/200301/kittterod.pdf

Kitterød, R., & Pettersen, S. (2006). Making up for mothers' employed working hours? *Work, Employment and Society, 20* (3),473–492.

Klinth, R. (2002). *Göra pappa med barn* [Making men into fathers]. Umeå, Sweden: Boréa.

Lamb, M., Frodi, A., Frodi, M., & Hwang, C. P. (1982). Characteristics of maternal and paternal behavior in traditional and non-traditional Swedish families. *International Journal of Behavioral Development, 5,* 131–141.

Lamb, M., Frodi, A., Hwang, C. P., Frodi, M., & Steinberg, J. (1982). Mother– and father–infant interaction involving playing and holding in traditional and non-traditional Swedish families. *Developmental Psychology, 19*, 215–222.

Lamb, M., Hwang, C.P., Broberg, A., Bookstein, F., Hult, G., & Frodi, M. (1988). The determinants of paternal involvement in primiparous Swedish families. *International Journal of Behavioral Development, 11*, 433–449.

Lammi-Taskula, J. (2006). Nordic men on parental leave. In A. Ellingsaeter & A. Leira (Eds.), *Politicising parenthood in Scandinavia* (pp. 79–100). Bristol, UK: Policy Press.

Lappegård, T. (2008a). Changing the gender balance in caring: Fatherhood and the division of parental leave in Norway. *Population Research and Policy Review, 27* (2), 139–159.

Lappegård, T. (2008b). *Couples' parental leave practices*. [Discussion Paper No. 561] . Oslo, Norway: Statistics Norway Research Department. Retrieved from http://www.ssb.no.

Leira, A. (2006). Parenthood change and policy reform in Scandinavia. In A. Ellingsaeter & A. Leira (Eds.), *Politicising parenthood in Scandinavia* (pp. 27–52). Bristol, UK: Policy Press.

Lewis, J. (2009). *Work–family balance, gender and policy*. Cheltenham, UK: Edward Elgar.

Livingston, G., & Cohn, D. (2010). *The new demography of American motherhood*. Pew Research Center. Retrieved from www.pewsocialtrends.org

Lundin, D., Mörk, E., & Öckert, B. (2008). How far can reduced childcare prices push female labour supply? *Labour Economics, 15* (4), 647–659.

Lundqvist, Å. (2011). *Family policy paradoxes*. Bristol, UK: Policy Press.

Låftman, S., & Ostberg, V. (2004). Barn och ungdomars sociala relationer ochpsykiska välbefinnande [Children's and youth's social relations and psychological well-being]. In M. Bygren, M. Gähler, & M. Nermo (Eds.), *Familj och arbete* [Family and work] (pp. 56–89). Stockholm, Sweden: SNS Förlag.

Melby, K., Ravn, A.-B., & Wetterberg, C. (2009). A Nordic model of gender equality? In K. Melby, A.-B. Ravn & C. Wetterberg (Eds.), *Gender equality and welfare politics in Scandinavia* (pp. 1–26). Bristol, UK: Policy Press.

Moss, P., & Deven, F. (2010). Country notes 2010: Overview. In P. Moss (Ed.), *International review of leave policies and related research 2010* (pp. 20–41). [Employment Relations Research Series No. 115]. London, UK: UK Department for Business, Innovation and Skills.

National Center for Health Statistics. (2009). *Changing patterns of nonmarital childbearing in the United States*. [NCHS Data Brief. No. 18]. Accessible at www.cdc.gov/nchs

Naz, G. (2010). Usage of parental leave by fathers in Norway. *International Journal of Sociology 30* (5/6), 313–325.

Nilsson, K., & Strandh, M. (2009). Skilsmässor och separationer [Divorces and separations]. *Sociologisk Forskning* [Sociological Research], *46* (3), 19–36.

Nordic Council of Ministers. (2011). The Nordic region. Accessible at www.norden.org

OECD [Organisation for Economic Cooperation and Development]. (2010a).

Quality of life: Income inequality and poverty. Accessible at oecd-library.org/ factbook-2010

OECD. (2010b). *Family database: Country snapshots.* Accessible at www.oecd.org

OECD. (2010c). *Gender brief.* Retrieved from www.oecd.org/dataoecd/23/31/ 44720649.pdf

Office for National Statistics. (2011). *Average age at first marriage.* Retrieved from www. statistics.gov.uk

Oláh, L. (2001). Policy changes and family stability. *International Journal of Law, Policy and the Family, 15,* 118–134.

Premberg, Å., Hellström, A-L., & Berg, M. (2008). Experiences from the first year as father. *Scandinavian Journal of Caring Sciences, 22,* 56–63.

Rege, M., & Solli, I. (2010, July). *The impact of parental leave on long-term father involvement.* [CESIfo Working Paper No. 3130]. Stavanger, Norway: University of Stavanger. Retrieved from http://ideas.repec.org/p/ces/ceswps/_3130. html

Reneflot, A. (2009). Do married and cohabiting fathers differ in their commitment to fathering? *Advances in Life Course Research, 14* (4), 162–170.

Roman, C. (2009). Academic discourse, social policy and the construction of new families. In K. Melby, A.-B. Ravn, & C. Wetterberg (Eds.), *Gender equality and welfare politics in Scandinavia* (pp. 101–118). Bristol, UK: Policy Press.

Rostgaard, T. (2010). Country note: Denmark. In P. Moss (Ed.), *International review of leave policies and related research 2010* (pp. 88–95). [Employment Relations Research Series No. 115]. London, UK: UK Department for Business, Innovation and Skills.

Rønsen, M., & Skrede, K. (2006). Nordic fertility patterns. In A. Ellingsaeter & A. Leira (Eds.), *Politicising parenthood in Scandinavia* (pp. 53–78). Bristol, UK: Policy Press.

Sayer, L., & Gornick, J. (2011). Cross-national variation in the influence of employment hours on child care time. *European Sociological Review, 27* (3), 1–22.

SCB [Statistiska Centralbyrån]. (2005). *Statistiska meddlanden migration* [Statistical information on migration]. Retrieved from www.scb.se

SCB. (2010). *På tal om kvinnor och män 2010.* Retrieved from www.scb.se

SOU [Statens offentligar utredningar]. (1978). *Föräldraförsäkringen* [Parental insurance]. Rapport #39. Stockholm, Sweden: Gotab.

Statistics Denmark. (2010). *Statbank Denmark.* Retrieved from www.statbank.dk/ statbank5

Statistics Norway. (2008). *Statistical analyses, Immigration and immigrants 2008.* Retrieved from www.ssb.no

Statistics Norway. (2010). *Women and men in Norway.* Retrieved from http://www. ssb.no

Sullivan, O., Coltrane, S., Mcannally, & Altintas, E. (2009). Father-friendly policies and time-use data in a cross-national context. *The Annals of the American Academy of Political and Social Science, 624,* 214–233.

Thomas, J., & Hildingsson, I. (2009). Who's bathing the baby? The division of domestic labour in Sweden. *Journal of Family Studies, 15,* 139–152.

U.N. (United Nations) (2010). *Marriage and divorce.* Accessible at http://unstats. un.org

U.S. Census Bureau. (2011a). *Marital status.* Retrieved from www.factfinder.census.gov

U.S. Census Bureau. (2011b). *Median age at first marriage for men.* Retrieved from www.factfinder.census.gov

Valdimarsdottir, F. (2006). *Nordic experiences with parental leave and its impact one-quality between women and men.* [TemaNord 2006: 531]. Copenhagen, Denmark: Nordic Council of Ministers.

Westerlund L., Lindblad J., & Larsson M., (2005). *Föräldraledighet och arbetstid* [Parental leave and work hours]. Stockholm, Sweden: Lands organisation en i Sverige.

Wiik, K., Bernhardt, E., & Noack, T. (2009). A study of commitment and relationship quality in Sweden and Norway. *Journal of Marriage & Family, 71,* 465–477.

Chapter Fourteen

Fatherhood and Fathering Research in the UK

Cultural Change and Diversity

Charlie Lewis
Lancaster University, Lancaster, UK

Case Story: David's Efforts to 'Become' a Father

As a 22-year-old medical student, David suddenly found that his girlfriend was pregnant and wanted to keep the baby. She was three years his senior and already in a steady job, while he was accruing debts as his studies continued. He moved in with her and tried to keep his studies going while caring for her and the home, and then also the baby. He could not combine all these tasks successfully, particularly because his partner needed to go back to work in order for the family to maintain an income and pay their bills. David decided to suspend his studies for a year or so, and then his partner became pregnant for the second time. David now found himself caring for two young children. He loved the boys and even enjoyed the daily routine, but he missed the intellectual stimulation of his training and found caregiving to be very socially isolating. He invited mothers and their toddlers who attended the same activities as his children to coffee, but they seldom came and never invited him back. He gradually sank into a depression that led to the breakdown of his relationship, and then his partner asked him to leave the house. Because the children were born before 2005 (when fathers in the UK assumed automatic responsibility when their names were on the birth certificate), he found that he had no legal redress and was not even allowed to see the children whom he had cared for with great diligence.

Slowly but surely David recovered from the depression and the pain of not being with his children full-time. His ex-partner "allowed" him to have contact and, at his children's request, they started to spend nights and then half the week at his flat. He trained in computer science (his dream of returning to medicine now a distant and unaffordable memory) and the job helped him furnish his rented flat so that his children enjoyed being there. As of the time of our last meeting, the children were entering their teens and had decided that they'd prefer to live with their dad full-time. Now at age 37, David admitted that for the first time in ten years his life was taking on a meaning that kept feelings of melancholy away, and that he was truly becoming a father.

Cultural/Historical Background of Fathering in the UK

In this chapter, I will show that current British (i.e., England, Wales, Scotland and Northern Ireland comprise the United Kingdom) fathering reflects a plurality of fathering styles. Fathering can only be understood within cultural and individual developmental processes that are shaped by a mixture of historical patterns. In many respects, fathering in the UK has always been diverse and shrouded in contradictions within popular debates about the family. Stereotypes of paternal involvement hold that the aloof Victorian father of the late nineteenth century was surpassed by the father as playmate depicted since the 1920s (see Figure 14.1), followed by gradual progress towards an involved father as the 'new man' of the past generation (see Figure 14.2). These images were inspired by the emergence of positive role models of fathering in parenting books in the 1920s (Walker & Walker, 1928), radio and television in the 1930s, and increasing numbers of parenting magazines since the 1950s, some of which were targeted at fathers.

There are several reasons why these depictions of British history tell only part of a more complex story. For a start, there is evidence to suggest that the Victorian father was much more involved in domestic life than we give him credit for. This was demonstrated very cogently in an oral history of fishing families at the turn of the twentieth century. Trevor Lummis (1982) showed that while these fathers were described as aloof and uninvolved by their children at the start of interviews, they were reported as highly involved at home when daily life at home was described in depth.

There is also good evidence to show that the twentieth century was not simply characterized by the gradual emergence of the 'new man' of the past generation. The century was plagued by economic recessions and two world wars. The Second World War was followed by a polarization of gender roles in which women were barred from positions in the labour force that they had occupied, and images of masculinity militated against involved fatherhood (Bowlby, 1954). Paradoxically, ethnographic reports of family life during this period of supposedly heightened sex differences at home and at work identified that men attended their children's birth at home and engaged in childcare (Bott, 1957; Newson & Newson, 1963).

Figure 14.1 A UK father and daughter in 1924. British men have always participated in rough and tumble play with their young children. The child in this case
(Catherine Lewis) remembered these events with great fondness throughout her
long life. Photo courtesy of Charlie Lewis.

After protracted periods of war and economic restraint acted as a cen-
trifugal force on men's family commitments, either temporary in active
service or permanent through casualty, a slow increase in divorce since the
1920s and rapid rise from the late 1960s imposed increasing restrictions on
paternal involvement (see e.g., Lewis, Papacosta, & Warin, 2002). Ironically
the increase in the divorce rate did not lead to a rapid rise in involved British
fathers competing for residence with their children (in the UK the term

"residence" is used instead of "custody" as it highlights the importance of caring for over ownership of children). Some men reported discovering the complexities of parenthood once they had to care single handedly when their children visit (Smart & Stevens, 2000), but only 10% of men attempted to obtain sole or shared residence (Maclean & Eekelaar, 1995).

In the mid-1970s a small group of Ph.D. students from around the UK got together to talk about an emerging theme in contemporary social scientific debates. They were not the first British scholars to focus on the role of the father (e.g., English & Foster, 1953; Walker & Walker, 1928), but they did make empirical analyses of the father the central focus of research attention. In many respects, the series of seminars and symposia that developed under the banner of the Fatherhood Research Group from 1978 to the mid-1980s reflected a number of themes that illustrated key features of the landscape of contemporary parenting. This group was inspired first by influences on fathering such as the rise in the divorce rate and pressures on men to keep them out of the home, as described above. These forces were accompanied by widespread social changes, especially the emergence of a much more obviously multicultural Britain, following widespread migration of families around the Second World War and of British subjects from many ex-colonies, particularly from the Indian subcontinent and the West Indies in the 1960s. Together these trends set the stage for the next thirty years of research on fathers.

The two architects of the Fatherhood Research Group, Margaret O'Brien and Lorna McKee, were inspired by both the feminism of the 1970s and their own highly involved Irish grandfathers. Their edited volume *The Father Figure* (McKee & O'Brien, 1982) was an attempt to bring together historians, social policy researchers, sociologists and psychologists to grapple with widespread historical misconceptions of paternal involvement which characterize many popular and academic accounts. *The Father Figure* explored why we continue to misrepresent men's domestic involvement and its influence, the experiences of "lone" (now called single parent) fathers, and how British society coped with the notion of fathering within a dramatically changing social policy frame work. A sequel, *Reassessing Fatherhood* (Lewis & O'Brien, 1987), showed that the 'new man' who took equal care of his children was more of an ideal than a reality.

Contexts of Contemporary Fathering: Sub-Cultural Variations, Economic Conditions and Social Policy Issues

Paternal involvement with children in the UK has always been a varied experience. In their seminal study of parenting between 1958 and 1961,

John and Elizabeth Newson (1963) found that some fathers fit the 'traditional' stereotype of being breadwinners, which can be traced back to before the Industrial Revolution (Houlbrooke, 1988), but the large majority did not. Sixty years ago, involved fathers used to care for their young children in the home but almost never in public. Today's fathers are more visible, but many still confine their involvement to the home.

As in other countries, a key driving force in the process of fathers becoming more visible as caregivers of their children has been the nature of men's and women's employment patterns (Lewis, 1993; Presser, 1989), in what Pleck and Masciadrelli (2004) termed a 'culture shift' towards greater male domesticity. British national data show a relative increase in British fathers' participation in childcare compared to mothers' involvement since the 1960s (Fisher, McCulloch, & Gershuny, 1999). This illustrates what Young and Wilmott (1973) termed the "Swing Door" effect of fathers entering the home to care for their children as part of the same process, as their partners entered the labour market in increasing numbers (e.g., David and his partner in the opening Case Story). By the early 1990s, Ferri and Smith (1995) found that fathers looked after their young children while their partners worked, more than any other individual or institution. This was not the result of an emerging ideological commitment, as their analyses suggested that blue collar fathers in the National Child Development Study (NCDS) were more likely than white collar workers to care for their children while their partners worked. Highly involved blue collar workers report reluctance in taking on the role of primary caregiver (Wheelock, 1990). The swing door arrangement allows couples to avoid childcare expenses which could swallow up one parent's earnings. These patterns have been shown to continue over the past twenty years since the NCDS data were collected in 1992. Margaret O'Brien (2005; O'Brien & Shemilt, 2003) has conducted two analyses of data from the Office for National Statistics on the involvement of men in dual earner households. Mothers reportedly still did more childcare (4.5 hours daily compared with 3 for fathers), but O'Brien's longitudinal analyses showed a gradual movement towards greater equality, particularly among parents of preschool children.

In two-parent households, paternal involvement has consistently increased since this type of information was first gathered in 1970s, while a similar increase in family separation has meant that large numbers of fathers do not have regular contact with their children. If we examine the numbers of divorces per 1,000 people, the UK is the divorce capitol of Europe with 3.08 divorces per 1,000 people (see, e.g., www.divorcereform.org). The UK law made divorce relatively simple to obtain in the 1960s, and by 1974 there were sufficient numbers of 'lone parent families' for the government to commission a report on this emergent family form

(Finer, 1974). This report found that 10% of one parent families were headed by a lone father, but in the rest contact between men and their children was variable, with one-third of fathers losing contact at any given time. Such contact depended more on the relationship between the parents and re-partnering than the ages of the children. Subsequent research showed that paternal contact with children must be seen as a continually changing phenomenon, with individual men often renegotiating contact after a period of distance when fathers move out of the family home (Maclean & Eekelaar, 1995).

Since that time there have been successive attempts to incorporate fathers into the post-divorce picture. By law, the Children Act (1989) established parental responsibility (i.e., a duty of care rather than 'custody') following divorce. Further, the Child Support Act (1991) ensured that men continued to support their children financially even if contact was prohibited. From 1974, the advocacy group Families Need Fathers (www.fnf.org.uk) has campaigned for equal parental responsibility, particularly after parents separate. However, the inertia in the system has been hard to overcome, because most men do not seek joint residence after separation. Although 50% of men who seek residence obtain it, public perceptions perpetuate the view that men are discriminated against, based on a few widely publicized cases where men did not gain joint residence. The emergence of radical pressure groups like *Fathers4Justice* in 2001, famous for stunts like hurling purple flour at Prime Minister Blair in the House of Commons in 2004, has placed non-resident fathers and conflicted divorce squarely in the public eye. Yet the establishment of a system of compulsory divorce mediation service in the Family Law Act (1996) was abandoned after a pilot project.

British divorce rates and their influences on families have received constant public attention over the last forty years. Another quiet revolution has been under way concerning the dissolution of formal family ties. These can be demonstrated in the seminal analyses by demographer Kathleen Kiernan on data collected by the Office of National Statistics and the Millennium Cohort Study, a longitudinal database on children born in 2000. In the early 1990s she identified an increase in couples who cohabit and have children (Kiernan & Estaugh, 1993; see also McCrae, 1993). Kiernan's research identified a dramatic trend in that by 2008 over 30% of children were born to cohabiting parents. In addition, the past ten years have witnessed the emergence of a growing minority of fathers who are non-resident at the time of their children's birth (Blackwell & Dawe, 2003). Kiernan found that in addition to the 25% of children born to mothers in cohabiting relationships in 2001, 15% had mothers who did not reside with the fathers (Kiernan & Smith, 2003). Both of these groups tend to be poorly educated (i.e., 28% of 'solo' men and 13% of cohabiting fathers leave school with no qualifications, compared with 8% of married fathers). In addition, Kiernan (2006) showed that cohabitees are predominantly young (37% of solo men and 22% of cohabiting fathers are under the age of 24, compared with 4% of married fathers) but non-resident fathers are older (two-thirds are over 25 when their children are born). Kiernan's research showed that fathers in these previously under-researched samples may go through various experiences, ranging from moving in with the mother (in 24% of households) to weekly contact (Kiernan, 2006). She also found that these family forms are much less common in Asian than White or African-Caribbean families (Holmes & Kiernan, 2010).

Shifts in family forms are not in complete synchrony with changes in the law. For example, the legal status of men who cohabit took parents by surprise. Many had assumed that British common law gave fathers parental rights over their children, when in reality it gave them no such rights. In fact, unless they went through the courts they had no recognised responsibility as parents. An unpublicised amendment to the law gave parental responsibility to all fathers named on the child's birth certificate after December 1, 2003, but they had to attend the registration for their name to be included (in the UK all births, marriages and deaths must be recorded at a local government registry). Such legal idiosyncrasies have consequences that I will discuss below (the laws that refer to above apply to England and Wales; Scotland and Northern Ireland are different jurisdictions).

Partly as a result of the complex changes in British social history over the past half century, it took a long time for fathers to occupy a central place within UK policy debates. Organizations like *Families Need Fathers* served special interest groups, in this case non-resident men struggling for contact with their children. However, a group of journalists, inspired by Adrienne Burgess' (1997) *Fatherhood Reclaimed*, set up a pressure group called *Fathers Direct* in 1999 (renamed the *Fatherhood Institute* in 2008). This group has been very successful at lobbying members of Parliament for family legislation to consider the role played by men within and beyond households in the care and development of their children. It emerged with the Labour administration (1997–2010) whose document *Supporting Families* in 1998 was dedicated in part to ensure that all family members, including fathers, received sufficient support to offset social division (see Scourfield, 2001).

The 1997–2010 Labour government's policy to reduce 'social exclusion,' the increasing numbers of population groups who did not have the means to participate in wider economic activities, included the establishment of the *National Family and Parenting Institute*. The Employment Act (2003) established two-week paid statutory paternity leave for all men irrespective of their occupations (see Figure 14.2). This family policy was

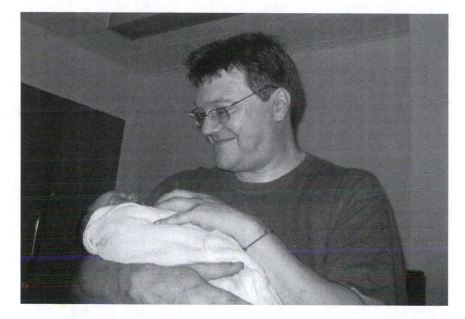

Figure 14.2 A contemporary father with his 1-hour-old infant (Catherine Lewis). British men are increasingly involved in child care even when their infants are young, partly as a result of the rise of paternity leave since 2003. Photo courtesy of Charlie Lewis.

spearheaded by the Sure Start programme, aimed at supporting families in the most deprived areas. Sure Start involved fathers and was targeted particularly at 'fragile families' with cohabitation and sometimes absent fathers. The current Conservative–Liberal coalition (2010–2015) is, as I write, reviewing many of these family-friendly policies with the aim of cutting budgets to reduce the national debt while still in theory protecting the family.

Many British fathers continue to work much longer hours than their counterparts, especially in northern Europe. More than 33% are regularly engaged in paid employment for more than 48 hours per week and 12% continue to work for over 60 hours. There are signs of a slight reduction in the numbers of men working such long hours (CIPD, 2003). However, most couples respond to the dilemmas of childcare and economic survival with fathers working longer hours than before the children were born and mothers returning to at least part-time work while the children are young. The Office for National Statistics (ONS, 2008) reports that 57% of women with children under the age of five are now employed, and this figure is 78% when children are in secondary school. Overall 38% of mothers work part-time. These figures compare with 90% of men who are employed regardless of the age of the child, with only 4% working part-time. More men than their partners want to spend more time looking after their children, compared with the past (Yaxley, Vintner, & Young, 2005). One-third of British fathers do not take paternity leave, with most claiming that their work commitments do not allow them to do so (Ellison, Barker, & Kulasuriya, 2009). Ellison et al.'s large scale survey suggests that contemporary British fathers are torn between the needs to provide and to fulfil the desire to care for their young children, a dilemma which also faces fathers described in numerous other societies described in this volume.

In conclusion, this review of patterns of British fathering suggests that while there has been a continuing gradual increase in paternal involvement in two-parent households, this trend has to be balanced by an increasing marginalization of some men, given some mothers' attempts to establish a household as single parents or following parental separation.

Research on Fathers in the UK

British research over the past 10–20 years tends to reflect the public debates and policy shifts described above. There has been a concerted attempt in UK research over the past decade to consider new ways of studying fathers. In keeping with the Fatherhood Research Group in the 1970s, a continuing wave of small-scale studies has attempted to get to grips with the complexity and diversity of fathering in the UK. The remainder of the chapter describes this initiative, since this is the research that has received policy-orientated funding. Recently, a small group of researchers has capitalized upon a unique set of longitudinal data bases to be able to tease apart causal influences on fathers. We will examine each of these research strands.

Research methods

The recent wave of research has witnessed a dramatic diversification of methods used in the study of fathering. Two approaches have a particular British flavour to them. The first concerns a growing number of investigations of children's perspectives on fathering. Over the past fifteen years, a series of studies has examined the perspectives of young children (e.g., Morrow, 1998), teenagers (e.g., Gilles, Ribbens McCarthy, & Holland, 2001; Langford, Lewis, Solomon, & Warin, 2001) and minors following parental separation, re-partnering and step family creation (Dunn, Cheng, O'Connor, & Bridges, 2004; Smith, Robertson, Dixon, Quigley, & Whitehead, 2001).

While these studies tend to involve sensitive interviews or even focus groups, some use more experimental techniques. Sturgess, Dunn, and Davies (2001) devised an interesting means of exploring children's perspectives on the effects of family division and re-partnering. In the sample of 258 children aged 4–7 years, 192 had parents who separated, divorced, and/or formed step- or blended-households. Children were asked to place all of their family members within five concentric circles on a piece of paper, using a method called the Four Field Map. They were shown an X in the center of the inside circle and told that (1) this X represented themselves; (2) the inner circles represented 'close' relationships; (3) the two outer circles indicated relationships that were 'not close.' The respondents seemed to grasp the aim of this exercise, and as they placed their respective kin members with care and attention some interesting patterns emerged. For example, in reconstituted families only 30% of the children put stepfathers in the inner two circles, but 62% of them placed their non-resident biological fathers there instead. This was comparable to the 67% of children who lived with their biological fathers. Not only did this suggest that biological fathers retained a closeness with their children after a stepfather enters the household, but it also showed how even elementary school-aged children can be very informative participants in research on the nature and closeness of complex contemporary families.

A second strand of research is particular in its orientation. Sociologist David Morgan continues in retirement to exert a key influence on how British social scientists conceive of 'the family.' He has emphasized the importance of conceptualising it not as a static institution with fixed roles and relationships, but rather as a continually changing process of shifting relationships across a number of dynamics (e.g., Morgan, 1998). He termed this approach 'doing the family' and his thinking has stimulated much research. For example, one recent study (Lee, 2008) looked at changing family processes and forms, examining the 2,600 respondents who have taken part in the British Household Panel Survey (BHPS) over the past twenty years. This analysis confirmed Kiernan's earlier analyses of other data bases that men are far less likely to live continuously with their children in British households now than they were in the past (83% of those born in 1900–1939, compared with 63% of those born in 1960–1979). However, the picture is more complicated than this. Lee's analysis of the BHPS reveals that men (and women) may go through a range of pathway shifts through their lives as partners and parents. She charted the nature of transitions in ways like this:

$$NR \longrightarrow BIO \longrightarrow NR \longrightarrow STEP \longrightarrow DUAL$$

This pathway depicts a man who becomes a father but does not at first live with the mother of his first child or children (NR). After a period of living with his child[ren] (BIO), he leaves the household (NR), becomes a step-father by cohabiting with another mother (STEP) and then becomes a bio-logical father again with a new partner (DUAL). According to Lee (2008), 37% of men can be seen to follow this sequence. Lee identified 81 differ-ent pathways in the BHPS, including the one shown above, indicating just how complex are many contemporary fathers' "careers" as parents. Therefore, when we take Morgan's idea of 'doing the family' we must not think about 'the family' in a solitary two-parent residential household, because many men and women may have multiple relationships across several households and these are all in a state of perpetual change and negotiation.

Understanding fatherhood

The methodological advances of Sturgess et al. and Lee formed part of a wider movement to grasp the theoretical complexity of fatherhood. Over the past decade, there have been concerted joint efforts across the British social science community to grapple with the meaning and implications of the increasing complexity of family forms, within policy debates and with regard to shifts in fathers' legal statuses (e.g., Dermott, 2008; Featherstone, 2009; Smart & Neale, 1999). This work has been influenced by the grow-ing visibility of men's groups, notably *Fathers4Justice* and the embarrass-ment its actions have caused the government since its inception in 2001, for example, scaling the Queen's Buckingham Palace residence. However, it also reflects a new feminist view of parenting that is consistent with the perspective taken within the fatherhood research group thirty years ago (see especially the chapter by Martin Richards in McKee & O'Brien, 1982). Dramatic increases in cohabitation, same-sex parenting, and both divorce and cohabitation breakdown have complicated existing family forms. If we add to these factors issues to do with paternity in assisted reproduc-tion, then it is apparent that traditional analysis of the biological, married father holding an authority over his child and displaying this through his detached masculinity (man as provider rather than caregiver) has become outdated if indeed such a prototype ever existed.

Richard Collier (e.g., 1995, 2009; Collier & Sheldon, 2008) has per-haps done more than any other contemporary British socio-legal theorist to reveal just how fragmented contemporary definitions of fathers have become. It is not the case that a legal paternal relationship to the child is established through a man's marriage to her or his mother. With assisted reproduction, there are different statuses accorded to the donor of sperm and the man who cares for the child. Increasing attention to the donor reflects what Collier (2009) terms "the geneticisation of fatherhood." A direct biological relationship between father and child establishes new responsibilities but also blurs traditional assumptions about the primacy of the mother's role. In a similar vein, Draper and Ives (2009) focus on the tension between 'social' and 'biological' fatherhood, reflecting upon the bioethical issues of sperm donation and the increase in paternity testing in the UK.

Collier's second area of interest concerns the legal issues involved in allowing or disallowing men to develop and maintain a relationship with their children. Not only are there issues of establishing paternity, but the law is often called upon to identify parental responsibility and residence or contact if men separate from their partners. In interpreting all these issues, Collier and his colleagues suggest that the processes initiated by policy makers, legislators and judges have a profound influence on the parental role and formal equality between men and women as parents:

> The symbolic power of law in relation to fatherhood, it is important to remember, has been explicitly recognised by the courts in recent developments in case law around the allocation of Parental Responsibility … where we find an acceptance in law of the view that the legal arena is an understandable focus for political frustration and gender equality claims. In relation to case law around Parental Responsibility Orders and Shared Residence under the Children Act 1989, for example, judicial statements have been made with regard to how the allocation of Parental Responsibility has an important symbolic element, a status that a father might understandably, and reasonably, seek to obtain.
>
> (Collier, 2009, p. 362)

As Collier (2010) and others (e.g., Featherstone, 2009) point out, displays of anger by men and a sense of loss at the separation from their children, have forced various branches of the law fairly rapidly to question traditional images of masculinity in terms of detached rationality and autonomy (two 'traditional' stereotypes attached to the roles of men). This might not seem obvious at first glance as only 10% of separated parents in the UK (about 140,000 per year involving children) go to court to resolve disputes over contact (Blackwell & Dawe, 2003). However, recent research shows that 10% of men in the UK now share residence (in the U.S., 'custody') of their children (Peacey & Hunt, 2008). Government-sponsored research has identified that issues concerning contact between non-resident parents and their children continue to be highly distressing for all parties, irrespective of whether the courts become involved, and perhaps more if there is shared residence. One recent assessment has suggested that 50/50 shared residence is too problematic for children (Harris-Short, 2010). Post-separation tension is perhaps even greater after 'cohabitation breakdown' where the child was born before 2003 (as in the Case Story of David), or if the father's name is not on the birth certificate (Lewis et al., 2002), since the father has no parental responsibility and therefore no automatic contact rights.

Theoretical analyses of the issues raised by Collier have tended to draw on an American model, Allen and Hawkins' (1999) 'maternal gate keeping' hypothesis, i.e., mothers play an important role in either facilitating or preventing paternal involvement. Dunn (2006) suggested that maternal gate keeping is central to our understanding of fathering and its effects, and Liz Trinder (2008) has argued that the hypotheses fits post-separation fathering well, in that most men have to negotiate involvement via their ex-partner. However, a long standing tradition of research has explored how parental responsibilities are negotiated using 'explanatory' demonstrations by the mother (Backett, 1982), which are copied by the father. Our recent interviews with parents of young children suggests that both mothers and fathers create and maintain the 'gates' (Zacharostilianakis-Roussou, 2010; Zacharostilianakis-Roussou & Lewis, 2012), because both parents construct the role of the mother as the 'gatekeeper' and the father as the 'helper' or secondary parent. Nevertheless, we must also remember that the hallmark of paternal roles (as shown in most of the chapters in this volume) has long been the individual variations between men in their involvement (Lewis, 1986; Newson & Newson, 1963). As Collier (2009, p. 368) suggested, 'Public policies based on outmoded stereotypes of both sexes are highly unlikely to address the real problems that parents can face in dealing with divorce and separation. Indeed, they are more likely to create barriers to communication if informed by increasingly outdated gendered assumptions about the lives of both women and men.'

Subcultural Variations in UK Fathering

Ethnicity and fathering

From the analyses described above it would be difficult to identify what normative paternal behavior is in 'ordinary families' in the UK. Fathering is particularly diverse when we take into account: (1) variations in patterns of activity over the life course (both children's needs and paternal availability vary); (2) unique life circumstances like separation and divorce which usually affect individuals' commitment to parenting, especially in the short term; and (3) societal shifts like the rapid increase in paternal involvement described by O'Brien and Shemilt (2003). Secular changes

need to be taken into consideration because they may reflect the temporary reactions of parents to outside forces like the recent worldwide recession, rather than a change in the nature of parents' roles.

Britain has always been multi-cultural, but over the past fifty years it
has witnessed an unprecedented immigration of Commonwealth families,
mainly from the West Indies (see Chapter 9, this volume) and the Indian
sub-continent (India, Pakistan and Bangladesh; see Chapters 3 and 5, this
volume) in the 1960s and 1970s. More recently there have been equally
large movements of population from within the European Union, particularly from the new Eastern European members, who are granted a right
to abode in other EU countries without having to assume British nationality. Such migration patterns have added to the diversity of patterns
identified in British ethnographies of the 1950s (e.g., Bott, 1957; Young &
Wilmott, 1957). Most of these new groups are 'traditional' in that they are
less likely to cohabit or engage in non-residential parenting (Goodman &
Greaves, 2010).

Given the massive migration in and out (particularly British nationals
emigrating to the New World and immigrants migrating back to Eastern
Europe) of the UK over the past half century, I would have expected copi-
ous research on patterns of fathering in different UK ethnic groups. Such
research would be particularly interesting because some groups, especially those originally from Southern Asia, tend to have more children
at a time when other communities are experiencing low fertility rates
(O'Brien, 2005). However, there has been more public debate about these
groups than research. Initial research suggested that Asian British fathers
appeared to fit the traditional stereotype, with a greater onus on men to
provide for their families (Warin, Solomon, Lewis, & Langford, 1999).
However, more detailed research has recently shown that parenting styles
in these communities are more complicated than this.

Salway, Chowbey, and Clarke (2009) compared fathers in four South
Asian groups living in the UK, to explore possible variations by religion
and culture: Bangladeshi Muslims, Pakistani Muslims, Gujarati Hindus
and Punjabi Sikhs. They examined the interaction between cultural, religious, social and economic influences on paternal involvement and men's
experiences. On some issues culture appeared to be important. For example, the four groups echoed the respondents in Warin et al.'s (1999) study
that economic provision is a high priority in the role of the father, but
two groups (Punjabi Sikh and Gujarati Hindu) also perceived this as an
integral part of mothering. Salway et al. found that men in all four groups
identified interaction with and care for their children as being central to
fathering, and explicitly rejected the stereotype of a 'typical (South) Asian
father' as a distant economic provider. Where the mother was employed,
men were more active in childcare (particularly among Gujarati Hindu

and Punjabi Sikh families), even though they felt that this was not sanctioned by members of their community. While these groups had a greater commitment to family obligations across national boundaries, Salway et al. (2009, p. 7) concluded: "These findings highlight the great family diversity that exists within ethnic 'groups'. Asian fathers also have much in common with dads from other UK ethnic groups, including white fathers. There is therefore a need to challenge the 'othering' and homogenising of minority ethnic fathers that can occur through the design of services and the attitudes of practitioners." Sulway et al.'s study showed that we must be careful not to assume general cultural differences (i.e., between 'Asian' and 'White' fathers) without considering other possible influences. Even where differences between ethnic groups are found, these are complexly influenced by a range of factors, including the child's gender and fathers' residence, as we see in African Caribbean families in the UK (Guishard, 2002; see also Roopnarine, Ch. 9, this volume).

Current Issues in Fathering Research

How does British fathering vary? Men's involvement ranges from those who have no contact with their children to 'role-reversed' men who are primary caregivers to their children while their partners are the main breadwinners, and to fathers who obtain residence following separation. In this section I outline the most visible recent and current projects that examine the nature of fathering in the UK and were not mentioned elsewhere in the chapter.

Teenage fathers

In the 1980s this group received much scrutiny in the U.S. (e.g., Lamb & Elster, 1986), but an attempt to study them in the UK was less successful (Lalonde, 1988). However, a more recent study by Quinton and Pollock (2002) in Bristol found the same sorts of variations as we saw in older fathers (Lewis, 1986). They identified that a large majority (60%) of young men became highly involved as fathers while the rest (37%) had no contact at the time of the interviews. Contact was predicted by the relationship between the expectant mother and father during pregnancy. Perhaps surprisingly, the new extended family (the mother's and father's families of origin) did not appear to influence the new father's involvement.

Fathers of children with intellectual disabilities

In the UK, a recent national survey conducted by a support group concluded that having a child with an intellectual disability in the family places pressure on fathers and on other family members. The fathers reported increased problems in terms of negotiating a work/life balance, because of the increased demands of parenting. They also reported heightened rates of physical and mental illness (Towers, 2009).

Fathers and substance misuse

Drug and alcohol abuse are often cited as factors that lead to family break up and continue to influence fathers' co-residence or contact with their children (e.g., Lewis et al., 2002; see also the Chapter 12 discussion of Russian fathers' alcohol abuse, this volume). Anne Whittaker's (2008) research and therapeutic work is premised on the fact that the research of drug abusing fathers is minimal compared to that on mothers, yet there are twice as many men who abuse drugs. According to the statistics of the Advisory Council on the Misuse of Drugs (2003), 240,800 children in the UK have drug-abusing fathers, whereas 117,900 have such mothers. Whittaker reveals that fathers who abuse drugs are most likely to experience other problems, including economic privation, unemployment and health issues. As a result, these fathers often find it difficult to remain actively involved parents. At the same time, for health professionals who are dedicated to preserving the parenting relationship, it is a major problem both to identify and locate these fathers and to ensure that the father–child contact is mutually beneficial.

Fathers in prison

Incarcerated men have attracted increasing international scrutiny (Boswell & Wedge, 2002). In the UK the prison population has expanded (Nicholls, 2006) and studies show that large proportions of this group are fathers (Dennison, 2003; Katz, 2002). This growing new literature has established that fathers' relationships with their children are stage managed or prevented by the mothers of their children (Clarke et al., 2005), and social organizations now have in place programmes to maintain and develop paternal contact and responsibility where appropriate (Katz & Stockdale, 2007).

Fathers and family service providers

Given that a main focus on British fathers has been funded by organizations with the social policy focus outlined earlier, there have been active attempts to facilitate paternal involvement over the past 30 years and (as also described above) particularly over the past 14 years. Policies for preschool children like Sure Start have been much less successful in reaching and helping fathers than more general invitations intended to increase social cohesion, e.g., programs for both parents to become involved in mainstream education. Two reports (Ghate, Shaw, & Hazel, 2000; Lloyd,

O'Brien, & Lewis, 2003) discerned that government attention to fathers of preschoolers did not seem to result in the development of many father-friendly services. Lloyd et al. (2003) found that Sure Start was only successful in including men in the few centres where the programme directors were motivated and employed a dedicated "fathers' worker" to facilitate father-related activities. There were also some beacons of excellence with many men becoming involved at various levels. Otherwise, the preschool setting remains a hostile environment for many British men. About 40% of fathers have some general contact with preschools (not including Sure Start), albeit for very short periods as in dropping their children off in the morning. Men do not participate in activities and often report that they do not become involved because male workers are absent from preschools; i.e., only 2% of employees at day nurseries and 1% at playgroups in Sure Start are male (Kahn, 2005). Fathers report that such services are run by women for women, and tend to focus on men's problems rather than the positive aspects of men's parenting skills (Cavanaugh & Smith, 2005).

As British children proceed through the school system fathers become increasingly involved (e.g., Scott, 2004). Goldman (2005) reported that men's involvement with children was predicted most strongly by their partner's level of involvement. Other significant predictors included a more harmonious mother–father relationship, better educational qualifications of the father or mother, whether the father was involved from early in the child's life, and when their child is in primary rather than secondary school. Factors such as whether their child's school is welcoming to parents and how well the child also were predictive of paternal involvement, in Goldman's study.

If we turn to what men do in school with their children, research has found little difference between mothers' and fathers' attendance or in terms of reading with children, helping with homework, helping out in classrooms, or feeling involved with schooling, once the parents' work hours are taken into account (Peters, Seeds, Goldstein, & Coleman, 2008). In our own research we found that men report coming into their own when children need their help with science, math and technology (Warin et al., 1999).

Hard to reach fathers

Several other groups of men are starting to appear on the research radar. For example, over the past twenty years there has been much written about mothers who were 'persuaded' to give up their children for adoption in the 1960s for the sake of the children's development. A trickle of studies has recently tapped the experiences of birth fathers (e.g., Triseliotis, Feast, & Kyle, 2005). Gary Clapton (2007) found that, even up to thirty years after the adoptions, his 50-year-old respondents reported the same feelings as mothers and reported feelings of loss and depression years later. A current study is investigating the children in these families to explore children's feelings towards their missing biological fathers (Hughes, Frosh & Seu, 2012).

Disentangling the Influences of Fathers

A smaller fathering literature in the UK is less inter-disciplinary and based mainly on experimental and observational research in the fields of developmental psychology and psychiatry. This group of researchers explores the nature of fathering not only as an inter-actional or relational style but also for its impact on the child's development. This research forms part of an international exploration of the dimensions of paternal styles (Lamb & Lewis, 2010). There are three areas of current British research on this topic.

First there is a research group which seeks to understand the nature of and influences on paternal styles, and covers the whole of development. For example, Malmberg et al. (2007) examined changes in parent–infant (10–12 months) play segments. They found that mothers displayed more positive affect in their interactions, but there was no concomitant reciprocity in their babies, who responded equally to both parents. This research uses multilevel statistical models to tease apart the relative influences of a range of factors on the interactions. To explore these influences, the team compared families where the man performed the main role of provider with those where he was the main caregiver to the children. They found that primary caregiver fathers used more positive affect with their babies, just like mothers, suggesting that parental interactional styles are determined by the time parents spend with their infant rather than biological differences between men and women. Even when they perform a secondary role, men may make a special contribution. Analyses of the Avon Longitudinal Study of Parents and Children study (ALSPAC) showed that infants' developmental progress was delayed when mothers returned to work before babies were 18 months old, except when the fathers were highly involved in childcare (Gregg & Washbrook, 2003).

These patterns continued over the first eighteen years of parenting. First, there seem from the research to be determinants of variations in parenting. Ferri and Smith's (1995) analysis of the relationship between the nature of parents' occupations and their family life showed that blue collar fathers in the NCDS were more likely than white collar workers to care for their children while their partners worked. According to their recent analyses of parenting, Coldwell, Pike, and Dunn (2006) found that a range of factors predicted paternal involvement with school-age children. For example, the warmth of men's relationships with their children was correlated with the quality of their relationships with the child's mothers. However, it was men's warmth in both blue and white collar families, combined with factors concerning the organization of the home that predicted behavioral outcomes in the children.

A second group is examining the clinical implications of the role of the father in the perinatal period, the effect of his adjustment to parenting, and its long term influences on the child. Using ALSPAC data, Paul Ramchandani and his colleagues have looked specifically at depression in men. They have found that fathers who experienced depression when their babies were 8 weeks old had children, especially sons, who were significantly more likely to display hyperactivity or conduct problems when the children were 3 years old. This correlation held even controlling for paternal and maternal depression, when the child was 3 (Ramchandani et al., 2005). However, this long term prediction was later found also to be related to the father's longer term history of depression. Ramchandani therefore concluded that the length of the man's depression and possibly its seriousness, rather than of the specific effects of postpartum depression on the immediate interactions with the infant, was the probable cause of these long term correlations (Ramchandani et al., 2008). We must not assume that it is only pre- or post-partum depression that has an influence. In the late preschool period, it has also been found that if a father is depressed his children are much more likely to experience problems in their peer relationships and behavior (Dave, Sherr, Senior, & Nazareth, 2008).

A third area of research has examined the possible influences of father–child relations on child development in families where the father had no presenting problem. While this derives from several data bases (e.g., Lewis, Newson, & Newson, 1982), much recent analysis has been conducted using the NCDS. Eirini Flouri's research has shown some concurrent correlations, e.g., British children in the cohort with more involved fathers had higher IQs at 7 years of age (Flouri & Buchanan, 2004). In the long term, Flouri and Buchanan also found a variety of relationships between patterns of father involvement, particularly in adolescence, and later measures of their child's psychosocial adjustment, even when a range of possible mediating factors (parental SES, family structure, maternal involvement, the child's gender and parental mental health) were taken into account. Father involvement described by mothers at age 7 predicted the child's self-reported closeness to the father at age 16, and lower levels of police contact as reported by the child's mother and teacher (Flouri & Buchanan, 2002a). This in turn predicted the children's reported satisfaction with their closest relationships and diminished psychological distress at 33 years (Flouri & Buchanan, 2002b). Teenagers' closeness to mothers at age 16 predicted only marital satisfaction seventeen years later. Flouri's

(2006) more recent work on a sample of 520 teenagers has examined the effects of paternal residence on adjustment. She found that the above concurrent patterns for non-resident fathers did not appear to apply as clearly as those for resident fathers, even when the amount of paternal contact with the child was taken into account.

These studies make a clear contribution to international theoretical and social policy debates on the role of the father. The UK is well placed to contribute to these discussions because its national cohort studies have focused on fathers over the past sixty years (since the 1958 National Child Development Study), and this contribution will continue.

Comparisons with Fathers in Other Societies

In this chapter I have sought to identify what is unique about British research on fathers. Much of the above discussion was about the changing patterns of fathering, and the research matches similar shifts in other industrial cultures. For example, in the U.S. and other industrial countries men who are primary caregivers were shown thirty years ago to interact more like mothers (Field, 1978), and debates about non-resident fathers in the 1990s (Blankenhorn, 1995; Popenoe, 1993) were similar to those in the UK reported here. However, there are distinguishing characteristics of fathering research in the UK, and I have focused on three particular themes. First, Britain is unique in terms of its particular waves of recent historical changes with reference to the roles of fathers. As one of the first cultures to industrialize, and then post World War Two to de-industrialize, British culture witnessed pressures on men to spend most of their working hours in paid work, which has meant that even contemporary family members express a belief in the father as economic provider (Warin et al., 1999). The specific mix of ethnic migration, large amounts of family breakdown and reconstitution, and government policies and legal changes to accommodate such changes, make the nature of this subject particularly complex. As I have shown, British men have always been active in childcare, and their role has increased since young mothers [re-]entered the labour force in large numbers over the past generation. Men's involvement continues to be somewhat private as this reality contrasts with images of the detached British man whose expertise is in economic provision.

Secondly, as a result of these complexities, British research has continued to adopt a multi-disciplinary perspective that is not clearly in evidence on similar countries. I have attempted to show that there is a great amount of British research on fathers, but because of its multi-disciplinary nature it is less visible than research on fathers in the U.S. Thirdly, as a result of our very detailed national data bases, like NCDS and the Millennium Cohort, British research is at the forefront of a move to identify unique positive and negative influences that fathers appear to have on children's long term development (Lamb & Lewis, 2010).

The research shows that men like David, presented in the Case Story at the start of this chapter, depict much that is more representative of contemporary British fathering than the stereotypes of the economic provider or the new man. David's contact with his children was in constant flux. He was highly involved and yet did not receive public recognition for the care which he gave his children, or for the personal sacrifices he made to become a father. While only one-third of UK men do not marry the mother of their children, David is a beacon for the emerging father of the 21st century. His parenting may take place within much looser 'family' relationships, but his commitment to fathering became clear when his children identified him as their primary parent. In most married British families men are highly involved in childcare and in forming deep relationships with their children. But given the continuing stereotypes of masculine and feminine roles, much of this involvement gets air-brushed out of most pictures of contemporary family life.

Summary

Fathering in the UK has been characterized by the variations between individual men at any point in time, shifting historical forces which promote or deny paternal involvement in childcare (notably economic forces and spousal relationships), and individuals' shifting patterns of involvement over the family life course. This chapter focuses on the complexities of the interacting influences on UK fathers. As a reflection of these processes, British fatherhood research makes a distinctive contribution because of its multi-disciplinarity, and its attempts both to chart the complexities of men's changing relationships with their children. Perhaps more importantly, the research also shows how fathering is the product of men's relationships with the mothers of their children and their own commitments to the labor force. Partly as a result, fathers in the UK have been more involved in childcare than many social commentators have given them credit for, and British research shows that men have particular and strong influences on their children's development.

References

Advisory Council on the Misuse of Drugs. (2003). *Hidden harm: Responding to the needs of children of problem drug users.* [The Report of an Inquiry by the Advisory Council on the Misuse of Drugs]. London, UK: The Home Office.

Allen, S. M., & Hawkins, A. J. (1999). Maternal gate keeping: Mothers' beliefs and behaviors that inhibit greater father involvement in family work. *Journal of Marriage and the Family, 61,* 199–212.

Backett, K. C. (1982). *Mothers and fathers: Study of the development and negotiation of parental behaviour*. London, UK: Macmillan.

Blackwell, A., & Dawe, F. (2003). *Non-resident parental contact*. London, UK: Office of National Statistics.

Blankenhorn, D. (1995). *Fatherless America: Confronting our most urgent social problem*. New York, NY: Basic Books.

Boswell, G., & Wedge, P. (2002). *Imprisoned fathers and their children*. London, UK: Jessica Kingsley.

Bott, E. (1957). *Family and social network*. London, UK: Tavistock

Bowlby, J. (1954). *Child care and the growth of love*. Harmondsworth, UK: Penguin.

Burgess, A. (1997). *Fatherhood reclaimed: The making of the modern father*. London, UK: Vermilion.

Cavanaugh, B., & Smith, M. (2005). *Dad's the word: A study of dads in Greater Pilton*. Unpublished ms. Strathclyde University, UK.

CIPD [Chartered Institute Of Personnel And Development]. (2003). *Living to work? Survey report*. London, UK: CIPD. Retrieved from http://www.cipd.co.uk/surveys

Clapton, G. (2007). The experiences and needs of birth fathers in adoption: What we know now and some practice implications. *Practice: A Journal of the British Association of Social Workers, 19*, 61–71.

Clarke, L., O'Brien, M., Day, R., Godwin, H., Connolly, J., & Leeson, T. van (2005). Fathering behind bars in English prisons: Imprisoned fathers' identity and contact with their children. *Fathering, 3*, 221–241.

Coldwell, J., Pike, A., Dunn, J. (2006). Household chaos: Links with parenting and child behaviour. *Journal of Child Psychology and Psychiatry, 47*, 1116–1122.

Collier, R. (1995). *Masculinity, law and the family*. London, UK: Routledge.

Collier, R. (2009). Fathers' rights, gender and welfare: Some questions for family law, *Journal of Social Welfare and Family Law, 31*, 357–371.

Collier, R. (2010). Masculinities, law, and personal life: Towards a new framework for understanding men, law, and gender. *Harvard Journal of Law & Gender, 33*, 431–475

Collier, R., & Sheldon, S. (2008). *Fragmenting fatherhood: A socio-legal study*. Oxford, UK: Hart.

Dave, S., Sherr, L., Senior, R., & Nazareth, I. (2008). Associations between paternal depression and behaviour problems in children of 4–6 years. *European Child & Adolescent Psychiatry, 17*, 306–315.

Dennison, C. (2003). *Parenting education for young fathers in young offender institutions*. Brighton, UK: Trust for the Study of Adolescence.

Dermott, E. (2008). *Intimate fatherhood: A sociological analysis*. London, UK: Routledge.

Draper, H., & Ives, J. (2009). Paternity testing: A poor test of fatherhood. *Journal of Social Welfare & Family Law, 31*, 407–418.

Dunn, J. (2006). Contact with nonresident fathers: Children's and parents' views. In Rt Hon. Lord Justice Thorpe & R. Budden (Eds.) *Durable solutions* (pp. 137–144). Bristol, UK: Family Law/Jordans.

Dunn, J., Cheng, H., O'Connor, T. G., & Bridges, L. (2004). Children's perspectives on their relationships with their non-resident fathers: Influences, outcomes and implications. *Journal of Child Psychology and Psychiatry, 45*, 553–566.

Ellison, G., Barker, A., & Kulasuriya, T. (2009). *Work and care: A study of modern parents*. [Research Report: 15]. Manchester, UK: Equality and Human Rights Commission.

English, O. S., & Foster, C. (1953). *Fathers are parents too*. London, UK: Allen & Unwin.

Featherstone, B. (2009). *Contemporary fathering: theory, policy and practice*. Bristol, UK: Policy Press.

Ferri, E., & Smith, K. (1995). *Parenting in the 1990s*. London, UK: The Family Policy Studies Centre.

Field, T. (1978). Interaction behaviors of primary versus secondary caretaker fathers. *Developmental Psychology, 14*, 183–184.

Finer, M. (1974). *The report of the Royal Commission on one parent families* [Cmd. 5629]. London, UK: HMSO.

Fisher, K., McCulloch, A., & Gershuny, J. (1999). *British fathers and children*. Unpublished html manuscript. Available at www.iser.essex.ac.uk

Flouri, E. (2006). Non-resident fathers' relationships with their secondary school age children: Determinants and children's mental health outcomes, *Journal of Adolescence, 29*, 525–538

Flouri, E., & Buchanan, A. (2002a). Father involvement in childhood and trouble with the police in adolescence: Findings from the 1958 British cohort. *Journal of Interpersonal Violence, 17*, 689–701.

Flouri, E., & Buchanan, A. (2002b). What predicts good relationships with parents in adolescence and partners in adult life: Findings from the 1958 British birth cohort. *Journal of Family Psychology, 16*, 186–198.

Flouri, E., & Buchannan, A. (2004). Early fathers' and mothers' involvement and child's later educational outcomes. *British Journal of Educational Psychology, 74*, 141–153.

Ghate, D., Shaw, C., & Hazel, N. (2000). *Engaging fathers in preventive services: Fathers and family centres*. York, UK: Joseph Rowntree Foundation & York Publishing Services.

Gilles, V., Ribbens McCarthy, J., & Holland, J. (2001). *Pulling together, pulling apart: The family lives of young people*. London, UK: Family Policy Studies Centre.

Goldman, R. (2005). *Fathers' involvement in their children's education*. London, UK: National Family and Parenting Institute.

Goodman, A., & Greaves, E. (2010). *Cohabitation, marriage and child outcomes*. London, UK: Institute for Fiscal Studies. Retrieved from http://www.ifs.org. uk/comms/comm114.pdf

Gregg, P., & Washbrook, E. (2003). *The effects of early maternal employment on child development in the UK*. [CMPO Working Paper Series No 03/070]. University of Bristol, Department of Economics. Retrieved from www.bris.ac.uk/cmpo/ workingpapers/wp70.pdf

Guishard, J. A. (2002). *Beyond father absence: An investigation into black fathering and child outcomes in Britain*. PhD Thesis. University College London.

Harris-Short, S. (2010). Resisting the march towards 50/50 shared residence:

Rights, welfare and equality in post-separation families. *Journal of Social Welfare and Family Law, 32*, 257–274.

Holmes, J., & Kiernan, K. (2010). *Fragile families in the UK: Evidence from the Millennium Cohort Study.* York, UK: Joseph Rowntree Foundation.

Houlbrooke, R. (1988). *English family life, 1576–1716: An anthology from diaries.* Oxford, UK: Oxford University Press.

Hughes, E., Frosh, S., & Seu, B. (2012). *The psychosocial implications on adopted women who have met their birth fathers in adulthood.* Birkbeck, University of London. Manuscript in preparation.

Kahn, T. (2005). *Fathers' involvement in the early years: Findings and research.* Report prepared for the Department of Education and Skills on behalf of the Pre-school Learning Alliance.

Katz, A. (Ed.). (2002). *Parenting under pressure: Voices of prisoners and their families.* Surrey, UK: Young Voice.

Katz, A., & Stockdale, D. (2007). *Young people: Prison to parenthood.* Surrey, UK: Young Voice.

Kiernan, K. (2006). Non-residential fatherhood and child involvement: Evidence from the Millennium Cohort Study. *Journal of Social Policy, 35*, 651–669

Kiernan, K., & Estaugh, V. (1993). *Cohabitation: Extra-marital child bearing and social policy.* London, UK: Family Policy Studies Centre.

Kiernan, K., & Smith, K. (2003). Unmarried parenthood: New insights from the Millennium Cohort Study, *Population Trends, 114*, 23–33.

Lalonde, S. (1988). *Child rearing practices and attitudes of adolescent fathers.* PhD Thesis, Nottingham University, UK.

Lamb, M. E., & Elster, A. B. (1986). *Adolescent fatherhood.* Hillsdale, NJ: Lawrence Erlbaum Associates.

Lamb, M. E., & Lewis, C. (2010). The development and significance of father–child Relationships in two-parent families. In M. E. Lamb (Ed.), *The role of the father in child development* (5th ed.). Chichester, UK: Wiley.

Langford, W., Lewis, C., Solomon, Y., & Warin, J. (2001). *Family understandings: Closeness, authority and independence in families with teenagers.* London, UK: Family Policy Studies Centre.

Lee, K. (2008). *Fragmenting fatherhoods? Fathers, fathering and family change.* PhD thesis. London, UK: City University.

Lewis, C. (1986). *Becoming a father.* Milton Keynes, UK: Open University Press.

Lewis, C. (1993). Mothers' and fathers' roles: Similar or different? [European Commission Report]. *Fathers in Families of Tomorrow* (pp. 87–106). Copenhagen, Denmark: Danish Ministry of Social Affairs.

Lewis, C., Newson, E., & Newson, J. (1982). Participant fatherhood and its relationship with career aspirations and proto delinquency. In N. Beail & J. McGuire (Eds.) *Fathers: Psychological perspectives* (pp. 174–193). London, UK: Junction.

Lewis, C., & O'Brien, M. (Eds.). (1987). *Reassessing fatherhood.* London, UK: Sage.

Lewis, C., Papacosta, A., & Warin, J. (2002). *Cohabitation, separation and fatherhood.* York, UK: York Publishing.

Lloyd, N., O'Brien, M., & Lewis, C. (2003). *Fathers in Sure Start.* [A report for the National Evaluation of Sure Start to the Sure Start Unit]. London, UK: Department for Education and Science.

Lummis, T. (1982). The historical dimension of fatherhood: A case study 1890–1914. In L. McKee & M. O'Brien (Eds.), *The father figure*. London, UK: Tavistock Publications

Maclean, M., & Eekelaar, J. (1995). *The parental obligation*. Oxford, UK: Hart.

Malmberg, L.-E., Stein, A., West, A., Lewis, S., Barnes, J., Leach, P., & Sylva, K. (2007). Parent–infant interaction: A growth model approach. *Infant Behavior & Development, 30*, 615–630.

McKee, L., & O'Brien, M. (Eds.). (1982). *The father figure*. London, UK: Tavistock.

McRae, S. (1993). *Cohabiting mothers: Changing marriage and motherhood?* London, UK: Policy Studies Institute.

Morgan, D. (1998). Risk and family practices: Accounting for change and fluidity in family life. In E. B. Silva & C. Smart (Eds.), *The new family?* (pp. 13–30). London, UK: Sage.

Morrow, V. (1998). *Understanding families: Children's perspectives*. London, UK: National Children's Bureau.

Newson, J., & Newson, E. (1963). *Infant care in an urban community*. London, UK: Allen & Unwin.

Nicholls, R. (2006). *Dads and kids: The inside story. Fathers in prison and their children*. Felixstowe, UK: Ormiston Children & Families Trust

O'Brien, M. (2005). *Shared caring: Bringing fathers into the frame*. Manchester, UK: Equal Opportunities Commission.

O'Brien, M., & Shemilt, I. (2003). *Working fathers: Earning and caring*. [Working paper No 18]. Manchester, UK: Equal Opportunites Commission.

ONS. (2008). Labour Force Survey, Q2, 26.09.2008.

Peacey, V., & Hunt, J. (2008). *Problematic contact after separation and divorce*. London, UK: Nuffield Foundation.

Peters, M., Seeds, K., Goldstein, A., & Coleman, N. (2008). *Parental involvement in children's education 2007*. [Research Report]. London, UK: Department of Children Schools and Families RR034.

Pleck, E. H., & Masciadrelli, B. P. (2004). Paternal involvement by residential fathers: Levels, sources, and consequences. In M. E. Lamb (Ed.), *The role of the father in child development* (4th ed.). Hoboken, NJ: John Wiley & Sons.

Popenoe, D. (1993). American family decline. *Journal of Marriage and the Family, 55*, 527–524.

Presser, H. B. (1989). Can we make time for children? The economy, work schedules, and child care. *Demography, 26*, 523–543.

Quinton, D., & Pollock, L. (2002). *The transition to fatherhood in young men*. Report submitted to the Economic and Social Research Council.

Ramchandani, P., Stein, A., Evans, J., O'Connor, T. G., & the ALSPAC study team. (2005). Paternal Depression in the postnatal period and child development: Aprospective population study. *The Lancet, 365*, 3201–3205.

Ramchandani, P. G., Stein, A., O'Connor, T. G., Heron, J., Murray, L., & Evans, J. (2008). Depression in men in the postnatal period and later child psychopathology: A population cohort study. *Journal of the American Academy of Child and Adolescent Psychiatry, 47*, 390–398.

Salway, S., Chowbey, P., & Clarke, L. (2009). *Understanding the experiences of Asian fathers in Britain.* York, UK: Joseph Rowntree Foundation.

Scott, J. (2004). Family, gender and educational attainment in Britain: A longitudinal study. *Journal of Comparative Family Studies, 35,* 565–589.

Scourfield, J. (2001). Constructing men in child protection work. *Men and Masculinities, 4,* 70–89.

Smart, C., & Neale, B. (1999). *Family fragments.* Cambridge, UK: Polity.

Smart, C., & Stevens, E. (2000). *Cohabitation breakdown: Non-marital separation.* London, UK: Family Policy Studies Centre (and Joseph Rowntree Foundation).

Smith, M., Robertson, J., Dixon, J., Quigley, M., & Whitehead, E. (2001). *A study of step children and step parenting.* London, UK: Department of Health.

Sturgess, W., Dunn, J., & Davies, L. (2001). Young children's perceptions of their relationships with family and friends: Links with family setting and adjustment. *International Journal of Behavioral Development, 25,* 521–529.

Towers, C. (2009). *Recognising fathers: A national survey of fathers who have children with learning disabilities.* Foundation for People with Learning Disabilities. Available at: http://www.learningdisabilities.org.uk/publications

Triseliotis J., Feast, J., & Kyle, F. (2005). *A study of adoption, search and reunion experiences.* London, UK: BAAF.

Trinder, L. (2008). Maternal gate closing and gate opening in post divorce families. *Journal of Family Issues, 29,* 1298–1324.

Walker, K. M., & Walker, E. M. (1928). *On being a father.* London, UK: Cape.

Warin, J., Solomon, Y., Lewis, C., & Langford, W. (1999). *Fathers, work and family life.* London, UK: Family Policy Studies Centre.

Whittaker, A. L. (2008). *The construction of fatherhood within the context of problem drug use.* PhD Thesis, University of Dundee, UK.

Wheelock, J. (1990). *Husbands at home.* London, UK: Routledge.

Yaxley, D., Vintner, L., & Young, V. (2005). *Dads and their babies: Mothers' views.* [Working Paper No. 41]. London, UK: Equal Opportunities Commission.

Young, M., & Wilmott, P. (1957). *Family and kinship in east London.* Harmondsworth, UK: Pelican.

Young, M., & Wilmott, P. (1973). *The symmetrical family.* London, UK: Routledge.

Zacharostilianakis-Roussou, I. (2010). *Paternal involvement within a relational context: Can mothers inhibit paternal involvement in child care?* PhD thesis, Lancaster University, UK.

Zacharostilianakis-Roussou, I., & Lewis, C. (2012). *The maternal gate keeping hypothesis re-examined.* Manuscript in preparation.

Part Six

Australia

Chapter Fifteen

Fathers in Australia
A Contemporary Snapshot

Bruce M. Smyth
Australian National University, Canberra, Australia

Jennifer A. Baxter
Australian Institute of Family Studies, Melbourne, Australia

Richard J. Fletcher
The University of Newcastle, Newcastle, Australia

Lawrence J. Moloney
Australian Institute of Family Studies, Melbourne, Australia

Case Story: Demands and Priorities

During school holidays, Tony (in his early 40s) and his 8-year-old daughter Jess enjoy fishing for trout together in a dinghy on Tumut Ponds, just down from the town where Tony grew up. Tony used to go fishing here with his father and now shares his special place with his daughter. Tony loves spending one-on-one time with Jess. But to do so requires coordination of his paid employment, voluntary work and family time. A complex mosaic of flexible work hours, working from home, part-time work, paid leave, school holiday programs, and mutual child-minding arrangements with other families helps the family juggle the many competing demands of modern life. All of this is further complicated by the fact that Jess's mother recently left her job to return to part-time study. Scrawled notes on the kitchen calendar bear testimony to the family's hectic schedule.

But the schedule collapses when Tony gets called out to fight bushfires. Two years ago he spent weeks travelling interstate fighting the Victorian bushfires. Contributing his skills and experience as a Rural Fire Service volunteer is extremely important to Tony. It also provides him with that archetypal domain of the Australian male – a really big work shed. Jess wants to be a fire fighter too one day, and Tony would like her to become involved in the Rural Fire Service. It encapsulates values that his father passed on to him and that he wants to instil in his daughter: self-reliance, a sense of competence, and community service. It also signifies the ability to distinguish the important things in life – like going fishing together – from the demands of daily life. Tony is a modern Australian father.

Like fathers in most Western countries, Australian fathers are immersed in a rapidly changing social landscape. In this chapter, we provide a contemporary snapshot of fathers in Australia and offer some reflections on the ways in which they might be similar to and differ from fathers in other societies. The somewhat fuzzy nature of this snapshot reflects the emerging though still piecemeal knowledge base about fathers in Australia.

The chapter is in six parts. Part 1 examines some of the ways in which culture, history, geography and climate shape contemporary fathering in Australia. Part 2 offers a brief demographic profile of fathers in Australia, and provides a present-day snapshot of fathers' roles within families. Part 3 examines two key areas of social policy of particular relevance to fathering, while Part 4 briefly explores some important sub-cultural variations. In Part 5, we reflect on some distinctive aspects of fathering in Australia, and Part 6 offers some speculation and concluding comments.

Cultural and Historical Background as It Influences Fathering

Australia is an island continent, with the bulk of its population of around 22 million people living in a small number of Eastern (and South Western) coastal cities separated by great distances. Because of its vast arid interior, Australia has the lowest population density of any continent in the world, with less than three people per square kilometre. It is also a very ethnically diverse nation. Since 1945, more than seven million people from more than 185 countries have immigrated to Australia (Commonwealth of Australia, 2009). In 2006, 44% of Australians were either born overseas or had a parent born overseas (Australian Bureau of Statistics [ABS], 2009a).

Since British settlement began in 1788, non-Indigenous Australian culture has retained strong links to its British founders. This is evidenced by Britain's monarch still being the Head of State, use of the English language and the Westminster system of Government, and the popularity of sports such as cricket and rugby. After World War II, however, the dominant Anglo-Celtic culture was progressively modified by successive waves of European migrants from countries such as Italy, Greece, Malta, Yugoslavia, and Germany. The change was even more pronounced when, following the abolition of the *White Australia Policy* (which restricted immigration by non-Whites) in the early 1970s, Australia opened itself up to large numbers of migrants from Asia, Africa and the Middle East. Globalisation has also brought a range of cultural, political, economic and social impacts from other countries that have become increasingly inter-twined with Australian culture. Australian fathering is not immune from these influences.

On a somewhat different level, it could be argued that the country's climate and geography have also shaped many of the activities tradition-ally associated with fathering in Australia. By virtue of being close to the equator, the northern half of Australia has a tropical climate, while Australia's southern regions are largely temperate. The climate itself sup-ports the many paternal (and maternal) recreational activities with chil-dren that take place outdoors. These include a wide range of water sports,

Figure 15.1 Father (early 40s) and son (15 years) fly a kite together at Pippi Beach, Yamba, New South Wales. Photo courtesy of Ricky Smyth.

ball sports and athletics, as well as camping in what is colloquially called "the great outdoors."

Within the large continent of Australia, families can be considerably mobile. For example, it is common for one member of a family associated with the mining industry to work on a "fly in/fly out" basis. These parents, most often the fathers, may have regular blocks of time with their children but then not see them for two weeks or more. In separated families, around one in four non-resident parents (again mostly fathers) live 500 kilometres (around 300 miles) or more from their children. Many of these separated fathers and their children travel large distances to see each other during school holidays and at other times of the year (Smyth, 2004). For 'intact' families too, it is not unusual to drive for many hours to a beach or holiday destination. Driving to a family reunion can take days rather than hours. It is perhaps not adequately appreciated that in Australia the car can be an important location for many meaningful father–child and family interactions.

What does the iconic Australian father look like? Does he wrestle crocodiles? Does he have a laid-back "she'll-be-right-mate" attitude, or is he stressed, exhausted and anxious from working 60 hours a week and racked with guilt because he's missed another school play? Is he of Indigenous descent, a newly arrived Sudanese or Lebanese father, or part of a family of mixed Asian, Indian or European descent? Is he a married father, a never-married father, or a separated father with children living elsewhere? The diversity of fathers in contemporary Australia shows us that any stereotypical image that comes to mind is likely to have many other equally valid competing counterparts. For example, a father like Tony in the opening Case Study, places a high priority on spending quality time with his daughter. But as we note later in the chapter, many Australian fathers feel obliged to place considerable emphasis on providing financially for their families. Some of these fathers do this at the expense of enjoying time with their children. Clearly, differences in approaches to fathering will vary across cultural groups, socioeconomic groups, life cycle stages and the messages that men take on board about their roles.

Review of Fathering Research

Until recently, fathers have been largely overlooked in many areas of research on Australian families. In this section we offer a brief demographic profile of fathers in Australia, and review recent Australian studies of fathering. For brevity, we focus on two areas of Australian research on fathers where good data exist: paid and unpaid work, and caring for children. We also review what we know about fathers and child wellbeing in Australia, acknowledging that the evidence base is in its infancy.

The demography of fathers in Australia

Increases in Australian life expectancy and the aging of the population are occurring alongside major changes in family formation. Marriage rates are falling while cohabitation and relationship dissolution rates are rising (Bacon & Pennec, 2007). Patterns of childbearing are also changing, with more women (and men) having their first child later in life and an increasing proportion of babies being born outside of marriage. These demographic shifts are not unique to Australia (some are found in both the Western and developing societies, as described in this book), and have important implications for the complexion of Australian fathering. In brief, Australian fathers are (a) less likely to be married than in the past, (b) getting older before fathering children, (c) fathering fewer children in individual relationships, (d) fathering children in more than one relationship, thereby having responsibilities in different families, and (e) taking on the role of 'social fathers' to other men's children (McDonald, 2003).

Specifically, in Australia, as in most other industrial countries, family formation, and thus fatherhood, is being delayed. In 2009, the median age of Australian fathers at the birth of a child in that year was 33 years, compared with 30.8 in 1989 (ABS, 2010). While teenage fatherhood is uncommon in Australia, at the other end of the age distribution, some increase in births to older men has occurred. It is noteworthy that fathers of Indigenous children are younger than other fathers, with a median age of 27.8 years at the birth of a child (ABS, 2010). Ideas about the best time to have children (e.g., after buying a house, or having good jobs) reinforce and fuel fertility trends (Hayes, Weston, Qu, & Gray, 2010), and having children later in life imposes limits on the number of children parents are likely to have. Families are thus smaller now than they were some decades ago, with the average completed fertility of women falling from 2.3 in 1964, to 2.0 in 1984, and 1.8 in 2004 (ABS, 2010).

A significant proportion of children in Australia are born outside of marriage. In 2009, 34% of births were ex-nuptial (ABS, 2010), although 90% of fathers were named on the birth certificate. Despite this high rate of ex-nuptial births, the majority (83%) of fathers who live with their children are married, with 13% cohabiting and 4% living alone (ABS, 2006a).

While most Australian fathers who live with their children also live with partners, these families vary in form. 'Intact' families, in which the family unit comprises two parents and their biological children, are still the most common family form in Australia, representing 88% of the families in which fathers reside (based on data from ABS, 2008). 'Blended' families make up 4% and step-families make up another 4% of fathers' families. Many Australian fathers live apart from their children because of parental separation or divorce. In 2006–07, there were almost half a million non-resident parents, of whom 82% were men (ABS, 2008). From the perspective of children, 18% of children had a biological father living in another household. This was most common among older children, i.e., 22% of children aged 10 years and over, compared with 18% of children aged 5 to 9 years and 11% of children under the age of 5 (ABS, 2008).

Australian-born non-Indigenous men make up the majority of Australian fathers (65%), although within this broad group of men are first- and second-generation Australians, who may strongly identify with the culture of their parents as well as with Australian culture. Indigenous fathers are relatively small in number, comprising approximately 2% of all Australian fathers (ABS, 2006a).

Father-time and child outcomes

What do fathers do with their children in Australia, and in what ways do Australian fathers 'matter'? Baxter and Smart (2010) recently sought to improve understanding of how Australian fathers in couple families with young children (aged 0–9 years) contribute to family life. Their analyses draw on data from the Longitudinal Study of Australian Children (LSAC), a panel study commencing in 2004 with approximately 5,100 newborns and 5,000 4- to 5-year-old children.

Baxter and Smart found that children in Australia spend an average of 4–5 hours each day with their father, albeit largely in the presence of mothers. For example, infants (aged 0–1 year) spend an average of 5.8 hours per day alone with their mothers, 30 minutes alone each day with their fathers, and another 2.7 hours per day with both parents. Even among 8–9-year-old children, the time they spend alone with their fathers is on average less than one hour each weekday, compared with 2 hours a day with both parents and 3.4 hours a day with mothers. Children obviously have more opportunities to spend time with their fathers on weekends, but that time is usually family time with mothers also present (Baxter, Gray, & Hayes, 2010; see also Russell et al., 1999).

Most father–child interactions involve meals, play and social activities, and going places (Baxter & Smart, 2010). For instance, almost three-quarters of fathers read stories and engaged in play, most commonly outdoor play, with their 4- to 5-year-olds on three or more days in a week. In addition, a substantial number of fathers had daily involvement in their child's personal care, e.g., 41% of Australian fathers of 2- to 3-year-olds reported changing nappies or helping their child with the toilet every day. While mothers had much higher rates of daily involvement than fathers, most fathers engaged in a range of personal care activities at least a few times a week. Baxter and Smart (2010) also found that a majority of fathers talked with children about their day on a daily basis or a few times a week (e.g., 85–93% of fathers with children aged 4–9 years), while a substantial proportion of fathers helped their children with homework a few times a week (40–45% of fathers with children aged 6–9 years) or a few times each month (another 35–36% of fathers). More broadly, within the confines of three biennial waves of LSAC data, fathers who were highly involved when their children were young tended to remain highly involved as their children grew (Baxter & Smart, 2010). In addition, fathers were more involved with children when mothers were in paid employment, especially when working full-time hours.

A related but equally important strand of Baxter and Smart's (2010) analysis was their focus on fathering and child wellbeing. They explored the links between fathering and wellbeing by examining two areas of child development: (a) learning outcomes (most notably, language and cognitive skills), and (b) socio-emotional wellbeing such as social competence, and internalizing/externalizing behavior problems. Using a series of multivariate models, Baxter and Smart (2010) found that children's scores on learning and socio-emotional outcomes were higher when the father was older or more educated. Children's socio-emotional outcomes were also higher when fathers: (a) worked in excess of 45 hours each week; (b) had an excellent relationship with their partner (which included a strong parental alliance over child rearing); and (c) had excellent mental health. By contrast and not surprisingly, children did less well developmentally and emotionally when the family was under financial pressure. Children's socio-emotional outcomes were also lower when the father was Indigenous or mainly spoke a language other than English. While these associations make sense, some results were counter-intuitive. For example, after taking other factors into account, children of cohabiting fathers had better learning outcomes than children of married parents. Baxter and Smart (2010) speculated that this finding might reflect unobserved characteristics of parents or families. For example, cohabiting families may have less traditional attitudes to gender roles and parenting, which might translate to a greater involvement of both parents in children's lives.

Fathers' parenting style was also found to be an important predictor of child outcomes. More paternal warmth was associated with more positive child outcomes; so too was a high level of paternal (and maternal) self-efficacy, i.e., the degree to which fathers and mothers perceive themselves to be good parents. It is noteworthy that the amount of one-to-one father–child time, or the time children spent in the company of their father, was *not* significantly related to children's development or their emotional wellbeing. This finding is consistent with prior work in the U.S. context (e.g., Amato & Gilbreth, 1999) that suggested that what fathers *do* with children during their time together and the quality of the parent–child relationship matter more than time *per se*. Baxter and Smart (2010) focused on fathers in couple families with children aged 0–9 years, but the extent to which the findings generalize to fathers of older children or to single non-resident fathers remains unclear. The study strongly suggests, however, that fathering in Australia is both multifaceted and important to child and family wellbeing.

Contemporary economic conditions that impact fathering

Any discussion of the role of fathers in Australian society must explain how this role is shaped or constrained by fathers' and mothers' engagement with the labour market. While Australian maternal employment rates remain lower than in many OECD countries, there have been considerable increases in these rates in recent decades, from 43% in 1981 to 63% in 2009 (ABS, 2009b, 2009c). A key feature of maternal – but not paternal – employment in Australia is the extensive use of part-time work. This not only has implications for the sharing of childcare, but it is also important for family finances. Many Australian families get by when mothers work part-time or remain out of employment because fathers' full-time employment provides sufficient family income. For instance, Baxter and Smart (2010) found that fathers in couples families with young children contribute more than two-thirds (70%) of the family income. They also found that in a large majority of these families (e.g. 76% of families with a 0–1-year-old child, and 67% with an 8–9-year-old child) fathers are the only full-time workers in the family. The breadwinner role assumed by the majority of Australian fathers thus continues to be pervasive, particularly when children are young.

Different patterns of employment by fathers and mothers result in different amounts of time spent in unpaid caring and household work, with mothers spending significantly more time on these activities than fathers (see Craig, 2006; Craig & Mullan, 2010; Craig, Mullan, & Blaxland, 2010). For example, in 2004 among parents with children under the age of five years, fathers spent on average 43 hours per week in employment (compared with 11 hours by mothers), 6 hours per week on housework (compared with 23 hours by mothers) and 16 hours per week on childcare (compared with 38 hours by mothers). For parents of older children, aged 5–14 years, time in employment was slightly lower for fathers (41 hours) but almost doubled for mothers (20 hours), and the childcare time of mothers and fathers decreased (Baxter, Gray, Alexander, Strazdins, & Bittman, 2007). Thus, for many Australian fathers, paid work frequently gets in the way of family time (Baxter et al., 2007; Hand & Lewis, 2002; Pocock, 2003; Pocock, Skinner, & Pisaniello, 2010; Russell et al., 1999). This also holds true for separated fathers. For example, according to an analysis of the LSAC data by one of the present authors (JB), of the almost 500 non-resident fathers who wanted to spend more time with their children, 40% said that their job demands were a factor in their not being able to do so.

The work hours of Australian fathers are long not only in comparison to Australian mothers, but also in comparison to some European standards. Thus, in 2009 full-time employed men in Australia worked an average of 44.8 hours per week. This figure was slightly higher than comparable figures from OECD countries such as Denmark, France, Germany, Ireland, the Netherlands and Sweden, all of which have averages of less than 43 hours per week (OECD, 2009). Pocock (2003) suggested that there has been a shift in recent decades in Australia towards a 'long hours work culture' whereby fathers feel pressure to work the hours of an "ideal worker" – i.e., a worker who is unencumbered by family obligations and can give priority to the demands of the workplace (Pocock, 2003). But fathers often report that they would prefer to work fewer hours than they do (Pocock et al., 2010), and many fathers who are dissatisfied with their hours or have a mismatch between actual and preferred hours experience a great amount of work–family strain (Baxter et al., 2007; Gray, Qu, Stanton, & Weston, 2004). Long work hours also directly affect time available for fathering. For example, Baxter and Smart (2010) recently found among fathers in couples with young children that longer work hours were associated with less time with children, less time doing childcare and domestic work, and being less of a resource or support to mothers.

Thus far we have not referred to fathers who are not employed. This is because it is relatively unusual in Australia to find 'stay-at-home dads' or fathers who reduce their involvement in paid work to assume the primary care of children (ABS, 2006b; Russell et al., 1999). For example, among infants in couple families in LSAC, 2.5% had a mother working part or full-time while the father was not employed (Baxter & Smart, 2010). This figure was only slightly higher for older children (4.6% of children aged 8–9 years). Most fathers who are not working do so because they are unable to find work, not because they have chosen to care for children. Nevertheless, because their time is less constrained than that of employed fathers, these fathers do spend significantly more time doing childcare and other household work (Baxter & Smart, 2010).

Generally speaking, however, the perceived association between good fathering and breadwinning in Australia is a strong one. Fathers' employment brings income, and because most Australian mothers are not employed full-time, men's income makes a major contribution to the wellbeing of the family. But although long work hours temper the nature and form of their involvement, many Australian fathers also make a valuable contribution to caring for children outside of paid work. The balance between work and family remains the greatest challenge for many fathers in contemporary Australia.

Social Policy Issues Related to Fathering

Post-separation fathering

Burgess (2005, p. 93) suggested that in the UK, the word *father* has been largely "colonised by the separated parents discourse." The same could probably be said of Australia, where more is known about separated fathers than about the great majority of fathers in non-separated families.

Around one in four (24%) of the Australian children under 18 who live separately from one parent sees that parent, most often the father, less than once a year or never (ABS, 2011). In short, father absence continues to be a common outcome for many Australian children in the aftermath of parental separation. This was a major factor prompting sweeping changes in 2006 to the Australian family law system, including new services, wide-ranging legislative and procedural changes, and a new Child Support Scheme.

Separated fathers' groups in Australia played an influential role in shaping the key reform elements but especially in lobbying for a greater legislative emphasis on shared parenting reform (Parkinson, 2010). Australian legislation has gone further than that of many other countries to encourage shared-time arrangements, that is, joint *physical* custody (Fehlberg, Smyth, Maclean, & Roberts, 2011). These legislative changes enshrine in law the need for Australian family law courts to begin with a rebuttable presumption of shared parental *responsibility* and if that is ordered, to consider orders for the children to spend 'equal' or else 'substantial or significant periods' of *time* with each parent where such arrangements are in children's best interest and reasonably practicable.

Not surprisingly, most separated fathers in Australia like the idea of 50/50 parenting (Smyth & Weston, 2004). Moreover, fathers with shared-time parenting and many co-parents typically report being happy with this arrangement and that their children are doing well (Cashmore et al., 2010; Kaspiew, Gray, Weston, Moloney, Hand, & Qu, 2009). But it is important to note that the relatively small group of Australian fathers and mothers with shared-time arrangements tend to have characteristics that make positive outcomes for their children more likely than other separated parents. Specifically, they are mainly well-educated parents who get along with and live near their children's other parent, are child-focused, avoid reliance on the legal system, and have a degree of financial independence and flexibility in their work hours.

As in the U.S. (e.g., Melli & Brown, 2008), a fascinating aspect of the Australian post-separation fathering landscape is that shared-time parenting has been steadily rising over the past decade, albeit from a low base level. In June 2002, about 6% of parents registered with the Child Support Agency exercised shared-time parenting; by June 2008 this estimate had doubled to 12%. The pattern for new child support cases is even more striking: in June 2003, only 9% of new cases reported exercising shared-time parenting; by June 2008, this figure had almost doubled to 17%. That said, shared-time parenting in Australia still remains a less common and less durable arrangement than more traditional patterns of care (Kaspiew et al., 2009; Smyth, Weston, Moloney, Richardson, & Temple, 2008).

There is no doubt that the once dominant sole (i.e., maternal) custody model of the past is gradually shifting. At the same time, the traditional 'standard package' of father–child contact, i.e., every other weekend and half of school holidays, is morphing into a more wide-ranging spectrum of arrangements that offer a diversity of parenting contexts for children and non-resident fathers (Smyth, 2005). This shift is significant because, as noted by Kelly and Lamb (2000), different parenting contexts facilitate children's social, emotional and cognitive development, and afford greater opportunities for parents to strengthen emotional bonds with their children. Less clear is the extent to which legislative changes in Australia that encourage shared-time parenting have in fact impacted on this shift.

A related policy issue of significance to post-separation fathering in Australia is the introduction of a new Child Support Scheme. The new Scheme uses the income of both parents to calculate child support liability, not just the fathers' income, i.e., the original 'percentage of father's income' model has been replaced by an income-shares approach. A strengthened enforcement regime was also introduced to ensure that child support is paid in full and on time. Preliminary evidence (e.g., Smyth & Henman, 2010) suggests that non-resident parents (mostly fathers) are more likely than resident parents (mostly mothers) to experience net gains under the new Scheme, when family tax benefits (i.e., child endowment payments from the government) and child support are jointly considered. These are gains intended to improve previous formula-related inequities and to encourage non-resident parents play an active role in their children's lives after separation. By and large, separated fathers seem to be more satisfied following implementation of this reform (cf. Kaspiew et al., 2009; Smyth & Weston, 2005).

Engaging fathers in services

There is some evidence in Australia (e.g., Gee & Melvin, 1998) that many fathers, and indeed men more generally, tend to avoid personal problems rather than face them, to not express their concerns, and be reluctant to seek professional help. Engagement with fathers thus remains a challenge for many Australian family services and programs (Berlyn, Wise, & Soriano, 2008). Systemic barriers to Australian men's engagement with services, linked to the fact that many family support services have been primarily oriented towards mothers and children, have been noted by Eardley and Griffith (2009). Australian men have been reported to feel frequently "alienated" by the way information is given to them (Russell et al., 1999, p. vii; see also Chs. 3 and 14, this volume, for comparable discussions about men's engagement with services in programs in Japan and the UK). At the same time, there is evidence that Australian men make better use of services when they are available, respectful and seen as relevant to their needs (Kaspiew et al., 2009).

In Australia, there has been a more recent emphasis on short-term, locally developed programs to engage fathers in services (Fletcher, 2004). The main foci of these programs have been on: (a) 'becoming a father' – prenatal and postnatal programs relating to newborns; (b) 'fathering practice' – discussion-based programs aiming to support involved fathering of children of all ages; and (c) 'fathering fun' – father-only play days and playgroups for fathers of young children. Fletcher found that the development of these programs and their delivery in a father-friendly style frequently relied on motivated individuals, many of whom were women. Programs were not always successful but when they were, they were generally not documented. Rather, they relied on word-of-mouth communication between practitioners for knowledge transfer. As a result, Fletcher suggested that Australian services for fathers remained fragmented, idiosyncratic and underdeveloped.

But while father-inclusive initiatives continue at the state and regional levels, outside the area of separation and divorce, Australian fathers have not established themselves as a legitimate interest group deserving of serious consideration in family-related services and policies. No senior politician has publically championed fathers' and men's issues in the way that U.S. politicians such as Presidents Obama and Clinton have done, and attention to fathers has not been included in key policies for children's services as has happened in the UK (see Chs. 11 and 14, this volume). Recent major Australian policy initiatives introducing change to early childhood, child protection and postnatal depression services have also failed to address the role of fathers.

Sub-Cultural Variations in Fathering

Indigenous fathers

The Indigenous cultures of Australia have the oldest surviving cultural history in the world (Maslen, 2005), estimated to date back between 40,000 and as much as 100,000 years (Gray, 2001). Traditional gender roles have been a feature of Indigenous families for much of this history. Typically it appears that adult men travelled considerable distances to hunt game while women, accompanied by children, foraged closer to camp (Hunter, 1993). While female children remained with their mothers through adolescence, male children were typically removed from contact with female kin prior to puberty and inducted into male-specific areas of knowledge linked to the specific geographical area of the clan. Social roles such as parenting were embedded in ceremonial responsibilities and practices (Gray, Trompf, & Houston, 1991; McCoy, 2008).

White settlement eventually disrupted virtually every aspect of Indigenous life. The role of men and fathers has been especially affected, with lands enclosed for sheep or crops denied to Indigenous men for hunting. Over a considerable period of time and driven mainly by ignorance or lack of concern about Indigenous culture, many young children were forcibly removed from their families and placed with white families or institutions. Parental contact was discouraged, which greatly weakened Indigenous knowledge of parenting and cultural practices such as male initiation ceremonies. This policy of forced removal from traditional lands and of children from their families has had a "devastating impact" on Indigenous Australians, including Indigenous fathers (New South Wales Department of Health, 2003, p. 5).

Figure 15.2 Father (early 20s) playing with his 3-year-old daughter in a park, at Bolton Point, Newcastle, New South Wales. Photo courtesy of Craig Hammond of the Family Action Centre, Australia.

In contemporary Australia, the Indigenous population is located in rural, regional and urban settings: in traditional tribal groups in the north, west, and interior of Australia, in small regional country towns, and in capital cities. Indigenous cultural practices continue to be recognised in varying degrees and in different parts of the country. Aboriginal males' identity as fathers stretches along a continuum from traditional Indigenous notions of male parental care bound up in ceremonial authority, to the biological and 'social' fathering recognised in mainstream society. Complex multiple 'parental' roles for men can include responsibilities for transfer of sacred knowledge, discipline, and provision of food and shelter to children not related by blood. Accordingly, Indigenous men may define themselves as having "fathering responsibilities" but not as biological fathers. Such extended family relationships remain critical to the way Indigenous culture is passed on to younger generations (Maslen, 2008).

In recent years, Indigenous fathers have often received negative publicity as a result of high rates of substance abuse, domestic violence, child abuse and neglect, and relationship breakdown. Poor health, low levels of education and social dislocation associated with poverty, poor housing, unemployment, and an incarceration rate 17 times that of non-Indigenous Australian men, have all had a significant impact on Indigenous fathering. Due to these compounding layers of social disadvantage, Indigenous men must overcome considerable obstacles to become involved fathers (Australian Institute of Health and Welfare, 2008).

Fathers from culturally and linguistically diverse backgrounds

While Australia is an ethnically diverse nation, knowledge of families classified by Australian researchers and policy makers as 'culturally and linguistically diverse' (CALD) is limited. Knowledge of *fathers* within these families is especially sparse. Furthermore, in this rapidly changing field, key pieces of research such as that conducted by Hartley (1995) and Kolar and Soriano (1999) are already somewhat dated. We know in broad terms that CALD fathers in Australia are often confronted by family and societal values and behavior that run counter to their own (McDonald, 1991). But little is known of the extent to which CALD families have integrated themselves into a broader Australian culture, or how fathers in these families have adapted.

Similarly, little is known of the particular issues facing fathers in Australia's most newly arrived families. Most of what *is* known about the current situation derives mainly from reports from the relatively small number of specialist practitioners and outreach staff members who work directly with fathers who are recent migrants or refugees from countries such as Sudan, Iraq and Somalia (e.g., Broadway, 2008). Although these groups represent less than 1% of Australia's population, they are nonetheless among the fastest growing part of Australia's population.

Broadway (2008) describes a common pattern among recently arrived Sudanese fathers in which they feel that their formerly well defined role as head of the household is diminished or even inverted. Children typically assume more adult roles than in their home country because they acquire language skills and learn about cultural expectations much faster than their parents; mothers often receive child and family payments directly from government agencies, thus further reducing the place of the father as key provider. Fathers in these families struggle over not only their place within Australian society, as do Indigenous fathers, but also with their very sense of purpose within their own families.

A significant research design issue is that even in large-scale population surveys, there are usually not enough respondents from particular groups to permit detailed examination of these issues. We need to understand each cultural group, and indeed the important intra-group differences, and the ways groups adapt to a mainstream environment, which is itself in a state of flux. Methodological approaches such as small scale qualitative work using in-depth interviews and ethnographic observations are useful in this context. In practical terms, the sort of small scale projects described above by Fletcher are likely to be the most effective way to both research and assist families and fathers from CALD groups, especially recent arrivals. As with Indigenous families and fathers, such research and assistance need to begin from approaches that reflect the principles of transformative learning (Taylor, 2007). By this we mean research that views the individual, including the researchers themselves, not as an object of study but as subjects who continually reflect and act on the numerous changes which take place in the physical and social worlds.

Reflections and Predictions for the Future

As noted, fathers in contemporary Australia come from a multitude of cultures, backgrounds and circumstances. Increasingly, this diversity is seen as an important part of the Australian story. It is part of what makes contemporary Australians who they are and it is by extension part of what makes any statements about Australian fathers problematic. Not all subgroups of Australian fathers will respond in the same way to the current opportunities and challenges that Australia offers. For example, the debate about Australia's materialistic culture and the tendency to over-consume impacts pointedly on fathers because as noted, they continue to make the major contribution to family income.

In addition to, or perhaps because of, a common expectation of a high standard of living, all Australian fathers must at some level respond to the following kinds of pressures: the growing housing affordability crisis and increasing costs of education; the tendency for extended family supports to dissipate due to high levels of mobility, and the 'tyranny of distance'; the high costs of childcare outside the home; and the ever-present threat – statistically speaking at least – that family relationships might unravel. Whatever their ethnic or cultural origins, there are society-wide pressures on Australian fathers to work long work hours to meet the high costs of living that our mainstream lifestyle demands.

Somewhat pessimistically, we speculate that changes in the employment participation and work hours of Australian fathers are likely to be minimal in the foreseeable future. Access to father-friendly policies such as a specified period of paid parental leave for fathers, are likely to change things only at the margins or encourage father involvement at very specific life cycle stages such as immediately after childbirth. Changes in the Child Support Scheme designed to encourage greater father participation may possibly create as many problems as they solve not so much because the Scheme itself is seriously flawed, but because the reality for most separating couples is that there is often simply not enough money to go around after divorce. Many separated fathers are faced with an even more acute version of the hard choice between earning money vs. personal investment in their children.

The other side of this coin is that Australian mothers are unlikely to relinquish the role of primary caregiver, at least while the children are young, and to give up part-time work for full-time positions. We may, however, see fathers spend more of their outside-of-work time engaged in care-giving activities as a response to the growing recognition that fathers can indeed be effective nurturers and that it is beneficial for fathers to spend time with children. This behavior may, of course, simultaneously support the increasing employment rates of mothers.

As noted earlier in the chapter, a distinctive feature of the Australian context is the extent to which the role of separated fathers has been recognised in legislation and policy. Prompted by concerns about father absence, and pressured by separated fathers' groups, Australia has gone further than many other countries in legislating to encourage shared-time parenting outcomes. Separated fathers' voices have indeed been heard and acted on by politicians and policy makers in Australia. It is much too early to predict the extent to which the Australian family law and child support reforms will reduce 'father absence' and might affect attitudes to fathers or enhance children's wellbeing more generally.

Twenty-five years ago, in his review of fatherhood in Australia, Russell concluded:

> … [T]he modal pattern [of fathering] is one of a traditional type, with fathers being much more involved

> in play than in childcare, and having responsibility for family financial support and traditional male household tasks. ... [A]lthough the future will likely see Australian fathers becoming more highly participant in childcare, this change is likely to be very slow indeed.
>
> (Russell, 1987, p. 354)

While Russell's comments appear somewhat prophetic in the light of the data summarised in this chapter, we would argue that the change has actually been more rapid than was predicted in 1987. For instance, there is an expectation in Australia that all soon-to-be fathers attend prenatal and parenting classes, and virtually all do. Further, the difficulties Russell (1987) claimed that fathers faced in accessing paid parental leave have been removed by recent legislation that guarantees leave. Most fathers take parental leave following the birth of a child, even if that leave is only brief. These and other indicators suggest that the involvement of Australian fathers is increasing at a faster rate than might have been predicted two decades ago. In fact, Russell and his colleagues (Russell et al., 1999, p. 40) later wrote that a shift had indeed occurred where fathers were "less likely to see their role in terms of breadwinning and more likely to perceive their role as providing emotional support to children." Of course, Australia has not been unique in this regard.

Concluding Comments

Within the confines of the limited Australian data available, we offer three tentative conclusions relevant to fathers. First, while the traditional gender division of labour largely continues to prevail in Australia, change is afoot. Parenting roles, expectations and responsibilities are in transition, and the defining features of the father's roles are expanding. While the main role for many Australian fathers continues to be that of economic breadwinner, their desire (and often the desire of their partners) for greater involvement in their children's lives present a series of challenges that may ultimately result in families looking somewhat different to how they look today. Greater father involvement is likely to increase our appreciation of the socialising and nurturing roles they are able to play with their children which in turn is likely to lead to further routine involvement and so on. We might expect to see fewer television advertisements that depict fathers as well meaning but quite incompetent when it comes to being 'hands on' with children. Second, if fathering in Australia takes on greater prominence, the diversity of the Australian population will ensure that expressions of fathering that have their origins outside the dominant

Anglo-Celtic culture will also be recognised. Third, it is axiomatic that fathering in Australia will continue to respond to pressures from global and national changes in the economy, industry, finance and technology. However, the growing but still very modest Australian research evidence relating to fathers' role with children, and the dearth of policy formulations specifically addressing fathers, suggest that change will probably continue to be sporadic in that it will be piecemeal and locally based.

Clearly there is still much that needs to be studied about fathers in Australia. While the Longitudinal Study of Australian Children is producing new insights about fathers with young children (see, for example, Baxter & Smart, 2010; McIntosh, Smyth, Kelaher, Wells, & Long, 2010), very little has been published in Australia about the processes of fathering and the resulting developmental outcomes for children, teens and young adults. Other longitudinal studies, such as the Household, Income and Labour Dynamics in Australia (HILDA) survey, hold much promise for improving our understanding of fathers' roles in Australian families with regard to issues such as decision-making about parenting and family finances. The HILDA survey will also offer insights about how, when, and to what extent fathers negotiate their work hours to accommodate their desire to participate more in the direct care of their children. Relevant to the issue of post-separation fathering, the Child Support Reform Study is about to break new ground on the close but complex links between parenting time and the financial arrangements that support children, and the ways in which money can act as a tracer for relationships within families. Meanwhile, the Longitudinal Study of Separated Families (Kaspiew et al., 2009; Qu & Weston, 2010) has begun to yield valuable insights on how different parenting arrangements (including shared-time parenting) function in the context of different family dynamics.

While these large-scale longitudinal studies are an important source of information about fathers, there remains a great need for stand-alone focused studies of Australian fathering. Several possible studies of Australian fathers have been initiated in the past but were sidelined by the research priorities dictated by competing policy imperatives. Our hope is that such studies will be reprioritised and made available soon, so that we can fill in the many large gaps in our knowledge of this important field.

Summary

Australian fathers appear to share a number of demographic similarities with fathers in other Western countries. Amidst a rapidly changing social landscape, they are increasingly: less likely to be married, getting older before they father children, fathering fewer children in individual relationships, fathering children in more than one relationship, and taking on the role of 'social fathers' to other men's children. In terms of role definition, many Australian fathers continue to place considerable emphasis on providing financially for their families. The long hours devoted to this goal can be at the expense of spending time with their children. On the other hand, though somewhat patchy, the available data suggest that fathers in Australia make an important emotional as well as financial contribution to child and family wellbeing. Finally, whilst Australia has become increasingly ethnically diverse, its dominant Anglo-Celtic culture remains over-represented in research on fathering. To improve our knowledge of Australian fathers, better data are needed on Indigenous fathers and on fathers from other non-dominant backgrounds.

Acknowledgments

This chapter uses unit record data from Growing Up in Australia, the Longitudinal Study of Australian Children (LSAC). The study is conducted in partnership between the Department of Families, Housing, Community Services and Indigenous Affairs (FaHCSIA), the Australian Institute of Family Studies and the Australian Bureau of Statistics. The chapter also draws on confidentialised unit record data from the Household, Income and Labour Dynamics in Australia (HILDA) Survey. The HILDA Survey is funded by FaHCSIA and managed by the Melbourne Institute of Applied Economic and Social Research at the University of Melbourne. The findings and views reported in this chapter are those of the authors and should not be attributed to any affiliated organisations.

References

Amato, P.R., & Gilbreth, J.G. (1999). Non-resident fathers and children's wellbeing: A meta-analysis. *Journal of Marriage and the Family, 61,* 557–573.

Australian Bureau of Statistics (ABS). (2006a). *Census of Population and Housing, Australia, 2006.* [1% cent sample file]. Canberra, Australia: Australian Bureau of Statistics.

Australian Bureau of Statistics (ABS). (2006b). Fathers and family balance. In *Australian Social Trends* [Catalogue No. 4102.0] (pp. 39–43). Canberra, Australia: Australian Bureau of Statistics.

Australian Bureau of Statistics (ABS). (2008). *Family Characteristics and Transitions, Australia, 2006–07* [Catalogue No.4442.0]. Canberra, Australia: Australian Bureau of Statistics.

Australian Bureau of Statistics (ABS). (2009a). *Perspectives on Migrants, 2009* [Catalogue No. 3416.0]. Canberra, Australia: Australian Bureau of Statistics.

Australian Bureau of Statistics (ABS). (2009b). *Labour Force Survey: Monthly family data, June 1994 to June 2004* [Datacube: ST FA4_jun94; Catalogue No. 6224.0.55.001]. Canberra, Australia: Australian Bureau of Statistics.

Australian Bureau of Statistics (ABS). (2009c). *Labour Force Survey: Monthly family data, from August 2004* [Datacube: ST FA4_aug04; Catalogue No. 6224.0.55.001]. Canberra, Australia: Australian Bureau of Statistics.

Australian Bureau of Statistics (ABS). (2010). *Births Australia, 2009* [Catalogue No. 3301.0]. Canberra: Australian Bureau of Statistics.

Australian Bureau of Statistics (ABS). (2011). *Family Characteristics, Australia, 2009–10* [Catalogue No. 4442.0]. Canberra, Australia: Australian Bureau of Statistics.

Australian Institute of Health and Welfare (AIHW). (2008). *Australian's Health 2008*. Canberra, Australia: Australian Institute of Health and Welfare.

Bacon, B., & Pennec, S. (2007). *APPSIM-Modelling Family Formation and Dissolution.* [Working Paper No.4]. Canberra, Australia: National Centre for Social and Economic Modelling, University of Canberra, Australia.

Baxter, J. A., Gray, M., Alexander, M., Strazdins, L., & Bittman, M. (2007). *Mothers and fathers with young children: Paid employment, caring and wellbeing* [Social Policy Research Paper No. 30]. Canberra, Australia: Department of Families, Community Services and Indigenous Affairs.

Baxter, J. A., Gray, M., & Hayes, A. (2010). *The best start: Supporting happy, healthy childhoods*. Melbourne, Australia: Australian Institute of Family Studies.

Baxter, J. A., & Smart, D. (2010). *Fathering in Australia among couple families with young children* [Occasional Paper No. 37]. Canberra, Australia: Department of Families, Housing, Community Services and Indigenous Affairs.

Berlyn, C., Wise, S., & Soriano, G. (2008). *Engaging fathers in child and family services: Participation, perceptions and good practice.* Canberra, Australia: Department of Families, Housing, Community Services and Indigenous Affairs.

Broadway, M. (2008). Family Structures: Insights for practice. *Migration Action, 2,* 19–22.

Burgess, A. (2005). 'Bringing fathers in': International perspectives on father-inclusive practice. In B. Smyth, N. Richardson, & G. Soriano (Eds.) *Proceedings of the International Forum on Family Relationships in Transition: Legislative, practical and policy responses* (pp. 93–98). Melbourne, Australia: Australian Institute of Family Studies.

Cashmore, J., Parkinson, P., Weston, R., Patulny, R., Redmond, G., Qu, L., … Katz, I. (2010). *Shared care parenting arrangements since the 2006 family law reforms.* Sydney, Australia: Social Policy Research Centre, University of New South Wales, Australia.

Commonwealth of Australia. (2009). *Department of Immigration and Citizenship Fact Sheet 4*. Retrieved May 27, 2011, from www.immi.gov.au/media/fact-sheets/04fifty.htm

Craig, L. (2006). Does father care mean fathers share? A comparison of how mothers and fathers in intact families spend time with children. *Gender and Society, 20,* 259–281.

Craig, L., & Mullan, K. (2010). Parenthood, gender and work family time in the United States, Australia, Italy, France, and Denmark. *Journal of Marriage and Family, 72,* 1344–1361.

Craig, L., Mullan, K., & Blaxland, M. (2010). Parenthood, policy and work-family time in Australia 1992–2006. *Work, Employment & Society, 24,* 27–45.

Eardley, T., & Griffiths, M. (2009). *Non-resident parents and service use* [SPRC Report

12/09]. Sydney, Australia: Social Policy Research Centre, University of New South Wales.

Fehlberg, B., Smyth, B., Maclean, M., & Roberts, C. (2011). *Caring for children after parental separation: Would legislation for shared parenting time help children?* [Family Policy Briefing Paper 7]. Oxford, UK: Oxford University.

Fletcher, R. (2004). *Bringing fathers in handbook: How to engage with men for the benefit of everyone in the family.* Newcastle, Australia: University of Newcastle.

Gee, T., & Melvin, T. (1998). *On the back foot: Men, relationships and accessing services.* Paper presented at the Relationships Australia Forum "Men and Relationships", Canberra, Australia.

Gray, A. (2001). Part II: Indigenous Australians – Demographic and social history. In J. Jupp, (Ed.), *The Australian people: An encyclopedia of the nation, its people and their origins* (pp. 88–93). Cambridge, UK: Cambridge University Press.

Gray, A., Trompf, P., & Houston, S. (1991). The decline and rise of Aboriginal families. In J. Reid & P. Trompf (Eds.), *The health of Aboriginal Australia* (pp. 1–36). Marrickville, Australia: Harcourt Brace Jovanovich.

Gray, M., Qu, L., Stanton, D., & Weston, R. (2004). Long work hours and the well-being of fathers and their families. *Australian Journal of Labour Economics, 7,* 255–273.

Hand, K., & Lewis, V. (2002). Fathers' views on family life and paid work. *Family Matters, 61,* 26–29.

Hartley, R. (Ed.). (1995). *Families & cultural diversity in Australia.* Sydney, Australia: Allen & Unwin.

Hayes, A., Weston, R., Qu, L., & Gray, M. (2010). *Families then and now, 1980–2010* [Facts Sheet]. Melbourne, Australia: Australian Institute of Family Studies.

Hunter, E. M. (1993). *Aboriginal health and history: Power and prejudice in remote Australia.* Melbourne, Australia: Cambridge University Press.

Kaspiew, R., Gray, M., Weston, R., Moloney, L., Hand, K., & Qu, L. (2009). *Evaluation of the 2006 family law reforms.* Melbourne, Australia: Australian Institute of Family Studies.

Kelly, J., & Lamb, M. E. (2000). Using child development research to make appropriate custody and access decisions for young children. *Family & Conciliation Courts Review, 38,* 297–311.

Kolar, V., & Soriano, G. (1999). *Parenting in Australian families: A comparative study of Anglo, Torres Strait Islander, and Vietnamese communities.* Melbourne, Australia: Australian Institute of Family Studies.

Maslen, P. (2005). *Aboriginal fathers/fathers' roles: Are they recognised in Australia's contemporary society?* Honours Thesis, Yoorang Garang: School of Indigenous Health Studies, The University of Sydney, Australia.

McCoy, B. (2008). *Holding men: Kanyirpinpa and the health of Aboriginal men.* Canberra, Australia: Aboriginal Studies Press.

McDonald, P. (1991). Migrant family structure. In K. Funder (Ed.), *Images of Australian families: Approach and perceptions* (pp. 102–121). Melbourne, Australia: Longman Cheshire.

McDonald, P. (2003). Australia's future population: Population policy in a low-fertility society. In S. E. Khoo & P. McDonald (Eds.), *The Transformation of*

Australia's population: 1970–2030 (pp. 77–103). Sydney, Australia: University of New South Wales Press.

McIntosh, J., Smyth, B., Kelaher, M., Wells, Y., & Long, C. (2010). *Post-separation parenting arrangements and developmental outcomes for infants and children: Collected reports*. Canberra, Australia: Attorney-General's Department.

Melli, M., & Brown, P.R. (2008). Exploring a new family form: The shared time family. *International Journal of Law, Policy and the Family, 22*, 231–269.

New South Wales Department of Health (2003). *Aboriginal Men's Health Implementation Plan*. Sydney, Australia: New South Wales Department of Health.

Organisation for Economic Co-operation and Development (OECD). (2009). *Average usual weekly hours worked on the main job*. [Online OECD Employment database]. http://stats.oecd.org/Index.aspx?DatasetCode=AVE_HRS

Parkinson, P. (2010). Changing policies regarding separated fathers in Australia. In M. E. Lamb (Ed.), *The father's role in child development* (5th ed., pp. 578–614). Hoboken, NJ: Wiley & Sons.

Pocock, B. (2003). *The work/life collision: What work is doing to Australians and what to do about it*. Sydney, Australia: Federation Press.

Pocock, B., Skinner, N., & Pisaniello, S. (2010). *How much should we work: Working hours, holidays and working life: The participation challenge*. Adelaide, Australia: Centre for Work+Life, University of South Australia.

Qu, L., & Weston, R. (2010). *Parenting dynamics after separation: A follow-up study of parents who separated after the 2006 family law reforms*. Melbourne, Australia: Australian Institute of Family Studies.

Russell, G. (1987). Fatherhood in Australia. In M. E. Lamb (Ed.), *The father's role: Cross-cultural perspectives* (pp. 331–355). New York, NY: Routledge.

Russell, G., Barclay, L., Edgecombe, G., Donovan, J., Habib, G., Callaghan, H., & Pawson, Q. (1999). *Fitting fathers into families: Men and the fatherhood role in contemporary Australia*. Canberra, Australia: Department of Families, Community Services and Indigenous Affairs.

Smyth, B. (Ed.) (2004). *Parent–child contact and post-separation parenting arrangements* [Research Report No 9]. Australian Institute of Family Studies, Melbourne, Australia.

Smyth, B. (2005). Parent–child contact schedules after divorce. *Family Matters, 69*, 32–43.

Smyth, B., & Henman, P. (2010). The distributional and financial impacts of the new Australian Child Support Scheme: A 'before and day-after reform' comparison of assessed liability. *Journal of Family Studies, 16*, 5–32.

Smyth, B., & Weston, R. (2004). The attitudes of separated mothers and fathers to 50/50 shared care. *Family Matters, 67*, 4–11.

Smyth, B., & Weston, R. (2005). *A snapshot of contemporary attitudes to child support* [Research Report No 13]. Melbourne, Australia: Australian Institute of Family Studies.

Smyth, B., Weston, R., Moloney, L., Richardson, N., & Temple, J. (2008). Changes in patterns of parenting over time: Recent Australian data. *Journal of Family Studies, 14*, 23–36.

Taylor, E. (2007). An update of transformative learning theory: A critical review of the empirical research (1999–2005). *International Journal of Lifelong Education 26*, 173–191.

Part Seven

Conclusions

Chapter Sixteen

Final Thoughts, Comparisons, and Conclusions

**David W. Shwalb and
Barbara J. Shwalb**
Southern Utah University, UT, USA

Michael E. Lamb
University of Cambridge, Cambridge, UK

We begin this chapter by identifying five themes that help organize and give coherent structure to the international literature on fathering.

1. Cultural and historical backgrounds and changes have a major influence on fathers.

The father's roles are a product of both recent and remote history. Instead of viewing social change solely as an immediate impetus for the transition from traditional to contemporary fathering, we have seen throughout this book that historical events and the evolution of cultures over generations, centuries, and even millennia all continue to affect the father's roles. The word "change" appeared frequently in every chapter and over 300 times in this volume, underscoring that fathering has changed and continues to evolve everywhere in the world. Such changes can be interpreted as negative or positive, and may occur at different paces, depending on a number of factors in each society. In fact, the sub-titles of four chapters (those on China, Japan, Brazil, and UK) all invoked images of change or transition. Thus, the most representative answer to the question, "What characterizes fathers cross-culturally?" would be "Change."

2. Research on fathers is of varying breadth and quality around the world, where we also see varying levels of enthusiasm for increased paternal involvement.

The contributors to this volume demonstrated, with few exceptions, that there is at least some discussion worldwide about the need for fathers to become more involved and to take more responsibility for their children. All of the contributing authors seem to favor this belief, although research shows that there is not universal public support for the "rhetoric of paternal essentiality" discussed by Joseph Pleck in his Foreword. Fathers were almost always portrayed as secondary to mothers, although their levels of involvement at home ranged from very high (Scandinavia) to very low (Brazil, India), and from total involvement to complete detachment within individual families. In addition, the research literatures on fathering worldwide are inconsistent in quality and quantity, and research on fathers still lags in most countries. Discussions of many societies were absent from this volume because no data whatsoever had been collected on the fathers in those countries.

This book filled a major gap in the fathering literature, but there is still a large discrepancy between the amounts of research on fathering in Western and non-Western societies. In several societies (e.g., Japan, Brazil, India), fathers have only recently become willing to talk to researchers or to be observed by outsiders. In sum, research on fathering is clearly expanding internationally, but is still generally limited in depth outside Western Europe and North America.

3. Social policies designed to affect fathering are prominent in some cultures but non-existent elsewhere.

Social policies and laws which affect fathers' roles have profound effects in some societies (as evidenced, for example, by the title of the Scandinavia chapter), while in other countries such policies appear to be of marginal importance (e.g., Brazil, India, and Arab societies) although the need for them may be recognized. As illustrated in the U.S., UK, and Scandinavia chapters, policies are sometimes informed and evaluated by researchers, but elsewhere (e.g., Japan, Russia, and China) important policy initiatives have arisen in response to political, ideological, or popular demand, with little connection to research. Many recent laws and policies relevant to fathering are concerned with three issues: the promotion of increased involvement by fathers (e.g., leave policies in numerous countries), establishment of paternity (e.g., Brazil), and the responsibilities and involvement of non-resident fathers (e.g., Australia).

Most discussions of social policy in this volume reflect the widespread assumption that fathers should spend more time with or take more responsibility for their children. Pro-fathering and egalitarian ideologies underlie many policies and interventions, even though such ideologies are not universally embraced within the cultures concerned. In addition, experiences in Japan have shown that media and non-profit organizations can stimulate changes in fathering roles more effectively than government policies, especially when the government lacks the resources to follow through on its initiatives.

4. Sub-cultural variation in fathering is universal.

The contributors all made clear that diversity is a fundamental characteristic of fathering across cultures. In fact, diversity describes fathering in societies once stereotyped as homogeneous or heterogeneous, with high or low levels of immigration, and characterized by large or small minority group populations alike. We can often discern cultural patterns of fathering, but it is also tempting to answer the question, "What are fathers like across cultures?" with one word: "Diverse."

5. Contemporary economic conditions affect fathering.

Economic conditions, the state of economic development, and living standards all vary widely among the societies represented in this volume. Among the countries listed in Table 1.1 (p. 5), per capita income ranged from $700 in the Central African Republic to $54,600 in Norway, with every other level of affluence between these extremes just as likely to affect paternal behavior and involvement. Some of the societies discussed are relatively stable in political, economic, and social terms, while others have experienced recent turmoil sufficient to turn life and paternal roles upside down. Economic disparities appear to affect the father's roles, and in some societies disparities in social status and affluence have been endemic over centuries or millennia (e.g., South Africa and India). In other societies, the economic disparity between rich and poor fathers is growing (Russia, U.S.) or may be imminent (Japan).

Changes in demographics such as family size and structure were often mentioned in this volume, and phenomena such as divorce, fatherhood outside marriage, non-resident fatherhood, shrinking family sizes, and the postponement of marriage and childbearing were each said to account for variability in fathering. Many contributors also referred to expectations regarding men's roles as providers. The effects of work on fathering, and the blending of the two aspects of manhood, were portrayed in a variety of ways. But whether the spillover was positive or negative, and whether work separated fathers from their children for a hundred hours per week or by a thousand miles, work (or lack of work) was always viewed as an important aspect of fatherhood.

Lessons Learned from Each Chapter

Every chapter added to our understanding of fathers from a cross-cultural perspective, and of fathering in general. We focus next on findings which appeared to be distinctive or surprising, and also compare the portrayals of fathers within each region.

East Asia: China and Japan

Li and Lamb (Ch. 2) showed us that diverse family structures (including both trends toward nuclear living arrangements, and the existence of a "floating population" of more than 100 million men who leave their families or never marry as they migrate to major cities in search of work) must be considered when attempting to understand Chinese fathers. These tendencies have multiple origins, including China's One Child Policy, urbanization, and its rapid transformation to a market economy. We cannot say that these factors are "causing" Chinese fathers to change, but the magnitude of such recent phenomena is impressive. In contrast, despite a common East Asian and Confucian/Buddhist heritage, Japanese fathers apparently departed from the traditional ideology of "strict father, affectionate mother" sooner in their history than Chinese fathers. Indeed, Nakazawa and Shwalb's (Ch. 3) depiction of the Japanese tradition of emotion-focused and permissive fathering helps us to understand contemporary accounts of nurturant and friendly Japanese fathers. Another aspect of Japanese fathering, also observed in several other chapters, is that popular rhetoric in favor of fathers' involvement in childcare at home was not matched for many years by parallel changes in paternal behavior. Research studies have not specifically tested the effects of decades of pro-fathering government policies, but it appears that the present generation of Japanese fathers is the first where behavior has changed dramatically. Nakazawa and Shwalb also illustrated the impact of non-profit organizations and the Internet on fathering, and we anticipate that such influences on fathers will become prominent in other societies in the near future.

India, Bangladesh, Malaysia, and Arab societies

Chaudhary (Ch. 4) portrayed Indian fathers as an immense, diverse (e.g., rural vs. urban) and changing sub-group characterized by "multi-voicedness" and "incredible variety." She also emphasized "distancing" and "awkwardness" whereby Indian fathers were purposefully detached from children and avoided open expression of emotions, so that they could maintain authority as family patriarchs. Chaudhary further drew attention to an intriguing lifespan pattern whereby fathers may be aloof and unemotional toward their own children but subsequently become openly loving and affectionate as grandfathers. She concluded (Chaudhary, this volume, p. 90) that the father's roles were "shared with a wide network of people including relatives, neighbours, friends or household helpers," a pattern reminiscent of Townsend's (Ch. 8) depiction of Southern African fathers. In his coverage of predominantly Muslim Bangladesh and Malaysia, Hossain (Ch. 5) observed that fathering is as diverse as in India. He then concentrated on another similarity between fathering in India, Bangladesh, and Malaysia: the combined influences of culture, religion, strong extended families, and patriarchy over thousands of years. Hossain also emphasized that traditional Quranic verses and traditional customs (*adat*) call for involved fathering, asserting that Islamic traditions and Westernization convey similar messages to fathers, and together may be "reinvigorating" father involvement.

Ahmed (Ch. 6) focused on very different Muslim populations from those in South Asia, in his examination of 22 Arab societies (citing research mostly from Egypt, Saudi Arabia, Kuwait, and Jordan). He reviewed a literature that was extensive but also piecemeal, and most of the data cited by Ahmed suggested that Arab fathering is correlated with the same aspects of child development (child adjustment, cognitive development, behavior problems, and aggression) as in Western countries that have been studied more extensively. Perhaps most distinctive in Ahmed's portrayal of Arab fathers was his emphasis on negative social trends and the adverse effects on fathers of immigration, death and divorce, although he concluded with a guardedly optimistic comment on the future of Arab fatherhood.

Africa

Fouts (Ch. 7) discussed small-scale societies of East and Central Africa, asserting that biology (genetics, evolution) and culture (belief systems, values) must both be considered to understand the father's roles. This biology/culture interplay was seldom mentioned by other contributors, yet Gray and Anderson (2010), like Hewlett (2010), have suggested that both factors must always be considered. Fouts' chapter was more theoretical in focus than most of the others, and also offered insightful comparisons between fathers from foraging, pastoral, farming and other communities, thereby underscoring diversity even within some of the world's smaller societies.

Diversity, separation, population migration, and historical change all were prominent in Townsend's (Ch. 8) descriptions of Southern African fathers. He emphasized that black Southern African men other than fathers are often *assumed* and *required* to be significant figures in children's lives (rather than looked on as *possible* alternatives to biological fathers), a pattern which Hewlett (2010) called "multiple" fathering. In this context, several men share aspects of what Westerners consider to be *the* father's role, with the magnitude of their responsibility varying by their age and life stage. Townsend also asserted that fathers are forced by economic "desperation" to separate from their children and that, as with African Caribbean fathers (Ch. 9), marriage is not the typical path to fatherhood in Southern Africa. His analysis of the difficult plight of Southern African fathers led to soberingly cautious projections for the future of fathering in that region.

The Americas

The concept of diversity was also notable in Roopnarine's (Ch. 9) descriptions of Indo Caribbean and African Caribbean fathers. Roopnarine used terms like "mating unions" and "mate-shifting" as often as "marriage," because they are so common in African Caribbean cultural communities. Many fathers never marry their children's mothers, and "social fatherhood" describes a large number of Caribbean men who act as fathers to other men's biological offspring. Roopnarine's chapter helpfully explained the father's role in an environment where men's lives diverge from those of men in middle-class two-parent families. His alternative model instead emphasized the "conceptual separation between what it means to be a good father and to be committed to a relationship with a woman" (p. 215). Further, because of the Caribbean history of immigration and emigration, Roopnarine's chapter can be viewed usefully in comparison to the contents of the U.S., Indian, and African chapters.

It is also worthwhile to compare the Caribbean context with that of Brazil, as depicted by Bastos and her colleagues (Chapter 10), because both chapters emphasized the 500-year-long history of colonization and patriarchy. In Brazil, however, there is a low divorce rate, and according to Bastos et al. "fatherhood remains associated with masculinity and is consequently connoted by power and control over one's wife and children" (p. 232). Although they highlighted contemporary Brazilian fathers' quests for a new identity (i.e., the "right to fathering as a life experience," p. 230), patriarchy and the colonial past still appear to cast a shadow over 21st century Brazilian fathers. Indeed, these authors concluded that "The socialization of boys does not support the emergence of a new father ..." (p. 245).

McFadden and Tamis-LeMonda's (Ch. 11) analysis of fatherhood in the U.S. emphasized the themes of freedom and equality, economic opportunity, and immigration and diversity. These cultural elements reportedly influence not only fathers' behavior, but also the focus of research on American fathers (e.g., father presence vs. absence, roles within the family system, the father–child relationship, and fathers from diverse backgrounds) as well as the goals of policy makers. Because American research on fathering is emulated around the world, the priorities reflected in American ideology, research topics, and policy goals help us to understand why certain assumptions, issues, and policies are also common in work on fathering in other societies.

Europe

Contemporary Russia (Ch. 12) presents one of the saddest portraits of fatherhood in this volume. Utrata, Ispa, and Ispa-Landa began by citing the "negative discourse on men" (p. 295) over a millennium of Russian history, also observing that fathers have become increasingly disconnected from their families in the Post-Soviet era when fathers became "objectively freer to opt out of this [paternal] involvement" (p. 297). As with Arab fathers, Utrata and colleagues observed more problems than opportunities for fathers, but the difficulties faced by Russian fathers (alcoholism, inability to earn enough money to be a provider, negative public image of fathers) differed from those in Arab societies. Utrata et al. concluded that the Russian father's roles are in transition, yet they were not optimistic about the future.

In stark contrast to the Russian portrayal, the obstacles affecting Scandinavian fathers seemed minor and surmountable. Haas and Hwang (Ch. 13) also illustrated that policy makers and fathering researchers, especially in Sweden, can work together to change fathers' behavior. They uncovered few direct cross-national comparative studies of Swedish, Norwegian, and Danish fathers, yet their chapter was unique in demonstrating what we can learn from within-region analyses of fathers and the contexts of fathering. According to Haas and Hwang, the father's roles in Scandinavia changed dramatically about 40 years ago in response to social welfare and family policies, thereby illustrating how policies related to fathers reflect political priorities and ideologies.

Lewis (Ch. 14) showed British fathering to be both diverse and in transition (probably the two most consistent themes throughout this book) by stating that "the hallmark of paternal roles … has long been the individual variations between men in their involvement" (p. 344). In addition, Lewis cited multi-disciplinary evidence that many UK fathers spend at least some time living apart from their children, thereby reminding us of fathers in the Caribbean, U.S., Southern Africa, and elsewhere. Lewis also emphasized historical changes in British fathering due to a recent influx of immigrant populations.

Australia

Smyth and his colleagues (Ch. 15), like Lewis in the UK, had the benefit of strong national data sets that provided a general 'snapshot' of contemporary Australian fathers, although they lamented the general 'dearth' of systematic research on fathering. Interestingly, 44% of Australians were reportedly born overseas or had a parent born overseas, a fact that underscores the diversity and mobility of the Australian population. This chapter (along with Chs. 7 and 8 on Africa) considered how climate and geography affect the father's role (e.g., a temperate climate encourages outdoor activities with children, while great distances between families and non-resident fathers make regular contact difficult), yet geographical influences may well apply in other countries. As revealed in several other chapters, work conditions also affect the behavior of Australian fathers, and Smyth et al. emphasized how hard Australian fathers must work because of the high costs of living. Finally, they stressed that in a large and mobile society father absence is a serious problem, requiring "distinctive" (p. 376) social policies and legislation to address the role of separated fathers.

How to Classify Cultural Research on Fathers

As we mentioned in Chapter 1, Hewlett (2010) identified three ways to categorize fathers and fathering research. His main focus was on small-scale cultures, but Hewlett's taxonomies can be applied regardless of the size of cultures. His first distinction was between three methodologies, the first of which was called evolutionary and focused on "how a father's and/or a child's reproductive fitness in particular ecological and cultural contexts influences his or her interactions" (Hewlett, 2010, p. 416). This approach was utilized only in the African chapters by anthropologists (Fouts in Ch. 7; Townsend in Ch. 8). However, several authors concluded that the father's role was changing and had an uncertain future, which reminded us of Gray and Anderson's (2010) conclusion about the evolution of fathering: "transformations in fatherhood are hardly complete" (p. 243). We believe that the evolutionary approach deserves more attention than it has received from psychological researchers interested in cultural aspects of fathering in large and small-scale societies alike.

The second methodology, "cross-cultural," involved analysis of pre-

coded data on fathers from a large number of cultures (Hewlett recommended samples of 50 or more cultures). This approach, for example based
on use of the Human Relations Area Files or Standard Cross-Cultural
Sample (e.g., Rohner & Rohner, 1981; Veneziano, 2000), was only cited
by Fouts (Ch. 8). Hewlett's third methodology involved ethnographic
case studies conducted in the field, and this approach was rarely referenced throughout this book (again, mainly in Chs. 7 and 8). In fact, the
large majority of studies cited in most chapters were quantitative psychological studies, usually based on self-report measures of fathers in single
cultures.

Two theoretical approaches were defined by Hewlett (2010): "adaptationist" and "cultural." According to Hewlett (p. 413), the adaptationist orientation "assumes that fathers' roles are functional in that they are
adapting to particular social, economic, reproductive, or demographic
conditions or contexts." Although Fouts (Ch. 7) was the only contributor
to use the word "adaptationist," this perspective was implicit in almost
every chapter. From a global perspective, the father's role clearly reflects
men's adaptation to social conditions (e.g., social norms of patriarchy in
Brazil; pro-fathering ideology in Scandinavia), economic conditions (e.g.,
transition to capitalism in Russia and China; Japan's economic miracle and
subsequent chronic recession), reproductive patterns (e.g., mate-shifting
in the Caribbean; multiple fathering in Southern Africa), and demographic
trends (e.g., decreasing family size in Europe, the U.S. and elsewhere).
Indeed, these and other adaptations are continuous.

According to Hewlett (2010), the cultural approach assumes a "configuration of beliefs and practices that are maintained by conservative
mechanisms of cultural transmission" (p. 414), and this approach was also
implicit in most chapters. Whenever chapter authors referred to historical legacies or traditions affecting contemporary fathering, they were in
fact alluding to inter-generational cultural transmission. For example, the
Confucian heritage of East Asia (Chs. 2 and 3), individualism and equality in the U.S. (Ch. 11), the negative narrative of Russian fathering (Ch.
12), and patriarchy in the Caribbean, Brazil, Bangladesh and elsewhere, all
involved a cultural "configuration of beliefs." We conclude that both the
cultural and adaptationist approaches are helpful for understanding the
view of fatherhood in every chapter.

Hewlett also delineated four specific patterns of fathering behaviors.
He categorized one type of fathering as "intimate," as men who are strongly
attached to their babies and spend significant amounts of time as caregivers. Trends toward greater paternal involvement in numerous countries
appear to reflect a worldwide increase in intimate fathering. By contrast,
"distant" fathers are primarily involved with discipline and economic provisioning. The concept of the distant father reflects the breadwinner and

provider roles that formerly typified fathers in many cultures, but this type of fathering apparently still predominates in Russia, India, Bangladesh, Brazil, and elsewhere. Fathers may be distant for a wide variety of reasons, including breakups of families and heavy workloads. Hewlett also identified a pattern called "multiple" fathering, which involved deviation from the assumption that an individual man was responsible for each child. Multiple fatherhood appears to be more common in cultures with low marriage rates (Caribbean), high rates of extra-marital child-bearing (Europe, Southern Africa), and normative extended family relationships (Africa and elsewhere). Hewlett observed all three of the preceding types of fathers (and a fourth group called "pastoral fathers") in ethnographic studies of hunter-gatherers and other small-scale cultures. We, too, can see fathers fitting into these categories in various cultures discussed in this volume.

What Is a Cross-Cultural Perspective on the Father's Role?

As we completed this book, we decided not to replicate Lamb's (1987) title (*The Father's Role: Cross-Cultural Perspectives*). Because very little of the data cited here was by conventional standards 'comparative,' some would argue that the word 'cross-cultural' was inappropriate. We have a high regard for comparative research, yet we also appreciate the value of single-culture research that is interpreted with cultural sensitivity. Can we have a cross-cultural literature comprised mainly of non-comparative research?

Matsumoto and Yoo (2006) provided a useful way to classify behavioral studies, into four types which they associated with "phases" in the growth of cross-cultural research. In the first phase ("cross-cultural comparisons") participants in two or more cultures are compared with respect to their responses on the same measures. Few studies cited in this volume directly compared different cultural groups, and the few such comparisons seldom showed *how* culture affected fathers. In the second phase of cross-cultural research ("identifying meaningful dimensions of cultural variability") different cultures are assessed using aspects of culture (e.g., individualism/collectivism) rather than nationality as the basis for comparisons. Most studies cited in this volume utilized measures derived from Western research, and when their results differed from Western expectations the findings were attributed to 'something' about the culture. But what aspects of culture predict fathers' behavior across cultures? Demographic factors, living standards, family structure, gender division of labor, and employment systems were suggested as possible antecedents in most chapters, although these antecedent conditions were seldom actually measured by researchers.

Matsumoto and Yoo labeled the third phase of cross-cultural research "cultural studies," which compare "relationships among variables across cultures, suggesting how variables function differently in different cultural contexts" (p. 236). This type of study is exceptional in cross-cultural research on any topic, but it was exemplified in Roopnarine's consideration of mate-shifting and family configurations in the Caribbean, Fouts' comparisons between different types of small-scale societies in Central/East Africa, and Hossain's discussion of the impact of poverty and Islamic values on Malay and Bengali fathers.

The final phase in Matsumoto and Yoo's taxonomy involved "linkage studies" which connect population differences in fathers' behavior to objective measures of aspects of culture. In our view, this type of cross-cultural research was not reported in our book. In fact, while the work cited included many examples of the first three types of cross-cultural research, this volume presents an international literature rather than a comparative cross-cultural literature. Most of the research was conducted to understand fathers *per se* within single societies, rather than to understand cultural aspects of fathering. We appreciated Joseph Pleck's comment in the Foreword that this volume advances fathering research by making it more "global" and "inclusive," but acknowledge that most researchers have been concerned with fathering and not with culture. We hope that the next generation of research on fathering across cultures will focus more on culture, which might be accomplished in some of the following ways.

Future Research

Some of the following recommendations for future research on fathers in cultural context also apply generally to non-cultural research on fathers.

Sampling: Wider geographical coverage and targeted comparisons

Although every society represented in this volume would benefit from more research on fathering from a cultural perspective, we also noted earlier that there has been *no* research on fathering whatsoever in many countries around the world. Our suggestions here would be especially useful for pioneering researchers who break further cultural and language barriers to conduct the first research on fathering in their societies.

Comparative studies within regions would enable scholars to make direct comparisons between fathers in different cultures, provided that there is a rationale for such regional comparisons. For example, comparative studies within Scandinavian welfare states, between Arab societies with discrepant living standards or common Muslim heritage, between

Brazil and neighbors with common colonial and patriarchal heritages, within East Asian states sharing a Confucian/Buddhist heritage, within African regions, or between South Asian societies with different or common religious heritages, would all enhance the fathering literature. Within-culture comparisons based on social class or regions are also warranted, for example, social class comparisons in India or Brazil, or urban/rural comparisons within China or Central/East Africa. A third type of comparison would be between populations that share problems or conditions that affect fathers. For example, comparison of the problems associated with emigration/mobility in Australia, Russia, and China might be extremely informative.

Research designs: Explanatory research with a primary focus on fathers and cultures

A second priority for cultural studies of fatherhood is the initiation of explanatory research. It is a convenient truth to criticize past research as descriptive, but at an early phase of research on any topic (including research on fathering across cultures) descriptive and correlational research provides a necessary foundation for future research. One glaring omission from most research reported in this volume was measurement of specific contextual or cultural antecedent variables. It is not sufficient to study fathers in two countries and to interpret differences in vague terms of 'something' about the cultures. We also appreciate the need to study mothers and children alongside fathers, but as we repeatedly exhorted our chapter contributors, we must keep the focus of fathering research on fathers.

Measurement: From derivative replications to new issues

We would prefer objective and standardized measurement approaches, but also respect a multi-method and multi-disciplinary approach in the study of fathers across cultures. We also value indigenous measures and the exploration of new topics about fathers suggested by analysis or consideration of non-Western populations. Research is guided by theory, but if the theory continues to derive exclusively from the U.S. and Western Europe, the fathering literature cannot avoid some degree of the 'U.S.-centrism' noted by Pleck (Forward, xv).

This volume reminded us that several important topics have been neglected by experts on fatherhood in different cultures. For example, a lifespan approach – that considers how fathers themselves develop over time and how fathers' roles change in relation to their life stages as well as the ages of their children (or the phase in the family lifecycle) – was rarely mentioned in this volume. However, Townsend (Ch. 8, Southern Africa), Chaudhary (Ch. 4, India) and others demonstrated that a lifespan approach would enhance fathering research in general, as well as research on fathering in cultural perspective.

Research on the effects of non-profit organizations, fathering classes, and the media, were rarely discussed in this volume, although we expect that they will have a growing impact on fatherhood in the future. For instance, media are ubiquitous worldwide and may also promote the homogenization of fathers' roles. In addition, evaluations of government policies are also necessary if interventions are to be effective in the future. Many of our contributors were unable to find any assessment research associated with the important programs designed to affect fathers in their cultures. This lack of connection between research and practice was sometimes as glaring as the dire need for effective policies and interventions.

Building a cohesive body of multi-disciplinary research

This and other volumes (e.g., Cabrera & Tamis-LeMonda, in press; Tamis-LeMonda & Cabrera, 2002; Yeung, in press) demonstrate that research on fathers has a long multi-disciplinary tradition, and that different academic disciplines have different priorities and purposes. For example, why do researchers in particular disciplines study fathers in different cultures? Is it their primary goal to better understand specific cultures, to understand cultures in general, to understand fathers and fatherhood, or to understand families? Do they conduct research on fathers in diverse cultures to build theories, to promote active fathering, or to evaluate fathering-related policies, or to understand child development? The contributors to this volume, and the hundreds of scholars whose work they cited, would probably answer these questions in a wide variety of ways. The incompatibility of some perspectives may make it impossible to forge a common agenda for future research, and a multi-disciplinary approach may consign future researchers to a piecemeal approach in which research cannot be integrated. Yet it may also make research on fathers richer and more meaningful.

Our first goal in planning this volume was to make the account cohesive. It was challenging for contributors to integrate their respective literatures, and for us to integrate their chapters. The main source of these difficulties was that fact that many researchers whose work is cited in this volume have paid little attention to the findings of other researchers. In the future, researchers need to learn from one another while building a cross-cultural knowledge base. Smyth et al.'s description of the Australian fathering literature as 'piecemeal' applies to research in most societies, and we urge researchers in all cultures to draw on the wisdom of their predecessors and peers.

Looking Forward and Looking to the Future

Shwalb, Nakazawa, Yamamoto, and Hyun (2010, p. 357) offered the following observation about Japanese fathers:

> ... the stereotype of fathers in post-World War II Japan changed to a weak figure who was physically or psychologically absent. Most Japanese families recognized that this absence was due to men's dedication to being good providers rather than to selfishness or negligence ...

This statement suggests that from the 1950s through the 1980s, Japanese fathers showed that they loved their children by being good providers, rather than through direct involvement with children at home. Some of these men were ridiculed for abandoning their families for the sake of corporate profits or national economic success. But the above quotation indicates that for the Japanese there was little distinction between the worker role and the paternal role. Workaholic men thus gained the respect of their wives and children through sacrifice and diligence (Vogel, 1996). Similar versions of the father's role were apparent here in portrayals of Arab and Bengali fathers who emigrate for work, separated South African fathers, non-resident Australian fathers, and some in the Chinese floating population, all of whom left their children in order to provide for their children. Almost every chapter contributor mentioned a movement (or at least change in mentality) in favor of fathers' increased responsibility and involvement in the home. But at the same time, while Pleck (Foreword, xvii) observed the possibility that the American rhetoric of "paternal essentiality" might spread worldwide through globalization the provider role may still be the essence of involvement in some societies. The Japanese poster (see Figure 4.1) asserting that "A man who is not involved in child rearing is not really a father" presents a view of the father's role that is still far from universal.

Are fathers outside North America and Western Europe still the "forgotten contributors to child development" (Lamb, 1975)? Is there now or will there be a global "emergent father" (Lamb, 1987)? This volume reviewed a far broader and more extensive literature of research on fathers across cultures than its predecessor (Lamb, 1987). But fathers still seem to be relatively unnoticed by researchers outside North America and the West, even as they are beginning to gain attention. Regarding the global emergent father, we recall that diversity was a dominant theme in almost every chapter of this volume, and that each of the Case Story fathers was unique. Globalization may lead many fathers to spend more time with their children in many societies, but globalization will not eliminate the importance of history, tradition, geography, culture, or individuality. We predict that 25 years from now there will be a very different story to tell about fathers in cultural context, and we expect that this story will be far more complex (and *not* more unified) than the story told in this volume. This prospect presents a growing and exciting challenge for researchers and for fathers.

References

Cabrera, N. J., & Tamis-LeMonda, C. S. (Eds.). (in press). *Handbook of father involvement: Multidisciplinary perspectives* (2nd ed.). Mahwah, NJ: Lawrence Erlbaum Associates.

Gray, P. B., & Anderson, K. G. (2010). *Evolution and human paternal behavior.* Cambridge, MA: Harvard University Press.

Hewlett, B. (2010). Fathers' roles in hunter-gatherer and other small-scale cultures. In M. E. Lamb (Ed.), *The role of the father in child development* (5th ed., pp. 413–434). Hoboken, NJ: Wiley.

Lamb, M. E. (1975). Fathers: The forgotten contributors to child development. *Human Development, 18,* 245–266.

Lamb, M. E. (1987). *The father's role: Cross-cultural perspectives.* Hillsdale, NJ: Lawrence Erlbaum Associates.

Matsumoto, D., & Yoo, S. H. (2006). Toward a new generation of cross-cultural research. *Perspectives on Psychological Science, 1,* 234–250.

Rohner, R., & Rohner, E. (1981). Parental acceptance-rejection: Cross-cultural codes. *Ethnology, 20,* 245–260.

Shwalb, D. W., Nakazawa, J., Yamamoto, T., & Hyun, J.-H. (2010). Fathering in Japan, China, and Korea: Changing context, images, and roles. In M. E. Lamb (Ed.), *The role of the father in child development* (5th ed., pp. 341–387). Hoboken, NJ: Wiley.

Tamis-LeMonda, C., & Cabrera, N. (Eds.). (2002). *Handbook of father involvement: Multidisciplinary perspectives.* Mahwah, NJ: Lawrence Erlbaum Associates.

Vogel, S. H. (1996). Urban middle-class Japanese family life, 1958-1996: A personal and evolving perspective. In D. Shwalb & B. Shwalb (Eds.), *Japanese childrearing: Two generations of scholarship* (pp. 177–207). New York, NY: Guilford Press.

Veneziano, R. (2000). Are cross-cultural codes for paternal proximity and paternal warmth measuring similar phenomena? *World Cultures, 11,* 138–151.

Yeung, W. J. (Ed.). (in press). Asian fatherhood. [Whole issue]. *Journal of Family Issues.*

Author Index

Subject Index